THE HABERMAS-LUHMANN DEBATE

THE HABERMAS-LUHMANN
DEBATE

GORM HARSTE

Columbia University Press
New York

Columbia University Press
Publishers Since 1893
New York   Chichester, West Sussex
cup.columbia.edu
Copyright © 2021 Columbia University Press
All rights reserved

Library of Congress Cataloging-in-Publication Data
Names: Harste, Gorm, author.
Title: The Habermas-Luhmann debate / Gorm Harste.
Description: New York : Columbia University Press, 2021. |
Includes bibliographical references and index.
Identifiers: LCCN 2020049327 (print) | LCCN 2020049328 (ebook) |
ISBN 9780231159142 (hardback) | ISBN 9780231159159 (trade paperback) |
ISBN 9780231550079 (ebook).
Subjects: LCSH: Habermas, Jürgen. | Luhmann, Niklas, 1927–1998. |
Political science—Europe—Philosophy—History. | Social sciences—
Europe—Philosophy—History. | Communication—Social aspects—
Europe—History. Critical theory.
Classification: LCC B3258.H324 H38 2021 (print) | LCC B3258.H324 (ebook) |
DDC 193—dc23
LC record available at https://lccn.loc.gov/2020049327
LC ebook record available at https://lccn.loc.gov/2020049328

Cover design: Chang Jae Lee

CONTENTS

Preface and Acknowledgments vii

I. A DEBATE UNLIKE ANY OTHER

INTRODUCTION 3

1. THE HISTORICAL CONTEXT OF THE DEBATE 25

II. MEANING, LANGUAGE, AND COMMUNICATION

2. HOW A DEBATE TAKES OFF 55

3. INTERSUBJECTIVITY AND LIFEWORLD 108

III. BETWEEN HISTORY AND EVOLUTION

4. HISTORY AND EVOLUTION: THE INITIAL DEBATES 133

5. EVOLUTION AND HISTORY: THE HARVEST (1977–) 166

IV. THE DEBATE ON LEGITIMACY

6. COMPLEXITY AND DEMOCRACY (1968–71) 211

7. PARADOXES OF LEGITIMACY: CRISES AND RISKS (1973–91) 231

8. "BEFORE THE LAW" (1992–) 284

V. FURTHER DEBATES

9. BROADER PERSPECTIVES—LUHMANN, HABERMAS, FOUCAULT, AND BOURDIEU 325

EPILOGUE: HABERMAS'S LIMITATIONS TO SECULARIZATION (2019) 347

Notes 365
Reference List 373
Index 397

PREFACE AND ACKNOWLEDGMENTS

The present book has been long in the making. As early as in 1977, after my bachelor's in political science in Aarhus, Denmark, I moved to Louvain-la-Neuve, Belgium, and there conceived a study of the self-legalizing, self-organizing, and self-steering systems of the European community critically delimited by autonomous processes of life and communication. I observed the first aspect with Niklas Luhmann's systems theory, and the second with Jürgen Habermas's theory of Legitimation Crisis and life-world. Twenty years later, one of my brightest students, Poul Kjaer (2006, 2010), now professor at Copenhagen Business School, took up a similar project and certainly embarked upon it much better than I would ever have been able to.

Aarhus University was central in Nordic sociopolitical critical debates. Certainly, there was a provincial deficit of enlightenment—which existed everywhere, and which there was a surplus of in the position of small countries such as Denmark, Norway, and the Netherlands, balancing hybrid research between the large German, French, and English traditions. However, throughout the 1980s, I followed Habermas and his scholars as well as Luhmann and his scholars at the famous conferences held in April at the InterUniversity Centre (IUC) of postgraduate studies in Dubrovnik, now Croatia—a meeting place for leading critical East European scholars and Western intellectuals. There, Habermas and Luhmann's controversy certainly was indirect and implicit. Yet in 1984, some of the North American scholars such as Thomas McCarthy and Dieter Misgeld criticized heavily what they saw as the "seducements of systems theory" that misled Habermas. I told them how they missed the point, but I certainly was too young and remote from Frankfurt, Bielefeld, or New York to affect the debate. My dissertation, finished in 1983, was about critique of legitimacy, and focused on Habermas, Luhmann, the Frankfurt School, Hegel, and the so-called "linguistic turn." It was quite a Habermasian project, yet Habermas taught me to read more Luhmann, and certainly Luhmann in the early 1980s embarked on gigantic projects of social theory.

At the same time, in Dubrovnik, conflicts and still darker clouds emerged between cosmopolitans such as Habermas and communitarians headed by the praxis philosopher and antiglobalist Mihalo Marković, later cultural minister of Slobodan Milošević. Luhmann developed his theory of world society at some distance from these conflicts. However, the drama was widespread, albeit strictly embedded in extremely sophisticated philosophies and social theories, which exploded in April 1986 and escalated into a civil war and secessions in former Yugoslavia.

More than a decade later, the terribly bombarded IUC building was completely restored—even the smell, if not the atmosphere, was there again. Then it was my turn to organize conferences in Dubrovnik, this time about the use of Luhmann's systems theory.

I have discussed quite a range of the basic ideas in the present book with Niklas Luhmann and Jürgen Habermas. Several times, I asked Habermas if he should rewrite his seminal *Theory of Communicative Action* now that Luhmann has reformed what systems theory is about, and each time he answered something like "yes, but younger scholars have to take over." Both Luhmann and Habermas were most kind and helpful in all possible ways, even though they were of course extremely busy; and in 1997, Luhmann became ill and died a year after.

At an IUC conference on hybrids observed with Luhmann's social systems theory in April 2009, the professors Michael King and Anton Schütz from Birkbeck College in London proposed that I write a book on the Habermas/Luhmann controversy. For me it was a peace project written while I wrote a sociological theory on war published in books and articles. Conflicts and dialogue, war and diplomacy, always were more to me than I can express in this book. I am most grateful to Anton and

Michael, who arranged the contact with Columbia University Press; without them, I probably would not have written the book. In particular, the patience of Wendy Lochner was helpful.

I am grateful to many scholars in the fields of theology, philosophy, and history of ideas in Aarhus and a great range of sociologists and political scientists; moreover, to Helge Höibraten, Dieter Misgeld, Hans-Ulrich Gumbrecht, Andrew Arato, Axel Honneth, Christoph Bartmann, Thomas Mertens, Inge-Johanne Sand, Roar Hagen, Antje Gimmler, Mathias Albert, Chris Thornhill, Poul Kjaer, Niels Åkerstrøm Andersen, Elena Esposito, Christian Borch, Klaus Dammann, Richard Nobles, David Schiff, Alberto Febbrajo, Hans-Georg Moeller, Carsten Pallesen, Steen Nepper Larsen, Heine Andersen, Øjvind Larsen, Mikael Carleheden, Erik Oddvar Eriksen, Nils Mortensen, Jesper Taekke, Lars Clausen, Klaus Laursen, and Hauke Brunkhorst, who have given so much inspiration and opened so many discussions, as have my sociology section in the Department of Political Science and the Department of Society and Culture at Aarhus University, as well as the many scholars in the workshops at Nordic Summer University and the systemic network in Aarhus and Scandinavia. Of particular importance has been the always-helpful secretariat at IUC. More than anyone, my wife Bernadette and my two daughters Hannah and Elise have helped in every possible practical way, yet also with indispensable intellectual advice. With them and with my parents, my uncle, and my Belgian in laws, I sought to find insights into perspectives about how to observe and understand European political and cultural history, both with Habermas and Luhmann and as a son to their generation, which was born into an extremely conflictual situation at the end of the 1920s. The word *de-bate* has its origin in French and is not about a bat but literally means "un-fight" or "un-battle." Therefore this book is about the constitution of meaning and validity in communication. The topic is what we can learn from the most important intellectual "de-fighting" from a German and European debate, which previously destroyed itself in battles.

THE HABERMAS-LUHMANN DEBATE

I
A DEBATE UNLIKE ANY OTHER

INTRODUCTION

There is nothing particularly new about comparing, weighing, and measuring social theories against one another. As far back as the memory of social theory reaches, university seminars and lectures, and sometimes public debates (particularly in Europe), have discussed the advantages of this or that theory or philosophy compared to another. Since 2008, the financial crisis extended this form of public discussion to the economic theories of Keynesianism and monetarism. Earlier examples include the long-standing and multiple exchanges between diverse Marxists and anti-Marxists, a confrontation that dominated social theory discussions throughout the 1970s, followed in the 1980s by further debates about postmodernity and, in other corners, about liberalism or communitarianism.

As another important cliché has it, one kind of polarity underlying all this debating has something to do with two models—a heavily sophisticated German social philosophy in the wake of Immanuel Kant and G. W. F. Hegel, and a more experimental, more passionate, and perhaps more makeshift social thought *à la française*. According to that same stereotype—which, once again, is not entirely off the mark—the Anglo-American debates were rather a neutral marketplace. Yet, they did contribute following a more analytical game of discussion in England and carried a pragmatic tune if they were directed at an American audience. Anyway, stereotypes are everywhere.

Among the reasons why pointed debates of this sort occur relatively often in university corridors or faculty cafés is that the great authors of the past, studied in classes, are seldom to be found in explicit dialogue with the other great authors who were their contemporaries. It takes open discussion, as can take place in cafés (or sometimes in seminars), to engage their conceptions with replies or rebuttals. Famously, Max Weber and Émile Durkheim, two contemporaries both equally keen to establish sociology as a major university discipline, never referred to each other.

WHO, WHERE, WHEN, AND WHAT?

Nevertheless, as with any rule, this rule has exceptions—one of which is precisely the theme, or at least the occasion, of this book. The German philosopher and sociologist Jürgen Habermas might be said to be the social thinker who made his mark on more than a half-century of intellectual history simply by virtue of having been engaged in several, if not most, major social, political, and philosophical debates of his time, whether public or scholarly. Over the decades, he analyzed and discussed such a large list of contemporary social thinkers that the French philosopher Jean-François Lyotard once complained about not having been cited by Habermas.

One might venture to discuss which other author is most important among all those discussed by Habermas, mindful of the pitfalls that threaten such metadiscussions. Some would probably mention the hermeneutician Hans-Georg Gadamer, others the moral philosopher John Rawls. Intellectual historians would perhaps prefer to mention his master, Theodor Adorno. Many would bemoan a debate with Michel Foucault that was never realized, despite having been planned and scheduled for a celebration in 1984 of the bicentennial of Immanuel Kant's short but famous article "Answering the Question: What is Enlightenment?" (Kant 1783/1977).

In Germany, however, there is one social theorist who, more than anyone else, is recognized as holding the position most important for comparison with the social thought of Habermas. This is the sociologist Niklas Luhmann, who was a professor in Bielefeld and a direct contemporary of Habermas (Habermas was born in 1929 and Luhmann in 1927). For a short period at the end of the 1960s, Luhmann replaced the father of the Frankfurt School, Theodor Adorno, as professor in Frankfurt. This paved the way for an amazing publication by Habermas and Luhmann, published in German in 1971, though it has never been translated into English (it has however been translated into Chinese). The book is *Theory of Society or Social Technology: What Is Attained by System Research?* (*Theorie der Gesellschaft oder Sozialtechnologie: Was leistet die Systemforschung?*), and it includes five contributions of unequal length (although the sum total of Habermas's two and Luhmann's three contributions is about the same). These can be seen as a succession of consecutive arguments. Over the first hundred pages, Luhmann provides a short discussion of sociological foundations, followed by a more extensive one about meaning as a basic sociological concept.[1] The third piece is a rather independent, mid-length piece by Habermas on some linguistic and pragmatic aspects of communication, perhaps a rough outline of a communication theory of society, with no clear relation to Luhmann's two preceding chapters. Yet the subsequent chapter is Habermas's 160-page comment on Luhmann's theory; and the final contribution is Luhmann's hundred-page response to Habermas. Counting all contributions together, the coauthored book is some four hundred pages. In the years that followed, Habermas and Luhmann continued to engage each other with both long and short articles and book chapters and with an incredible number of references and remarks in their numerous—indeed, continuous—publications. Habermas and Luhmann were both highly prolific authors, who, at least initially, seemed to differ on series of similar subjects aside from their voluminous output. If Habermas has written more than forty books, Luhmann wrote no less than seventy. In both cases, most of them are seminal studies. The more important are included in the list of references at the end of the present book.

Here I do not aim to present the theories of Luhmann and Habermas in any comprehensive way. A voluminous literature already introduces Habermas's social theory and philosophy to an English-speaking audience, with the standard being set in 1978 with the publication of a classic introduction by Thomas McCarthy. Fewer introductions to Luhmann have been published (Rasch 2000; King and Thornhill 2003; Mueller 2006, 2013; Borch 2011). Rather, the present book is about their debate and its stakes. The point is not to declare one or the other to be the major social thinker of their generation, or, even less, to say who was the "winner" or the "loser" of their debate. By far the most enlightening contribution of their debate is how they proceed in order to build up a social theory. Most of their comments on each other were published yet happened to be fruitful at a time when their positions still had yet to reach final maturity. Indeed, their theoretical developments did not stop until, if not beyond, Luhmann's death in 1998. To say it in an extremely reductionist phrase, their debate concerns whether we should ask for pragmatic logics of communication and use of language, or for systems of broken politeness. My take is that both authors, like a series of other authors in continental Europe from their generation, were immensely influenced by questions that emerged with totalitarian experiences, in particular experienced in Germany; yet at the same time they reflected how modern conditions are to be conceived beyond that situatedness. In this sense, be it particular or constitutive, I find that the two authors have more metaphysics in common than what divides them—in comparison with readers from another generation. Thereby they reconstructed classical questions from the Enlightenment posed by social thinkers such as Immanuel Kant and developed in social theory ever since.

This opens a window. It implies a series of reconstructions in social thought and theory. What is truth about? What is meaning? What is legitimacy and social procedures? How can we understand communication, dialogue, and intersubjectivity in situations of simultaneity? Which social systems does communication refer to, take for granted, or react to and reform? What are collectivity and individuality, cooperation, power, and exclusion? Not the least, how can we argue about law? Such issues and several others certainly were at risk in Europe and in particular in Germany after 1945. They were in need of reconstruction. Notwithstanding, they are classical themes in social sciences and political philosophy. They are core topics in the extremely civilized controversy or dialogue between Habermas and Luhmann. Amazingly, they all happened to be targeted in the televised debacle between Donald Trump and Joe Biden, September 2020. Hence, such questions still have to find answers.

AGREEMENT ABOUT DISAGREEMENT: CONSENSUS OR DISSENSUS

In the 1970s, when students, especially in Germany, discussed Marx, both Habermas and Luhmann asked what should replace not only Marx but also the entire classical legacy of social theory. Not unlike their contemporary French master thinkers Michel Foucault and Pierre Bourdieu, beginning in the late 1960s they strived to conceive a social theory or analysis founded on what was to be called, in the language of later twentieth-century philosophy, a "communicative turn" or a "linguistic turn." Two further themes were also common to both Habermas and Luhmann—although they fundamentally disagreed about how to answer them. The first was how to appraise what systems theory actually achieves (or "accomplishes," or "attains," or "contributes"—the German *leistet* refers to all types of services or performances). Second, both Habermas's and Luhmann's elaborations closely depended upon the analyses of meaning and intersubjectivity provided by the phenomenologist philosopher Edmund Husserl. Thus, three themes seem to constitute the foundations of what, right from the start, both believed was indispensable in giving rise to a renewed social theory: communication, meaning, and systems. These were closely followed, first, by the question of evolution and the historical emergence of modern society and, second, by themes of democracy and power.

At this point, then, it looks as if there was something like a basic agreement between Habermas and Luhmann on the key matters of social theory. At the very least, the commonality of their themes and their common critical proximity to Talcott Parsons's work should have been sufficient to provide their discussion with a common object and interest. In fact, it quickly turned out that their disagreements were not reconcilable. In this regard, many commentators immediately point to political disagreements between the two thinkers. Indeed, it was characteristic of Western intellectual comprehension in the 1970s to first search for political roots as the most probable motive underlying any discussion, an approach particularly widespread in Germany. However, in the case of Luhmann and Habermas, this standard account was marred by misconceptions and mistakes right from the start, and blocked the possibility of understanding rather than making it easier.[2] The reason why both discussants did not have to be moved by opposing political motives was, simply put, that they did not agree about agreement and disagreement. The issue, puzzling for many interpreters, is that Habermas and Luhmann actually disagreed about whether communication in and of itself aims for consensus or, to the contrary, for dissent.

Later chapters will examine the philosophical and theoretical constituents of this consensus/dissent problem. In a concrete sense, however, what was it about? To say it pragmatically, the fact is that, among friends or among colleagues, in widely shared public debates or in short, personal interactions, we often experience how communication strives to find a common ground. At the same time, debates also strive to defend positions even where it is clear that disagreements and misunderstandings will remain. Competitive arguments about who is right and wrong, and about what exactly they are right and wrong about, are bound to emerge, and are unlikely to go away—other than to be displaced by some other, more urgent argument.

To illustrate the point with an anecdote at the organizational level, it became popular a number of years ago to stage public policy summits, or so-called "consensus conferences." At these, a number of experts would come to the fore, utter their opinions, and argue eventually in favor of or against each possible decision, while laymen evaluated the facts, norms, and values underpinning the judgments they had to hand down. Yet has it ever been the case that these consensus-producing ventures have actually produced a consensus? One may look to the climate change summits of recent years (the COP 15, 21, or 24), which were summits of rather indisputable global importance, and argue that the impossibility of reaching a consensus may lead to global disaster. Despite the objective facts and normative grounds necessitating consensus and action, people and systems disagree. In fact, dissent—including on such a vital point—is just as foreseeable as the sun rising in the east.

This, however, does not stop Habermas from arguing that the need for consensus and coordination, as well as the requirement to strive for it, is inescapably inherent in any effort of reasoning and arguing. Power-invested officials cannot publicly legitimize the positions they hold and the actions they impose by simply declaring, tautologically, that they have the power and therefore the authority to do as they did. Procedures of "reason-giving" are instituted to help out. Indeed, if we look into the praxis of dictatorial régimes such as Hitler's, we see that even they try to supplement their cocktails of violent policies, aggressive gestures, and mass killings with important efforts for providing legitimacy—at least symbolically, by means of rhetoric and propaganda (Walzer 1977).

Luhmann explains that legitimization and justification follow different and sometimes even opposing criteria. He grounds this in the notion that, all things considered, there is usually more than one way of making sense of, let alone deciding about, a particular situation. The last European aurochs was killed in Poland in the seventeenth century, during the Thirty Years War, in what appears to us to be an ecological sin or biological disaster. Yet probably, the poor hunter who did it also had an ethically watertight argument: namely, he had to feed his family. One might object that this example oversimplifies by reducing the history of a long decimation to one ultimate hunting feat, but sociologists know that big social happenings, at some point, always boil down to small effective decisions. There is little hope that the codes of communication and criteria for reasoning that are in place at any particular point in history, always complicated and makeshift, could provide one comprehensive common ground capable of making contentious decisions or judgments a thing of the past. If such a common ground could be found, this would signify a return to the arrangement of centuries past (in Europe): that in which God was a supplier of one unique, or "best," course of action to be chosen. God, once, was thought to authorize the one correct way of acting. Yet today we know that good solutions are often identified from a range of possible options, both good and bad, and not handed down in the unison chorus of a superior "one best."

On one level, the question at stake between the two thinkers—which, at least in its most dramatic formulation, boils down to whether society is possible because of consensus or, to the contrary, because of dissent—might appear to be a red herring. The disagreement over consensus and dissent orientations between Habermas and Luhmann is readily explained in pragmatic terms. Both authors recognize that normative efforts and commitments are more than just window dressing on idealized moral concepts. What is more, both understand that normative insights are usually generated on the basis of diverging interests, and, as a consequence, both resist the temptation of privileging any singular set of descriptive criteria.

Underlying the normative level, we find the analyses that Habermas and Luhmann have devoted to the concept of meaning, and especially to the meaning of communication and the communication systems that differentiate and specialize meaning. In order to prevent or cure the abstract character of such analysis, however, Luhmann and Habermas link them to historical inquiries about how modern communication has evolved.

As Friedrich Nietzsche first detected, history has a specific power to blur into illusions, and not only, as Immanuel Kant had suggested, to enlighten us and make us capable of developing appropriate philosophical views on historical tendencies and evolutions. Of course, we do establish such philosophies of history; what the strong legacy of social theory since Karl Marx, Émile Durkheim, Georg Simmel, and Max Weber enables us to do is to develop hypotheses about historical evolution. We can thus reconstruct positions and possibilities about learning processes and mistaken developments in history. Social theory appears, in this view, to be a form of communication developed in society and necessary for societies that try to organize and institutionalize themselves. The very notion of "power" emerged first as a concept, then also as a code in communication used to talk about what to do and what to "empower" in society—and the means for this offered by society.

Accordingly, Habermas and Luhmann do not only discuss, agree, and disagree about common themes of communication, meaning, and systems. They also discuss and analyze what it means to construct social theories about the development of societal communication, social meaning, and social systems—by means of communication. Analyzing the processes of differentiation, rationalization, system formation, and power formation in the course of social evolution, they take account of the obstacles and possibilities for theories handling such questions.

AN INTRODUCTORY RECAPITULATION OF HABERMAS'S AND LUHMANN'S SOCIAL THEORIES

Many academics, within and outside of the social sciences, are familiar with Habermas's writings; some—probably far fewer—with Luhmann's.

There are many different ways in which introductions focus on the gamut of ideas of one thinker. The basic textbook framework and approach to main concepts is just one of them. The present framework, which needs to open the way to two thinkers at once, does not aim as high: Here in this section, I aim simply to introduce (for the newcomers) or recapitulate (for those with some basic knowledge). Habermas, in any case, has been widely read and discussed by philosophers, sociologists, political scientists, lawyers, aestheticians, and even theologians. Exactly the same thing can be said about Luhmann as well. Both have so prolifically published that a scholar can rarely be found who has full knowledge of both. In the case of Habermas, we can say that this is alleviated by the fact that his work has a certain politico-philosophically inspired idea about how a society worthy of the name should look. In the case of Luhmann, a thinker for whom differentiation, not community, plays the main role, it is method, style, form, and wit, more than content, ideal, or community, that hold the multiple facets of his work together. Apart from his own notion (and interpretation) of "systems theory," it is not easy to find a comprehensive formula for his work. Characterizing it—and Habermas's social thought too—is rather like the famous story about the Indian elephant and the five blind people touching it while they try to describe the animal to the others. One holds a leg, another one holds an ear, a third one the tail, the fourth a tusk, the fifth the trunk. What they agree on is that the animal is of cylindrical shape, and rather thin. Nevertheless, Luhmann's theoretical performance is impressively coherent; yet of course, it developed over more than thirty years. In introducing Luhmann's systems theory to first-year students for more than twenty-five years, my experience is that his analyses never fail to be easy to grasp for first-year students—a bit like Foucault and Bourdieu. Habermas is more difficult. Also to translate.

In Habermas's writings however, there is a thread from his first major publication, *The Transformation of the Public Sphere*, to the last ones more than fifty years later. Habermas enjoys going to cafés to discuss. In fact, in his analysis of public spheres, Habermas took the role of a guide to café discussions in early Enlightenment Paris and London, showing the reader how new information and arguments were discussed, demonstrating how newcomers were to be welcomed and how discussion procedures were sufficiently established even to the point of being possible to alter. In early modernity, ideas emerged about valid discussions, about cognition, about norms dealing with practical matters such as whom one has to listen and talk to, and about being honest enough to be considered trustworthy. Throughout his incredible number of intellectual analyses of political culture, figures, and issues, he has stayed extraordinarily participative and engaged at a level superior to any other commentator, such as Jean-Paul Sartre, Francis Fukuyama, or Slavoj Žižek. One of the secrets behind this is certainly Niklas Luhmann's push toward a second-order disengaged observation. What is realistically observed to be the judgment—not just any judgment but the judgment, to which rational decisions should listen—that is the challenge! Another background is the unmatched philosophical heritage from Immanuel Kant and Georg Wilhelm Friedrich Hegel.

This picture of café discussions represents a lasting theme in Habermas's writings. Ever since his first writings, Habermas has focused on the three Kantian forms of cognitive reason, normative reason, and reasoning about situated judgments. The early Habermas distinguished between the three types of interest that constituted knowledge as technical, practical, and emancipative. Shortly after, he introduced the distinction of validity claims with regard to truth, justice, and truthfulness. Communication has to operate with such distinctions in order to be meaningful, though there are borderline cases where the clear-cut order of meaning is blurred. A man who orders the most expensive wine on the menu will face additional questions, such as whether the bottle actually is in the restaurant's cellar, whether he will be able to pay for it, whether his gesture fits well into the normative horizon of his companions, and, first of all, whether he authentically meant what he said by ordering it, or was simply making a joke.

More crucially, the problem that Habermas is continuously preoccupied with is how to deal with political and organizational issues about coordination in a society that at its core is a creature of its capacity to communicate and its approach to communication. Political society is about will formation. What is possible and acceptable to do together is conditioned by the means and limitations of communication. Communication is, in this sense, "out of one's hands," uncontrollable (for Luhmann the same diagnosis applies, as we shall see, if for wholly different reasons). Communication is conditioned by communication. Furthermore, any communication about coordination needs conditions by ideas of free speech and respectful argumentation, which alone can emancipate it from domination and manipulative rhetoric. However, to stay inside Habermas's framework of the public sphere, it is not only journalism and the mass media that have fallen under the domination of capitalist constraints: power is, on the whole, invested in steering systems that, like money and law, are eminently exposed to manipulative temptations. Modern communication is constantly exposed to the danger of becoming twisted and distorted. In Habermas's view, modern communication has become split into a purely functional form on the one hand. It is mediatized according to the strategic imperatives imposed by a rationality that is governed by the preferences of steering and production. On the other hand, modern communication is mediatized into an interpretative form that alone could still reproduce what communication can mean if meaning survives in an undistorted way.

Communication itself is thus split into a sphere of system communication on the one hand and the open horizon of a lifeworld on the other hand. It is only that second constituent that offers a background for effective speakers to open up the broader possibilities inherent in intersubjective dialogue. Modernity emerged with this differentiation and rationalization of communication into distinctive forms, each giving rise to distinct validity claims while being connected to more or less open or restrained forms of communication. Along with Durkheim (1893/1930), Habermas claims that modern society primarily is differentiated based on separate spheres and divisions of labor, and at the same time has had to develop forms of social and cultural integration (Habermas *Communicative Action* 1987, 2:97–122; 1981, 2:118–40). Thus, system differentiation is, for Habermas, only possible if some kind of social integration of norms about communication within and between systems has emerged (Strecker 2018; Neves 2018b). While this, it is conceded, can barely be upheld as a precise scientific notion, the task that Habermas assigns to social research is to demonstrate more accurately which forms of system differentiation and communication developed, as well as where and when they did, outline their conditions, and explain what happens when they fail. Moreover, more specifically, what happens when norms do not develop adequately and society loses its capacity to establish sufficient forms of communication?

Looking back to the time when the Enlightenment movement was at its peak in the 1780s, we see Immanuel Kant claiming that reason must be taken as a goal to be sustained, not simply as a means to achieve a goal. A century later, sociologists, and Max Weber more than anyone, described how modern society has been subjected to processes that forwarded dominant ideas of instrumental or formal means and goal/means-rationality at the expense of value-oriented or material rationality. Habermas's work needs to be placed within the pursuit of this sequence of interpretations of rationality. Rationality is not only instrumental and strategic or indebted to realization of values. It forms, Habermas has argued, the basis of a communicative rationality and thus is the indispensable starting point and base for all aspects of the evolution of modern society. For Habermas, if there is no communicative rationality, there is no society, entailing that it is not even possible to argue for any another opinion without presupposing such a form of communicative rationality. The conclusion is that there is an argumentative ethics inherently embedded in social communication. In argumentation, communication strives to communicate about communication conditions in what Habermas calls discursive ethics: for example, to avoid what today often is called "fake news."

If so, then a major point for discussion is, of course, exactly what is meant by the expression "communicative rationality"? Does it imply that stronger forms of discursive ethics have to be observed, and do such discursive ethics impose any definable forms and conditions for what coordination and cooperation can be in modern society? These questions give rise, in turn, to further examinations: Are argumentative criteria stronger in science and in politics than they are in aesthetics? How have such conditions evolved? And perhaps most importantly: How can they be developed outside of the realm of their own emergence, say, in view of today's geopolitical issues, in negotiations between Western and non-Western governments?

The later Habermas, starting in the mid-1980s, elaborated a theory about political and organizational forms of communicative rationalities led by a conception of institutional arrangements, mainly based on one theory dealing with the legal paradigm and one about the separation of powers. Between sociocultural integration and system integration, we find forms of political, organizational, and legal integration that have developed. In social thought, after the days of Kant and Hegel, but well before the post–World War II flourishing of the communication-based sociologies of Habermas (and Luhmann), Ferdinand Tönnies (1887/2010) suggested three rather well-known German concepts to describe society sociologically, according to a tripartition of the modalities of modern society: Society is to be viewed as a community, a *Gemeinschaft*. Yet society is also a societal system, a *Gesellschaft*. Finally and often forgotten, society is a political society, a *res publica* or republic, a *Gemeinwesen*. It is this third form, the one once (around 1900) framed in Durkheim's political theory in terms of a "political society" with a "deliberative democracy," that the later Habermas aims to reconstruct (Durkheim 1908/1969, chaps. 9–11).

Habermas is indeed a politically minded thinker. He is engaged in political discussions, participating and commenting repeatedly on current political issues: whistle-blowing, Iraq or Syria interventions, European integration, the bracketing of universal law in a state of exception by George W. Bush, genetic modification, minorities' rights, and so on. The role of the intellectual, as he understands it, is to be a participant and to establish criticism by exposing themes deemed acceptable in some—eventually distorted—forums. He finds his vocation in a continuous reasoned critique of political legitimacy. His conception of the role of the critical intellectual or theorist consists of explaining, interpreting, and translating the political stakes and historical meanings within a communication, and in dissolving them and recovering and reconstructing what could or should be meant or promoted *instead*.

In the political society of public reasoning, argumentation cannot simply be open-minded to an "anything goes" procedure of making statements. Declarations about what concerns others, for instance, the legislation about Jews in the Third Reich, or toward blacks, homosexuals, or minorities in apartheid regimes, have to be submitted to public argumentation. If they cannot be sustained by reasons acceptable to all concerned, then those statements are invalid. Sometimes such criteria may appear simple, yet they can easily lead to conflicts and confrontation.

Yet the society in which Habermas is going about his critical-theoretical work is also one in which unexpected complexities emerge that resist, in diverse ways, the critical-theoretical approach. Technical issues have to be dealt with before any critical argument can be tested, unintended and unexpected effects appear, precaution measures impose themselves, precedence in decisions needs to be examined, and so on. Modern society gives rise to many differentiated and specialized discourses. It also gives rise to many translation issues between experts and groups of politically motivated laymen, such that a critical position informed by everyday life and interaction touches the limits of society's communication competence. It is one thing to analyze how such different discourse forums communicate internally and according to which validity claims, standards, and norms; it is another thing to analyze the "external relations" among them and how their mutual differentiation develops over generations, in different places, between countries or powers, or between different social spheres.

Turning to Luhmann's work, we find that communication is just as essential here. To a certain extent, it is even tautological to claim that communication is important for society, since, in Luhmann's view, communication *is* society. All social theories and all social research take place in the medium of communication and are conditioned by the possibilities of communication. Yet communication cannot communicate about every matter at one single moment. Luhmann distinguishes between material complexities, social complexities, and temporal complexities. All of them always ask too much from the limited means of the system of society (or from any system whatsoever, social or otherwise). "Reducing complexity," the suggestion that underlies Luhmann's theory, is the secret recipe of successful communication, a secret recipe that is, as it happens, omnipresent, infinitely at work in any process or evolution. An obvious application of the need for reducing complexity is the fact that communication cannot take place between seven billion people, less so about every issue or in one synchronic single moment. However, this modest observation has its immediate applications to matters of decisions regarding any number of subjects: climate change, the war in Syria, or even harmonization of cable codes for electric systems.

A basic piece of advice for anyone keen to approach Luhmann's systems theory and his conception of modern society is to focus on his essential topic, social communication. Social communication can only have meaning if complexities are reduced. While Habermas, as we have seen, was led by Kant to distinguish between three forms of reason, Luhmann was led by Kant to distinguish everything that happens, according to its material, social, and temporal complexities. Communication reduces complexity; reduction of complexity selects the communication code that seems able to distinguish meaningful from meaningless communication. For example, communication in the classroom is not able to handle every matter at the same time, yet in fact, the classroom is an invention remarkable for its capacity for teaching children how to communicate in a society. It provides opportunities to communicate together in classes of, say, twenty children; their communication themes are selected according to topics (biology, music, or mathematics); the schedule is differentiated according to time, so as to describe when something is achieved and how long it takes in minutes, hours, weeks, months, years, and stages. A classroom reduces the complexities of social communication in a social, material, and temporal way and offers a certain form of social communication. At the same time, pupils, as organic, psychic, and communicative systems, observe what is going on. At a second-order level, all systems observe those operations that define systems. The late Luhmann tends to focus on this distance of observation to communication and inside communication. Whereas Habermas participates in communication, Luhmann observes communication.

This is much more of a remarkable and unexpected achievement than meets the eye at first glance—one could even say it is an improbable result in historical terms. Nevertheless, in modern society quite a number of such improbable forms of communication have been successfully realized; if it were otherwise, neither social research, nor science, nor reason-based communication would have been possible. Social theory thus has to find out, first, exactly which forms of communication have developed; second, how they become stabilized in certain forms of communication; and even, third, how they develop into systems of communication that organize themselves around their own specialized communication codes. These specialized communication codes are well known today, for example, as money, rent, payments, credit, taxes, and finance in the economic system, or law, contracts, legal/illegal, punishment, guilt, judgment, and so on in the legal system. Many communications are loosely coded, for example, the topic of "carrying bags on streets," or the question of whether neighbors should help each other in doing so. Other things are strictly coded and rely upon stabilized concepts and semantics in social systems. Take, for example, the improbable yet well-established competition of running a marathon, staged by society's sporting system. The form, say, of carrying boxes has not been firmly codified and established as a sport, but marathon running has. Which systems, forms, codes, and semantics we have is a matter of selection, which is open to empirical and historical analyses. Nevertheless, it is possible to compare systems and analyze the strengths and weaknesses of their communication codes and forms. In the Olympic Games, the process of selecting which games should be included and recognized for competition is a game in itself.

Luhmann's theory of social systems describes how such communication systems have emerged by means of their increasing differentiation from one another. He also described how they developed, in a sense, commonly, by means of their division from one another ("structural coupling"). Modern society emerged constituted by these differentiations, which have led us to be able to distinguish political communication from religious communication, sport from war, art from law, science from love, economy from education, mass media from organization, and so on. It is an open question how many such relatively easily recognizable self-regulating and self-referential social systems historical evolution has hitherto allowed. Luhmann himself, at any rate, has analyzed ten or eleven (others, working in his wake, a further five or six), depending on the criteria used.

It is, of course, also an important research question to find out what exactly conditions the forms of communication that make it possible to distinguish between such systems. What do we mean when we use the words *credit* and *creditworthy* today, as distinct from the religiously inspired *belief* and *faith*? Why is it that we cannot go into a bank and ask for a loan with the simple claim that we are believers? Historically, we can observe that, once, in late medieval society, both forms of communication occurred in the form of "credibility," and religious communication was decisive for credit systems to develop.

It is important to remember, in this context, that the system underlying Luhmann's theory of systems is different from the so-called exchange systems of Talcott Parsons's theory (Parsons 1971).[3] To Luhmann, social systems communication is basically not about exchanges among actors. Social systems have emerged when communication codes have appeared in forms that have become self-referential. Of course, the importance of language and, later on, texts was understood as essential to such self-referential communication. Language and texts could stabilize what communication was about, who was addressed, and what was expected to be selected and stabilized as meaningful. An individual on one's own cannot, of course, invent such communication forms alone. The point of communication is that it develops anonymously and stabilizes itself throughout history—it has taken certain social systems hundreds or thousands of years to emerge. The individuals can observe that some communications have taken form; and individuals as psychic systems can have thoughts about such communication. Language is indeed a form of structural coupling that has developed to stabilize how we think and what we think about—yet we also think in pictures, in music, and in infinitely complex sensations.

Distinct from Habermas, Luhmann distinguishes sharply between the self-reference of individual psychic systems and the self-reference observed in communication systems. Both operate with meaning, but meaning in communication is not always, and perhaps even rarely, the same as meaning experienced in one's consciousness; the difference between the experiences psychic systems first perceive and then subsequently communicate about offers a good example. This is different from what we see with Habermas. For Habermas, we have to mean what we are able to express, and we cannot accept and legitimate what is meant beyond this threshold of expressibility, at least in political communication (which is the paradigm of Habermas's philosophy of meaningful communication). For Luhmann, the point of departure is just the opposite, since he aims to observe how individuals became free from such premodern forms of communication that claimed to be able to interpret whatever the individual meant. For Luhmann, this differentiation of a human right to individuality was indeed only possible as part of a wider differentiation process that began when religious communication allowed legal communication, research communication, economic communication, communication about war and power, and so on to separate from religious authorization (Thornhill 2007b, 314–43; Backhouse-Barber 2017).

If, to Luhmann, social systems are self-referential, this means that they are also self-observing, self-describing, and self-organizing. In the later part of his work he also called them "auto-poietic," meaning self-reproducing and, indeed, self-producing. These words seem harmless and obscure. Nevertheless, the claims they involve are far sharper and more revolutionary than one would think. Take, for example, a human individual. One certainly can observe oneself, describe oneself, and organize oneself. The fact that one does so, however, is not what constitutes one as an individual. If one takes leave from all these activities, and is no longer doing any deeds, making any decisions, or conveying any communications, this might be a bad idea in many respects, but one would not cease to be; one's existence, self, and identity would clearly survive it. Social systems, according to Luhmann, are different in precisely this respect. They *are* the activities that they consist of. The point is not that communication transfers messages between psychic systems, but the opposite: because our thoughts are not identical and remain more or less alienated from communication, communication is possible. The magic is that we can communicate even when we have different thoughts: for example, in the classroom when pupils do not have the same thoughts as their teacher. Communication between Luhmann and Habermas can go on for decades exactly because they do not have the same thoughts but only deal with what is selected in communication, by communication, and for communication, in the self-reference of communication.

The operations that Luhmann identifies under the term *communications* are the social system itself. The self of the social system is something that takes place, which has no other self than that of the events that constitute it. The social system "is" nothing other than the result of its earlier operations, which also means that it chooses its operations at every moment by reference to its own earlier operations. Accordingly, systems are not, strictly speaking, adaptive systems: they might later turn out to have been "adapted" (or not) to their "environment," in Darwin's sense. In the course of the game, so to speak, they don't adapt—be it to an external "world" or to the actions of other actors. They are not instruments or means to achieve certain externally fixed goals or causalities. This is why communication cannot be rendered correctly in terms of a causal explanation; to try to do so makes no sense, or at best only very limited sense, which fails to account for communication's effective performances. After all, one can also causally explain what goes on in a brain, for instance, by means of biochemical formulas, but here, too, one has to admit that the effective performances of a brain almost entirely escape such an approach.

This being said, it is perfectly true that any performance, even just the process of writing this phrase, would not be possible without—and is thus causally related to—any number of things, such as nerves, cells, water, light, even electricity (since the phrase is written on a computer). The link between meaning and communication has turned communication into an indispensable self-referential form. This form is what Luhmann tries to understand, calling it "society."

Among the issues of crucial importance for our topic is of course the question of how either of the two theorists deals with the issue of the constitution of systems. In Luhmann's view, everything in systems theory is predicated on one's capacity for coming up with a nonreductionist notion of systems. Systems in his sense are not subject to a sovereign environment to which they would have to adapt, nor are they masters or steersmen of their fate, as earlier systems theorist have argued they are, and as Habermas sometimes still seems to suppose in his first reactions to Luhmann. That social systems, to Luhmann, are self-referential means precisely that they are neither adaptive systems nor steering systems.

Looking into Habermas, a somewhat different image emerges. Social systems are dominated by power in the mediatized form of money or law; they can be transcended by other forms of communication committed to opened lifeworld horizons of communicative meaning—in a clear phenomenological sense. Luhmann concedes that loose communications are factually situated within a lifeworld (*Lebenswelt*); he admits the requirement to give meaning to such communications. He objects, however, to the notion that social communication systems can unfold their communication codes according to some form of external "control" to which they are subjected. Even loose commitments are predicated on the presence of more strictly coded forms. Thus, modern universalist morals have been able to emerge only because legal communication has given rise to a self-referential code. Does this mean, for Luhmann, that we are able to expose the law to these modern universalist morals, as Habermas would suggest? If so, then only insofar legal communication admits it.

Luhmann's conception of self-referential systems implies that no system can control or steer another system. This "uncontrollability" is the condition of a modern, functionally differentiated society, and it is certainly a condition framed in terms of separation of powers. If this is the case, however, we are left in a situation haunted by paradoxes. The political system, to start with, is in charge of leading and coordinating society and claims to synchronize with itself, since it makes use of the state as the dominant organizational system of society. This, at least, is what is claimed by its internal codes. The paradox here is that the only way in which this claim can be manifested, demonstrated, and reproduced by the political system is by distinguishing it from other social systems. The latter have become differentiated from the political system *as* self-referential systems, or in other words, they are themselves self-referential and autopoietic, no longer dominated by the political system. Law, education, research, art, love, economy, mass media, and so on all have emerged as self-referential systems operating, no less than the political system, by claiming and putting into daily practice an undivided competence both decisional and interpretational, regarding every item that occurs within their (functionally defined) zones. Each of these systems communicates according to its own code, without relying upon, and without subjecting itself to, any superior or overarching or ultimate instance (a role once played by the political system, at earlier moments of societal evolution). A totalitarian society, such as Nazi Germany or the Stalinist Soviet Union, dedifferentiate the distinctions between such separated functional systems.

In a time where the experience of a financial crisis and the pandemic crisis that globally exposed the powerlessness of the political system is still painfully present, there is no need to insist upon the prima facie plausibility of Luhmann's relevant claims, patiently developed since before 1970. There is no one in charge of society at large—government itself is, as is the case of any other functionally differentiated system, only dealing with its own, functionally defined patch. In this precise sense—that contemporary politics no longer can offer to take up the role of steering, or perhaps of "being master in its own house"—Luhmann's teaching on the political system corresponds perfectly to Hans Christian Andersen's fable about the emperor's new clothes. In today's society, the political system, like any other system, can govern only itself. The venture of acting beyond its limits to control what happens in economics, science, law, or religion (though perfectly in keeping with traditional images of "politics" and "political power") can at best have the effect of "irritating" these other systems—including at the price of destructive effects on the meaningful communication inside them. However, if this Luhmannian description of the conditions in modern society is correct, then the question to which it gives rise is the Habermasian question: How should we react to such a situation?

INCLUSION AND EXCLUSION

In Luhmann's essay, "Women, Men, and Spencer Brown," he in 1987 introduced the particular deconstructivist logic of the British mathematician George Spencer Brown and offered a vision, which could resemble the Yin-Yang version of Chinese Daoist philosophy. The point is that distinctions are made. "Draw a distinction!" as Spencer Brown says. Distinctions are unavoidable. So are indications and that means asymmetries. Otherwise communication stops. Yet this does not mean that those asymmetries are rational, meaningful, or true. On the contrary. They imply paradoxes and deconstruct any privileges. No observation is rational and good per se, yet observations might be unavoidable. Science cannot avoid taking a stand in favor of science, communication has to invite communication, and so on.

From this, Luhmann embarks upon a social theory of inclusion and exclusion. All social systems try to communicate about their own communication and include their own communication in themselves, and ex-communication opposes communication. However, this means that they take stand upon ex-communication and give meaning to it. So it seemed in orthodox interaction systems, where inclusion and exclusion concern religious meaning and members of congregations. In organization systems membership was hierarchized. In functional systems, as they emerged with Enlightenment, inclusion was to concern merely communication codes. Not individuals. Therefore functionally differentiated systems enlighten in a universalist and in principle extremely anti-discriminatory way. In this sense, Luhmann's theory offers a strongly modern claim about morality. Moreover, the most interesting perspective sociologically seen is that he in the important study on "inclusion and exclusion" and in "Causality in the South" warns against the falling-down effect. That is the implication that exclusion from one system, for instance, the economic system, might lead to exclusion from a health insurance system, to exclusion from habitation, from voting, from education, and so on. Functional systems differentiate.

When he says that "integration appears at the exclusion side in modern society," this means that, by living in the environment, systems implode all kind of externalities, for the unemployed, the ill, blacks, the uneducated, the imprisoned, the unhealthy, the young, the old, females, and so on.

With their, so to speak, inborn antiracist and antidiscriminatory ideas of inclusion and exclusion, both Habermas and Luhmann, if anything, took issue with the rule of law of welfare states in Europe and in the United States with the endeavors that arose with Eleanor Roosevelt and Martin Luther King.

To Habermas the *Einbeziehung des Anderen* means literally the inclusion of others (see *Inclusion*). This implies more than the participation rights of everyone. Communication has to speak, and to speak on behalf of those concerned who somehow are ex-communicated. Communication has to listen. We find, inherent in the universalist principles of Habermas's discourse ethics, the "principle of expressibility," that one should be able to say what one feels and thinks about social issues and in particular about others with whom coordination and cooperation will take place. Moreover, and more hidden in Habermas's philosophy, is a focus on a "principle of listening," for instance, to those metaphors that appear in art or religion, in grief and sorrow. To this Luhmann—but also Habermas—would include "silence" (Luhmann "Silence" 1989). The victims of concentration camps cannot speak—not even in poetry, as Adorno would say. If George Floyd is a human being, then he ought to have rights. To identify a human being is to identify will, and that means commitment to self-preservation rather than slavery. Commitments are about rights. Will is about time and the self-preservation of the form of will in the medium of time.

1

THE HISTORICAL CONTEXT OF THE DEBATE

To read German social and political thought, whether philosophical or sociological, is often a less obvious undertaking than is understood by Anglo-American readers. It is as if German social thought is as complex as German history. Germany is only recently reunited—for the second time after 1871. Way back, the Roman Empire of the Holy German Nation should have integrated, but could not unite mid-Europe from Sicily to Schleswig under a complex and disintegrated umbrella of several hundred city states, "lands," duchies, and counties. Catholicism and Protestantism, past and present, North and South, East and West. Differences and differentiation often took the lead. Yet still higher levels of integration were invented, sometimes unfortunately, as Europe and the world realized, in the German intellectual spirit, as well as in powerful political realities. Spirit became critical to illusionary realities. Many layers are implied and are still present. As Chris Thornhill (2007b) describes it, the orthodox form of the pre-Reformation social orders created a metaphysics that paved the way for Martin Luther's Reformation in such a way that German Idealism was born. In addition, quarrels and dispute developed between the confessional cultures to a level of unprecedented political and military rivalry. In that vein social thought in Germany has been so serious business that it is a relief to be at some distance to it and to participate in it from that distance.

To take a look into the many books of Habermas and Luhmann is somewhat similar to a walk in Berlin: the difficult past is all over. And so it is in the writings of many a great German scholar. Moreover, they carry an intellectual heritage that started with Immanuel Kant and G. W. F. Hegel, which in their combination constituted an almost insurmountable foundation. This heavy heritage is certainly present in the writings of Habermas and Luhmann; perhaps it is more felt in Habermas's linkage and debates with almost all possible legacies from past and present. In Luhmann it is somewhat different, yet the heritage is certainly there; it is bearable, though the entrance level into Luhmann's style of reasoning seems difficult—at least in the first impression, which often scares many older scholars. But after some short concentration, it starts to display an immense clarity. It is fascinating to see the heavy burden of German history in the writings of Habermas, as much as it is enlightening, in the writings of Luhmann, to deal with a European heritage in a definitive modern way with a fresh distance to the cultural burden of the amazing and scary German legacy.

POLITICAL AND SCIENTIFIC DEVELOPMENTS SINCE WORLD WAR II

When Niklas Luhmann and Jürgen Habermas in 1945 witnessed the liberation after the downfall of the Third Reich at the end of the Second World War, they were seventeen and fifteen years old respectively. They were part of the so-called Flakhelfergeneration, used in counterattacks against Allied planes. In addition, Luhmann had been conscripted in 1943 as a member of a Hitler Youth battalion yet thought that the war would be lost for the Germans. He was a prisoner of war of the American forces close to Marseille. There he felt the betrayal of jus in bello, only to realize that Holocaust was of another category.[1] He had already completed high school (*Gymnasium*) a year earlier in his hometown of Lüneburg, southeast of Hamburg, so shortly after he was released from captivity on September 5, 1945, he was able in 1949 to get university law degree from Freiburg. Habermas—again unavoidable—had the experience of serving in the Hitler Youth during his school days in Gummersbach, a town some fifty miles south of Ruhr. Both their families were provincial, higher middle class, and Lutheran (though Luhmann's mother was from a different background, namely French-speaking Switzerland). As far as we know, no member of either family had been active in the Nazi party; on the other hand, their parents were a clear distance from the Nazis though they were not involved in anti-Nazi movements. During his regular visits to Switzerland, Luhmann learned to observe Nazi Germany at some distance. Habermas has had a cleft palate since youth, which is particularly difficult to deal with for children, but was certainly so in a Nazi context, which despised and excluded people if they appeared as handicapped, as Habermas did whenever he spoke. Both experiences tell us more than a long discussion would and need to be reflected on by the reader—like Foucault's experience with homosexuality, Derrida's with a Jewish heritage, and Bourdieu's background in "deep France" too.

In 1945, Habermas was still in high school. He later studied philosophy, history, psychology, and literature at Bonn and then Göttingen universities. Throughout the early 1950s, Luhmann worked in the provincial governmental law court in Lüneburg as a researcher for one of the judges. At the same time, he worked on his doctoral thesis. Just after Luhmann finished his thesis, his supervisor, Walter Hallstein, a supporter of the first postwar German chancellor, Konrad Adenauer, was appointed Head of the European Commission. One consequence of this was that Luhmann took over his work on critical legal issues concerning the rehabilitation of former officials from the Nazi regime, such as questions of stolen modern (*entartetes*) art. Meanwhile, Habermas, after having written doctoral dissertation on the Romantic philosopher Friedrich Schelling, worked initially as a journalist until 1956, when he became a research assistant to Theodor W. Adorno, one of the two leaders of the Frankfurt School.

Germans refer to 1945 as "die Stunde Null" (Year Zero), which is to say, a time of special significance when everything had to start again. On the ground in Germany, everything was a disaster. We have all seen the pictures of almost totally devastated cities. All the centers of modern life were destroyed. Moral standards had collapsed in every possible way, beyond what anyone at the time could have imagined. In the prevailing social and economic conditions, the path taken by Luhmann and Habermas was nothing extraordinary. Like many Germans at that time, they were trying to find a way back to normal life and a career; in their case the path they chose was university study. Both were successful students, and both prospered at the start of their careers from the German postwar economic miracle (*Wirtschaftswunder*). At the same time, each of them was a witness to the major changes occurring in their homeland (Habermas *Philosophical* 2018, 123ff.; Luhmann *Archimedes* 1987, 125ff.). To Habermas the Nazi experience certainly was about morality; to Luhmann, it was more about contingency; from this distinction, perhaps, a major difference emerged between Habermas's striving for participation and Luhmann's striving for observation.

Both Habermas and Luhmann read extensively both German and non-German social theory and philosophy, and along with many other intelligent young Europeans at that time, they developed an outlook on the world that departed radically from that of previous generations of intellectuals. From the distance of the twenty-first century, we could well ask what were the particular experiences shared by the generation of European intellectuals born at the end of the 1920s—a generation that includes Michel Foucault, Pierre Bourdieu, Jean-François Lyotard, Gilles Deleuze, Jean Baudrillard, Jacques Derrida, and Zygmunt Baumann. Perhaps we should go further and ask what effects their experiences of continental Europe at that time had on *the way they observed the world*, their attitudes toward events in that world, the questions they asked, and the answers that they subsequently came up with. If there is one clearly identifiable characteristic that applies to all of them, even if it is only in a general way, it is that they were all fervently antitotalitarian. They were horrified by what they saw as the vulgar political rhetoric of totalitarian regimes. This horror may go some way toward identifying the common root of their respective endeavors—the study of communication and language. Still, until a new German generation born and raised after 1945 began to write, the silent taboos of power distorted communication with a paradoxical form of "invisibility" (Luhmann, *Politik* 2000, 33–35). To both Luhmann and Habermas the experience with Nazi rhetoric stayed too invisible as the real—communicative, but tacit, hidden, and secret—power of power. To act and produce, not to speak, was the power of the German *Wirtschaftswunder*.

Before 1933, German scientific and social research institutions had indisputably provided the most productive and vibrant academic environment of their time, in most if not all disciplines. Of course, the natural sciences had flourished under the Nazis mainly to the extent that they were necessary and useful to the regime. Social science and the humanities, however, had largely been regarded as opposed to the objectives of the state and almost all the leading intellectual figures in these fields had fled, mainly to the United States.[2]

Among the groups of émigré social scientists, two became particularly important for the debate that later took place between Habermas and Luhmann. The first, the "Frankfurt School," which worked within an intellectual framework called "critical theory," had been able to obtain private financing and, as a consequence, survived the early years of Nazi rule and later established itself in New York as the Institute for Social Research, the predecessor to the New School of School Research (Horkheimer 1937/1968; Jay 1973). Jürgen Habermas tells us that "if it was possible to locate any Frankfurt School in space and time then it would have been in New York, between 1933 and 1941, in building number 429 made available by Columbia University on the West side of 117th Street" (in *Profiles* 1981, 414). Among the staff was Max Horkheimer, the director, and his close associate, Theodor Adorno. Herbert Marcuse was another member. He later left for San Diego and then stayed for the rest of his career in Berkeley, California, having spent some years in the State Department. Neither Horkheimer nor Adorno returned to Frankfurt until 1949 (Jay 1973, 282). Hence, it was in the 1950s that the Frankfurt School and its research programs were really established.

While the story of the Frankfurt School has been recounted on several occasions (Jay 1973; Hoy and McCarthy 1994), the same cannot be said of the exile of systems theory from Germany (Emery 1970; Baecker 2017). There were among systems theorists a number of German scholars working independently in several very different fields. They left for the United States before and during the war, and most of them never returned. Versions of systems theory at the time these scholars left Germany existed within several disciplines. Although one of its leading proponents, the Austrian biologist Ludwig von Bertalanffy, had set down the general ideas of the theory as early as 1932, one cannot really speak of an Austrian or German intellectual school of systems theory. Moreover, as already mentioned, there was no return to Germany from the United States, as was the case with critical theory. While Habermas was able to take over from Adorno and Horkheimer and establish a second generation of critical theory in Frankfurt, Luhmann could not claim to be carrying the baton for anything that could be described as a German school of systems theory. Nevertheless, it is certainly the case that German research methods did have a considerable effect on what later emerged at the end of the 1940s and in the 1950s in the United States under the name of systems theory.

Probably, modern systems theory had its origin in the transformation away from neo-Kantianism in the aftermath of the First World War.[3] Even the young Max Horkheimer in his dissertation of mid-1920s began working on a system-theoretical reconstruction of forms of knowledge (Horkheimer 1922/1987, 1925/1987, 95ff., 126–44). Many were occupied with evolutionary systems and systems as a form of knowledge, explanation, and understanding. Luhmann was certainly as influenced by earlier system theory as Habermas was by the earlier Frankfurt School. However, both in their respective ways transformed their theoretical traditions. In particular, their orientation toward the concept of communication was highly significant in both of these transformations.

During their years of struggling for survival in postwar Germany, Luhmann and Habermas, like many other the students, sought answers to the questions concerning recent social events. Both described how important the Nuremburg Trials were in their lives. However, Luhmann saw his task as a systematic observation at distance, as he, as a lawyer, strove to reestablish the rule of law in the postwar German administration. Habermas by contrast saw his role as engaging directly with the politics of his day through his writings in the field of political philosophy. In fact, it was partly for political motives that Habermas first embarked on a university career in 1954. He became so enraged by the famous German philosopher Martin Heidegger's refusal to renounce his publications from the 1930s, which appeared to endorse National Socialist ideas, that he wrote an article denouncing Heidegger's conduct (Habermas *Veröffentlichung* 1953/1981; *Profiles*, 65–71), which helped him to his first academic post.

THE POSITIVIST DISPUTE

At the same time, there was another intellectual context that was equally important to both Luhmann's and Habermas's subsequent development.

This took place within the German universities. Germany was liberated from the National-Socialist regime by both the Communist Soviet Union and the capitalist Anglo-American forces. This would later, in 1949, result in the division of Germany between East and West. These opposing ideologies provided the background for developments within German academia during the 1950s and 1960s and resulted in a parallel opposition between Marxist and positivist forms of social science. This division deepened particularly during the Vietnam War. Those philosophers, sociologists, political scientists, and the like in West Germany (the Federal Republic) who referred to themselves as Marxists certainly developed their sophisticated ideas at a distance from the ideological models that dominated party thinking and policy in the Soviet Union and its satellites, including East Germany (the German Democratic Republic). Hence, the neo-Marxism of Adorno and Horkheimer, in particular, was far removed from the simplistic determinism of the so-called dialectical materialism that permeated communist parties in East Germany and throughout Europe.

We have here to be extremely careful, however, to keep the Frankfurt School concept of "positivism" distinct from most or all of the many concepts of positivism currently in use. What Horkheimer and Adorno, and following them Habermas, referred to and rejected under that name, has absolutely nothing to do with, for instance, the positivism of the protosociology of Auguste Comte, or with the legal positivism of Jeremy Bentham, J. L. Austin, H. L. A. Hart, and the more neo-Kantian Hans Kelsen. We should bear in mind that the positivism that figures as the main target of the critical attacks of the Frankfurt School related only to two distinct but interconnected sources. One was the Vienna Circle, generally held to be the cradle of analytical philosophy, which described itself at the start of the twentieth century as "logical positivism." This was the legacy of researchers and philosophers such as the young Ludwig Wittgenstein, Rudolf Carnap, Otto Neurath, Karl Popper, and Carl Hempel. Second, and perhaps more pertinently in political terms, were the ideas put into practice by social scientists mainly of the Anglo-American traditions, from the 1950s and 1960s onward, namely empiricism, behaviorism, objectivism, quantitative research methods, and rational choice and hypothetical-deductive explanatory models of causality. Much of this, however, came as a heritage from the early exiled Frankfurt School too, for example, with the sociology of Paul Lazersfeld.

All these ideas were beginning to take hold and be developed at this time in the universities of West Germany as well as elsewhere in Western Europe and the English-speaking world. The specifically German campaign against "positivisms" gained in momentum until it culminated in the famous, if rather unproductive, clash set out in *Der Positivismusstreit in der deutschen Soziologie* (Adorno 1969/1976). This publication and the meeting of the German Association of Sociology (Deutscher Soziologentag) were the precursors of the Habermas-Luhmann debate.

That influential collection of essays was edited by Theodor Adorno. The principal opponents in this earlier debate were Adorno and Karl Popper, who in 1961 at the German sociology conference could not agree on "the logic of social science"—a theme later, in 1967, rephrased as a book title by Habermas. It is instructive to take a look at what occurred in this debate, as this will help to inform our examination of the subsequent disagreements between Habermas and Luhmann. First, the Frankfurt School featured as one of the contestants in both the earlier "positivism" and the later German intellectual debates at that time. Second, it explains the otherwise surprising frequency with which the issue of positivism appears in the discussions between Habermas and Luhmann. Positivism acted as a cluster of theoretical and methodological ideas, which in West Germany at that time operated as a demarcation line separating those who endorsed and those who rejected its general empiricist and behaviorist teachings. Most importantly, it cast its shadow over the Habermas-Luhmann debate and the battle over positivism (*Positivismusstreit*) in a way that provided the overall framework in which broader intellectual circles initially interpreted this debate. Yet this should not lead us to assume that there was any basic incompatibility between the claims of the one side and the claims of the other. Adorno and Popper agreed on some basic concepts, as did Habermas and Luhmann. The crucial difference lay, rather, in the logic or style of the respective arguments, and in the whole idea about what social research is capable of achieving. Today, the debate and criticism of, for instance, New Public Management (in the position of positivism) is similar to, yet not close to the aggressiveness in, the previous setting. Indeed both Habermas and Luhmann mostly take issue with the Adorno side in the positivist dispute, albeit by transforming it into renewed differences.[4]

The debate ended in regular conflicts, including the notorious student protests in the 1970s. It was observed politically as a debate between left and right, between critical theory and positivism, between social movements and technocratic administration, between conservatives and progressives, against or for the Vietnam War. At the time, it was a debate without any possible resolution. The positions were extremely aggressively held, and could be compared with two opposed incommensurable paradigms in the Kuhnnian sense (Kuhn 1962).

This was a debate that predated the whole development of social thought around communication. Phenomenology and hermeneutics certainly served as easier positions to balance against positivist positions, when neo-Marxism was more fiercely and polemically opposed. Habermas, more than Luhmann, saw philosophy of language and developments in philosophical logic from Wittgenstein to W. V. O. Quine, Gilbert Ryle, J. L. Austin, Peter Strawson, John Searle, and Michael Dummett as a tool breaking the walls of positivist philosophy of science in a way irrefutable for even hard-core positivists. Since every form of theory and research is expressed in language, research simply has to respect the rules of language in order to express valid and meaningful statements. In this context Habermas was supported in Germany by the then important Erlangen school of argumentative logic around Paul Lorenzen and especially by his former teacher and good friend Karl-Otto Apel. Perhaps more than any other, Habermas intended to have an extremely social cooperative mind and had many close colleagues that worked with him, often to the benefit for their career. Some of them, like the political scientist Claus Offe, later went to Bielefeld, while others like Hauke Brunkhorst and Ingeborg Maus have developed positions in between Habermas and Luhmann.

Luhmann too was among the critics of positivism and technical reductionism. This is in particular obvious already in his first pathbreaking article, "Function and Causality" from 1962, which preceded his first major publication about philosophy of social science, *Goal Concept and Systems Rationality* (*Zweckbegriff und Systemrationalität*) from 1968. In 1969, he published the article "Theory as Practice" ("Theorie als Praxis") where he especially attacked three notions common to positivist social science. This is his first article commenting on Habermas's endeavors. The positivist strand focused on causal necessities as explanations between causes and effects, and at the same time positivism tried to document and verify hypotheses about such explanations in stochastic statistical measures. To Luhmann, however, on the one hand, social life and social acts are less about "necessities" than ideas about causalities suggest; and on the other hand, social life and acts are also far less contingent and stochastic than statistical variance allows for. Social meaning reduces complexity in another way between absolute necessities and absolute variance. The span of contingency is handled with meaning and makes social interaction probable without falling into absurd causal explanations of absolute necessity in social action or absurd stochastic variation.

Luhmann criticized the Frankfurt idea of critical theory since it, according to Luhmann, had to reflect more sociologically on how its criticism is part of the society criticized. Yet I do not, as Chris Thornhill in his brilliant *German Political Philosophy* (2007b, 328), see Habermas's *The Structural Transformation of the Public Sphere* (1962) as any decisive publication that framed Luhmann's early writings already in the mid-1960s. Luhmann, in an article from 1967, had argued for a "Sociology as a Theory of Social Systems" (SA 1, 113–36). There he argued that "the capacity to criticize is and stays an essential element in scientific theory" (113). To criticize society is to describe the limits of social systems. However, these limits expose also how a critical theory is placed not outside a complex society but exactly inside those complexities that can never take the form of a unity, and when such a united total form is exposed, it can be criticized. Moreover, there is no safe place for a theory which says that it is good and society is bad. This would simply expose a lack of self-criticism (*Praxis* 1969, 257).

The third criticism Luhmann launched concerned Max Weber's famous notion on "value freedom." In fact, in neo-Kantian terminology "free values," strictly speaking, means obligatory commitments, and Weber was much to his own irritation misunderstood as a "value relativist." To Luhmann, meaning established selections in the complexities of variance with the aid of preferential values. Without values, selections cannot offer any meaning to our acts. Yet social life lives by means of such valuable selections. Values do not mean normative values; but we cannot avoid values, and even the idea of value freedom is in social research observed as a value that allows for "intersubjective transition" of acceptable suggestions.

In the concluding part of *Goal Concept and Systems Rationality* (1968), Luhmann criticizes the overall idea about a distinction between empirical descriptions and normative prescriptions. As a consequence of the overall argumentation forwarded in this important book, the duality is conditioned by the system that holds them together: descriptions of the past and prescriptions of a future are like past and future held together by the difference from the present moment that unites their differences. Empirical descriptions have no sense if they are not guided by such classifications, which the observer ought to use.

In a close parallel to this argument, Habermas, in the conclusion of *On the Logic of the Social Science* (1967), could claim that descriptions of what "is" "ought" to follow normative standards. Expressed in Durkheim's classic terms, to which both Luhmann and Habermas subscribe: *If* A "is" a society with a division of labor, *then* it "ought" to enable communication in such a differentiated society (Watts Miller 1996).

Habermas in fact took his famous notion of "knowledge interests" (*Erkenntnisinteressen*) from Weber's conception of value-directed research (Weber 1904/1984, 161, cf. 181; Habermas, *Erkenntnis*; *Knowledge*). To Weber values are a precondition for directed research. However, Weber himself followed a rather subjectivist interpretation of neo-Kantian moral philosophy and was skeptical toward the possibility of a moral social science. Moral philosophy could only lead to very abstract imperatives ("thou ought not to kill") but not to norms about which studies to undertake, where to live, and so on. Here Durkheim subscribed to a French social variant of neo-Kantianism, developed by his philosophy teacher Charles Renouvier, and was much more offensive; he argued that a still-ongoing division of labor has severe normative implications about tolerance for variation and reflexivity of norms as well as abstraction processes in coordination and cooperation. On this important point Habermas still more follows Durkheim's lead and early on in a discussion from 1964 criticized the Weberian notion that in the meantime had turned into a dogma about a so-called "natural fallacy" about normative deductions from factual statements ("from 'is' to 'ought'") (Habermas, *Logic*, 313–21). While Luhmann never began to develop a normative theory about moral values, Habermas became still more critical toward Weber's skepticist version.

I shall discuss the different stands of Habermas and Luhmann later on; yet about this early stage, some would be surprised to see that Luhmann, with the article "Reflective Mechanisms" published in 1966, began a Durkheimian argumentation about the reflection of norms in a functionally differentiated society that came to a more full development in his article "Self-Thematization of Society" (1975/1982), originally published in 1972. In communication practice, learning processes have to cope with reflexive abstraction processes of selection that reduce complexities in order to allow for variance, or in other words, norms and communication codes have to develop in order to allow for cooperation. Any form of coordination employs such codes. In fact, much later, Habermas has taken this argument to his very heart as "the normative content of modernity" (Habermas, *Discourse* 1987, 341–49; 1985, 396–404).

PARSONS IN THE UNITED STATES

In the United States, Max Weber's and Émile Durkheim's writings became known very much through the use the Harvard sociologist Talcott Parsons made of them. The meaning of social action in Weber's sense and the differentiation of functions in Durkheim's sense should reconcile action theory with systems theory. In fact, Parsons undertook a range of research projects in order to find a decent way of coping with analyses offered by systems theory and actions. Different symbolically generalized actions could be handled by differentiated systems, but how? The aim here in this book is not to expose Parsons's different versions. Rather, the point is that Habermas and Luhmann both were very inspired by Parsons, and not only in the 1960s, like so many others, but also and perhaps even more later on. More than any other, they today have authorized ideas about how Parsons's analyses can be used.

Parsons was part of a much wider current in systems theory after the Second World War. In fact, while the early Parsons, even in his book *The Social System* from 1951, preferred to base his analyses on action theory and on small-scale ego-alter relations, he soon after reconstructed social theory with systems theory. Not only Parsons but also other system theoreticians, for example, the Czech-American Karl Deutsch and David Easton, based theory analyses on open systems theory. Indeed, in the social sciences in the 1960s there was a widespread use of open systems theory based on the transformation of input into output with outcomes in an environment and feedback into the system. As mentioned, modern systems theory developed as a consequence of German researchers that flew into United States in the 1930s. Many of them came with philosophical schemes that went beyond neo-Kantian ideas for an objectivist natural science and subjectivist humanist studies. Kantians worked with a distinction between form and material, whether the materials were observations of nature or will-formation, and this distinction could be used to establish a distinction between system and environment. Observation was systems observation. Parsons, too, learned about such Kantian schemes when he studied in Heidelberg from 1925 to 1927 under Marianne Weber and the shadow of Weber, who died in 1920.

Parsons tried to undertake a quite rationalist or even speculative way of understanding system differentiation from the basis of a temporal distinction between presence and absence and a spatial distinction between inside and outside. Hence, actions as well as systems could be observed according to modalities about their fourfold combination of absence-inside, absence-outside, presence-inside, and presence-outside; and this paved way for his famous AGIL distinctions between adaptation, goal-achievement, integration, and latency.[5] Parsons certainly tried to find ways to think about rationality and social systems in ways that surpassed, for instance, the economist rationalist way of thinking about rational action and economic systems. Action systems were divided into the cultural system, the social system, the personality system, and the behavioral system; actions systems were again one of four systems and the social system could also be divided into four subsystems (economy, polity, latent pattern-maintenance, integrative). It is not surprising that many found such fourfold subdivisions too speculative. The English-speaking sociologists as Alvin Gouldner in *The Coming Crisis of Western Sociology* (1970) and, later, Anthony Giddens in *New Rules of Sociological Method* (1976) gave Parsonian systems theory a negative reputation as speculative. Gouldner's penetrating critique was above all that the system as a whole was established ex cathedra before the empirical investigation of its parts according to an idea of equilibrium and adaptation to an external world; this gave systems a culturally conservative form (Gouldner 1970, 210–13).

EUROPEAN INTERESTS IN SYSTEMS

Habermas and Luhmann insisted that there was a lot to learn from Parsons. They could reconstruct the philosophical underpinnings of Parsons's theory, and in this sense the speculative heritage from Parsons did not threaten their undertakings. Yet another reading was as important, since Parsons's approach was also very pragmatic; instead of simply applications of ad hoc distinctions upon empirical materials, he tried to think about what difference a distinction gave not only inside a targeted domain but also to other domains. Parsons made experiences with theory and often, in fact, Parsons did operate quite empirically. Later we shall return to Parsons's theory of social evolution.

The scale of Parsons's project was important for the two Germans, and later Germans, such as the younger neo-Parsonian professor and sociologist Richard Münch, were impressed. We cannot leave social analysis and social theory only to micro- and middle-range (meso-) studies. We imply Grand Theory even in more simple undertakings. In a more pragmatic way, Parsons was not only speculative; he also had a strong sense for fantasy. In particular Luhmann underlines that Parsons's way to play with thoughts and social phenomena always was in a move for new forms of observations. More than many other social thinkers in the 1960s, Parsons was aware of the symbolic construction of social life. For example, in his theories of power and of money, both were symbolically generalized media. Yet they were conceived as media for interchanges and not for communication as such. In their first debates, Habermas and Luhmann did not discuss Parsons intensively, although both recognized a need for a more communicative transformation. Communication is not simply about interchanges; and the problem of system boundaries and system identity was for Parsons stated prior to the communication theory and not inside communication or constituted by communication.

As mentioned, in 1967, Luhmann wrote the path-breaking article "Sociology as Theory of Social Systems," in which he defended systems theory as a theory that could be criticized in its "universal claim." In the article, he outlined how to reconstruct the basics of Parsons's theory. For Parsons and most of the sociological community, the paradigm discussed and so often criticized was "structural functionalism." In Parsons's version, the problem was that the ex cathedra structure of the AGIL dimensions defined the system and the subsystems before the functions. Luhmann's early criticism centered on the functions, how they emerge and evolve. In the German language, Parsons's former problem of reconciling action with system appears solved with "Germanistic" expressions like "actionsystems" (*Handlungssysteme*); later Anthony Giddens (1979) became famous when he coined the similar idea of "actor-structure duality." Yet already the early Luhmann saw how the evolution of semantics created functions that lead to structures; accordingly he transformed "structural functionalism" into "functional structuralism." This transformation goes back to early disruptions in neo-Kantianism, such as Ernst Cassirer's path-breaking treatise *Funktion und Substanz* from 1911. The relation comes before the substance, ontology after action.[6] The point is to look for the meaning of differentiations and the variance or contingencies of the functions they could establish. If we imagine a school class, we may figure the room, the twenty-five pupils, the teacher, and six hours a day throughout a year or so as the structure altogether. However, we may also think about the relations and communications going on, the thematized discussions and paperwork, the moments of concentration before computers, some times more formal, sometimes more informal; and this is the functional perspective.

To Luhmann in 1967, "social systems shall be understood as a meaningful connection of social acts that relates to one another without being delimited by an external environment" (*Sociology* 1967, 115). Here Luhmann repeats Max Weber's influential concept of "meaningful connections" or "connectivites" (*Sinnzusammenhänge*). This invokes descriptions of interconnections in meaning that give sense, known or unknown. The decisive point is, first, that it is the connections that establish the meaning and not some fixed ontological substance, and, second, that one or another form of meaningful interpretation or observation of such connections is a condition for the detection of such connections. The connected meaning establishes a difference from the horizon of possibilities in an undetected world.

Habermas, in *On the Logic of Social Sciences*, coped with Ernst Cassirer and Max Weber. Cassirer, who today is much more recognized than he was in the 1960s, was praised for his analysis of symbolic forms that presented a level of analysis beyond the distinction between natural science and humanities. However, Habermas at that time did not see Cassirer's analysis of historical semantics during the Enlightenment or even before. Cassirer directed the historical Wartburg archives in the late 1920s and, on that basis, undertook important analyses of conceptual history (Habermas *Liberating* 1997/2001, 1–29). Thus, without taking conceptual history too serious, Habermas directly focused the heritage of meaning analysis in the sociological path of Max Weber's idea of "interconnections of meaning" (*Sinnzusammenhänge*).[7] For Habermas this was a question of communication and linguistic meaning and not so much one of evolution and history and differentiations between "interconnections of meaning" that could have their own rationalities. Habermas, rightly, was critical toward Weber's dualist rationalities of instrumental goal rationality and subjectivist rationality, but at that time, he was not so empirically oriented that he saw how different "interconnections of meaning" established their own rationalities of connectivities. To Habermas the problem of connecting rationality and meaning was and continued to be a philosophical problem of constituting meaning in language before the empirical history was detected. Later I'll give an example involving discussions in courts of how the early Habermas and the early Luhmann differed on this point.

INTRODUCTION TO LUHMANN'S AND HABERMAS'S RESEARCH PROGRAMS ESTABLISHED IN THE CONTEXT OF 1968

HABERMAS'S VIEW ON ENLIGHTENMENT AS EMANCIPATION

Until the transformation years between 1965 and 1970, Habermas and Luhmann had intellectual careers not so different from several others in the same generation. Yet, it is interesting to compare their inaugural speeches as professors in Frankfurt and Münster. Discovered by Helmut Schelsky, who more than any other was responsible for the reconstruction of German sociology in the 1960s, Luhmann shortly was appointed to a chair in sociology in Münster before he in 1968 came to Bielefeld. In 1965, Habermas made his inaugural speech in Frankfurt, published under the programmatic title of "Knowledge and Interest" in his booklet *Technics and Science as "Ideology"* in 1968 (partly translated as *Toward a Rational Society*, however without this article) at the same time as the magisterial *Knowledge and Interest*.

Habermas conceived a dualist heritage in Western philosophy going back to a Socratic conceptualization of theory distinct to the world. Without pushing the history of that well-known heritage too far, he reestablished a criticism of it that invoked the late Edmund Husserl's phenomenology of a lifeworld that in 1936 delimited what Husserl called the crisis of Western science—of course in opposition to the German derogation after the catastrophic Nazi takeover. While Husserl's criticism conceptualized the notion of a reconciliating lifeworld as a presupposition of every form of meaning expressed in theory and science, the young Max Horkheimer simultaneously established the program for Frankfurt's critical theory with a likewise famous analysis of "Traditional and Critical Theory." In both cases, the point was to avoid a dualism that placed science and research at the outskirts of societal life and practice. The practical lifeworld constituted the metalanguage and background activity of any form of conceptualized research whatsoever. To Habermas, this meant that language and knowledge invoked a dialogue with a lifeworld emancipated from dominated figures of meaning and embedded into forms of language and dialogue in which communication could be valid. Accordingly, Habermas conceived three differentiated validity claims: a technical interest in knowledge, a normative practical interest, and an emancipative interest in knowledge. This triangular form of validity claims has remained decisive for Habermas ever since.

In a more empirical form, it was already central in *The Structural Transformation of the Public Sphere*, in chapter 2, where he took the reader with him into the cafés of Enlightenment in Paris and London. There Habermas described how argumentation and reasoning had to be open toward new information and arguments, toward new participants, and toward new procedures. These analyses were recapitulated by

Habermas in the famous phrase that began his book *Knowledge and Human Interests* (1968): "a radical critique of knowledge is only possible as social theory" (Habermas *Knowledge* 1971, vii). Yet, to establish such a theory of society, Habermas found it obligatory to work himself through a kind of self-reflection in social research. Thus, Habermas first wanted to establish a metatheoretical reflection.

To Habermas, the practical validity claims expressed in everyday life imply a logic of emancipation that reflects at a distance those forms of domination that rule everyday life: that is to say, linguistic rules oppose dominating rules. Though Habermas indeed admits the importance of a theory of society, to him enlightenment passes through the analysis of an emancipatory logic expressed in the pragmatic use of language, that is, in its intersubjective social use in the everyday lifeworld.

LUHMANN'S VIEW OF SOCIOLOGICAL ENLIGHTENMENT

Luhmann called his inaugural speech on January 25, 1967, "Sociological Enlightenment," and later this became the name for a six-volume series of books, which included a number of Luhmann's articles (*Soziologische Aufklärung* [*Sociological Enlightenment*], 1970–95). He published the inaugural speech in the first volume. While Luhmann reflects enlightenment in the intellectual heritage of freedom from traditions and prejudices, sociology, he says, should observe the limits and constrains on such enlightenment. Enlightenment means reason and rationalization, but sociology detects limitations to rationalization. Thus, sociology observes how society always subverts reason and is critical to a forward reasoning that imposes plans and steering programs.

Together with the first volume of *Sociological Enlightenment*, Luhmann published another book at the same publisher, his much-used Westdeutscher Verlag (which translates to West German Edition), titled *Political Planification* (*Politische Planung*). Typical of Luhmann's ironic sense in his titles, the book is about the improbability of steering and control. Luhmann reflects this in the inaugural speech. To get knowledge about society is to get distance from society. Society not only opens a path to knowledge, reason, and consensus, but also subverts such projects. This, however, Luhmann does not conceive as a critique that understands itself, on the one hand, as enlightened, free and meaningful, and valid, or, on the other hand, as invalid, meaningless, and an object for criticism. In a second thought, there is no valid unity that serves as a yardstick to measure society. Luhmann then invokes Marx, Freud, and Nietzsche. Sociology can describe latent functions and thus enlighten enlightenment, or preferably "clarify enlightenment" (Luhmann SA 1, 70). Luhmann observes enlightenment and reflective mechanisms as parts of modern and early modern society. Theories are in society, in society's own reflection of itself, in its distance to itself, and society contains and is that self-reflection and self-distance.

Indeed, the era of disruptions from 1965 to 1975 contained an overwhelming range of conflicts and forms of dissent, but also hopes of consensus directed against a perceived false and forced consensus, as if the postwar fearful conformity embedded in instrumental growth scenarios was not only cognitively to be constated but normatively to be hoped for too. Habermas hoped for another form of consensus and tried to find it already and a priori embedded in social life. Luhmann respected this, yet made it clear that this would-be hope probably risked disappointments.

Accordingly, we can establish a first kind of summary of themes established in Habermas's and Luhmann's research programs as they took form right before they met each other. Of course, they both reflect the common themes discussed in intellectual social research, stemming from Marxism, psychoanalysis, positivism, Parsons, Nietzsche, Weber, Durkheim, and Simmel. Embedded in this conceptual legacy, they aimed to discuss quite a great range of themes that all can be found in Luhmann's inaugural lecture: universal validity of social theories, the notion of critique, the possibilities and limits of enlightenment, rationality, and meaning and intersubjectivity in a heritage from the philosophical logic of Husserl. Furthermore, they more and more started from a theory of communication, a theory that itself was to be established in the medium of communication itself.

Some of these themes certainly were worth a major debate. When Luhmann visited Frankfort in 1969, both authors had a kind of surprise. On the one hand, Luhmann found the seminars less occupied with political or politicized quarrel, and more with decent occupation with an honest search for forms of valid argumentation. On the other hand, the Frankfurt students, and Habermas too, found in Luhmann a systems theorist and a gifted organizational sociologist and lawyer with a far broader and more enlightened range of interests than they ever believed possible. Luhmann replaced Adorno for a semester with a seminar not on planning or on formal bureaucracy, but on the history of love, not in the sense of some flower-power sociologist, but conducted with a penetrating knowledge about history and the impact of ideas and semantics in history. For his seminar, Luhmann made a booklet, *Love—a Sketch* (2010).

In these years, Habermas mostly wrote about philosophy of language and tried to find and reconstruct theories and philosophies occupied with language and communication. The communicative turn certainly was common for both Luhmann and Habermas, yet in the context of an exploding interest in Marx studies among students, few themes could seem so remote and abstract as studies of language and communication. However, this orientation toward language, discourse, and symbols was broader. Part of it was driven by Oxford philosophy of language and the endeavors to constitute sociology and social research in line with whatever happened in philosophy and philosophy of science.

Certainly German philosophy, ever since Kant and Hegel, through Edmund Husserl, Martin Heidegger, and Hans-Georg Gadamer, was much more in touch with sociological themes than English philosophy, which tended toward more narrow discussions about logic, and sometimes discussions strictly about logic. In Paris, however, poststructuralists—like Jacques Derrida, Michel Foucault, and the still quite unknown Pierre Bourdieu—were all occupied with language, discourse, and symbolic practice with the same energy that was going toward Marxist studies of work, class relations, commodity forms, and political practice. For a generation of scholars that had their youth embedded in Nazi society, the challenge to stay away from mainstream intellectual currents was perhaps not always as difficult as we today imagine. We talk about a generation that challenged the dominant forms of research and dominant issue agendas, yet also a generation with unprecedented career opportunities in the booming years of the 1960s.

ENLIGHTENMENT AS A DISCUSSION OF DISCUSSIONS

In 1969, Luhmann and Habermas were the two upcoming young stars on the German Milky Way to the intellectual Heaven of Kant and Hegel. In just a few years, they wrote a large amount of important work, Luhmann more than Habermas since Luhmann not only covered metatheoretical and philosophical themes, especially with his classic *Zweckbegriff und Systemrationalität* from 1968, but also published other classic studies, such as the book *Trust* (*Vertrauen*) in 1968. (Some of the books written at that time were published only much later and a few indeed only recently.) *Trust* is probably his most typical sociological book and exposes themes particularly from interaction sociology in a highly original way. His distinction between trust in systems and confidence in experiences of the past is widely used, and later became foundational, for instance, for Anthony Giddens in *Consequences of Modernity* (1990), thought he never admitted the intellectual influence and weight of Luhmann. In *Trust*, Luhmann was still occupied with action theory and symbolically generalized media. At this point, communication was not really established in the core of his theory.

Another series of studies undertaken by Luhmann during these years was about sociology of law. Those studies had a tremendous impact upon not only Luhmann's but also Habermas's arguments and later developments. In 1969, Luhmann published *Legitimation durch Verfahren*, which linked a theory of courts and their procedures and processes with a more general theory of decision-making in administration and politics. The point was not to make still another theory of law to be used in law, but to reestablish a sociology of law at a higher and more abstract level of social research. The study of decision-making in law was undertaken as a step toward a broader series of studies, and actually Luhmann's contributions to his book with Habermas were written while he wrote a broad and widely recognized book published in 1972, *A Sociological Theory of Law* (*Rechtssoziologie 1-2*). Recently, in 2013, his study *Contingency and Law* (*Kontingenz und Recht*), written in 1971, was published. Already in 1964, in *Folgen* (295–303), Luhmann, like Weber, was concerned about the "rights of the social situation" that broke the formality of, for instance, bureaucratic organizations and bracketed requirements for consensus in favor of dissent—an important pragmatic condition in the coming controversy of Luhmann and Habermas. During the late 1960s, Luhmann wrote quite a range of articles in sociology of law on themes like evolution, positive law, separation of power, functional differentiation and decision-making in law, "subjective rights," and rule of law. The arguments developed in these analyses are often reproduced in his comments to Habermas.

In the following chapters, we will return to some of these themes. Therefore, it is convenient to treat a simple and quite concrete description of the issue to be analyzed now. For instance, according to Luhmann, positive law, as it developed in the eighteenth-century Enlightenment, paved the way for an innovation in decision-making, namely, in courts' deliberations and discussions about how a present situation and theme could be judged and be distinguished from past legacies. Since formal positive rules became homogenized and settled, deviances from them were more easily discussed, and discussions emancipated from earlier privileged positions could take place. Court practice deliberated precisely because its autonomy was emancipated by the efforts to establish positive law, for instance, in the early enlightened French chancellery and the Paris High Court. In fact, this argument is not far from the young Habermas's analysis in *The Structural Transformation of the Public Sphere* of early modern distinctions:

> The bourgeois public's critical public debate took place in principle without regard to all pre-existing social and political rank and in accord with universal rules. These rules, because they remained strictly external to the individuals as such, secured space for the development of these individuals' interiority by literary means. These rules, because universally valid, secured a space for the individuated person; because they were objective, they secured a space for what was most subjective; because they were abstract, for what was most concrete. At the same time, the results that under these conditions issued from the public process of critical debate lay claim to being in accord with reason; intrinsic to the idea of a public opinion born of the power of the better argument was the claim to that morally pretentious rationality that strove to discover what was at once just and right. (*Transformation*, 54; 1962/1975, 73)

The obvious difference from Luhmann's analysis is that Luhmann analyzes discussions in the context of courts, whereas Habermas treats literary discussions or debates in theaters and about theatrical performances. However, the differentiation between theatre and court was far less established than it is nowadays. Thus, the point is that formal expositions, the written law, the written piece were subject to treatments and they, in turn, could become subject to discussion. A sociological analysis will start in the institutionalization of the court (or the theater) and describe how this led to the construction of the setting, the proponents, the turn-taking in interaction, talking time, the specter of arguments, their content, and the expectations about what was discussed, who was to be included, and for how long time. On the metalevel, another theme is the positive objectivization of codes and the subjective experience of them and their adequacy or inadequacy. Likewise, a very important theme is the differentiation of themes and the function it has to differentiate between, for instance, court and theater; and again, we observe differentiations from discussions in academies, bourse negotiations, discussions in parliaments or estate assemblies, and not least discussions in the forecourt of courts, theaters, corridors and streets, cafés, meeting rooms and salons, journals, and newspapers. On the philosophical level, the theme is the temporality of the present situation, reasoning as reason and rationality, universal validity and the validity claims, and whatever can be meant by such claims.

Habermas's path-breaking analysis of the emerging public sphere of reasoning owed much to the conceptual history of Reinhart Koselleck (*Critique and Crisis*, 1959/1988) and the somewhat more philosophical heritage of Hannah Arendt (*The Human Condition*, 1958). While Habermas in the 1960s more and more was led to reconstruct enlightenment as a philosophical heritage and to take a philosophical stand on the communicative and linguistic logic of the enlightened learning processes, Luhmann preferred to hold the line of historical sociology and saw philosophical enlightenment as part of a social differentiation of functions. Logic is part of society, yet society can only be studied in accordance with some pragmatic logic. To formulate these opposite strands in an exaggerated way, in Frankfurt, philosophers were surprised that Luhmann knew more about philosophical enlightenment than they did, while sociologists in Germany were surprised that Habermas knew more about sociological theory than they did.

HOW DO HABERMAS'S AND LUHMANN'S THEORIES DIFFER IN THE CONTEXT OF 1968?

Though there are a number of parallel interests, we can also observe how Habermas and Luhmann characterized each other when each began to see the other as holding a different or opposed position. Luhmann often characterized Habermas's ideas of discussions emancipated from dominance as some kind of utopian and conservatively romanticized idea of premodern discussion, as if Socratic discussions could be used as guidelines to understand modern society. On the other hand, Habermas viewed Luhmann's analyses as much too involved with established conventions in law and dominating forms of organization or management, and too influenced by conceptions of natural science in the form of a system theory that cannot be connected with modern philosophy. In the worst case, each viewed the other as having betrayed the enlightenment. Furthermore, students in the extremely heated discussions of these years used them as straw men for whatever problematic tendency they wanted to argue against.

During the years after 1968, many students saw law as an almost hopelessly conservative way of approaching society. For many students whose views on law followed Max Weber, law could not rescue modernity from the Nazi abuse of law.[8] However, of course, this was exactly why the enlightenment of law (which had been so important in Germany, more than elsewhere in fact) became so extremely important—and the resistance to its distortions so exaggerated. Thus, Luhmann with his background as a lawyer seemed at odds with Marxist debates, which all concerned an illegitimate class structure as the veritable constitution of law. As challenging were Luhmann's many studies on organization. In 1970, he published a series of articles in a book called *Political Planification*. As already mentioned, the title is in fact ironic, since the book is one big argument about the impossibility of steering, control, and planning. Nevertheless, in combination with systems theory, many observers took the title at face value and read Luhmann through the lens of his being one more bureaucratic freak defending top-down control in state administration, not to say capitalist firms. However, Luhmann, more stubbornly than Habermas, insisted that modern society cannot be described or understood, let alone changed or transformed, without an adequate interpretation of its organizations and the complexities they are involved in. Habermas assigned the students in seminars Max Weber's theory of bureaucracy, which to some degree was already critically accepted by those students who had read Georgy Lukacs's combination of Weber with Marx (in *History and Class Consciousness*, 1923/1971).

Yet Luhmann offered an extremely more informed range of organization studies. Accusations during these years that Luhmann's views were conservative were linked to his double defense of positive law and formal organizations and their routines. His point is that formalized procedures can be transformed, whereas informal decision-making is difficult to identify and therefore difficult to change—less in chaotic procedures, not only by totalitarian regimes.

Even worse for many students, Luhmann used systems theory. One popular notion is, of course, that systems are evil and nonsystems are morally better. However, systems theory was also a research trend that subjected natural science and social research into a common framework of general theory. It was therefore easily observed as a continuation of positivism, with its postulates about how natural sciences proceeded and about how social sciences should proceed—as if humans could be interpreted according to hypothetical-deductive laws and causalities and as isolated atoms. Nothing was more remote from the heritage of systems theory—in particular in Luhmann's reinterpretation—than this picture. Nevertheless, students of social science were often told—and in the United States this misperception still prevails, for example, in military research—that systems were about linear transformations of input into output. This narrative had—and still has—some truth, though it leads to abuses and misunderstandings. For instance, in Vietnam at the end of the 1960s, from McNamara to Nixon, students could see how the U.S. government used ideas of systems theory to make causal predictions of victory as output by sending more bombs as input. Under Rumsfeld, this linear road to victory still ruled in the U.S. military organizational system—and failed. Paradoxically it was possible to predict that this form of causal prediction failed in its self-blindness.

However, this picture of systems theory was and is hopelessly wrong. Systems are considered to be complex and do indeed break up, on the one hand, with the idea of some causal necessities that lead to foreseen effects. On the other hand, systems interrupt the reverse stochastic and statistic idea that human behavior is only stochastically predictable in an infinite space of possibilities for variance. First, systems reduce such complexities; second, they do reduce external complexities because they themselves are constituted with an internal complexity. Therefore, they cannot be steered or planned; they control themselves. The core of the problem is, what is the form of those selections that establish those reductions of complexities? In the solution to this core problem, Luhmann deviates from those systems theories that directly used natural science.

Of course, already with Kant (and in particular with Marx) cultural systems are also natural systems. Thus, we should explain how they differ from natural systems; and we can follow another, more precise solution and indicate a form of systems inside natural systems that simply can only be interpreted according to their own ways of reducing complexities. Now, so far the ideas of systems and their complexities do not deviate from the classical solutions offered by Georg Simmel and Max Weber. In short, Luhmann used Talcott Parsons's classic receptions of Weber to describe how social systems are based on "values"—an inspiration to Weber from the neo-Kantian philosopher Heinrich Rickert.

Yet to Luhmann and much linguistic philosophy, "value" is not sufficiently precise. Values (as is the case for Kant and Nietzsche) are about everywhere and indicate what is in a system as well as outside a system. Preferably to value, "meaning" is the decisive concept for finding the form of reduced complexity established by society. Weber used the concept of complex "interconnections of meaning" (*Sinnzusammenhänge*) to describe what he looked for. Meaning connections could be distinguished according to cognitive purified "ideal types," and their "conceptual systems" could be detected in empirical research (Weber 1904/1975). In his article "Sociology as Theory of Social Systems," published in 1967, Luhmann describes such complex "interconnections of meaning" and their differentiations as functional systems with their own internal complexity. Accordingly, economy, research, law, love, art, and a series of other meaningful interconnections have their own complexities and describe meaning according to differentiated selections of whatever becomes meaning in economy, research, law, love, art, and so on. In principle, it is not meaningful in a court to discuss communications as if they were only theatrical performances, though in fact they may often appear so, but their meaning is established according to a strictly differentiated form of meaning that keeps theater far from law, and law far from theater (Nobles and Schiff 2013, 237–50).

The Habermas/Luhmann controversy about systems theory is very abstract and it may appear to be only metatheoretical debate. Yet it shouldn't be forgotten that it is also a historical and sociological debate about extremely concrete experiences and evolutionary learning processes about how to differentiate between audiences. Furthermore, it is a debate that attempts to find a way to observe how sense and meaning have been established in social communication. At the same time, we have to be aware that the debate is already established in communication, as if it has sense and offers meaning to its participators. Hence, the next part will treat this foundational challenge about meaning and intersubjectivity.

This was the historical context in which the Habermas-Luhmann debate began. In one sense, it was a relief from all the heat and the little light that had preceded it. However, the risk was, of course, that with its heated argument over technology in light of the ongoing Vietnam War, it could be seen as a continuation of the Marxism-positivism quarrel with "the media of communication," with systems theory being viewed as an extension of the two sides in the old debate. The important Habermas scholar Thomas McCarthy later published an article titled "The Seducements of System Theory" (1985) that seemed to run very close to such a misreading, which I will discuss later. Habermas, on his side, repeatedly told his students (according to a personal communication in 1982 with Axel Honneth, Habermas's follower in Frankfurt) that they "should read more Luhmann and still more Luhmann." In Germany, the first edition of the book from 1971 was followed by manifold reprints and sales of several hundred thousand copies. It was also followed by a number of commentaries by other authors (Eder et al. 1973; Narr et al. 1973). From a retrospective view, most of these can be seen today as noticing that "something had happened," but with an implied "but we don't know what it is." With all of the different positions that the two protagonists took in the books and articles that followed so rapidly during the 1970s, it was almost impossible to outline any comprehensive overview before new developments made them obsolete. Jean-François Lyotard, the French philosopher, has outlined some of the consequences in his well-known and still worthwhile booklet, *La condition postmoderne* (*The Postmodern Condition*), published in 1979.

Today that debate about the sense of quantitative social research methods is clearly moderated by thousands of research projects that have paved the way for qualitative research, such as interviews, text analysis, and discourse analysis: i.e., analyses starting from the communicative facts in a communication society. The blind alleys of the quarrel about positivism rapidly became famous in all Western research traditions. When we think about what science and research mean in Germany and indeed Europe, though, we have to remember that that will change our terms a bit. The German legacy speaks about *Wissenschaft*, which, though untranslatable to some degree, means something like "knowledgeability." The German *Wissenschaft* distinguished between natural science and cultural research, *Naturwissenschaft* and *Kulturwissenschaft*. Social research is such a *Kultur-* or *Geisteswissenschaft*.

II

MEANING, LANGUAGE, AND COMMUNICATION

2

HOW A DEBATE TAKES OFF

For readers not accustomed to social philosophy, the coauthored Habermas/Luhmann book certainly involves some hard reading and lengthy discussion. It had to do with the preconditions of social forms of reasoning before anything close to a result was achieved. It was certainly a work in progress, yet it is interesting to look into the laboratory.

In the following, I have reconstructed the debate between Habermas and Luhmann according to a double principle. On the one hand, I follow a chronological narrative. From literature, music composition, and movies everyone knows that such a structure is not simply linear, since past problems reappear in later developments. This complexity destructures, and it will interrupt the simple story of the debate. On the other hand, a number of themes appear and reappear. Some develop far beyond others. Since the initial debate was very metatheoretical, I will begin at that indeed—sorry to say—abstract level. The later chapters, on evolution and history, on democracy and complexity, and on law, discuss history and social research more.

THE DEBATE'S METATHEORETICAL TAKEOFF

What is all that about? Let me quickly recapitulate. Some students of social analysis and social theories may wonder why it is necessary with such penetrating elucidations of theoretical work as what we witness with Habermas and Luhmann starting in the early 1970s. Yet the point is double. On the one hand, we may admit that every corner of scientific work and research is embedded in language and communication. Rather than simply using a toolbox we do not understand, analyze, or examine, Habermas and Luhmann examine closely this toolbox to observe its parts, coherence, function, and meaning.

On the other hand, society is certainly, as many observers claim, embedded into language and communication. It would be difficult to claim that society could function without language and communication. Admittedly, it is an idea necessary to examine, if linguistic communication is the very core of the construction of the social analysis of society. To misuse communication performance is to misuse society and the way it creates its inner core, its coherence and meaning. In Europe, and certainly in Germany, such destruction was experienced in the 1930s and 1940s, when Luhmann and Habermas were young. Hence, for the generation of Habermas and Luhmann, it is compelling to understand the way society uses language and communication.

Luhmann recapitulated systems theory in the first two chapters (one hundred pages), and subsequently somehow Habermas felt it compelling to expose some kind of a link between philosophy of language and sociology. This theme Habermas discussed at length in the Princeton lectures planned for February 1971. The insights from those lectures may have resulted in a push from Habermas's side toward Luhmann in favor of an ambition for more in-depth reflection on communication and interaction conceptions. Should social theory build upon a theory of action and interaction or upon a much more pure theory of communication?

In their coauthored book, Habermas certainly pushed toward a stronger concern with communication as language than did Luhmann, who soon after, in *Power* (1975), on the other hand fully made the transition to communication that Habermas never followed. Yet in fact the positions are somewhat more complex than a simple notion that Habermas stayed closer to the communicative theory of action discussed in the H/L book. We can divide the debate into three phases: an interaction-oriented sociology before 1971; a concern with communicative action starting in 1971; and for Luhmann a more pure communication theory from 1975 onward. Certainly, after 1971, Habermas reconstructed the core of his theory upon the metacommunication function of a discourse theory about truth and ethics. Luhmann's transition probably began in the important article "The Self-Thematization of Society" (originally published in 1972, and republished in *The Differentiation of Society*, 1982). We will see that Luhmann in his reply to Habermas in their coauthored book also began to transform the classical action theory toward a more abstract and pure theory of communication.

In a certain sense the debate began for real when Habermas's students proposed to publish the contributions, namely, Luhmann's two articles (totaling about a hundred pages) on modern systems theory and on meaning as a basic concept in sociology, as well as Habermas's forty-page preliminary remarks recapitulating the idea of linguistic philosophy as the basis for a theory of communicative competence as well as Habermas's 160-page remarks on Luhmann's theory. Habermas's remarks were actually papers from a seminar and not meant for publication; they were seeking something no one had done before, somewhat in the wildness, and sometimes Habermas even expressed himself somewhat aggressively, though not arrogantly.

When Luhmann heard about the publication plans he accepted, yet he wanted to comment Habermas's comments. In this way Luhmann, probably more than Habermas, cleared the ground for a much wider and ongoing debate. In particular, the first fifty or sixty pages of Luhmann's hundred-page comment offer some kind of platform. In response, Habermas's famous *Legitimation Crisis* can be read as one long comment on Luhmann's remarks. Accordingly, what follows now is essential in the debate, but it is also a metatheoretical interlude about whatever it takes to establish a theory about legitimacy and politics.

OVERVIEW OF THEMES IN H/L

Habermas:

- The status of systems theory
- The coordination of coordination and Language
- Truth

- Ideology
- Intersubjectivity
- Self-reflection

Luhmann:

- Complexity
- Discussion
- Truth
- Evolution
- Universality
- Critique and Ideology

MEANING AS SOCIOLOGY'S BASIC CONCEPT

The only chapter of the coauthored book that has been translated into English is Luhmann's second chapter, "Sinn als Grundbegriff der Soziologie"; it is translated as "Meaning as Sociology's Basic Concept" and appears as the second chapter of *Essays on Self-Reference*, published in 1990 by Columbia University Press. Interestingly, there is no indication in this book of the fact that this is a translation of the piece from 1971. Strange too is the fact that no translator is named, but slightly less so considering that no reference is given to the original publication. The other interesting aspect of this republication of the early essay arises from the fact that Luhmann saw it fit to make available in English, an essay written twenty years previously, before he had fully developed his ideas on self-reference and long before he had begun to label his systems theory as autopoietic. In this respect, it presents clear evidence of continuity in his conceptualization of systems between his pre- and postautopoetic work, for the hyperproductive Luhmann had no need to repackage his earlier writings just to satisfy the demands of a book publisher. He would only have allowed his essay on meaning to be translated and published in English in 1990 if he felt that the ideas that it contained were still important and relevant to the way he was thinking at the time *Essays on Self-Reference* (ES) was published.

In this chapter, Luhmann sets out his intellectual wares in his typical style. He moves from a philosophical elucidation of the concept of meaning to an account of the way that systems develop through the reinterpretation of selected meanings and the negation or exclusion of other possible meanings. The concept of meaning in his scheme "refers to the way that human experience is ordered and not ... to some particular fact or matter in the world" (Luhmann *Self-Reference* 1990, 26). Everything that is communicable must have meaning or, put the other way around, if it can be communicated it must carry some kind of meaning. "The efforts some make to confront us with meaninglessness," he writes, "ultimately serve only the increasingly difficult production of astonishment; and the positivist who labels a Christmas carol as 'meaningless' is merely formulating the limits of his own maxim" (26). To label something as "nonsense" or making no sense still has meaning and is still an ordering of experience.

What is referred to as "complexity," by contrast, cannot be communicated and, therefore, in its raw form cannot be communicated. "The term *complexity* is meant to indicate that there are always more possibilities of experience and action than can be actualized" (26). They cannot all simultaneously be ordered and conveyed as meaning. For complexity to be accessed, there needs to be a process of selection whereby meaning is extracted, or rather created, from all those possible ways of understanding events (including people's actions). Yet, for Luhmann, "what is special about the meaningful or meaning-based processing of experience is that it makes possible *both* the reduction and the preservation of complexity" (26): that is, it provides a basis for selection that prevents the ordering of the external world into meaning from "shrinking down to just one particular content of consciousness" (27), one person's way of understanding things.

Luhmann then goes on to show how systems, based on meaning, signify that they are able to evolve an increasingly complex framework for making sense of complexity, and so give meaning to what would otherwise be incommunicable. In Luhmann's seminal *Theory of Society* (*Theory* 1997; 2012, 1:142), we find a continued insistence about this characterization that links meaning to the reduction of complexity.

Moreover, he distinguishes between meaning and information. "Unlike the concept of meaning, information is always to be understood in relation to a currently given, constantly changing state of knowledge and to an individually structured preparedness to process information" (*Self-Reference*, 31). Identical configurations of meaning can, therefore, result in quite different information, depending on when and by whom it is used to update experience. As Luhmann states, "what one person takes for granted might be surprising to someone else; and the same is true across time" (31).

While systems generate meaning through their selections, they in no way determine and have no way of determining what use is made of information contained in (meaningful) communications. For example, the information provided by the communication "the USA has invaded Iraq" will depend on the particular mind-set or communicative context of those receiving it. It may denote, for some, a colonialist suppression of a small nation in order to seize its oil production or its Sunni-based government, while, for others, a liberation of an oppressed people. This information will differ according to events that have preceded it and how they have themselves been internalized as information. Though meaning and information are clearly distinct, it is the case that, through making possible the communication of meaning, systems generate information, which may be retained within the system: for instance, the different ways that political parties in the United Kingdom responded to the invasion of Iraq as information within politics or interpreted it with other systems, whether individual conscious systems or social systems—for example, in psychiatric health systems according to those who are psychically unwell or in the economic system according to an increased risk of oil scarcity within.

The final parts set out the new sociology, which Luhmann claims should no longer focus on action but upon the role of meaning in what he calls "a functionally conceived systems theory." Here, "human action does not appear as a causal factor acting or acted upon in accordance with certain laws, but instead, human action is oriented on meaning, and becomes predictable only by way of system-structural restrictions of the possibilities" (*Self-Reference*, 63). The explanation and prediction of actions are not, he tells us, exclusively the task of a science, which sees itself as "confronting an explainable and predictable reality. It is first and foremost a matter for *real* systems themselves and, *within these*, something to be balanced against other interests" (63, italics added). Meaning is decisive, not action.

What Luhmann appears to be saying is that a science of sociology would be better off treating systems as if they were *real*, rather than assuming that there exists some ultimate reality that makes it possible to explain and predict people's actions. In making these explanations and predictions, science accomplishes only "the reconstruction of a rationality" of its own selections (based on meaning): that is, those selections and only those selections that the system of science recognizes as giving rise to possible explanations and prediction. "It does not have the function of predicting action *per se* and must be able to reflect the fact that in *real action systems* the predictability of action" is not achievable (63, italics added). Actions and predictions relate to reality, only as far as these are recognizable as real possibilities within the system making them. Only within the system are they are regarded as the only possible explanations and predictions, because all other possibilities have already been excluded by the system's prior selections.

Only two times in this chapter does Luhmann mention Habermas and then only in passing. Apart from relating Habermas to the hermeneutician Wilhelm Dilthey, Luhmann associates Habermas with Ludwig van Bertalanffy, the Austrian-Canadian biologist who founded the interdisciplinary idea of open systems theory, with Ross Ashby, the psychiatrist and pioneer in cybernetics and complex systems, and with Herbert Simon, the American social scientist who contributed enormously to the development of the study of complex systems, organization theory, and artificial intelligence. All four, according to Luhmann, are "tied to the limits of the classical notion of causality and to the limits of available logical calculi." Because this approach does recognize those meaning selections that are at work in any attempt to attribute causality, they can only offer limited success "when applied to highly complex systems and are thus unable to fully neutralize the subject as decision-maker and interpreter" (62). Although they may accept the existence of systems in their schema, they do not go so far as to see these systems as actually making causality statements possible through their selections of possible meanings and negation or their rejection of everything else. In this way, they do not escape from the notion of human subjects as decision-makers and interpreters because they do not recognize that their decisions depend on the meanings that different systems make available. Luhmann here contrasts their approach, first, with his own rejection of the human subject as the central or principal unit for sociological analysis and, second, with his insistence that systems as the source of meaning should be the starting point for sociology. Hence, the task of the sociologist should be to determine how meaning is constituted—herein, Luhmann will go along with Dilthey and Habermas. As such, it is a compliment to Habermas, who moreover is being mentioned in the same breath as three of the most celebrated systems theorists of the twentieth century. At the same time Luhmann makes it quite clear that all four—Habermas, Bertalanffy, Ashby, and Simon—have misled themselves into believing that sociology is able to retain the Enlightenment notion of the human subject at the center of any theoretical account of society or any of the systems that make up society.

Although in this article Luhmann does not engage in any direct confrontation with Habermas's theoretical ideas, he in passing does draw a clear line between Habermas's use of the term *social systems* and his own. Unfortunately, this distinction becomes neglected or totally lost in the ensuing debate. According to Luhmann, Habermas simply assumes that both he and Luhmann are dealing with interpretations of a given reality, of a real external world, of a true state of being, that exists and can be accessed. "The true function of meaning resides for many—as it does for Habermas, in *Knowledge and Human Interests*, 1968—in deciphering the in itself inaccessible experience of others. This is one-sided insofar as meaning, and even the expectation of expectations, can also be used to 'by-pass' the subjectivity of others without looking in" (75n47). There is also little acknowledgment that a conceptual gap exists between, on the one hand, Luhmann's idea of communicative meaning from complexity and, on the other, Habermas's use of systems as networks of communications. Habermas's hermeneutics, then, was more in accordance with the subjectivist interpretation of Dilthey and less with Gadamer's focus on dialogical systems.

HABERMAS'S TAKE

In the following three subchapters, I reconstruct Habermas's take and sometimes-sophisticated comments to Luhmann. There is one rather evident reason why Habermas became so preoccupied with the structures of linguistic performance in intersubjective dialogues. The differentiation of propositional content and the performance dealt with in the intersubjective construction of a social reality already suggest how intertwined or entangled the circular structure is whenever communication is about the social realities of communication. The perspective is that communication is used to treat communicatively constituted realities, for instance, whenever social coordination is sought, reformed, and altered by means of social coordination itself, that is, in forms of "preparedness for cooperative understanding" (Habermas, in H/L, 117).

The point is less simply that social coordination is about communication and about the use of language too. The more sophisticated point is that coordination is used to transform coordination. This happens by way of distinguishing. Strategic rhetoric and the powerful use of communication in change should be distinguished from a certain form of the linguistically defendable use of performative language in dialogues between those possibly concerned by that very change. Habermas does not look for all forms of linguistic use. He restricts his concern to a particular yet indispensable part of linguistic communication that concerns the change of coordination by means acceptable to all those concerned.[1] Therefore, Habermas aims to distinguish between, one the one hand, a pragmatic form of communication and, on the other, a metacommunicative discourse about more justified (and that means sharply differentiated) forms of communication. In this idealized form, people communicate explicitly (and that means linguistically) according to distinctions between a language of constatations, representations of motivations, practical regulations of intersubjective relations, and pragmatic talk about understanding linguistic performances (Habermas, in H/L, 111–12).

Whereas Habermas distinguished between the three linguistic competences (constating propositions, social performatives, and authentic presentations of motives), Luhmann distinguished between communicative selections according to their material, social, and temporal dimension. These three forms should be compared, though they are different and not as similar as they may appear. Luhmann has used the form of those so-called reductions of complexities all along. This may have inspired Habermas, and both Luhmann and Habermas refer to Karl Bühler's book *Sprachtheorie* from 1934 with its distinction between the referential functions (*Darstellung*), conative functions (*Appel*), and expressive functions (*Ausdrück*). Yet Habermas more often explicitly referred to J. L. Austin's speech acts theory in *How to Do Things with Words* (1962). Of course, Kant's distinction between three forms of reason in his three critiques is a main reference too. Kant's distinction between three forms of interchanges in the Third Analogy of *Critique of Pure Reason* could appear to have some foundational role, though Luhmann would never accept such an external foundation. In Simmel's *Sociology*, the tripartition of social forms of interchange certainly could be traced to Kant.

Why are such elaborated distinctions important to Habermas? Because Habermas aims to make clear when we have a real orientation toward consensus and a deceptive consensus. Habermas's philosophy of an emancipative orientation in a domination-free idealized discursive situation is famous, but not always well understood. It is not an empirical theory about certain empirically identified situations. It is not about an actual consensus about some contents of propositions. It does not forward a claim that consensus can be obtained for certain in a short span of time. Rather, it is a philosophy about the counterfactual conditions in use whenever claims about norms, meanings, and motives for coordination are communicated according to procedures that could become accepted by those possibly involved in decisions. Thus, it is not a theory of just decisions, but a theory of justifiable norms that are in use when counseling about decisions is undertaken in communication (Wellmer 1992).

Accordingly, Habermas offers his bid of what ideology is. Ideology is "blocked communication" (Habermas, in H/L, 120). Indeed, this theory certainly does not tell us that everything thought can be communicated, or that everything experienced can be communicated, or even that everything experienced should be subject to communication. On the contrary, it is a theory about the unavoidable conditions for political and organizational cooperation, i.e., coordination of coordination. Nothing more and nothing less. Only cooperation that claims acceptance needs a form of communication that differentiates what acceptance means according to propositions about truth and justification.

Durkheim, in his *Division of Labor* and *Professional Ethics and Civic Morals*, had already focused on what he called democratic deliberation in a theory about coordination as cooperation, and later John Rawls did so in *Political Liberalism* (1993). Later, Habermas found a more explicit starting point in this idea of deliberative democracy.

Hence, in communication, expectations emerge that those motivations and intentions about norms that are claimed to be valid for others also express and explain concerned or implied facts. Moreover, communication should also explain why and how those norms should be valid for others. This "expectation of legitimacy" (*Legitimitätserwartung*) has to include how presuppositions in this case could be justified in an unrestricted discussion to follow. "At every moment, accountable subjects should be able to withdraw from problematized connections of acts in order to enter a discourse" (Habermas, in H/L, 119). This, of course, is a counterfactual claim. The point is not at all that we always would enter a discussion. Nor is it that we always could. But the proper claim is that this could be a claim asked of us. Or it could be and should be, or actually is, a claim we have on ourselves, which filters motives and intentions we have about norms and meaning, which we, in this case, could forward in given social situations. All those concerned know that, for instance, a president could be subject to such questions, yet ideologies may prevent an audience from being subject to such questions.

We could say that this, in particular, is the experience of a German generation that was troubled about the problem of convincing Nazis. This concerned the need for reflection about motives and for a rational argumentation that followed norms of reasoning rather than propaganda, rhetoric, or pure violence. In this sense, the aim is to constrain ideology as blocked communication and to deblock communication. As such, Habermas's analysis became extremely forceful in Germany. Furthermore, it influenced a younger generation of students quite deeply and became part of a Marxist rebellion against preunderstood conventions and privileges.

Whereas Luhmann created a sociology of pragmatic situations, for example, in organizational coordination (Luhmann *Folgen* 1964, 293–304), Habermas developed a philosophy of communication in a situation of broken politeness. The normal preunderstanding we can have about our fellow citizens' motives is not always to be trusted. Hence, a forceful model of thought for Habermas and many others during these years was translating a Freudian psychoanalytic therapeutic speech into expectations of social communication. Motives might be blocked, hidden, rejected, privileged, neurotically occupied with recognition, frustrated, and so on. The sociological and philosophical purpose of such a compelling post-Freudian motive is to advocate for an ongoing communication about what could be said and reflected, beyond the surface of a so-called polite social life. In general, such communication is needed to enlighten what society does to itself. Of course, Germany was an extreme case; yet socially and politically repressed arguments and reflections are well known everywhere.

AN INTERLUDE WITH PHILOSOPHY OF LANGUAGE

In Habermas's critique of legitimacy, the ethics of discourse has a decisive and indeed constitutive position as the ground for the reconstruction of motivations. Feelings of injustice, the experience of neglect, stopped communication, and unreasoned proposals or decisions could become justified, criticized, rejected, or reconstructed. The point is not that all norms are always justified, but that norm change, if unjustified, could become justified, rejected, or reconstructed. This puts a heavy burden of proof on the shoulders of linguistic performance beyond whatever rhetoric allows doing. A critique of legitimacy does not accept simple legitimation or consent: a rhetorically produced form of political legitimation, no matter which political regime we are actually dealing with, does not lead to legitimacy in the critical sense of a political proposal that could stand for further proof. Just or correct politics is not actual consent; instead, it leans upon the counterfactual possibility of proposals and decisions that could be sustained.

The well-known argument directed against any discourse-ethical claim, that time does not allow so much discussion, will not—as Luhmann would say—hold against the easily observable and much-observed fact that, today, discussions can take days, weeks, months, years, decades, a life span, or even generations. Discourses devoted to the search for proof can go on for hours and eternities. For example, there is the still-frequent discussion about just war. For almost twenty-five hundred years, insights have developed about whether there was anything that the Melians could have replied to the military emissaries of Athens in order to avoid being slaughtered, and if so, what. Habermas allocates a decisive importance to the use of shared or coordinated language about what should or could be done in order to get acceptance or dissent from everyone implied by proposals. In principle, it should be possible to explain and publicly defend the motives and intentions behind proposals that have implications.

This was stated by Immanuel Kant in *Toward Perpetual Peace*. Kant's argument can be explained with the help of problems today. Habermas doomed it to obsolescence in 1995; yet after the Iraq Invasion in 2003, he developed a far stronger and more adequate Kantian interpretation (Habermas *Inclusion* 1998, 165–202; *Divided West* 2006, 113–93; Harste 2009). In this version, Kant's classical argument is the following: If Iraq is to be attacked, then George W. Bush, Colin Powell, and Tony Blair should in principle be prepared to defend this decision in a public debate. Herein, "public" means nothing more or less than that it must include the Iraqi soldiers, mothers, and children (in other words, the victims to be of the planned offensive) in addition to the American and English soldiers who will inflict harm on them. A third group would be military experts, of which it might be hoped that they have some adequate knowledge of Clausewitz and Sun Tzu. However, successful proponents cannot limit themselves to sustaining an argument with a reference to what has already been explained, since that explanation is always conditioned by the acceptance of categories and concepts used *in the present moment*. In order to make it sustainable, there needs to be lurking behind every argument *the transcendent claim that still further arguments could* be found. It seems that discursive ethics is in need of an extended temporal theory.

Now if this is how political legitimacy is judged, this criterion of analysis implies an extended debate about why language, discourse, communication, and the like are important, as well as about the form they impose. What exactly is meant by meaning, by norms, by rules? This had, in fact, been a much-debated question when the twentieth-century turn toward a philosophy of language began. Some refer to the late Wittgenstein's disheveled *Philosophical Investigations*, published in 1952; others to Ernst Cassirer's multivolume *Philosophy of Symbolic Forms*, published in the 1920s; others again to Gottlob Frege's short article "On

Sense and Reference" ("Über Sinn und Bedeutung") from 1892. Yet tracks can even go way further back, until we arrive at Hegel's *Phenomenology of Spirit*, or alternatively, as the young Habermas, at Hegel's earlier writings from the Jena period, or at Wilhelm von Humboldt's pioneering work on language. If the point is the criticism leveled by the late Wittgenstein's argument against private language and in defense of public language, Kant's *Critique of Judgment* (§§19–22, 39–40, and 54–56, 59) can be invoked.

Another aspect is how this paradigmatic shift influenced social science and in particular sociology with its all-embracing social theories. Certainly Max Weber, in his famous article "'Objectivity' in Social Science" from 1904, led to a renewal of conceptual history and apparently defended discursive knowledge. Émile Durkheim began a similar turn toward communication around 1900, as his political theory—outlined in *Professional Ethics and Civic Morals* from about 1908 and *The Elementary Forms of Religious Life* from 1912—makes sufficiently clear. Yet, a hundred years later, large fractions of the social sciences, especially in economics and political science, still proceeded as if positivism were the unique, natural, and normal form to be used in explanations of knowledge, meaning, motivation, acts, causality, and so on. Habermas, in *On the Logic* from 1967, carefully explained why this does not hold for social research, and his arguments were strengthened over the years to come. This is well explained and continued in writings from his colleagues: Karl-Otto Apel's *Transformation of Philosophy* (1973), Albrecht Wellmer's *Critical Theory of Society* (1969), Richard Bernstein's *The Restructuring of Social and Political Theory* (1976) and *Beyond Objectivism and Relativism* (1981). Many more could be mentioned.

Niklas Luhmann also attacked the idea of causal explanation as inadequate for social research, and this before Georg Henrik von Wright's *Explanation and Understanding* (1971). Luhmann in his seminal book from 1968, *The Concept of Goal and Systems Rationality*, moved to center stage arguments that seem to actualize Ernst Cassirer's reconstruction of the temporal dimension of explanation. Luhmann displayed how mainstream social science was trapped in a linear focus on causality that did not observe the temporal fact that every explanation has to explain the past from the present moment.

THE TRANSFER OR INTERSUBJECTIVITY DEBATE ON TRUTH

The underlying challenge here is to find an adequate concept of truth. And Luhmann's efforts to provide himself with such a concept as those turning on function, functional method, causality, ideology, and the like go back to the 1960s—in this case, to the article "Selbststeuerung der Wissenschaft" (*Self-Steering* 1968). This article is extensively discussed by Habermas in their common book from 1971. It is undeniable that dealing with these topics, more than with many others, Luhmann's thought appears to be relatively close to Habermas's—despite Luhmann's quite outspokenly functionalist conception of truth, where truth appears in the guise of a medium serving the transfer (*Übertragbarkeit*) of meaning (233). And Habermas recognizes this proximity, for instance, when he quotes Luhmann's passage: "As far as we can think back, it has been the claim to intersubjectively compelling certainty that has endowed true knowledge with the character of a convincing demonstration of knowledge, *that is to say, of its assured transferability*" (233; Habermas, in H/L, 222, italics added). As it appears in this passage from Luhmann, which Habermas quotes, the "convincing" character of its capacity to function as a proof, in Habermas's understanding, is clearly synonymous with the classical Weberian conception of "intersubjectively recognized knowledge." Even "a Chinese" should understand argumentation in Western research (Weber 1904/1985, 155). Yet, as the line put into italics makes clear, it may appear, on the contrary, to be a much more pedestrian task, namely, the capacity of the meaning involved to be transferred, passed on, communicated, with all the consequences of this possibility (especially that of constituting a generalized, shared knowledge).

On the one hand, Luhmann explicitly stipulates that truth is about "intersubjectively compelling certainty." Yet, on the other hand, far from being rooted in anything lifeworld related, or simply in anything that would transcend the realm of communication, this intersubjectively compelling character is defined by Luhmann simply as the ability of truth to be transferred to another person (*Self-Steering* 1968, 234). The question is thus, for Luhmann, merely about transfer (*Übertragbarkeit*), not about an experience that would be able to examine, measure, or warrant the content of what is passed off as truth, while for Habermas it is clearly that possibility of verification (*Überprüfbarkeit*) which every other question depends on. For whoever looks into these texts, the stake here is a double one.

On the one hand, we have to find what precisely Luhmann's position was in 1968—especially in light of later evolutions of his own thought. On the other, there is the question of how we should qualify, in retrospect, Habermas's interpretations of that position, since Habermas refers to the "transfer" rather negatively and mockingly as the "transport concept of truth" (Habermas, in H/L, 223). On the first account, there is an obvious ambiguity in Luhmann's notion of "transferability." It is likely that Habermas's reading in 1971 of Luhmann, in its critical part, triggered the latter to abandon the idea of linking either meaning or communication to anything that could be seen, no matter from how far or how close one looks at it as a "transfer." Even so, it is both possible and instructive to solve the riddle of what was the "intended meaning" in that "transport concept" of truth, which is an irresistible lookalike of a transmission theory of messages passing from a sender to a receiver. On the one hand—and this alone adds a serious question mark to the "transport concept" that Habermas reads into Luhmann's theory of transferred meaning—Luhmann is careful to qualify his "transfer" criterion by explaining it as *intersubjectively* compelling certainty. On the other hand, Luhmann follows a much stricter sociological (and, in one sense, less philosophical) agenda than Habermas, sticking always to the *difference in sociological terms* that any difference, or any feature whatsoever, is capable of making. The attribution of truth to a claim to validity on the basis of a consensus obtained through unconstrained and unlimited communication, as Habermas suggests (H/L, 223), means less to him than the possible operations that a truth allows or that empower communication to operate. In other words, the truth concept that Luhmann discovers at the heart of modern society is co-original with his understanding of the concepts of functionality and functional equivalence; however, truth is not about functional utility. Racist theories are utilized but not true. This also explains Luhmann's interest in *trust*. And it is well known that the way in which truth animates the operations of science has something in common with certain kinds of trust in shared meaning.[2] Habermas, on the other hand, gains from being understood as chiefly concerned by the search for an alternative to the positivist correspondence theories of truth.

There is no doubt that, much later on, when Luhmann established his sharp distinction between consciousness and psychic systems, on the one hand, and social, communication-built systems, on the other hand, he submitted his position to a radical and sharpening improvement. In 1968, he suggested the following, almost classically humanist interpretation: "Truth is something that no one can deny without thereby manifesting himself as a human person without sense and reason, and without thereby excluding himself from the community of world-carrying, meaning-constituting humans" (*Self-Steering* 1968, 233). Truth is the ultimate, that is, the nonrejectable discursive reality that society is dealing with. "Truth in the strong sense is a communication that is accepted by everyone" ("eine Kommunikation, der jedermann zustimmen muss"; 234) Yet the system formed by science or research is "emancipated from anguish" and can "continue to legitimate meaning even on the basis of high uncertainties that establish some firm intersubjectively transferred working condition" (247).

Arguably, what is offered by the largest part of Habermas's critique of Luhmann is a series of attempts at sharpening the understanding of what is meant by validity claims that concern "a communication that is accepted by everyone." This notion is at the heart of the extensive development of the consensus theory of truth in Habermas's elaborations over the following years. This work is rooted in his bid for a theory of validity claims for truth as well as for justice (*Richtigkeit*). Habermas's hypothesis developed throughout the 1970s, starting from the intuition that the motivations, norms, and possibilities that govern linguistic performance, and that thus offer themselves as a rational base of any theorization, are the fruit of the development of the coherent meaning that is imparted on them by social relationships such as coordination and cooperation. The theoretical proof of that intuition amounted to the rather formidable task of offering a coherent explanation of communicative rationality.

In hindsight, what is rather unquestionable today is the fact that, since the late 1960s, the evolution of Western culture, or at least of its discursively most active zones or sites, has undergone a powerful evolution of *Versprachlichung* (literally, "linguistification"), an unprecedented increase in the social "difference" "made" by discourse. Emotions, motives, thoughts have found ways of expression that give rise to communicative rationalization. The width and relevance of this tendency can barely be overrated. For instance, a person's concern for politics, political movements, or motivations is no longer simply accepted as a simple "feeling," an intimate and ultimately irresponsible affect or emotion: it has to be subjected to a social form—the omnipresent forum of rational argumentation (though without always being clear what is meant by this). Another aspect of the same tendency is the increase of communicative accountability (*Zurechnungsfähigkeit*). Habermas: "If we *wish* at all to take heed of the other person with whom we enter into an interaction, then we *must* assume that our interlocutor *could* tell us why he chooses to behave in the manner he does" (H/L, 118). The strength of that argument lies less in its philosophical novelty than in the correct description it offers of what might be understood as a new, near-omnipresent figure of social rhetoric. In the 1970s, it became a common and universalizable, if not universal or universalized, experience for everyone that entered into some kind of deliberation.

Whereas Luhmann's systems analysis has generated a powerful observatory of social evolution, including in its capillary detail, that is second to none, it might be argued that Habermas's account of the conditions of the newly emerging consensus about social existence today and the claims to validity bolstering them offers an invaluable hermeneutic assessment and self-assessment of the new aspirational grammar of consensus that characterizes modern society in our times. In Habermas's work, contemporary society mirrors itself as a result of communication, validity claims, and the acceptable and unacceptable sources of legitimacy in decision processes.

In 1970–71, Habermas developed a new, comprehensive recapitulation of the possibilities for a reconstruction of social theory in common with philosophy of language in *Reflections on the Linguistic Foundation of Sociology* (*Vorlesungen zu einer sprachtheoretischen Grundlegung der Soziologie*). This was developed in lectures held in February and March 1971 at Princeton, later (1984) to be published in the *Vorstudien und Ergänzungen zur Theorie der kommunikativen Handelns* (11–126), which forms the third part of *Theory of Communicative Action* (1981) and was probably written soon after finishing the manuscript of his contributions to the Habermas/Luhmann book.

In his Princeton lectures, Habermas writes a fully fledged homage to the sociologist Georg Simmel, a contemporary of Max Weber, for having contributed to the sociological study of society as a whole, and for having given it the form of a knowledge based upon the intersubjectivity constituted in the form of social interchanges. "This turn in the argument has a noteworthy implication. If the system of social life is constructed out of cognitive acts, then it rests on the facticity of the same validity claims as posited with every form of knowledge" (*Pragmatics*, 22). The "construction" inherent in the continuous building up of a society, its facticity, is constitutively in need of claims that are invested with a certain validity. Referring to them as "facticity," Habermas transforms a heritage from the neo-Kantian philosopher Heinrich Rickert (1910) that distinguishes between values and facts. Later, Habermas will use the (better-known) German title *Faktizität und Geltung* (*Between Facts and Norms*).

Habermas makes two equally important yet separate points: First, society is constitutively in need of a valid form of communication; in other words, society has "an immanent relation to truth" (*Linguistic*, 33). Second, the form of communication can be studied according to a philosophy of linguistic acts. To this second point, the idea is that linguistic acts can be studied in relation both to the notion of meaning and to the notion of truth. Some years later, Habermas added the notion of justice as validity claim. With regard to meaning and truth, meaning has been a core concept in sociology all the way back to Weber, Wilhelm Dilthey, and Georg Simmel, as well as in the philosophy of language too. Ludwig Wittgenstein and especially the Oxford school of Herbert P. Grice, Peter F. Strawson, J. L. Austin, and John Searle claimed "meaning" to be the core concept of a philosophy of language, while that school that starts with the work of Tarski and is in a sense continued by Donald Davidson claimed truth to be the more important concept. A few years later, the two schools ran together in the philosophy of meaning and truth proposed by Michael Dummett (1976), which Habermas used in his formal pragmatics. I mention these facts and events, if only within an overly schematizing recapitulation of English philosophies of language, in order to allow for an approximately correct appraisal of Habermas's in-depth discussions of those different schools. Things became even more complicated when Habermas combined them with the borrowings from phenomenological sociology, from Simmel and Weber to Alfred Schütz, Peter Berger, and Thomas Luckmann. The receptive performance—the sheer amount of doctrines, schools, and traditions recapitulated by Habermas—would deserve a chapter of its own, a chapter, however, that cannot be included in the present study, since its topic, Habermas's discussions with Luhmann, does not centrally refer to these philosophical backgrounds—otherwise the differently organized background of Luhmann's contributions would require the same amount of attention. All this needs to be left for another work. Pragmatically, one may add that no two persons read the same books.

LUHMANN'S RESPONSE TO HABERMAS: COMPLEXITY AND DISCUSSION AS SYSTEM

At the end of the common book, Luhmann answers Habermas with a hundred-page reply. To sum up, first it should be acknowledged that the debate certainly did not end with a conclusion that simply could be stated as if Luhmann accepted systems theory whereas Habermas did not. Habermas needed and needs systems theory in order to establish a theory of communicative action about modern society and what communication means in a complex society. Second, as Luhmann states in the beginning of his reply, the result does not appear as a contrast between an apology for an existing social order or a critical neglect of such an order. Systems theory, in Luhmann's version, is not an apology that simply adapts descriptions to society for useful purposes. We have already seen how Luhmann, from the very beginning, conceives systems theory as critique in the sense of the delimitation of conditions and possibilities inherent in modern society and its development. Neither Luhmann nor Habermas would accept the legacy of the Frankfurt School legacy of critical theory, yet Habermas would moderate and revise it, whereas Luhmann's aim was to reconstruct the entire program of not only a critical theory but any social theory about modern society.

Of course, such an endeavor became useful for Habermas. Our authors certainly dealt with a number of common themes such as communication, meaning, system, and evolution. Whereas Luhmann's program of building an adequate social theory to *observe* modern society certainly, on the one hand, is larger in scope than Habermas's, Habermas, on the other hand, has greater intentions about *what to do* with such a reconstruction in terms of normatively embedded action and participation programs. Habermas would establish a theory about how to act in a modern society and *participate* in its transformation. Accordingly, in order not to act naively, he needed systems theory, but he also delimited those parts of systems theory that were useful for such a politically oriented program.

This, too, is the background for the still-ongoing debates in the Habermas camp about, for instance, aesthetics. Habermas did not need an aesthetical theory; however, his close colleagues like Peter and Christa Bürger, Albrecht Wellmer, and Martin Seel who were concerned about art and aesthetic experience have had to expand Habermas's theory of communicative rationality into one of aesthetic rationality. This has been a fruitful endeavor that has led to important contributions. Yet for Habermas the political rationality of cooperation and coordination was the point of departure. For Luhmann, however, *Art as a Social System* (1995/2000) is as important as *Law as a Social System* (1993/2004) and *Politics as a Social System* (2000/still not translated). Luhmann himself developed an original theory of aesthetics. Habermas's core theme concerned conditions for coordination and cooperation, whereas Luhmann never accepted a certain political cluster concept to be more important or decisive as a departure point for the observations of modernity. Law, aesthetics, economy, science, love, religion, and so on are equally important. Organization has a somewhat similar position. Yet this does not mean that all those social systems are conceived in the same way.

Accordingly, in the first part of Luhmann's reply, the theme is "complexity." The problem is a paradox, which Luhmann observes in Habermas's conception of politics and domination (*Herrschaft*). Habermas aims to establish a critical position on domination that enlarges a description of political domination into one of a technical instrumental rationality that constitutes the backing of such forms of domination. To replace one form of domination with another form, however, does not entirely solve the problem. To start from conceptualizations and problems of political coordination is too obvious as answer to the problem of domination in Luhmann's conception (H/L, 399). If anything, perhaps the point is in the complexity inherent in modern society, since complexity says that modern systems cannot be dominated. Habermas's critical opposition to domination forms of modern society inherits Marx's idea of a capitalist system that dominates; and this idea inherited the idea of an organizational hierarchy of domination in a long-gone estate society. Yet, the form of society has changed. This does not mean that systems of capitalism, or war, or mass media, or what have you are incapable of domination. All systems are able to dominate communication scenes. Yet some have developed capacities to neglect more easily than other systems have. Money does not care, war does not care; but health systems care, aesthetics and law care. In short, "complexity" is not merely a catchy word useful to describe society. The conception of complexity demands a clash with a classical, if not traditional, reductionism, and a full development of not only one single fully integrated social system, which conceives a unitary whole of society, in the classic Hegel-Marx-Lukács sense of a totalizing unity. On the contrary, "the whole is less than the sum of its parts" (Luhmann *Differentiation* 1982, 238). The complexity of modern society is that it is not integrated, but differentiated into different systems.

One the one hand, Luhmann observes the problem of complexity with the system concept that is based on the formula "reduction of complexity." However, there are many forms of reduced complexities and each system establishes its form of reduced complexity, and hence, its own form of meaning, whether in law, economy, politics, art, science, or law. A problem is observed with a particular system formula that is used to reduce the complexities of the problem and solve it in exactly its specialized form: we may say, "do not cry, we still love each other," or "do not cry, here is some money," "do not cry, we can still complain to the court," "elect a new politician," or "change paradigm," and so on.

On the other hand, Luhmann accepts that Habermas is not satisfied and cannot find a solution to the problem of worldly experience with such formulas. This was what led Habermas to stick to Edmund Husserl's notion of lifeworld (*Lebenswelt*), a notion Luhmann also uses. Kant's world "as such" (*Welt an sich*) transcends our imagination (H/L,

297). In their later discussion, a certain "theological" observation of the correspondence between one system, one world, and one God appears. Here, Luhmann only mentions it. His observation is that differentiated systems may lead to differentiated imaginary forms of what they are not. If the world is not an economic system, and not a political system, we discuss the imaginary idea of a world as the common theme of what is "not an elephant" and "not a mouse": the world becomes an unidentifiable horizon.

This theme, conceived phenomenologically, as lifeworld, became increasingly decisive especially for Habermas as a consequence of the debate. Yet, already at this point in their discussion, the theme is not the one of one system and one world, a theme so much later to be discussed by Thomas McCarthy in his article "Complexity and Democracy, or The Seducements of Systems Theory" (1985). The idea of such a totalizing unity has been observed from a theologically described system, but this has nothing to do with the sociological notion of differentiated complexities.

Habermas and Luhmann agree that the sociological notion of a systemic reduction of complexity cannot be conceived from the basis of organic ideas of system or biological life. Bio-organic life is indispensable; however, it does not indicate what can be meant by meaning as a core concept for reduced complexity. Yet "to take the basis in linguistic rules of intersubjective communication, such as Habermas does, to coin the identity of meaning is insufficient, since the problem of meaning lays deeper than that of rules, because rules themselves have to be meaningful, in order to argue why the question of argument and justification of arguments and so on has a meaning" (Luhmann, in H/L, 302–3). Of course, Habermas could reply: What are the rules for Luhmann's argument? This was the typical argumentative style of Habermas's teacher and friend Karl-Otto Apel. Still, such a form of argumentation emerged historically. However, the problem is not sociological, whether or not rule-following is conventionally well established in linguistic forms. In the debates of philosophy of language, a major quarrel has been about a problem that comes from Ludwig Wittgenstein's *Philosophical Investigations*. Habermas and to some extent Luhmann have been aware about this, Habermas first in his Princeton lectures in 1970–71 and later in *Communicative Action* (2:30–39). Peter Winch's *Idea of Social Science* (1957), Saul Kripke's *Wittgenstein on Rules and Private Language* (1982),

G. P Baker and P. M. S. Hacker's *Scepticism, Rules and Language* (1984), and numerous others books (by people such as Jacques Bouveresse, J.-F. Lyotard, and Ernst Tugendhat) were concerned about this. A satisfying solution to this debate is, for Habermas and Luhmann and their sociological undertakings, to conceive rules as implicit rules implied in social communication. It is so basic to sociology from Durkheim to Harold Garfinkel's ethnomethodology and Erving Goffman's analyses of rules in everyday life that it is close to defining the core of all sociology and indeed certainly that of Habermas and Luhmann. However, in 1971, the philosophical debate was not completely settled; the point here is, however, that this does not constitute any major difference in Habermas's and Luhmann's views.

If anything, the divergence is indicated in Luhmann's note about the position of language to thought and perception:

> The opposite view of Habermas is a good example for our divergence: Habermas postulates that perception processes in principle (!) are possible to reconstruct in language because he is led by a counterfactual interest in argumentation. To me, the proper quality of perception, and for example its high speed in comparison to speech or thought, is more to the foreground, because the respective complexities treated cannot be replaced functionally. For such an interest, the exact relation between perception, speech, and thought is an empirical problem due to rather complex organized systems without any evident sub- or superordination. (Luhmann, in H/L, 303)

Speech cannot replace thought and vice versa. There is no functional equivalence, but only interpenetration as "structural coupling" (a later concept) between, perception, thought, and language. There is a difference in the form of complexities. Perception and thinking are undoubtedly much faster than speaking when complex matters are to be operated. With Husserl's phenomenology, perception and thought are not only about speed, but about synchronic holist operations. This difference does not neglect that speech refers to thought and thought is stabilized by speech or by perceptions. This differentiation has important implications for Luhmann and Habermas, since Habermas basically focuses thinking according to a principle of expressibility,[3] according to an idea that whatever can be meant about cooperation with others has, in principle, to be possible to be not only expressed but also defended in a communicative discourse. Yet of course this constitutive principle does not imply that the principle holds for everything that takes place in society; but it is, according to Habermas, necessarily and unavoidably an ideal principle for one form of meaning in and about communication in society. Whereas Luhmann with this argumentation finds operating with a sharp distinction between psychic systems and social systems obvious (Luhmann in H/L, 317), Habermas intends to find a middle area where thoughts, language, and communication systems overlap or ideally even integrate into one form of orientation.

This linguistic principle is constituted on a metacommunicative level with extremely idealized notions about whatever communication can be about. However, Luhmann prefers to take as his sociological starting point a much broader conception of communication. In the Habermas/Luhmann book, Luhmann still conceives of communication in terms of "meaningful action and experience with prelinguistic roots" (Luhmann, in H/L, 303). Communication operates with the distinction, for example, between words about bread and bread as on object for eating. Language takes the linguistic departure in the meaning of the word *bread* according to its use.[4] For Habermas, this difference is useful when political cooperation should be reduced to whatever can be defended linguistically. However, for the political sociologist Luhmann, the perception of, say, the rhetorical voice of Nixon, Reagan, or G.W. Bush compared to that of JFK or Obama could be about the difference between the rhetoric of confidentiality and a rhetoric of argumentation as forms of persuasion without a possibility of reducing the complexity of the problem to the problem of linguistic argumentative speech devoid of perception.

In their coauthored book, Habermas reproaches Luhmann that a philosophical conception of world should be radically different than a conception of world complexity, as it can be operated as a contingent world for those selections coped with in systems. To this, Luhmann answers with a conception from Husserl that distinguishes between action and experience (*Handeln und Erleben*). The world can be experienced as contingent on selective reductions that distinguish between system and environment (*Umwelt*), yet also on distinctions between what is determined or undetermined. Thereby Luhmann operates with four possibilities: undetermined environment (i.e., "world"), determined environment, undetermined systems, and determined systems (Luhmann, in H/L, 301). Remember that in German the environment of a system is designated as *Umwelt*, which literally means "surrounding world."

To sum up, communication acts through speech, in such a way that "thought" and "perception" are experienced as such a "surrounding world." Habermas and Luhmann diverged on the distinct ways to handle the problem of system and world; in fact, both authors used the German philosophical tradition from Gottfried Leibniz to Immanuel Kant to Edmund Husserl in order to describe whatever could be indicated as "world" (Luhmann, in H/L, 313). However, Habermas mistrusted systems theory in using an instrumental or organic-biological paradigm to describe the distinction between system and environment. This, nevertheless, does not correspond to Luhmann's reconstruction of world experience compared to those acts; it operates with clearly determined and reduced selections, later described in the form of "codes," a designation value Luhmann used for the first time in their coauthored book (H/L, 345). From this, it is clear that both Habermas and Luhmann aimed to preserve phenomenological ideas about world and lifeworld. Habermas did not find the idea of reduced complexity useful to his purposes. Luhmann operated with that idea because his conception of meaning aimed to operate with an extremely broad spectrum in his communication theory, whereas Habermas ideally focused a very particular form of counterfactual communication in consensus-oriented speech situations. Luhmann agrees with Habermas that intersubjective communication, in the form of dialogues, cannot be conceived with technical concepts.

> However, our arguments for this are very different. Whereas Habermas refers to a practice of linguistically argued communication as nontechnical action and eventually of a discourse of idealized implied possibilities of understanding, I do see the problem not in an opposition between technique and practice as models for action, but in the insufficient concepts of action whatsoever, which is in the distinction between action and system. Thereby we arrive at a central point in our controversy: This depends more precisely upon how a systems-theoretical interpretation

of the personal and social constitution begins and how argumentations could defend its superiority or inferiority in comparison with a linguistic approach. (Luhmann in H/L, 318–19)

Luhmann and Habermas both find that "the inter- in intersubjectivity" and "interaction" cannot lead back to any subjective philosophy of consciousness (Luhmann, in L/H, 319; see further SA 6, 169–88). Luhmann could be wrong in the statement that Habermas sought intersubjective rules, but only if such rules were reducible to explicit communication rules, as in discursive argumentation.

Yet in 1971, Habermas had not fully developed his conception of discourse and communicative action. Habermas's philosophy of discursive argumentation primarily should be conceived as an idea of a differentiation between explicit argumentation and the implied presuppositions. Moreover, if this differentiation operates in discourse-ethical argumentation at the philosophical level, it is, according to Habermas, more penetrating than sociologically observed differentiation in its communicative operations at the level of a socially integrated lifeworld. Habermas's point is not any reductionist version that deduces communication from explicit argumentative discourse, or one that infers from presuppositions of a lifeworld to communication. The point is in the differentiation *and* in the distinction between the sphere of argumentation and the sphere of the presuppositions developed already and simultaneously implied, whenever language is in use.

Of course, Habermas could not lead his intuitions about communication into a direction where only explicit linguistic performances were idealized. Such a position would be much too vulnerable to rhetorically powerful speech and would be far from Habermas's personal experiences. Rather, to the contrary, his model of an idealized speech situation tries to save a possibility of a social life embedded in communication that at least in principle would be free from the domination of charismatic talk, spin doctors, and brilliant speech without sustainable content. That is why he holds validity claims as a criterion for meaningful speech.

According to Luhmann, this (sometimes-agonizing) intuition might be right. However, in Habermas's sociological observations of society, it also brings up the question, of whether this orientation toward argumentative speech needs a general theory about how communication processes develop in society *independently* from our eventual hopes of domination-free ideal speech. Communication processes have to be observed in their own autonomy as self-regulative communication. In fact, Habermas repeatedly reproached the rebelling students after May 1968 that they forgot to observe society with that cool distance Luhmann furthered. If hopes could replace distorted realities, it would only happen if such realities were observed as conditions for the hopes. There is no functional equivalence, and both Habermas and Luhmann tried during those years to teach their students about realism. Perhaps exaggeratedly, one may say that Habermas was a spokesman for a minimum of realism, whereas Luhmann pled for a maximum of realism. The description of societal conditions and the possibilities they can sustain must be coped with if we want to enlighten and be clear about the differentiation between explicit argumentation and implicit presuppositions. In which systems does such explicit argumentation occur? Discussions are also systems.

> The meaningful constitution of the world in human social life does not depend on the argumentation [*Begründung*] of validity claims in acts; rather, to the contrary, the argumentation and even the questions about argumentation and interests in it depend upon the intersubjective constitution of the world. Therefore, intersubjectivity has to be conceptualized as a social dimension as such that is more abstract and independent from argumentation. [In a note Luhmann adds, "Habermas here lacks a temporal language for the temporal dimension of meaning. This would finally disrupt the subject/object dichotomy."] (Luhmann, in H/L, 321)

The linguistic dimensions of meaning are comparable whenever Habermas and Luhmann elucidate the social and material (cognitive) dimensions of language. The difference is in the temporal dimension. To Habermas, Husserl's notion of intersubjectivity is about dialogue, whereas intersubjectivity for Luhmann is in temporal copresence, simultaneity, and synchronicity, and also in personal encounters in the sense that Goffman discusses them (Luhmann, in H/L, 329). Martin Heidegger wrote about "cobeing" (*Mitsein*). Luhmann refers to "colife" (*Mitleben*), life in simultaneity. The interaction system is to be found in the double contingencies of interchange (*Wechselwirkung*), not between two subjects or two actors, but in the action itself as interconnection (Luhmann, in H/L, 322–23).

A certain discussion theme concerns Parsons's conception of double contingency as a form of double negation (Habermas, in H/L, 187ff.; Luhmann, in H/L, 324). To Habermas, the point is about the famous capacity-to-say-no (*Nein-sagen-können*; cf. Habermas *Religion*, 60–66). To Luhmann, the point is the negation of the experience of the other as identical to my experience, which I, furthermore, cannot use in an identified connection with the other. Hence, the identification in communication does not pass only based on the one or the other, as if something meaningful becomes transmitted, but because a common theme occurs in communication.

Kant's famous example of an aesthetical judgment, "this is beautiful," is a statement about communication, and is like saying, "In communication this can be described and defended as beautiful—the 'thing it self' is not identical to the judgment about it; yet my compassion, or your compassion, with the thing (the salad, the mountain, the picture) can be filled with horror." To Habermas, the starting point here is the conditions for expression, as if the point is "the law is beautiful"; to Luhmann, the starting point is the distinction between the experience (*Erlebnis*) of the psychic system and the action handled by communication according to the conditions established and differentiated in communication systems (such as art, law, politics, love, tourism, and so on). Habermas finds that Luhmann here is fixed to a monological psychic system. However, Luhmann's point is different: Luhmann's position is that the individual psychic system is allowed to experience whatever it may, exactly because an aesthetic symbolization has become "differentiated, generalized, and respecified" in, for example, art or politics. If such differentiated forms do not emerge, judgments may lead to severe conflicts; however, I can discuss performances of an orchestra according to aesthetic standards, even if my personal experience is made horrible because of a headache. In fact, it is exactly this differentiation that allows me to have a headache and be concerned about it as a condition for experience and judgment. Yet in political discussions (and here Habermas finds his point), my disgust for a certain politician cannot be defended with a reference to the voice of a politician being similar to that of my repressive schoolteacher.

Neither the schoolteacher nor the politician dominates any form of authority for my judgment; therefore Habermas's point, according to Luhmann, should not be about domination-free discussion, but about freedom of constraint, since discussions *as systems* may be led by ideas of problem-solving with external purposes. To Luhmann, this means that discussions in their nonconstrained form have to be what Luhmann defines as internally self-regulated systems. And yes, "there are systems" ("es gibt Systeme," a phrase famously repeated by Luhmann in his introduction to *Social Systems*; Luhmann, in H/L, 325; *Systems* 1984, 16). Whereas this autonomy of system communication could satisfy Habermas's claim about free discourses, the closure inherent in this autonomy is, according to Luhmann, exactly not what Habermas wants to plea for. Habermas, according to Luhmann, opts for an argumentation form that can use the individual experience as a resource for further arguments (Luhmann, in H/L, 326–27). Selections in the closure of social systems are one thing; another is about reasoning that is committed to still further argumentation based on a presupposition that individuals can add still further reasons behind their claims.

To Luhmann, argumentation as communication system involves further system operations, whereas, for Habermas, argumentation involves the experiences of individuals who participate in discussions. In a certain sense, this difference is very simple and we know it from discussions and how they proceed: The discussion can evolve as such whereas people as observers can observe how themes and stories emerge around the table. Or people experience how they participate with their stories and their contributions. To Luhmann, this distinction is about "themes" and "contributions" (Luhmann, in H/L, 331–33), and he refers to interaction sociology in order to invoke our everyday life experiences. Yet what are the repercussions of this tiny difference between the observation of discussion themes and contributions from participants?

Here we have to remember that we're still talking only about interaction systems and encounters in intersubjective meetings and not about the self-regulation of financial systems, legal systems, or war systems. When Luhmann in a much later final speech at Bielefeld University in 1994 asked, "'What is the case?' and 'what is behind it?,'" he not only depicted two leading trends in modern sociology; he also indicated that the case may be about huge, complex systems, which evolve behind our immediate experience of our everyday life and the discussions that occur in it.

TRUTH

In Luhmann's third chapter of his final six chapters, which replies to Habermas, he discusses "Truth as a medium of communication." The initial theme is about Habermas's idea of a so-called "ideal speech situation," and the first problem is whether this ideal has something to do with truth; the second problem is whether it has anything to do with real conditions in the real world. Habermas tends to solve this double problem with the idea of an implied consensus. Yet as we have seen, Luhmann himself describes consensus as a real empirical phenomenon to be found in the world. Among citizens, firms, public authorities, and so on, there is probably a consensus in modern society that there should be roads. This empirical finding, of course, could have something to do with the idealized principle that there argumentatively should be roads in a society; and if the question arises whether they should be paid for publicly or privately, certainly some divergences could occur and dissenting opinions would find a place. Yet how could argumentation about such questions develop in any rational way? Habermas tends to argue with a model, which since Kant has been named "an a priori synthetic statement": reasonability and idealized conditions for argumentation do in fact occur! What form they could have is then still to be clarified. The telos of rationality is in fact somehow already there in society, as when theology found that perfect virtues were around or neoclassical economists got the idea that firms somehow behave according to instrumental rationality. Communication occurs as if some form of communicative rationality is embedded, and is so, above all, in dialogues.

In a long note, Luhmann breaks down those problems into four claims about the fact that intersubjectivity in social systems is not necessarily equal to ideal speech situations and that intersubjectivity may lead to dissent, quarrel, and conflict. Likewise, consensus is often not ideal, but imposed or simply false. At the same time, Habermas should search for those real conditions that function as presuppositions for valid idealized consensus. We can place Luhmann's concepts used to describe Habermas's position in a table.

TABLE 2.1 Consensus, Dissent, and Intersubjectivity

	Nonideal risky reality	Intersubjectivity
Conflict	False invalid consensus	Valid dissent
Anticipation	Facticity, pragmatic conformity	Habermas's ideal speech situation (true valid consensus)

Luhmann finds the problem in the notion of consensus where the ideal speech situation should be distinguished from that of achieved consensus. An achieved consensus may be false and illusionary, and an idealized speech situation (with infinite discussion and so on) may lead to dissent and quarrel. Of course, we shall remember that Habermas, at that moment in 1971, was only at the beginning of his research program about a critique of legitimacy. Habermas sought an idea of consensus to find the moral criteria of achieved acceptance in the communication of coordination.

Here, Luhmann's position could be to establish the acceptance of dissent possibilities, or what Habermas has called the "capacity-to-say-no" (*Nein-sagen-können*), and to say, "I am not convinced," as the German foreign minister Joschka Fischer famously did in a debate with the U.S. secretary of defense Donald Rumsfeld before the Iraq invasion in 2003. Similarly, Colin Powell's speech in the UN Security Council in February 2003 may be treated by all kinds of differentiated communication systems (law of nations, mass media, political systems, war systems, economical credit markets, governmental administration systems, families, and so on). Its validity claims became subject for all those systems and were treated accordingly.

Luhmann's reconstruction of Habermas's discourse model should not be confused with his often-repeated oversight model of what communication implies, a four-box figure, which he puts into use right after his criticism of Habermas (Luhmann, in H/L, 345). Communication in an intersubjective situation is about more than what occurs in dialogues.

Thought and perception are added to the explicit use of language. What other people do may occur to me through perception and thought; likewise, what I do to others, and what we do with one another, may be the object for thought and experience without any direct translatability into language.

LUHMANN'S FIGURE (H/L, 345)

TABLE 2.2 Luhmann's Figure

	Ego's experience	Ego's action
Alter's experience	Ae—Ee (truth; values)	Ae—Eh (love)
Alter's action	Ah—Ee (money, art)	Ah—Eh (power)

The classical idea was that the experience of truth was embedded in the facticity of experienced realities. Truth was basically about ontology but became subject to questions about the knowledge of these realities, which is a knowledge that ideally was claimed to be true or false, dichotomized in the binary schema of yes/no as a code (Luhmann, in H/L, 350). Before the linguistic turn, this was seen as a reflexivity of thought: the truth of thought could be subject to thought in the reflexivity of thinking about thinking. This reflexivity could then repeatedly be the subject for theoretical statements. Language is able to repeat.

In German, the word "perception" is *Wahrnehmung* and the word for "truth" is *Wahrheit*; thus perception literally means "truth-taking" or "take-as-true." This is why the experience in perception is linked to truth in a sense that can become external to linguistic action. Luhmann includes this conception in his "general theory of communicative media" (Luhmann, in H/L, 353). There cannot be sanctions against such a thing as false experience, but only against lies and false statements. For example, if Colin Powell's agents had experienced weapons of mass destruction in Iraq before his famous speech in the UN Security Council on February 5, 2003, the speech could not be contested as a lie, but the invented statements about what was claimed as perceptions could be subject to contestations.

According to Luhmann, this is decisive for differentiations between truth claims and claims for justice. Those two claims have to follow separate criteria and codes in communication. "Therefore I do not see that there is a danger of a conceptual fusion between truth and power in my conception, which is based on a differentiation of media and corresponding differentiations of subsystems in society" (Luhmann, in H/L, 353). Luhmann, here, probably tries to push Habermas toward a differentiation between a communicatively embedded discourse theory of truth, a discourse theory of justice and practical normative claims, and a discourse ethics. Such a differentiation was not yet established by Habermas. Yet his response to Luhmann's suggestion came with the next two major contributions from Habermas's hand: the long, important article "Theories of Truth" (1972) and *Legitimation Crisis* (1973).

In his reply, Luhmann repeatedly tries to elucidate the roots and motivations behind Habermas's suspicions toward systems theory in general and Luhmann's theoretical developments in particular. Often Luhmann states the points and presuppositions they have in common, but several times Luhmann has to describe why they come to misunderstandings. Luhmann finds some reasons in their views about "technique."

In *Technology and Science as "Ideology"* (1968) Habermas tries to reconstruct the modern transformation of science into the means of production, which gave a new role to interaction superior to or functionally equivalent to instrumental work. Yet Luhmann in *Goal Concept and Systems Rationality*, published the same year, points toward the misfire in the use of instrumental concepts about input-output, cause-effect, and means-goal. He showed that linear causation models should be replaced, and accordingly, systems theory in Luhmann's version was reconstructed. Science as system does not operate instrumentally to any external goal. Therefore, an ideal of whatever truth can mean to science cannot be built adequately as an idealized conception dependent on classical notions about a knowledge that is used in technical instrumental action. The triangular notions of domination-free idealization, power, and systems of science have to recognize that science is not a tool for craftsmen used instrumentally in a power system, which tries to dominate in such a way that, in opposition to that, a domination-free search for truth is adequate. There is no "implicit zero-sum" with some authentic true experience to be searched for (Luhmann, in H/L, 359). Research systems function in another way.

As Habermas and Luhmann during these years discussed the function of research and adequate validity conceptions in modern research, the Popper-Hempel model was being replaced by Thomas Kuhn (*The Structure of Scientific Revolutions*, 1962), by Hans-Georg Gadamer (*Truth and Method*, 1960), by Paul Feyerabend (*Against Method*, 1975), and Georg Henrik von Wright (*Explanation and Understanding*, 1971), and still new philosophies emerged such as Michel Foucault's *Archeology of Knowledge* (1969). In Germany Karl-Otto Apel's *Towards a Transformation of Philosophy* (vols. 1–2, 1973; English translation 1998) and the constructivist Erlangen School around Paul Lorenzen (1974) for a while became extremely influential, especially for Habermas. A few years later, those debates were further enlarged with pragmatically oriented publications such as Richard Rorty's *Philosophy and the Mirror of Nature* (1979), and in the present context in particular Jean-François Lyotard's influential *The Postmodern Condition* (1979), which in fact appears as one coherent, or at least refreshing, reconstruction of part of the Habermas/Luhmann debate. The important point here is not to summarize all those contributes, but to make clear that the system of science became restructured with new standards about what research was good for. Luhmann much later published a huge book *Die Wissenschaft der Gesellschaft* (1990; *Science as Social System*), which had a major impact on the history of science in Germany, especially through the research of his pupil Rudolf Stichweh (1991).

UNIVERSALITY

Luhmann's fourth chapter in his reply, "Evolution and History," touches upon another theme in their debate and will be discussed later. The fifth chapter is named "Universality and Possibilities to Argue for Systems Theory."

Habermas several times used the theme of universality. In 1970, he published an important reconstruction about the "universal claims of hermeneutics," and later he coined the concept of "universal pragmatics" in the long article "What Is Universal Pragmatics?" (originally published in 1976, collected in *Pragmatics*, 21–104). At the same time, he became more and more occupied with the universalizable claims in a discourse ethics. Yet to Luhmann, the term *universality* is used to describe the cognitive scope of a systems theory in social research. If systems theory is used more or less everywhere in other sciences with a universalist claim, this certainly is a theme external to Luhmann's endeavor.

Luhmann's aim is to establish a systems theory, which can cover all fields in social research, or at least in sociology broadly. This includes economical sociology, sociology of law, political sociology, educational sociology, and management, just to mention some of the major fields covered by departments of law, economy, political science, education, and organization; but humanities (arts), religion (theology), and history are also important subjects that Luhmann aimed to cover and eventually managed to make important contributions to.

Luhmann finds that one of the reasons for the debate with Habermas is the probably somewhat uncertain view that Habermas had about Luhmann's ambitions and probably about his capacities too—and one is tempted to say vice versa too. Even in a respectful debate, a certain mistrust could find its way if it was questioned whether even the most brilliant heads could cover as many fields as Luhmann and Habermas eventually managed. Perhaps Luhmann even more than Habermas penetrated deeply, in the sense that Habermas oriented himself, though broadly, toward conditions for social and political coordination.

Luhmann is tempted to say that communicative claims toward a constitution of world relations in this respect are more ambitious for Habermas than for Luhmann (Luhmann, in L/H, 379). At the same time, Luhmann delimits himself to not take a "totalizing" approach: Luhmann's ambition is to observe what can be observed with systems theory and not to observe what cannot be observed with systems theory yet perhaps could be with other theories. He does not claim that his theory is or should be the sole valuable or useful theory. In this dual sense, Habermas's claim is much more universally penetrating, however, with a strength in ambitions about cooperation about coordination of acts. Luhmann finds that Habermas sinks into a "problem of dissolution of contingencies" (*Kontingenzausschaltung*), when he dissolves contingent experiences. This happens whenever Habermas claims to reconstruct valid claims about interlinkages between political domination and reasoning (Luhmann, in L/H, 380–81). Or, to say it far more bluntly than Luhmann would, Luhmann probably here claims that Habermas risks an intolerant position.

Luhmann placed this criticism after his chapter "Evolution and History" probably due to the important argument by Luhmann that any idea of reasoning under idealized conditions is based upon historical suppositions in which we today unmistakably have our starting point, but nevertheless also our conditions and limitations (Luhmann, in H/L, 382). As far as I can see, in the continued debate, this reproach became more important some years later for Habermas, when he changed his claims of, for example, a "universal pragmatics" (1976) toward a so-called "formal pragmatics" (in *Communicative Action*, vol. 1) and also renounced claims about "universality" in discourse ethics in favor of "universalization" of claims.

Luhmann finds that the problem is not that questions of validity disappear or get dissolved. The problem is, if anything, that contingent experiences become regulated by systems, which code what is recognized as accountable valid communication (Luhmann, in H/L, 383). This happens not only in science as a system but all over with all kinds of systems. Remember that Luhmann does *not* say that systems are "good"; he is not particularly in favor of systems and does not claim their normative or even cognitive superiority, only that they establish codes for problem treatment and communication.

Accordingly, systems theory too can be treated as a subject for systems theory where it becomes obvious that systems theory has to delimit itself and even criticize itself in its inabilities to see what it cannot see (Luhmann, in H/L, 386–87). Therefore, Luhmann can reply to Habermas's reproach that Luhmann does not reflect upon the bracketed validity in the use of systems theory in self-reflection (Habermas in H/L, 226–32) by saying that this is no problem. Later, in 1990, Luhmann, in the little speech "I See What You Cannot See" (named after a German game for children) celebrating the Frankfurt School's fiftieth anniversary, reversed the criticism and claimed that the Frankfurt School (in particular Max Horkheimer) should have established a description of society to explain how such theories as critical theory became possible.

Luhmann's point is that society develops self-descriptions, including (self-critical) theories, in order to establish and develop itself. Habermas found that systems theory confounded theory with action and mentioned systems structures as being as inherent in reality as in theory. Yet Luhmann, the sociologist of law, took legal positivism as it emerged in the eighteenth century as an example and claimed that a systems theory of law can perfectly well describe how legal positivism led to stabilized structures. Such structures can be reformed and transformed due to their positive formalization—and this can be a subject for a systems theory, whether such reforms then use systems theory or not (Luhmann, in H/L, 388). This indeed is no limiting condition for systems theory. Nor is Habermas's use of descriptions of public mass media a delimiting condition in *Structural Transformation of the Public Sphere* (1962).

THE DEBATE ON IDEOLOGY

Of the four hundred or so pages of their coauthored book from 1971, each author, Habermas as well as Luhmann, devotes about twenty pages to the question of truth. Habermas's chapter carries the title "The Systems Theoretical Concept of Truth—and the False Unity of Theory and Practice" (221–39). He begins with a discussion of some of Luhmann's earlier conceptions about truth, without, however, discussing "Truth and Ideology—Proposals to a Renewed Discussion" ("Wahrheit und Ideologie—Vorschläge zur Wiederaufnahme der Diskussion"), Luhmann's first article on the subject, written in 1962, and featuring a subtitle that sufficiently indicates Luhmann's aim, namely, to resituate the discussion in the field in which it had started, sociology of knowledge (*Wissenssoziologie*). Luhmann's "Truth and Ideology" explains that, in historical terms, the theme of truth was, primarily, about being and ontology. It lost its privilege only at the point at which, throughout a long-extended movement triggered by Plato and Aristotle, epistemological questions about knowledge and truth took the place of ontological questions about being and turned the main discussion into one of method. Truth transformed into a function of knowledge and methodology. At a much later moment, after the French Revolution, truth acquired separate grounds and became distinguished from ideology.

Whereas ideologies were characterized as internal and rather short-lived furniture of a world itself characterized by the rapid change of its conditions and parameters. One ideology, in other words, could be replaced by another one, and factually was replaced, whenever goals and means were contested.

In this way, ideologies acquired a *functional* definition. Moreover, one ideology was deemed to be the functional equivalent of another one. Luhmann determines the function served by ideologies as that of externalizing goals in such a way as to form a chain ideology-goals-means-consequences. By the same token, ideologies also serve to rationalize choices within chains of interrelated decisions in order to exclude the threatening specter of other possibilities that might claim to be taken into account but that, for whatever reasons, official or unadmitted, are unwanted. Ideology generally operates as a justification of the possibilities that are actually chosen, as opposed to other ones. Accordingly, the move that comes closest to what might be called a critique of ideology consists in consistently asking the question of *other possibilities*. Luhmann explains:

> Yet, besides [every ideology's exposure to the critique emanating from] hostile ideologies, what emerges is the possibility of a different scientific-knowledge-based critique of ideology that focuses upon ideology's *function*. Ideology poses peculiar form-related problems; any insights about these are independent from this or that particular ideology and the value decisions it caters to. Insights of the sort are general enough to be impervious to the literary weapon of satire and to the political weapon of censure, both of which an opponent can always use against whatever specific ideological claim. (*Wahrheit* 1962, 60)

The reasoning that animates Luhmann's early critique of ideology can thus be characterized by the distinction between two levels: on the one hand, every ideology factually excludes other ideologies, while potentially it could be replaced by one (or some or perhaps any) other ideology. Conversely, every ideology has a function if and only if the command chain ideology-goal-means-consequence is accepted and excludes any type of relationship or arrangement different than the one foreseen by the ideology at work. Considering both together, the word *ideology* appears to refer to a peculiar procedure, which is founded upon a double exclusion. An ideology is a protection device with the function, first, of excluding other possibilities and, second, of excluding any competitors for the function of excluding other possibilities.

On both levels, the use of ideology consists in eliminating or bracketing contradictions or problems by means of raising the level of generality of the reasons, arguments, and motivations invoked, until the point at which their problem character is out of sight, or the contradiction is no longer perceived as a contradiction.

Compared to "truth," ideology is, in other words, a loosening of the criteria required for validity claims. It goes without saying that this diminishes its performances as a problem-solving device. All ideology can do is diminish the social or communicative presence of other possibilities, if they were deprived of their ideological shield and subjected to mere reasoning or argument. On the other hand, by doing exactly this, by preserving an integrity or, at least, a level of unquestionability, ideology does accomplish a function (which is not challenged by the fact that one could qualify this function, in some, many, or most cases, also as dysfunction). Luhmann's later position is the consequence of his dismissal, already in 1962, of claims that the ideological era had been a mere historical intermezzo, fated to disappear, a dismissal criticizing Raymond Aron's and Daniel Bell's diagnoses in "Fin de l'âge idéologie" (1955) and *The End of Ideology* (1961), respectively. The function of ideology has not disappeared; hence the counterposition that asks for truth is still valid.

In Habermas and Luhmann's joint publication *Theorie der Gesellschaft oder Sozialtechnologie?*, Habermas—skirting Luhmann's article from 1962 devoted to the matter—undertakes a lengthy examination of ideology as a concept and as an object. Since 1962, discussions about ideology had been anything but forgotten, especially in critical theory—an internal direction in social theory that sometimes even went under the name "Critique of Ideology." In 1968, Habermas had published *Technology and Science as "Ideology"*, a collection of articles that drew its title from its main, or at least longest, article, and attracted an immense audience in Germany. Published quasi-simultaneously with it was his *Knowledge and Human Interests* (1968), a study that in spite of its greater difficulty and complexity was almost equally widely read.

Here, Habermas developed a conception about interaction as a sociological core concept, which, he argued, should be given a status and a position equivalent and complementary to those attributed, in the sociology of neo-Marxism, to the concept of labor (*Arbeit*). Technology and science evolve as results of forms of interaction and communication. Therefore, Habermas argues, communication carries a claim to be classified, in neo-Marxist categories, among the productive forces, more exactly among the forms of *communicative rationality* and not among their commodified side forms called *instrumental rationality.*

Communication has become productive for the benefit of capitalist society; however, communication follows two paths, a commendable one—which Habermas calls "undistorted interaction"—based on an endeavor to orient interaction toward consensus, and a deeply regrettable one, called "strategically distorted interaction and communication." It is among the branches of the latter one that we find forms of technique: they are therefore defined as subject to a purely instrumental rationality. In practical research-related terms, it is the orientation toward instrumentalist objectivity, positivism, and causal explanations that distorts human communication into strategy. Therefore, social science is constantly on the brink of turning into an instrumentalist social technology—or, in other words, of becoming a distorted, reified, commodified, and, in short, alienated form of human communication. Ideology is identified as one of those *distorted forms of communication.*

The question at stake in Habermas's analysis is thus whether a particular social theory is subject to what is called "strategically distorted communication." As social systems theory was among the leading social theories and methodologies already of the immediate postwar era, it was not particularly astonishing that it would be subjected to the question of distorted communication and interaction, and of whether it is therefore to be criticized and discarded as an "ideology." This is the question posed in chapter 5 of Habermas and Luhmann's book, Habermas's thirty-page intervention: "The Systems Theoretical Concept of Ideology, and Systems Theory as a New Form of Ideology."

CRITIQUE OF IDEOLOGY AS CRITIQUE OF UNENLIGHTENED VALUES

Habermas goes back to Luhmann's article from 1962 "Truth and Ideology" and seems clearly to overstate, or misread, several of its points.

First, he reduces Luhmann's functionalism to a version of the age-old conception of causality, identifying "function" as a chain between cause and effect. He then identifies Luhmann's systemic outlook as a version of input-output relations. It is, incidentally, quite obvious how each of these overstatements contributes its share to the overall verdict of "social technology." Finally and perhaps most decisively, Habermas's ideology-critical outlook leads him to overlook Luhmann's own critique of ideology. In fact, here's what Luhmann said:

> By means of choosing "function" as a vantage point, one can confront every ideology with other possibilities, which concerns not only other possibilities in matters of action, but other possibilities in matters of ideological justification as well. The effect of this is that ideology itself becomes part of the category of objects that can be criticized, improved, replaced—that it becomes something that can be subjected [*fungibel*] to all types of operations. (*Wahrheit* 1962, 59)

Apparently ignoring this point, Habermas (in H/L, 258) quotes another phrase from the same page of Luhmann's article, which deals with examples of ideologies. Luhmann here explains the difference between two constructions of ideology—that of the contemporary Soviet Union (his article, once again, is from 1962) and that of National Socialist Germany. In the passage referred to by Habermas, Luhmann argues that, in contradiction to the Soviet manner of conceiving the world of social goods according to the notion that anything, as long as it is "productive," is justifiable as a means of social progress, in the Nazi case "a nonsensical [insane, *unsinnigen*] outsider value—the Nordic race—is given top status while everything else is downgraded, in a maneuver where the nonsensicalness/insanity of the chosen top value reveals ostensively that the stake is not that value in itself, but the neutralizing effect and the enlargement of the domain of admissible means that it allows to obtain" (*Wahrheit* 1962, 59). The meaning of the passage can be determined by saying that the "value" of racism is nonsensical/insane, and serves, precisely by this means, as a neutralizer of all alternative values, "manifesting" that neutralization by means of delivering the "proof" of power that it epitomized by its successful, general, unlimited imposition. The Nazi ideology says, "we're good because you're bad." This reading, however, is very distant from the way in which Habermas interprets the meaning of the passage. According to his reading, the choice of race ideology as an example of ideology proves that

> Luhmann is not able to conceive the essential phenomena in the formation and reproduction of ideologies: namely, that ideologies are prevented from being publicly questioned and that they can be maintained only by way of systematically restraining the communicational exchange of wills and intentions. Yet, even so, the example of the Nazi ideology—which fits the functionalist concept of ideology insofar as, here, the manipulators themselves do not believe their own artificial product—throws a clear light upon the control of language and the regulated selection of allowed communications that are at work [in ideology]. (Habermas, in H/L, 258).

The point at stake in the dispute is an instructive one. It is easy, today, with the hindsight of half a century, to understand it as turning on the position "beyond," which each of the interlocutors silently supposes, either as a potential path leading out of the ideological condition, or at least as a viewpoint from which the phenomenon can be observed.

Habermas, taking up a long tradition of antirepression militancy and critique of power, sees the "way out of ideology" in establishing conditions of unrestrained possibility to publicly communicate ideas, critiques, points of view. He thus approaches the issue of ideology on the basis of the assumption that the population is divided into two components according to a subject's stance (active and passive) with respect to power. Ideology is a matter of power or domination exerted, schematically speaking, by one limited group—the group that, for independent historical reasons, factually holds power—over another, much larger group, which includes everyone else. By sidelining repressive power and resolute action against the restraint of public discourse, society can overcome ideology and establish itself in an ideology-free space.

Luhmann, on the contrary, is animated by the ambition *not to need* a—necessarily fragile—assumption of the sort. For him, ideology is not explained as long as it is seen as an accompanying phenomenon of a foregoing structuration of society into power haves and power have-nots. On the one hand, Luhmann fails to take up the idea or ideal of a society that would be transparent to itself—or free from ideology. On the other hand, the issue of *ideologies*, in the plural, is given a much larger space than that of ideology. What is at stake in the appraisal of any empirical ideology is the question of *which* justifications it selects as acceptable or relevant. Center-staging the "Nordic race," Nazi ideology accepted *race* as a relevant justification, both necessary and sufficient; by showing the example of how easily an uncontrolled reduction of complexity can be enforced, it created the conditions of an exorbitant ease in the execution of any type of operation of maneuver that could be referred to as the racial reference. Luhmann criticizes that ease. Yet what he criticizes and rejects about the National Socialist ideology is less ideological characters as such than the extremely simplified and reductive ideology offered by National Socialism. The fact is that his general suggestion at this early moment, the suggestion to replace ontological with functional thinking, dispenses Luhmann from any antiideology crusade, and leads him even to interpret ideology as an (always-replaceable) solution to the problem of orientating action and behavior.[5]

In his criticism of this Luhmannian position, Habermas, or so it looks today, became overly absorbed by the suspicion that functionalism is about an instrumentalist control of causes and effects, inputs and outputs, similar to the strategic relation between goals and means that plays an important role in his own argumentation. Luhmann, since his first article ("Function and Causality," also from 1962, in SA 1), had opened up the instrumentalist "black box" between the two poles, goals and means, inputs and outputs, or at least "colored the box white."

By means of replacing their state of *mixte mal décomposé* with a neatly divided polarity between time for communication and time for reflection, Habermas presented a different conceptual distribution according to which "worldviews" (= that could be acceptable) "are always ideological" (= not acceptable) worldviews to the extent that "they serve the function of legitimating domination." He accused Luhmann of giving in to, subjecting himself to, those "restrictions imposed upon communication" (*Kommunikationssperren*) that were erected not only by Nazi ideology, but by bourgeois ideology generally speaking, thereby stopping a process of enlightenment from happening, which alone would succeed in abolishing ideologies by depriving them of their power-legitimizing performance (Habermas, in H/L, 259).

In fact, it is undeniable that Luhmann concentrated his own critical potential on the analysis of the social conditions of more specific phenomena, such as insane ideologies and the modalities of their accession to power, the analysis of the power structures involved, and so on. In this perspective, such later works as Zygmunt Bauman's analysis of the Holocaust as a continuation of bureaucracy by other means have grown out of an interest in the specificity of the National Socialist formation that has more in common with Luhmann's analytical take than with Habermas's politics-suffused one. Translated in straightforward, flat political terminology, the question of which one of the two viewpoints is more correct in its assessment of Nazi ideology must remain undecided. Equally undecided remains the question of to what extent they are able to own up to the position that they appear to have been identified with in each other's eyes. And which of the two reveals himself as cooperative and which insists on tolerance? Can they go to the restaurant together? If they do, is there a certain Carl Schmitt sitting at their table as well? And if so, who of the two has invited him?

It is difficult to follow Habermas when, in one of his less-convincing argumentative moves (in H/L, 242–43), he identifies this Luhmannian conceptualization of positive law as something like a side form of the German lawyer's Carl Schmitt so-called "decisionism." Luhmann in no way accepts the unity of a decision-making moment; on the contrary, according to Luhmann, decisions always, intrinsically, refer to former and later decisions; their only *reality as decisions* is to be decisions of other decisions (*Entscheidung* 1978/1981, 335–89; *Organization* 2000/2018, chaps. 4–5). It is difficult to see what a decision is, what relevance it has, if it is not either repeated, approved, or abrogated by another decision, later on—and tested upon such later decisions. Contrary to what for Schmitt is obvious, decisions are not a momentary matter; they take a span of time and construct the moment as a moment of a past presence with a future presence. It is not easy to find, in the entire experience of twentieth-century social and legal thought, two other thinkers so opposed, or, one should rather say, so disparate, to each other as are Carl Schmitt and Niklas Luhmann. Schmittian thought does not lead to any "realism"—as some philosophers might have it.

In the modern situation, ideology has the function of establishing a form of coordination useful to political parties, a coordination that is capable of connecting wishful ideas and firm principles with party organization and bureaucratic administration. This is what explains that Luhmann could criticize materialist ideologies in banks and bureaucracies by suggesting that their habitual tendency of neutralizing certain norms as external to decisions results in an unwished-for and unseen reduction of the complexities implied in their decision-making. At the same time, he also criticized Marxist dialectical materialism (in its Leninist version) for practicing just the opposite reduction of complexities: material experiences (work), equally externalized, were made into a symbol carrying all-compassing value. "Power and 'public opinion' need to be steered in such a way that agendas be set as to make sure that they do not question the domination of a certain group of values and norms, and therefore leave discussions alive only with respect to concern about technical and instrumental issues" (*Positive* 1967, 194).

Ideology reappears as a smooth form of communication that covers conflicts, problems, and unsolved complexities under a layer of vague words that are hardly concepts. Ideology should be enlightened with claims for truth and, as in the case of positive law, with claims for justice. However, the problem is that such a critical enlightenment is only possible and adequate on the premises of social differentiation. Values of justice and truth do not serve and cannot serve to unite and reconcile modern society; they do not have this kind of encompassing causal effect on society.

Where Luhmann observes truth as ontology or epistemology and registers these two possible directions, outlining their factual succession in history, Habermas objects that this distinction fails to do justice to practical reasoning about what to do. Yet, in order to correctly locate the level of the disagreement, it is necessary to take account of several layers of perfect agreement between the two. First of all, it is clear to both authors that the somber tones of Max Weber as a theorist of contemporary society were not simply those of a relativist—of a relativist who neglected, or had forgotten, that value-freedom in a strict Kantian sense means the value *of* freedom, and not the value of being exempt from any determination. More accurately, Weber was a pessimist right from the start: in his view, it was not possible for the sociologist to rely on morals in order to derive a complete social theory from Kant's categorical imperative.

Weber's much less "pessimistic" antagonist on this level was, of course, Émile Durkheim, who based his entire theoretical construction of society and solidarity on a coextensiveness of the social and the moral. For Habermas, Weber's pessimism about morals is unnecessary. For Habermas, social coordination is not separable from intersubjective communication and the need for norms that are compatible with different social and work conditions at the same time as they reflect a more abstract integration among different persons. This legacy of thinking about social rules, norms, and codes in a complex society characterized by a social division of labor and functional differentiation is also Luhmann's (Luhmann *Self-Thematization* 1972; Habermas, *Discourse*, 1985, 396–404; 1987, 341–49).

Thus both Luhmann and Habermas have received the Durkheimian legacy of social thought.[6] So why were they, Habermas and Luhmann, dissatisfied with the solution offered by the tradition of their field?

The answer to this question is that Habermas wanted more and expected more than the tradition did from moral analysis. Luhmann, on the contrary, expected less from morals. According to Habermas, norms could be subject to practical reasoning. Hence, rather than downgrading ideology to the pariah status of being related to a mere input-output conception of the decision-making process, as he accused Luhmann of doing, norms should, according to Habermas, rather be the subject of justification processes. Already at this level, however, Luhmann's focus on time, and his notion of time as simultaneity in coordination, trust, and intersubjectivity, should have made clear that Luhmann's work was simply not correctly located at the level at which Habermas located and criticized it. In fact, it looks somehow strange that Luhmann's extremely complex and careful construction of modern society could, even superficially, seem to correspond to the extreme simplicity of the input-output scheme in which Habermas tried to locate it. And did Habermas's own paradigm, the model of a critically enlightened and reasoned ideology, correspond to the refined sobriety of Luhmann's version of the systems theory? Rather, the level at which the questions at stake between Luhmann and Habermas could really open up is that of the relationship between positive law and ideology. As a matter of fact, "Positive Law and Ideology" (*Positive* 1967) is the title of an article by Niklas Luhmann. Jürgen Habermas discusses this article extensively (H/L, 242–45).

The problem is how, in the course of the upheavals and reforms of the Enlightenment, positive law has turned natural law into a universal norm, or form, of reasoning. This happened exactly at the moment at which another form disappeared from the stage: virtues. Virtues became subject to more abstract reasoning, or were dissolved into contingent norms—or ideologies. With this differentiation, positive law could no longer be criticized, from the position of a coherent daily life and its norms or from an overly abstract *Vernunftrecht*—based on a Kantian categorical imperative—or from the new ideologies emerging at these times. "Marx saw that positive law was simply an ideological instrument" (Luhmann *Positive* 1967, 178). However, to Luhmann such causal schemes are not anywhere close to getting at the point of what really happened at this moment. The problem is that if moral reasoning could emerge at this moment, this is because it simultaneously differentiated from positive law, at the same time as law became positive. The same is true about ideologies and about the newly emerged, more contingent and autonomous sets of norms in modern everyday life. We shall see later on that Habermas (in *Facts BFN*) adopted an important aspect of the simultaneity or co-originality idea, since people's sovereignty and human rights, in Habermas's conception, also emerged in a form that can be either related or opposed to "co-originality" ("Gleichursprünglichkeit"; *Facts BFN* 1996, 104, 122, 127; 1992, 135, 155, 161). The attempt to capture the radical transition that happened during the Enlightenment by reference to the instrumental chain linking ends and means, input and output, goals and instruments must fail. What is at the core of the newly emerged ideology is not the fact that there are ideologies, or that positive law made itself independent by emigrating from, or, as Luhmann says, "differentiating out of," the ecumenical totality of normative institutions. Rather, the effective ideological machinery acting from behind the mere surface of the main empirical ideologies of the time is the form of the pretended "causal chain" by means of which ideologies could be used as the goals that would fit the legal instrumentarium provided by the law. In other words, ideologies should supply the necessary conditions for decision-making processes. That was not the case with virtues. When ideologies replaced virtues—if they did so—a series of problems and paradoxes emerged.

Yet, at the most modestly empirical level, decisions are made about decisions; norms develop in a space freed from the fetters of feudal privileges or moral claims. Taken together, this means that what enables abstract moral claims to make a difference, to be used in the way in which claims are used, is the fact that they are differentiated from positive law, from organizational decisions, from political decisions, from everyday norms, from old-fashioned virtues, from ideologies. In this modern condition, we should not ask for one chain of decision-making to replace another one. Yet we need to understand the paradox here at work before we move on. Luhmann claims that

> a meaningful critique of the situation at hand is only possible as an immanent critique of systems, including the society-compassing system. It is possible only as systems analysis, as an uncovering and reproblematizing of the problems that are solved by habitualized norms, roles, institutions, processes, and symbols, and as an exploration of other, functionally equivalent possibilities. In this sense, one can speak of a sociological enlightenment. (Luhmann *Positive* 1967, 198)

An important analytical contribution can be found in Habermas's long comment on and against Luhmann, understood as an addition to Habermas's own discursive ethics and thus as a part of his own work about justified decisions, and not as an addition to the understanding of systemic thought. As far as Luhmann is concerned, we have to assume that Habermas back in 1971 failed to take on board some main points, including both Luhmann's idea of functional differentiation and his concept of the paradox that underlies the justified critique of legitimacy in modern, differentiated legal systems in modern society, where they coexist with political systems.

Habermas's later reappraisal in *Between Facts and Norms* of Luhmann's early conception comes much closer to an appropriate understanding of Luhmann. Yet, it is conspicuous that in his first reaction, in the coauthored book from 1971, Habermas still believed that Luhmann was a fully fledged adept of the older conception of decision-making processes based on input-output. One might argue in his defense that this mistake was difficult to avoid, as, at this time (the early 1970s), input-output models enjoyed an almost-universal recognition in the social sciences. Even so, it is almost impossible to escape the impression that Habermas contributed rather heavily, with some effort and artifice, to sculpting Luhmann into the straw man that fit best the image of Luhmann he needed in order to develop his own position. Luhmann's seminal book *Zweckbegriff und Systemrationalität* (1968) offered the most penetrating criticism then on the market of input-output-oriented versions of systems theory and of the reduction to causal schemes and orientations toward externalized goals. Though in Germany Luhmann's book ranked prominently among the pioneering works of sociological theory, Habermas preferred to categorize Luhmann's endeavors in the same box as those theories that Luhmann had just subjected to uncompromising criticism! Even today, the impression can barely be resisted that Habermas read Luhmann according to a stereotype inherited from the version of systems theory that, at the time, was considered "normal."

How can this misreading, both radical and rather consequential, be explained? One might suppose that Habermas cherished the idea of providing himself the decisive criticism on diverse points of these theories that, differently from those criticized by Luhmann, could be understood as directly "value"-related. Luhmann was always critical toward the notion of "values." In his understanding values are notions with contingent forms, located beyond the zone of meaningful communication. A value is by definition difficult to distinguish from its opposite, offering itself, as it cannot help doing, as a premise for communication before communication; a "value" is always sitting on the fence between the inside and the outside, between meaningful and not meaningful communication. Values are held to be ("be"!) beyond communication; nevertheless, they occur in communication. In a sense, values should be about theology (even if, in fact, they are a far shot from being so). Importantly, the discussion between Habermas and Luhmann follows a long line of relevant theorizing. For Nietzsche, at the uttermost opposite of Habermas's view, the notion of "values" (*Werte*) had been a matter related to demons and false gods. For Max Weber, on the contrary, it is not a contradiction to speak about values that could be rational or that could become subject to rationalization. Even so, in comparison to his French colleague Durkheim, it is conspicuous that Weber always remained critical (if not indeed skeptical), with respect to the possibility of elaborating, determining, identifying justified values.

Unlike Luhmann, Habermas seemed to praise Parsons's notion of "cultural values," claiming, however, that they should be filtered by an intersubjective form of reasoning. To Habermas, values become legible only if considered against the background of the cultural reinterpretation of anything that in itself can be located in the sphere of instincts, desires and material interests (H/L, 250). Values are also a matter of dissent and are subject to conflicting interests. Thus Habermas distinguishes between values that are subject to strategic action and those that are subject to communicative action (and, thus, to possible reinterpretation). A common understanding of what is entailed, say, in the project of going to a restaurant together could be supported by a consensus about norms of common dining; yet any such consensus is exposed to the danger of splitting off again and dividing into divergence of interests as soon as some are hungry and some not, or, especially, as soon as some have money to pay for good restaurants and some don't. At this point, consensus may turn into strategic and competing dissent. Here is also the moment at which Habermas presents his definition of *power* as the capacity to hinder other individuals or groups to orient themselves toward their interests (H/L, 254). In this sense power negates free will formation by means of communication in the same sense as ideology. Desires are always prone to be ignored and counteracted, already at the unconscious psychic level. Then, as well, desires are equally easily excluded from acceptable communication (e.g., the desire to eat at a strip-tease restaurant). The repressed desires may be excommunicated from any acceptable public sphere whatsoever. Indeed, overly vulgar desires can become the object of comparisons to good taste.

In his rejection of Luhmann's theory from 1971, Habermas criticizes Luhmann for what he sees as Luhmann's failure to open up a debate about goals and values. There is something particularly wrong or bizarre in this account, even in comparison with other weak renderings of Luhmann found in Habermas. In fact, it is Luhmann who, already when he briefly taught in Frankfurt in 1969, devoted his seminar not to any potentially strategic topic about systems or functions, but to love, the result of which was eventually published as *Love—a Sketch* (2010). And in fact, it was Habermas who, during that same year, taught his seminar about Weber's theory of bureaucracy. Later on, Luhmann extended the booklet on love into a major historical study (*Passion* 1982/1986). Nor was Luhmann's preference for themes that are, in fact, much closer to expressive than to instrumental interests satisfied by this. He also developed a highly elaborated aesthetical theory (in *Art* 1995/2000).

If we now turn back to Habermas, there is certainly nothing problematic about his critical stance with respect to the old and, in a sense, effectively "very German" neglect of value discussions, which had been discussed in the social sciences since Max Weber. What one is struggling to understand is how Luhmann can be suggested as the target of such an accusation, the culprit of such a misdeed. If the reproach of a narrow outlook on public matters and of a resulting preference for "institutional" over "cultural" matters made any sense at all, it would rather work in the opposite direction—Habermas at best focuses upon a sociology of art and not on the perplexities of aesthetics after *The Structural Transformation of the Public Sphere*. Of course, among the numerous pupils and collaborators of Habermas, there are many, notably Peter and Christa Bürger and, later on, Albrecht Wellmer and Martin Seel, who have developed their author's theory of communicative rationality into a theory of aesthetic rationality; yet it is clear that, for Habermas, the core point has always tended to remain limited to the inquiry into valid norms for social coexistence and cooperation.

Think of a group of people looking for a restaurant in order to have dinner together. How do you solve the fearful problems that irresistibly emerge owing to factors such as different tastes in matters of cuisines, different views of what a dinner together should look like, and different desires on a personal level? The problem can reach an importance that may indeed put an end to the common project of an evening meal. Moreover, if the members of the group, in their efforts to solve it, insist each upon her or his own understanding, including about what is the best solution for the endangered harmony to be restored, then the cure will be even worse than the disease. Hence, all the efforts that have started out of commonality and cooperation can turn, in a worst-case scenario, into a mutual crusade. For, where else should each of them look for solutions other than in their own repertoire, their own history? Yet, these repertoires and experiences differ irremediably from person to person: How should the solutions suggested on this basis fail to provoke even more disharmony?

In sum, their coauthored book did not result in any kind of final conclusion. Rather, to the contrary, if any conclusion can be drawn, it is about the obvious motivation to continue to develop research programs about systems, communication, and communication about communication.

Any theory is expressed as communication; thus, theory development about society is communication about communication or metacommunication. This was actually the research subject undertaken by Habermas immediately after the book. In fact, it was part of a major transformation in Habermas's research projects. He moved himself south to Munich to become director of the Max Planck Institute of Research in Societal World Conditions in 1971, a position he had until 1981. There he got a dozen assistants and could expand his program into research fields that covered philosophy as well as social science and their interlinkages.

There is much more to the initial opening debate between Habermas and Luhmann than their coauthored book, and I still need to discuss a couple of crucial chapters in it, Habermas's chapter 6 (270–85) and Luhmann's chapter 4 (361–78) in his final part of the book. I will continue that discussion below in chapter 4, yet before that, I investigate some of the more metatheoretical discussions coped with by Habermas and Luhmann in those years.

3

INTERSUBJECTIVITY AND LIFEWORLD

HABERMAS'S DISCOURSE THEORY ABOUT TRUTH AND COOPERATION

When Habermas and Luhmann's coauthored book was written, Habermas began to build a new fundamental social research, with philosophy of language as the core tool for conceptual considerations. In the Princeton Christian Gauss lectures, "Reflections on the Linguistic Foundation of Sociology" (in *Pragmatics*), Habermas concluded the fifth lecture with an analysis of the societal consequences of linguistic truth claims. Language does not only represent an external reality. The use of language, in particular in so-called speech acts, constitutes a social reality. Verbs are more central to this reality than nouns. If society is mediated in communication, speech acts about communicative interpretations should be recognized as valid. Hence, the questions arise about what can emerge and should emerge about adequate forms of validity. If the President declares, "we will invade Iraq," questions may arise if it is doable, if it is allowed, and if he sincerely means it.

Validity claims are posed in communication and Habermas distinguishes between four such forms: truth claims, claims for justification, claims for authenticity, and claims about comprehension. "These claims converge into one: that of reason [*Vernünftigkeit*]" (*Linguistic* 1998, 85; 1971/1984, 104). The point is not that history leads to reason, but that such idealizations are differentiated in the development of a societal communication that implicitly uses such communicative and linguistic claims.

Habermas's indeed very decisive point is that the implicit use of speech in communication can be subject to questions, oppositions, and transformations that require some demands for explicit linguistic explanation in the medium of argumentation. Habermas may be right that "the paradigm of all claims to validity is propositional truth" (*Linguistic* 1998, 86; 1971/1984, 105). Neither a correspondence theory of truth nor an evidence theory of truth escapes presuppositions about a prelinguistic ontology of truth.[1] Presupposed certainties are well known in our everyday experiences. Yet we know of doubt about such presuppositions and claims for argumentation ("we could eat dinner in town now"—"oh yes, but are the restaurants open, and are we already hungry"?). We all have that experience, yet we could withdraw, but whenever doubt emerges in communication we tend to ask for argumentation. To sustain Habermas's further elucidation of his research program, the next point is that this tendency is more than a temptation; it indeed is embedded in the very meaning of communication. Communication implies rules to follow without which the meaning of a social life in communication is lost.

> The validity claim of constative speech acts, that is, the truth that we claim propositions to have by asserting them, depends on two conditions. First, it must be grounded in experience; that is, the statement may not conflict with dissonant experience. Second, it must be discursively redeemable; that is, the statement must be able to hold up against all counterarguments and command the assent of all potential participants in a discourse. The first condition must be satisfied to make credible that the second condition *could* be satisfied as required. The meaning of truth implicit in the pragmatics of assertions can be explicated if we specify what is meant by the "discursive redemption" of claims to validity. This is the task of the consensus theory of truth. (Habermas *Linguistic* 1998, 89; 1971/1984, 109)

This claim is quite demanding in scale and scope. Note that this is about truth in its universal extension and does not concern validity claims for a cooperative society about the terms of cooperation: "The condition for the truth of propositions is the potential acceptance by *everybody*" (*Linguistic* 1998, 89; 1971/1984, 109).

According to Luhmann's criticism, this condition obviously and evidently becomes difficult to sustain in case the communication participants live in worlds somewhat different. This we always do: one observer observes the long side of the table while the other observes the short side. In the phenomenological analysis, observation therefore claims that perception, in order to be intersubjective, lets our perception and lifeworld transcend our individual positions. This is well known to Habermas; and therefore Habermas also immediately admitted the embedded paradoxes and had to explain his position in far more detail. The forerunners who claimed transcendental conditions inherent in valid communication were Habermas's friend Karl-Otto Apel, Charles Sander Peirce, and Immanuel Kant. A community of interpreters functions according to some presupposed rules about what can be asserted.

Remember that the claims are posed in communication and they refer with four different validity claims to four different realities, social, subjective, objective, and linguistic. Communicative claims may approach disagreements in four different ways, and before anything else, the metacommunicative claim is that communication in order to be meaningful implies a differentiation between such claims. According to Habermas, this is a pragmatic differentiation, though it may express a number of logics.

In 1971, it was obvious to start such a discussion about differentiated validity claims with the then still almost common agreement that inferences from descriptive statements about truth led to a fallacy if they concluded in normative claims. What to do cannot be inferred from descriptive statements, but implies another logic. A description of a hunger situation in Leningrad in 1943 may be right or wrong, but what to do about it is a different issue and it is—so it was commonly supposed in social sciences—not in itself a normative question whether hunger is subject to constatation.

In fact Habermas changed his position on truth claims some years later, in *Communicative Action*, vol. 1. Inspired by the British philosopher Michael Dummett (1976), he claimed that descriptions should be possible to assert. Descriptions are subject to some assertability logic about what is done with such descriptions. This means that descriptions that are strictly impossible to verify are simply not true or false, but meaningless. Yet Durkheim had already established the strength of such inferences: if some division of labor is in a society, then some norms do exist about cooperation in that society (Durkheim 1893/1930, xli). Hence, we infer from "is" to "ought" (Watts Miller 1996, 251–62; Durkheim 1924, 117–41). This assertability logic, however, does not dedifferentiate the distinction between truth claims and claims of justice; preferably it constitutes the distinction embedded in the pragmatics of communication. In 1971, Habermas's more original point was first to save claims of justifiability from the idea of a normative relativism that validity claims were only about truth claims. Second, in both cases he states that validity claims anyway are subject to discursive argumentation (*Linguistic* 1998, 93; 1971/1984, 113). Though Habermas of course admits that consensus criteria cannot be used in the case of claims for authenticity, still the claim for consensus seems to demand more than we normally attain for.

In the discussion about discourse theory, Habermas seems to operate with two sets of arguments. Habermas's first set of arguments is preferably sociological and not as abstract, transcendental, or philosophical as is often supposed. The idea is to explain how it in fact often is the case that we use some kind of common-sense agreement. If my wife asks for a glass of water when I am going to the kitchen anyway, she operates with a presupposition that we both know about what this implies, even if I come back with a cup when a pan of water would be of the record; and if such misunderstandings occur often, she may begin to mistrust me even at the level of insanity, as if I have lost my mind and ability to reason. In this explication, I may presuppose that the reader knows that a glass is not a horse, and therefore that we share some common forms of categorization picked up when we learned how to use language. We cannot even question such practical knowledge about presuppositions without questioning that we are able to understand what it means to use language and act with language in our daily communication. In this sense, Habermas claims that communication operates with presuppositions of an ideal speech situation. The idealizations are already, so to speak, hermeneutically embedded in our presuppositions. Ideally we could discuss what was meant by a glass of water (clean, warm, glass of milk, and so on), and Habermas's standpoint is that we then ideally would claim that each one had a say and could speak for himself. My wife would expect me to explain why I came with a cup with juice and I better be ready to offer some explanation. Of course, underneath those simple examples of glass and water, among Germans from the generation of Habermas and Luhmann, we can find questions about the validity and rhetorical abuse of language—the so-called "newspeak"—of Goebbels and Hitler. This is exactly why the simplicity of a philosophy of language is so tempting for Habermas and in another way for Luhmann. It is similar to the more recent discourse of "fake news" that started with Trump; here we tend to enter into metadiscussions about the use of language.

This is why Habermas and Luhmann both go back to another classical legacy, one from Germany between the world wars, namely, that of phenomenologist Edmund Husserl's foundational constitution of language and meaning in the experience of "intersubjectivity" explained in the chapter 5 of his *Cartesian Meditations* from 1928. Social language and communication are about interaction. Yet Habermas and Luhmann have two very different perspectives on Husserl's analysis of intersubjectivity. Habermas focuses on dialogue, whereas Luhmann focuses on presence or rather copresence. In everyday interaction cooperation is about dialogue and copresence.

Somewhat close to Luhmann's temporal idea of simultaneity in intersubjective situations, Habermas rightly supposed that we *could* pose questions to one another. The hermeneutic interpretation of the suppositions of the other person does not have to wait in some anticipation for any future reconciliation. This is a hermeneutic challenge too, and this anticipation was supposed by one of Heidegger's pupils, the important hermeneutic philosopher Hans-Georg Gadamer, in his dialogical interpretation of text reading: A reader, in order to understand a text, anticipates that a fuller interpretation will be possible in the future. In the intersubjective situation, questions can be posed in the present moment of the dialogue. My wife may trust me to bring the glass of water, and in case she does not, she may begin a dialogue about water and cups. In the sociology of nursing communication, these questions of the meaning of intersubjectivity are decisive: Does the nurse have to enter a dialogue with the patient, or can she communicate in silent awareness of the situation? Luhmann points to the importance of the pragmatics of tacit communication (*Folgen* 1964, 296).

Furthermore, we simply—eventually tacitly—presuppose that each of us could explain somewhat further what could be meant by a glass of water—say, if I came back with some warm water in a cup and had to explain about that; the patient patiently could presuppose that a nurse found it more healthy. Habermas's point is the inherent supposition that we could go on in such discursive argumentation: that me and my wife or the patient and the nurse have still further arguments or could develop still further arguments in an elaborated defense of our positions (*Linguistic* 1988, 99, 101; 1971/1984, 121, 123). It is presupposed that we may change and revise them ("oh yeah, you're right, now I understand what you mean"). In our communicative practice, Habermas accordingly claims that we are able to bracket the communicative situation about how to act and, accordingly, we are able to enter into a metacommunicative discourse in which the object of communication is communication and only communication.

Remember that Luhmann after their coauthored book began to puzzle over a completed communicative turn in social theory. Actions of individuals were to be cut in two: one part was absorbed into communication systems (interactional, organizational, or societal) whereas another was embedded into the experience of thought, perception, and feeling. This bifurcation is different than Habermas's bifurcation between communicative action and discourse, yet it may be questioned how different it is. Habermas's distinction occurred to many commentators as extremely complex when it came to a larger social theory. To give a quick summary, in anticipation of the following elaboration, it probably was much clearer in the more narrow political theory than in the larger social theory. We may suppose that those with whom we act have intentions with what they do and can defend those motivations in terms of acceptable recognized norms whereby presupposed expectations of legitimacy may be subject to discourse discussions (*Linguistic* 1971/1984, 124).

Yet we may be wrong about the claim for consensus in more complex situations, since they concern how to cooperate in a complex society. Yet Habermas first strengthened his arguments almost beyond any reasonable measure of what a sociology of communication would ask for. However, we should remember that the analysis of communication as a philosophy of argumentation is implied in the need to find a way in a dialogue with a Nazi or a former Nazi or, today, with someone who insists on the Western privileges toward the excluded.

This endeavor Habermas undertook with the long article "Theories of Truth" ("Wahrheitstheorien," in *Vorstudien*). There Habermas claims that an orientation toward "cooperative readiness for understanding" is what discourses are about (131). Yet this article does concern a philosophy of science and its theories of truth inasmuch as any theory about social cooperation does; and Habermas therefore here contends that his theory of truth has a far wider scope than only the human sciences. "Facts" are statements and not "objects." In this sense valid facts are about what can be recognized as truth and accepted as valid in a society of scholars, but not only accepted according to common-sense standards that may be utterly false about allegations of race or a flat Earth. Far more demanding conditions have to be fulfilled, and Habermas turns philosophy of science indeed into a social undertaking that demands valid legitimacy or what the Europeans calls *Legitimität* (German) or *legitimité* (French), as distinct from pure conventions about "Legitimation." Experience would not suffice as a justified claim; discursive argumentation has to follow. Validity is far more than consensus.

This refers to the second set of arguments about validity claims in a complex society. We may have a discourse about truth claims to objective knowledge and statements, but discourses about societal norms concern intersubjective social norms and realities. Norms about social expectations may have a "facticity" (*Faktizität*) in what counts as valid (*Geltung*) (Habermas "Wahrheitstheorien" 1972/1984, 146). Statements concerning "culture" are different from statements about "nature" in the sense that the first statements concern valid norms, even if they are about, for example, the amount of debt the United States has with China, since at the bottom line even such "facts" concern norms and rules of socially constituted payments. Descriptions of payments may involve normative claims for repayment, as already stated by John Searle (1967) in a well-known article. The implied claims a priori found in the concept of "payment" are synthetically present in the facticity of society, according to Habermas. Whenever we describe society, such a facticity of norms and their validity is implied. This may be correct, since the claim "if this is a table" also implies a priori and synthetically "therefore it should be possible to place something on the table"; we infer "if ... is" to "therefore ... should"; yet "should" is not "ought." Accordingly, Habermas distinguishes a practical discourse about the modalities of socially valid norms from the validity such norms could have in "social systems" (Habermas *Wahrheitstheorien*, 146). The constitutive descriptions of norms valid in a society with its systems can become a subject for discourse, in case such descriptions are questioned.

Whether these "should"- or "ought"-conditions are part of a systems condition or a normative discourse later became subject to an important discussion between Luhmann and Habermas in *Cardozo Law Review* (1996). Habermas's argument in 1972 was that the form and procedures, in the medium of argumentation, in themselves are subject to argumentation (Habermas *Wahrheitstheorien*, 171); this exactly is what culture is about: that it establishes its own truth conditions. It could be a culture of the "force in the better argument." Yet already to Luhmann in *Legitimation* (1969, 60ff.), systemic conditions of proof, evidence, procedure, opponent roles, and so on are established in communication. Systemic conditions about what counts as legal argumentation in courts may be subject to such a certified argumentation. Nevertheless, this authorization is not always established, for instance, not in aesthetical or mass media–oriented communication. Yet in principle, and at least since the early Enlightenment, if not already in the twelfth-century canon law, only argumentation that counts as legally valid counts as legal argumentation, and this means that procedures govern and authorize legality. This is close to a priori tautological, but is not obvious and, as a matter of fact, is an improbable evolutionary fact. If this condition of differentiated forms of argumentation is not accepted, then the very idea of argumentation and reasoning, distinct from rhetorical or violent communication, dedifferentiates and breaks down. In the Nazi regime, courts accepted a dedifferentiation of legal and political argumentation, as we today can be witnesses of in the movie *Sophie Scholl*, or read about in Michael Stolleis's *Recht im Unrecht* (1994). Later (in *Law* 1993/2008), Luhmann extended this analysis.

The second set of arguments is far more difficult to grasp and they developed almost two decades later, somewhat as a conclusion to the initial discussion. Since Habermas developed his theory into a still more refined and complex undertaking that involved a rather comprehensive group, especially of German philosophers, it would be futile to go through all those refinements. The contributions are counted in the hundreds. Hence, I follow the temptation to describe the standing of the discussion about two decades later, just before Habermas published *Between Facts and Norms* (in 1992). One of Habermas's closest discussion partners since the years with the Positivism Quarrel was Albrecht Wellmer, professor in Konstanz and later Berlin. His elaborated contribution was published in the book *Ethik und Dialog* (1986). In April 1990, at a conference, furthermore, he made a kind of summary (Wellmer 1992), which offers some standard that Habermas seemed to have followed, especially later (in *Truth* 2003). Wellmer simply stated that there is a strong and a weak version of the idea of linguistic understanding as an immanent telos in social communication. I will summarize his argumentation in three parts.

Wellmer and some from his strand of discourse theory pointed toward a logic of aesthetic rationalization that developed claims about good taste as something to be argued about in interpretations of art. However, this kind of discourse does not imply any consensus, just a rationalization, refinement, and differentiation of distinctions, clarification, and the like. This first point is not about any endeavor to reach any kind of consensus, and one may, as Luhmann does, claim to strive for dissent as well, for opposed views that elaborate the field of possible interpretations. Indeed avant-garde art is highly oriented toward a broadened scope of possibilities even if it implies provocations in the medium of ugly art (Karl-Heinz Bohrer), kitsch, garbage, or what have you. After Kant, art has been about something more than just acceptable decorative beauty. However, at the same time, Wellmer's second argument is that communication about political cooperation contains far stronger claims about consensus, since proposals may have implications for others besides the proposer herself. The third argument is about the differentiation between those two forms of discourses, the aesthetical discourse and the cooperative political discourse. Wellmer claimed that this rather idealized form of differentiated discourses is sustained by differentiated institutions. Since Montesquieu and Hegel, the spirit of different discourses has been supported by differentiated sets of institutions. In our everyday life, we discuss aesthetical judgments of taste and political claims, which concern what to do with others in a complex society, but we refer to discussions in institutionalized forums about politics and aesthetics. Of course, other forums are references too, courts, mass media, economical, and religious or research forums, for example.

Luhmann's example, in 1969, was about law courts, and the simple question then is how our culture of "the better argument" developed in such institutionalizations or systems of communicative argumentation. Habermas does not deny this learning process. However, two problems appear. Do everyday discussions and argumentation about, for example, water in glasses or cups add a decisively different transcendent perspective to systemically and organizationally embedded discourses? And, vice versa, are everyday discourses disrupted or transformed by institutionalized discourses, systems differentiations of discourses, and the like? In sum, is enlightenment, philosophical or sociological, reducible to a perspective that tells us that one of these discourses has a kind of preponderance in neglect of the other? Are we not all, in everyday life and practice, a kind of philosopher and sociologist who to various degrees learns and has learned to handle such discussions and reasoning procedures?

The debate between Habermas and Luhmann did seem to follow a line that, broadly speaking, favored the plus-sum of meaning constitution in a defense of the more complex double view on discourses. Institutionalized discourses develop and stabilize everyday discourses about even simple validity claims. Yet back in the 1970s, still a number of commentators saw systems communication as some kind of instrumental or strategic communication that never could resemble any kind of discourse of reasoning. On the other hand, discourses embedded in the lifeworld of everyday communication appeared to some as the road of universal reason and the yardstick of everything. This double neglect of institutionalized, not to say systemic, enlightenment of discourses may have been typical for some student movements. It favored, probably too easily, a zero-sum game view on systems communication and lifeworld communication.

In this book, I will not enter into a discussion of whether Luhmann's 1132-page book *Systems Theory of Society* (*Systemtheorie der Gesellschaft*), written in 1975 and published posthumously in 2017, adds additional perspectives to the Habermas-Luhmann debate. If Luhmann handed the manuscript to Habermas—as our two authors often did before publication—and Habermas responded to it, an analysis would be necessary. Seemingly, Luhmann was not satisfied with the construction of social theory in the version from 1975. For one thing, Luhmann, in the unpublished manuscript, appears to have discussed, for example, problems of intersubjectivity extensively and the problem of organizational history. As with several of his books that were only published posthumously (*Macht als System*, 2012; *Politische Soziologie*, 2010), the manuscript appeared ready to hand over to the editor. Yet, Luhmann still puzzled over the right solution to the reconstruction problem, which Habermas too worked with, as is obvious in the transition from Habermas's only partly translated *Rekonstruktion* from 1976. What we find as a representation of what he puzzled over in these years from Luhmann's hand is the short book *Power* (translated in *Trust and Power*, 1979).

Three aspects appear to me to have been touchstones for further developments. The first is that the version from 1975 is far less empirical than Luhmann's writings in the 1980s and 1990s and in particular the final magnum opus, *Theory of Society* (1997, chaps. 2–5), or, more precisely, it is deductively rather than abductively carried through. In this respect, the importance of Reinhart Koselleck's frame and research program of conceptual history seems to have intervened in the Habermas-Luhmann debate in such a penetrating way that we can speak about a first phase of the debate until 1975 and then a second phase between 1975 and 1986. Koselleck was a Bielefeld colleague of Luhmann, but certainly was also, as we shall see in chapter 4, invoked by Habermas. Koselleck, who was born in 1923 (and who died in 2006), was four years older and served as a voluntary regular soldier in the Wehrmacht and was a Soviet prisoner of war until 1947. He is probably the most important continental historian and got his professorship in Bielefeld at the same time as Luhmann.[2] However, still, Koselleck's grip on conceptual history did not cut deep in the unpublished voluminous book.

Yet Luhmann's later analyses developed probably from unresolved conclusions about what he called "self-thematizations" (a discussion elaborated on extensively in *Systemtheorie* 2017, 913–83). In this chapter, he, as a second aspect, developed the notion of "self-reference" as a differentiated reflection. Yet, almost immediately, afterward, he developed the research strategy with which he proceeded over the next decades, which as described in *Funktion der Religion* was finished in December 1976.

The third aspect that appears of importance for looking at the debate with Habermas is a longer chapter on intersubjectivity (*Systemtheorie* 2017, 627–75).

INTERSUBJECTIVITY AND LIFEWORLD: THE QUESTION OF METHOD IN HERMENEUTICS AND SYSTEMS THEORY

When sociologists as professional researchers touch upon concepts like intersubjectivity and lifeworld, it is very often in connection with methodologies of interviews. Since Anthony Giddens wrote *New Rules of Sociological Method*, published in 1976, and Richard Bernstein published *Social and Political Theory* the same year and *Beyond Objectivism and Relativism* in 1981, hermeneutics from Hans-Georg Gadamer to Habermas has been some kind of standard for interpretative qualitative research. The idea to use hermeneutics in social research came from Habermas's article "The Hermeneutic Claim to Universality" from 1970.

The basic approach in interpretative methodology is to enter a dialogue with historically given texts. In Gadamer's *Truth and Method* (1960/2004), an interpreter read a text whose origin is in the past; hence, the problem is how it is possible to understand the text. Gadamer's idea is that understanding is possible because the reader is situated in a context, a lifeworld, which historically is connected to the context in which the text was written. Gadamer's hermeneutics was extremely important to Koselleck too. The classical hermeneutical example is Erasmus and Martin Luther translating and reading the Bible in the Renaissance. The writer lived in the context of a lifeworld that constituted his background knowledge and the horizon in which he wrote. The interpreter finds himself in a lifeworld, the Renaissance, other than that of the Bible, which is before and under the Roman Empire in the Eastern part of the Mediterranean. These two historical horizons, Antiquity and the Renaissance, are interconnected and the interpretation can only offer some validity to its method if they become interconnected in what Gadamer (1960/2004) called a "melting of horizons." Of course, the reader does not understand the text as well as the author, but, reading it repeatedly, he will—in a hermeneutical circle—be able to see parts of the text in view of the whole, including the context. In addition, the reader knows the aftermath of the text, and therefore is able to see consequences following from the text and the future of the past context. Therefore, the reader also understands the text better than the writer does. He could also anticipate how he in a later future will be able to reconcile questions and answers to the reading.

Habermas sees this interpretative model in view of contemporary social research. His model is a psychoanalytical dialogue in which the analyst can ask the client, who has to clarify and open up his context and lifeworld. From an asymmetric dialogue, in which the analyst can have suspicions about conflicts in the clients' lifeworld, the dialogue may end up establishing a symmetric dialogue, where client and analyst have the same interpretation of the clients' lifeworld. Roughly speaking, the Gadamer/Habermas model is basic to open-ended qualitative interviews with one difference: The interview takes place in present time. The interviewer may ask the interviewed about her lifeworld, and pose further and still further questions, presupposing that the interviewed somehow is able or could be able to answer, and could be willing to interpret and change her lifeworld.

So, how would that look, according to Luhmann's methodology? Gadamer, Habermas, and Luhmann all have the idea to observe the interpretation from the background of the possibilities conditioned by the dialogue. It is neither the consciousness nor the will of the observer nor the consciousness and will of the observed that constitute meaning in the dialogue. Meaning is constituted in communication as such. To Luhmann, the interview forms a copresence and each participator, as a psychic system, may think whatever she thinks and perceives. However, the communication, the dialogue, constitutes a form apart from the experiences perceived by each psychic system. Also in psychoanalysis, the analyst can never get to any identical perception of the thoughts and feelings experienced by the client; it will never be the analyst who has been raped or traumatized. The psychic systems, even if they plunged into the deepest empathy, would never find a full identification with the thoughts of the other. Thinking and feeling are far too complex and fast for any linguistic dialogue; and the silent simultaneous copresence offers as much interpenetration and structural coupling between the two psychic systems.

Yet in the communication form, new and former narratives may appear. Some of them will claim that the participants in principle should be able to express their thoughts and perceptions to make them valid in communication; and this is the position of Habermas if those thoughts should achieve any political or organizational validity. Other narratives, forwarded by the Luhmannian observer, will talk about tolerance and offer a scope of absurdities and bizarre traumas and experiences that do not exclude the lifeworld of the observed. The observed may get a new confidentiality and find trustworthy narratives about her position on the brink of societal communication systems. The point is not to establish a consensus between the analyst and the client, but to allow for a difference and even admit dissenting perspectives on the lifeworlds.

In fact, this point is even stronger in its focus on presence. Luhmann refers to the French phenomenologist Maurice Merleau-Ponty's classic *Phenomenology of Perception* (1945/2012) to explain that the perceptions of the psychic systems and of the bodily living systems do not in any linear way have access to dialogues, but rather have access to another form of copresent communication. Let us take an example: Two people lift a ladder together. What is experienced here as a form of communication? They perceive their positions; they may—even quantitatively—know about their strength and age; and they may trust each other's experiences, one perhaps more than the other. They perceive their sense of orientation and balance, of walking and climbing when the ladder is placed up against a tall tree. Their climbing sense is a completely different form of social sense, material sense, and temporal sense; it reduces the complexity of communication with a very different form of communication than that form, which reduces the complexities to a question of verbalized dialogue.

With this story of interpretation from Luther and Gadamer to Habermas and Luhmann, we see a line of somewhat similar yet in the end also quite different views. Of course, the methodologies described are far from a positivist, causal, and quantitative form of methodology. However, the conceptual tools of the methodologies are not as neutral as they may appear at first sight.

In the article "Intersubjectivity or Communication" (SA 6, 169–88), Luhmann once again—as in 1968—discusses the theme of "intersubjectivity." This theme was part of Habermas and Luhmann's coauthored book, and it was also, previously, subject to analyses in Luhmann's elucidations in *Trust* from 1968. Yet in the meantime, their mature theories had developed. Still, the opposing readings of Husserl's philosophy of intersubjectivity in *Cartesian Meditations* (chapter 5) stand as a difference. Habermas still sees intersubjectivity as linguistic dialogue between subjects; and Luhmann observes intersubjectivity as communicative copresence in simultaneous time.

After stating that Habermas and he both use the German linguist philosopher Karl Bühler's classic tripartition of language (Bühler 1934, 28–30), as "exposition, expression and appeal," in a note Luhmann recapitulates his view on their theoretical developments in a few phrases:

> Habermas, too, departs from Bühler's three functions or components, in particular in the rigid version of linguistic theory. This leads him to the idea, in the three functions, to see orientations in which the speaker claims validity to be proved in a discussion free of dominance. This should not be doubted. However, this approach merely captures a much reduced part of communicative possibilities. (Luhmann *Intersubjectivity* 1995, 179n28)

Habermas may accept Luhmann's use of Bühler; yet, there are two ways to go from there. On the one hand, in sociology, there are good and healthy concepts. The concept of good could very well be a good concept, and it is surely healthy to speak about health—yet sometimes also unhealthy if such speech dominates every discourse. Concepts as "rational" could be rational, but the temperature of the word *warm* is probably not higher than that of *cold*. Action seems to be an active word, while passive passivizes and reliable is a reliable word. Social science is filled with such concepts that more or less in between the lines are considered as positive concepts, which should be favored and used in those paradigms to forward and use for next year's declaration of presidency in the national sociological association or in school committees. Concepts like lifeworld and intersubjectivity, along with concepts such as integration and commonality, meaning and communication, are among those presidential positive words. Trust is to be trusted and fear is to be feared. On the one hand, utterances imply self-references. Words act. Hence, even constative words are not neutral, but imply ideas and form normative realities.

Increasingly, Luhmann began to be very reluctant with the concept of intersubjectivity: What is in fact meant by "inter-"? His first point is that communication is not transition from a sender to a receiver, or from one subject to the other. Communication is far more, and "inter-" does not capture what is meant by the social realities of communication. Indeed, the sociophilosophical concept "meaning," does not mean you + me. On the contrary it is basic before any constitution of me or you and is found in language and experience. His second point is that the idea of intersubjectivity still offers some kind of idea that the reflexive subjects, by their thoughts, steer and control communication. Compared to the full-blown communication theory—established by Luhmann and perhaps also according to Habermas' conception—"intersubjectivity" is a "conceptual form of embarrassment" (169). It leaves too much control to subjects, as if communication does not organize itself, but could be reduced to thoughts. However, the autopoiesis of consciousness, thought, and feelings is of a very different and much more subjective art than whatever happens in communicational forms such as language: "The process from thought to thought and the process from communication to communication do not run in the same system. The connectivity is regulated completely differently. What is known as subject can never be part of a social system" (181).

Self-reference in communication should be differentiated from self-reference in psychic systems. To Luhmann the concept of subject is so radically different from what goes on in society: "To me, Habermas always underscores the consequences of this radicalization—above all in the assertion that still has some signification if the subject becomes bound or not bound by universally oriented argumentation. . . . Intersubjectivity is no alternative to subjectivity" (169).

Here Luhmann refers to a long criticism Habermas wrote about Heidegger's distance to subject philosophy (in *Discourse*, 158–90), but claims that this criticism would be stronger if Habermas could refer to a better alternative than "inter-." Luhmann comes back to the question in *Theory of Society* (vol. 2, 2013, 169–74; 1997, 870–76) where he again concludes that intersubjectivity at best can be interpreted (with Husserl and Kant) as contemporarity and copresence, concepts that fit with his systems theory.

To Luhmann, Habermas abuses the concept of subjectivity to conclude that some entity called identity can be found in this intersubjectivity, not to say some form of collectivity such as "complex societies." Identity is what is "invisible" for external observers. At best, as in some form of religious communication, "silence" is what represents what cannot be represented (Luhmann *Intersubjectivity* 1995, 184). Subjects can be silent together at the same time, and that is a form of communication, which in religion is known as prayer, contemplation, or meditation in common. In theological history, we speak and God is silent, yet we speak about this silence and communicate about perfect noncommunication replaced by sacred symbols. The sacred secrecies are kept silent and invisible and are certainly not identifiably evident in societal communication, as is well known from debates about the Eucharist. In Luhmann's *Speech and Silence* (*Silence* 1989) he continues an argument from Wittgenstein and Adorno to Lyotard: that the victim does not speak, but is kept in silence and doubt. The "identity of a symbol" (Habermas *Communicative Action*, vol. 2, 1981, 31; 1987, 16) is not the same as the identity of an individual. The victim cannot always say why she stays silent, for example, about rape. In care too, presence and silence constitute meaning, yet in a way other than interrogation and dialogue. A hand on the shoulder can say as much as a word in the mouth.

The concept "lifeworld" is as important in Luhmann's philosophy as in Habermas's. Like the concept of "intersubjectivity," "lifeworld" too has its origins in Edmund Husserl's later writings. Both concepts have something intuitively appealing; they are warm and social and seem to be concrete and substantially sociological. Furthermore, "lifeworld" has some horizon to it; it deals with the wider horizons of life, meaning, truth, and everything it is worthwhile to fight for. At the same time, a lifeworld may indicate something secure and homebound. Yet Luhmann in his article "The Lifeworld—in Sight of Phenomenologists" remarks on something that may one think about the melancholy of the song "Strangers in the Night" ("Lebenswelt," 1986/2000, 268–89).

Husserl wrote his analysis of lifeworld in an analysis about *The Crisis of European Sciences and Transcendental Philosophy*, based on an exile lecture in Prague in 1935. There are home and horizon at the same time: the given place is not at home, bound and secure; only abroad, in the horizon of a new world, is it possible to find a foundation for true science—and another security. Husserl felt he was too old (seventy-seven years) to accept a professorship in California. According to Luhmann, a lifeworld is not a reconciled upheaval of a difference between subject and object, but is only possible in a difference. In that sense, system and lifeworld have an internal connection; they are not objects to be identified as meaningful and meaningless, as pure science and life science. A lifeworld is part of science; there is no world outside the world of a lifeworld. To Luhmann, this is the same for Habermas's conception of communicative acting and lifeworld, which are complementary to each other (*Discourse* 1985/1987, 396/342). Yet in Habermas's conception, the horizon, implied in a lifeworld, conditions the possibilities of a dialogical consensus, since dialogues refer to experiences implied in the horizon of a lifeworld. According to Luhmann, such a background horizon can never offer any determined and given idea of one singular horizon. To Habermas, this is one world implied in our dialogues, whereas the world, for Luhmann, stays a horizon.

Under the sea, all islands meet—according to a Habermasian view. However, according to Luhmann, words in communication are "like ships observed from an infinite oceanic deep" (Luhmann *Communication* 1992, 123). This controversy about the role of lifeworld is probably not the most divergent to be found in modern social science; their positions seem to be close. Yet it is a bit amusing that Habermas in their coauthored book from 1971 criticized Luhmann as offering a too simple and shortened view on the concept of "world": namely, when Luhmann spoke about the environmental world (*Umwelt*) of system. Luhmann, however, in 1986 accuses Habermas of operating with a reductive view on the world of lifeworlds. The closer the observers came to their object, the more views and perspectives they got. As discussed by Ulf Mathiessen (1983) and Bernhard Waldenfels (1985, 94–119), when we go on, into the horizons of the lifeworld, we do not come home. The context of a text does not guarantee a consensus.

Such a consensus in the lifeworld was not the idea of Habermas. If anything, his combination of a discourse ethic for dialogues and a theory of lifeworld is constituted in the idea that we could continue our dialogues and find new ways and new comfortable connections of meaning. Indeed this is a (counterfactual) precondition in argumentation that we can continue to discuss, but our worlds will not break down, but rather become different. We leave the small waters where we used to find ground between the islands, but in the meantime we have learned to swim and build boats and ships, and can continue to feel comfortable. Yet Luhmann's point is a bit sharper: The disabled war veteran or traumatized person also lives in a lifeworld, but she cannot communicate it in any clearly well-ordered and integrated way. The victim lives in a lifeworld—even if she does not learn to communicate about her experiences. Habermas presumes that thoughts and feelings after some therapy are within the reach of language and expressive competences, but this is far from always being the case: thoughts, feelings, and nightmares have their own autopoiesis. This is extremely important for a social psychology of care and welfare.

At this point, we should not forget that Habermas's project is to avoid certain overly egoist, privileged, and distorted views to get into political decisions about social coordination. This seems to be recognized by Luhmann: "Communicative action can be conceptualized as participation in a communication that makes contradictions to obvious reasons incommunicable" (*Intersubjectivity* 1995, 174).

One argumentation line, heard from Gadamer to Habermas, sustains the view that we refer to a lifeworld that "always already is given as a well-known horizon of pre-understood background knowledge." Luhmann finds too much of a home metaphor in such phrasings. He aims to leave us "in the empty space" of Kierkegaard's water fifty thousand feet deep. In his article "Lifeworld," Luhmann uses the distinction and form analysis of George Spencer Brown (1969) for the first time in order to swim into the deep waters of the existentialist Søren Kierkegaard: draw a distinction and let the distinction between the marked and the unmarked reenter into the marked side. This move condenses meaning and trustworthiness. In an unknown world, the observation is at least more known to itself and achieves an inert trustworthiness.

This of course sounds extremely abstract, yet this narrative is exactly what Luhmann finds in historical myths used to establish trustworthy symbols and stories about language and meaning. By means of their own involution and innovations, they condense meaning and lead to evolution. Hence, Luhmann's aim is to describe how a world is built, namely, in distinction to a system that consists in its provision of self- and other-descriptions in relation to such an external world. These are harsh conditions in an utterly absurd and unknown world. Hereby Luhmann "rejects a subsumption of critique into only one side of a distinction of which the other side is that of a lifeworld. The distinction trustworthy/criticizable pushes heterogeneous phenomena into an opposition;

and it postulates, furthermore, a false reciprocal exclusivity. No area of a lifeworld is immune to criticism; and no criticism could operate without a lifeworld (*Lebenswelt* 1986/2000, 280).

THE SOCIAL FORM OF REASONING

Discursive argumentation in Habermas's sense may involve personal experience, yet if they should have any validity in the realities of social systems, arguments have to get a form that can occur as selections in social systems (Luhmann, in H/L, 327). On the other hand, discursive argumentation should certainly not be attached to a legacy of reasoning as if a reasoning master could teach a less-reasoning subject (Hegel's knight) about what counts as reason. The form of reasoning as such appeared during the Enlightenment as a self-regulating form of communication and reflexivity. There is some form of Kantian mind before Kant (Koskenniemi 2006). Here, a common ground for Habermas and Luhmann could be Reinhart Koselleck's fascinating and accurate description of enlightened reasoning:

> The entire period under discussion presents the picture of a uniquely powerful process. In the eighteenth century, history as a whole was unwittingly transformed into a sort of legal process. This occurrence, which inaugurates the Modern age, is identical with the genesis of the philosophy of history. "In critique, history turns automatically into a philosophy of history" (Ferdinand Christian Baur). The tribunal of reason, with whose natural members the rising elite confidently ranked itself, involved all spheres of activity in varying stages of its development. Theology, art, history, the law, the State and politics, eventually reason itself—sooner or later all were called upon to answer for themselves. In these proceedings the bourgeois spirit functioned simultaneously as prosecutor, as the court of last resort, and—due to be of crucial importance to the philosophy of history—as a party. From the outset, progress always sided with the bourgeois judges. Nothing and nobody could evade the new jurisdiction, and whatever failed in the bourgeois critics' judgement was turned over to moral censors who discriminated

against the convicted and thus helped to carry out the sentence. (Koselleck 1959/1988, 9–10)

In Luhmann's redescription, political legitimation is due to the legitimacy (*Legitimität*) produced in the reasoning form and not to the empirical acceptance offered by participating individuals. Individuals may reason from the background of their personal experience but this can only be accepted for others in the form of generalizable grounds if it can be selected in the form of reasoning. Luhmann's argument seems pretty close to Habermas's about discourse ethics, yet in this lesson taught by this theme, Luhmann learned how important it was to establish a sharp distinction between psychic systems and social systems (Luhmann in H/L, 317, 325, 328). For the first time, he draws that distinction with a clear understanding of all its implications, though sometimes the distinction in an abbreviated form appears in previous writings (Luhmann *Normen* 1969, 36).

The logical theory about argumentative assertability conditions could be described as reasonable, or as unconditional for a valid statement whenever language is used to defend truth claims. However, Luhmann's argument does not follow the philosophical tradition, not because he cannot accept its arguments, but because of the suspicion that a legacy of logical rules follows a moral etiquette about what reasoning is about (Luhmann, in L/H, 333). The form of reasoning and the form of logics may appear indispensable to us, but we have them learned due to a civilizational history about interaction rules in which the lords dominated weaker and subordinate people to follow their forms of speech in order to appear as reasonable and logically accountable subjects for communication. Reasonable opinions Rawlsian-style probably ignore the fact of whether they have emerged as normative and ethical due to a history of moralistic domination. Kant's ethics and its practical reason claim universalizability, yet it appeared at an evolutionary moment where law courts and their ennobled estates and lawyers taught a broader public about good, decent, and honorable behavior and argumentation. Luhmann later developed the historical sociology of this argument much more in detail, and it became well known from Pierre Bourdieu's sociology of judgment too. Luhmann clearly pinpoints the sociological realities that present difficulties for a theory of discursive argumentation: "In the case of moralization, the question is when contributions to a theme become a theme—not because of the esteem for the contributors but because of their argumentation" (Luhmann, in L/H, 334). The idea and form of "universalization" may be unavoidable in logics, yet even logics is indebted to the improbable evolution of social communication.

Certain themes have received designation values, which stabilize them with concepts such as "God, reform, justice, love, truth, democracy, freedom, etc." (Luhmann, in H/L, 335). National security, fear, and terrorism are other highly valued themes that are presented as themes beyond question. The forms of other contributions can be criticized for not fulfilling the criteria of validity claims comparable to those that set the standards for good acceptable argumentation. Possibilities to beg the question are widespread, and this probably was the reason why Habermas and his many colleagues who contributed to discourse ethics in Germany continued for years to find a form of argumentation that transcended the rhetorical power in communication. Note that the point is not that Luhmann does not accept Habermas's argumentation for a discursive ethics. Luhmann's focus is on the conditions that establish the institutional possibilities and the differentiations in systems communication drawn upon in a discourse ethics that actually aims to give a contribution to a theory about social and political communication.

Finally, Luhmann points to a weak point in Habermas's theory of discourse ethics, which, nevertheless, maintains a strong hold on the theory. Many commentators have seen a weak point in it, but in fact, Luhmann's theory could contribute to its solution. The point is about temporality, which, compared to Luhmann's, is the really weak and opaque part of Habermas's theory: How long time is used in discussion in order to fulfill criteria for a meaningful and valid argumentation (Luhmann, in H/L, 336ff.). Luhmann seems to be aware that discussions may take much more time than we normally think whenever we cope with normal encounters in, for instance, meetings. However, discussions about, for instance, the theme "free will" may continue for hundreds or even thousands of years. Sometimes, we observe that silence comes and that every necessary part of a discussion theme has been repeated a sufficient number of times without new contributions and without added value. Yet Luhmann also states that we forget the contributions; hence summaries and memories appear as necessary. Thus, in fact, discourse ethics is desperately in need of a temporal theory of argumentation. Luhmann himself contributed extensively with such a theory as to what concerns decision-making; yet discourse ethics, Habermas-style, is not about decisions, or even about political decisions, but about counseling in "situations" that may endure for centuries. Reason may drown in history, though reason and reasonability emerged in history and as the results of historical narratives. Habermas and Luhmann both saw that research had to escape from the fatalities of the twentieth century, became aware of its risks, and hope for its promises, yet without naivety. The two chapters to follow investigate those conditions and possibilities.

III

BETWEEN HISTORY AND EVOLUTION

4

HISTORY AND EVOLUTION

The Initial Debates

THE DEBATE IN THE COAUTHORED PUBLICATION

Unsurprisingly, one of Habermas's most cited references to Luhmann's writings is the speech "Society" ("Gesellschaft"), which Luhmann gave at the German Conference of Sociology in 1968, and Habermas quotes it at length in his chapter on evolution in their coauthored book. Luhmann published the article in an important publication from the conference, *Industrial Society or Late Capitalism* (Adorno 1968). Here, Luhmann analyses how concepts of society have emerged, and how sociology should study this "improbable" development. Since Greek Antiquity, it has no longer been possible to simply understand society as a city, a polis, or a larger form of friendship in any segmented form. This conceptual challenge is about the name of what we have become used to calling "the society." Hence, it became the initiating theme of Habermas and Luhmann's book in Luhmann's first contribution (H/L, 7–9).

The discussion about the evolution and history of "society" in the book invoked a lengthy debate with several other participants and a number of ever more penetrating contributions from both Habermas and Luhmann. In Germany, theories of social evolution were necessary to escape the sticky, tragic, and much-too-recent history that embraced social research and historical research. As in America, the problem is finding a form of history that goes beyond the *Stunde Null*, or the Zero Point of 1776, the American equivalent of the German problem with 1945, yet of course very different (with 1865 presenting another possible American threshold). Might 2020, the Year of the Pandemic, obtain a similar position? On the one hand, German sociology and history were in need of distance and abstraction, not to mention the conceptual clarification of overburdened political ideas and words, too heavily filled with dark and heavy history together with hopes for enlightened utopian miracles. On the other hand, history and social research needed reconstruction, as did the political enlightenment of debates. This German debate enlightens abroad too, since all of us are more or less embedded in hopes, aspirations, crises, and disasters. For Luhmann and Habermas, the debate has several phases: the initial book, a range of articles throughout the 1970s, and a mature phase characterized by the masterpieces they each wrote in the 1980s and 1990s. Eventually, Habermas's philosophical "testament" (*Auch* 2019) will probably be brought to the fore.

Habermas discusses the theme of evolution in his section in chapter 6 in their coauthored publication ("Luhmann's Contribution to a Theory of Societal Evolution," H/L, 270–90); and Luhmann discusses the theme in the second part of chapter 4 ("Societal Evolution," H/L, 361–78). Before *Auch eine Geschichte der Philosophie* (2019) and his late preparations for that late study, Habermas's contributions seemed to end with *Communicative Action* in 1981 ("Second Intermediate Reflections"). Before that, it culminated in a sixty-page article, "History and Evolution" ("Geschichte und Evolution"; "History" 1979), which offered an answer to Luhmann's article from 1973, "Evolution and History." Luhmann's contribution seems to have found a new continent after 1977 with his four-volume series *Gesellschaftsstruktur und Semantik* (*Structure of Society and Semantics*), to which later were added two more volumes, including *Love as Passion* and the posthumously published *Ideenevolution* (*Evolution of Ideas*). He resumed these endeavors in his two-volume magnum opus, *Theory of Society* (1997). In this sense, with the weight of scholarly publications, Luhmann undoubtedly said much more than Habermas concerning the themes evolution and history. Whether Habermas's more recent later writings add to his previous analyses will be the subject of debate for years to come.

In his article "Society," Luhmann elucidates, first, that society cannot sufficiently become described in terms of unifying formulas, such as the city or its political form (*polis*), or by its economic principles (*oikos*). Neither by love, nor by *kononia* (the Greek term for friendship), nor by a religious principle such as the Jewish concept of community or St. Paul's "holy community." Moreover, adding some kind of hierarchical core or organizational form to such principles is of no help. We probably mostly know about these reductive political descriptions when we describe societies in terms of democracies, monarchies, and dictatorships, and that means describing them not even according to their state organization but only their governmental form. This criticism of reductionism was already important to Durkheim in his political theory, *Professional Ethics and Civic Morals* (1908/1969, 110–11), in which Habermas and Luhmann find important common ground.[1]

Second, Luhmann proceeds with three features: meaning, differentiation, and evolution. These features characterize how society has emerged as an improbable system as a part of the world, as a part with its own environment, and as a part that (for quite some time, in fact since the end of the sixteenth century) has been described as a "system." In a slightly different version, these three features structure Luhmann's entire social theory until *Theory of Society*.

The third feature is about evolution. There are many versions of evolution theory. With Durkheim, Luhmann rejects the most widespread version, the Darwinian, though he does use a few very important conceptual devices that entered into theories of social evolution from Darwin through the conceptualization of Herbert Spencer.[2] From Darwin and Spencer, Luhmann took the advice to look for variation, selection, and stabilization. Evolution did not emerge simply as exogenous random variation; rather, it is *improbable* yet *indispensable* that variations are selected, and endogenous stabilizations allow for a greater range of variations, among which selections are drawn. Luhmann reformulates Durkheim's classical example of law in *The Social Division of Labor*; in Luhmann's reformulation, the stabilization of law allows for more varieties and deviances from expected normalities (*Theory of Law* 1972/1985).

Social evolution is therefore neither about stochastic randomness nor about exogenous external causality as compelling necessity (Luhmann "Evolution des Rechts" [1970], in *Ausdifferenzierung* 1981, 15). Humans are not billiard balls; and even worse, for any theory of independent variables, social theories imply themselves regardless of what we may think about their possible external determinations: From the point of view of social theory (or any theory), we cannot expect that social theories cannot emerge. This self-implication is constitutive to another branch of evolution theory that emerged with Immanuel Kant (1790/1974, §§61–86; Düsing 1968). This was already decisive for the classics in social theory, Durkheim (1893/1930), Simmel (1892/1989), and Weber (1920), as well as Norbert Elias (1939/1976) and Talcott Parsons (1978). The constitutive idea is that the self-implication of social theories is improbable, albeit indispensable.[3] While they are a fact, we must suppose, as a first hypothesis, that they say a few million years ago were improbable when human prehistory began. Hence, we must work with a second set of hypotheses, namely, about how the paths of societal evolution have attained form and developed with what Parsons (1963/1969) called "evolutionary universals." We communicate and reason about social historical development, and this is an indispensable characteristic of communication and reasoning. Yet we have to pose the question as to how communication could develop and attain such forms, which allows communication to communicate freely about societal development and form hypotheses about it.

Luhmann's contribution to a theory of societal evolution consists of the discovery and clarification of the evolutionary universals to which he refers, which are useful for the analysis of a world-historical process for the extension of the control and capabilities of self-control in social systems. Luhmann offers a starting point in *Sociological Enlightenment* (SA 1, 151–52), which Habermas quotes at length in their coauthored publication (H/L, 274–75):

> In the complexity gap between social systems (including society itself) and their environment, we have seen that regulators to a tolerable degree are institutionalized within the social system. With these functions, and through them, society becomes that social system in which evolution takes place. Social evolution is the increase in the complexity of society, which is the increase in complexity that is necessary for society and its different social systems to accept as it relates to its environment. This statement holds true, first of all, with regard to those structures that allow society as a system and its subsystems to achieve higher complexity in environmental stability. Here the theory of system differentiation provides a way of continuing the argument. We

have seen that the form of system differentiation contributes to the complexity that the system can achieve. As enabled in organic systems, as well as in systems organized according to meaning, functional differentiation allows for a higher complexity than systems ordered according to segmental differentiation. The result is the historically verifiable hypothesis that social evolution is connected with a restructuring of society from systems of primarily segmentation toward those of primarily functional differentiation.

This puzzle concerns the core question for social theories of evolution. It deals with the first two features: meaningful communication and differentiation. For instance, about the differentiation of society in such a way that independent research has turned out to be possible. In the Habermas-Luhmann debate, it sometimes appears as if they are competing for the best answers to the questions that arise with this self-implication. But their competition also extends to others, including the classical Frankfurt School, in particular Horkheimer and Adorno, as well as French authors such as Foucault and Bourdieu. For instance, Habermas attributes to Luhmann that he "does not see" this or that in his own undertaking (H/L, 176), and Luhmann replies in the same vein (SA 5, 228–34). The great problem for sociology is that it must develop beyond the philosophical question of self-implication to offer insights that solve the puzzle. Evolution is a multistaged learning process. In this endeavor, Luhmann and Habermas agree to use the "learning processes" concept to describe social evolution. Another very important agreement is that social evolution is about what Weber called "interconnected complexes of meaning" (*Sinnzusammenhänge*), their rationalities (Weber), and their differentiations (Durkheim), and that such cohesive forms of meaning find their forms in communication and even in some form of intersubjectivity. Nevertheless, we could identify many different and even opposed cohesive forms of meaning.

In Luhmann's interpretation, to work with hypotheses of how to arrange an analysis of the self-implication of evolution is to observe varieties and conflicts among them. Conflicts should be observed either as destructive or, in the context of evolution, as paradoxical in the sense that new solutions emerge, for instance, when conflicts are absorbed by courts that do not dissolve conflict but offer a new form and new codes for social conflicts (*Law* 1993, 153). To Habermas, the self-implication of evolution means that evolution is led by a certain a priori reasoning and treatment of conflicts in the courts. This implies that argumentation in the form of language is approved, if not among the inflicting opponents then at least by their lawyers. Moreover, this involves the form and procedure, if not the substance, of consensus. The discussion of the form and process of evolution can also be found in the interpretation of discussions as forms of dissent and consensus. This theme is treated in chapter 8.

Habermas suggested hypotheses that use Karl Marx's historical materialism. On the one hand, it is difficult to see exactly how the short reconstruction Habermas makes of Marx's theory of productive forces and production relations does a different job than what could be undertaken as task for a systems theory of economy as capitalist economy. Habermas says little about the instrumentalist side of technology, nor did he ever, whereas Luhmann wrote small conceptualizations of technology as forms of reduced complexity to bracket distinctions between past and present, means and goals. Thus, Habermas's reappraisal of Marx seemed to demonstrate how Habermas, with Marx, coped with the question of evolutionary hypotheses. This Marxist vein was one of the two ways Habermas reconstructed evolution theory in the early 1970s.

The other way differs greatly from historical materialism, although it also invokes a stage theory of evolutionary learning, albeit with a departure on the microlevel of preconventional, conventional, and postconventional cognitive learning processes (Jean Piaget) and moral learning processes (Lawrence Kohlberg). In addition, Habermas reconstructs these microlevel theories about individual learning at the level of the macroevolution of societies.

While Habermas claims that Luhmann deals with the evolution of steering systems, he often also describes Luhmann's conceptualizations of such systems as "self-regulating systems."

A final theme is about the cumulative learning processes of evolution. In the article from 1968 on society, Luhmann spoke about a construction (*Aufbau*) of social forms of interconnected complexes of meaning, which in the course of evolution happened to become a reconstruction (*Umbau*). Forms of meaning are reformed (and even revolutionized); but we establish our hypotheses about their reconstruction and reform from a point of view *after* the improbable reconstruction: our analyses are based on *ex post* reconstruction.

Thus, Habermas—in between a philosophy of history and historical sociology—reconstructs three evolutionary stages in a Marxian model, which should be comparable to Luhmann's distinction between segmentary evolution, stratified evolution, and functionally differentiated evolution.[4] Marx—but not Habermas—is renowned for finding one dominating system in the modern functionally differentiated form, namely, capitalism. Luhmann had not claimed that such findings are false; rather, they expose a hypothesis, and we, in addition, should observe other forms (e.g., law, science, art, war, transport, organization, and politics) before we can claim that one functional system dominates. According to Luhmann, the main problem is less the suggestion of capitalism as a strong system and more the conceptualization of dominance (*Herrschaft*) as an obsolete old-European concept based on the ontology of land and preurbanized social order.

In his reply to Habermas, Luhmann suggests a thorough abandonment of naturalistic explanations in evolutionary theories. Hence, not only Darwinian causal and stochastic explanations of variance and evolution but also Marx's explanations of productive forces and furthermore cultural traditions as a continuation of natural history into cultural history are all abandoned as past explanations of present evolution. The point is to describe evolution on a more abstract level as the liberation of the present complexity from the past. Hence, evolution is redescribed through systems distinguishing themselves from the past by means of their internal complexities. Habermas and Luhmann certainly agree with Kant that meaning cannot be explained in causal ways. Accordingly, however, a complex system differentiated from its environment will also transform the environment of other systems. Evolution is this cosimultaneous dynamic transformation of systems. Of course, such transformations are not harmonious, but rather risky; disorder and dissent rather than consensus might easily be the result. Of course, then, the emancipation from the determinations stemming from the past must find a form of new stabilization. This might sound like an extremely abstract research project. However, Luhmann's overall question is whether a wider empirical research program can sustain this (very abstract) description. Luhmann's methodological devices show that cultural presuppositions are not neglected by systems theory; on the contrary. Luhmann's "proposal for societal systems is to observe the mechanism of variation primarily in language, the mechanism of selection primarily in communication media, and the mechanism of stabilization primarily in the system formation of society" (Luhmann, in H/L, 364).

This is an approach for empirical research that is close to conceptual history. As a side note, at that time, with neither Luhmann nor Habermas writing much about it, a young Michel Foucault proposed somewhat similar research projects in *Archeology of Knowledge* (1969, 32–33) and *The Discours on Language* (1970).

Luhmann's first theme is to observe variance and innovation in linguistic processes and to detect how grammatical codes begin to appear, operate, and disappear again. Accordingly, the use of language contributes to dissent as well as to consensus.

The second theme is to discover how codes are selected as communication and achieve certain "forms." Such selections could also take place (or not) in the motivation of psychic systems, although communication selects possibilities for otherwise-improbable communication, whether in matters of passion, power, conflicts, trust, or mistrust.

The third theme is to observe how "media" (e.g., money, love, power, law, and truth) and the form of media are stabilized by system differentiation. This does not erect identities or unities, but rather complexities that are stabilized in order to reproduce such complexities. For instance, communication about false theories is part of system stabilization in research. The negative side is part of the complexity to be reproduced, and system stabilization cannot dismiss it. Luhmann suggests that even in a remote phenomenon, as in Chinese law, accidents are counted as the opposite of stabilized expectations; he therefore discussed such evolution of coded selections in *A Sociological Theory of Law* (1972/1985) shortly after the Habermas-Luhmann book.

Important for their further debate, we find Luhmann's conclusion to his elaborations on systems theory and evolution. Luhmann proposed that the whole is less than the sum of its parts and that system differentiation is decisive for evolution. This means that there is no easy meta-theory available to judge how to select distinctions between system references. In systems theory (in the year 1971), no such theoretical development was available, for example, he cannot find it in Parsons's writings on social evolution.[5]

With this statement in mind, Luhmann explicitly opens a path to Habermas to suggest a path forward. From Luhmann's perspective, Habermas's theoretical developments in the following five years fulfill a range of those theoretical requirements necessary to investigate. These concerned discussions of discourse ethics and theories of truth, and they link discourse to the limits of systems reproduction in crises; in addition, they reconstruct moral philosophy and cognitive evolution as if macrodevelopments in societies could follow equivalent evolutions from preconventional, to conventional, and to postconventional principles; moreover, we see Habermas's incessant endeavors to develop a linguistic theory of communication. However, Luhmann did not find satisfying answers to these investigations, though some of them, such as Habermas's analysis in *Legitimation Crisis* (1973), were very systematic and have enjoyed long and very respected recognition among scholars (Kjaer, Teubner, and Febbrajo 2011).

If anything, paradoxically, Habermas's reconstruction of Marx's historical materialism, in the tumultuous 1970s, seems to have had fewer repercussions on reconstructions of Marx's logic of capital than Luhmann's later (1987) theory of self-referential credit systems (Baecker 1991; Esposito 2011). Luhmann proposes that the temporal structure of money, capital, and credit is more decisive to capitalism than its material basis, a result that Marx also deals with in the third volume of *Capital* (*Das Kapital*) (Luhmann, in H/L, 373–74). According to Luhmann, social theory in general, and systems theory in particular, ought to occupy itself with the temporal horizons of society (*World-Time* 1975, 289–323). The capitalist economy transforms what is to be expected of the temporal future. Societal evolution concerns conflictual claims to temporalities; in his book *Trust* (1968), Luhmann had already conceptualized this as "risks," a concept much more developed in later German sociology (Beck 1986; *Risk* 1991; *Shocked* 1996).

Habermas and Luhmann both oriented their research toward the communicative reconstruction of meaning in the historical processes of everyday varieties, as they have influenced and constituted system developments and themselves been subject to such developments. Accordingly,

Luhmann proposed to investigate the conceptual foundations used in social theory, such as "life" in "life-experience" (*Erleben*) and "lifeworld" (*Lebenswelt*), a concept he claims remains metaphorical upon an organic origin (Luhmann, in L/H, 372). Another concept is that of domination (*Herrschaft*), and the conceptualization of important theoretical devices such as "domination-free" is to remain within the range of concepts from a stratified premodern society, since *dominus* is a medieval concept about upper-hand possession of land (Luhmann, in H/L, 380).[6] As early as Durkheim (1895/1937, chap. 2) and the critique of ideology in the classic Frankfurt School, a number of proposals emerged that research should examine semantic and linguistic conceptualizations, in order to reconceptualize and reconstruct all of the important concepts of social theory. This early take-off in a "sociology of conceptual history" probably owed much to Weber's path-breaking and important study "'Objectivity' in the Social Science and Social Policy" (1904/1985).

Systems theory claims universality exactly because of such a program of the reconstruction of an infinite number of social concepts, codes, media, and forms and their modulations after the modern establishment of differentiated systems.[7] "Life" and "domination" are mere examples of such premodern concepts; others include "communication," "inclusion and exclusion," "power," and "institution." Luhmann finally (in H/L, 378) seems to observe Habermas's endeavor in this context as one of finding the "good" concepts and the positive legacies rather than the bad; reason rather than vanity.

The Habermas-Luhmann debacle on systems theory is sometimes said to have been unfruitful, including by Luhmann and Habermas themselves. Nevertheless, it pushed metatheoretical observations toward the reconstructions in conceptual history. Foucault's writings about a genealogy of discourse and power are famous today, yet far more penetrating were the German endeavors to establish a conceptual history and to reconsider the origins and developments in societal and political concepts. This, in particular, centers on the heavy, and indeed untranslatable, eight-volume Historical Basic Concepts (*Geschichtliche Grundbegriffe*, published in paperback edition in 2004), which began taking form around 1970, with the first volume published in 1972 (with Otto Brunner, Werner Conze, and Reinhart Koselleck as editors). Some of Luhmann's students, such as Hans-Ulrich Gumbrecht (now at Stanford), also took part. In their realm, British historians such as J. G. A. Pocock and Quentin Skinner have developed similar, linguistically based conceptual studies.[8] The tremendous effort to establish a conceptual history of modern society obviously demanded the historical interpretation of texts, whether hermeneutically or systemically, yet the clarification of social structures of communication was important too. Habermas and Luhmann intervened in both research fields. The sociological context was once again Parsons, yet other sociologists were also available as the battlefield for theoretical developments.

THE CONTINUED DEBATE ABOUT EVOLUTION AND HISTORY

As already mentioned, Habermas and Luhmann changed their views on evolution and history after their coauthored publication. Nevertheless, it is important to identify two contexts for their undertakings: Parsons's understanding of evolution and Marx's view on social history. In 1966, Parsons published the minor book *Societies: Evolutionary and Comparative Perspectives*, and a second book in 1971, *The System of Modern Societies*. The first was about "primitive societies," whereas the second was more concerned with evolution from Antiquity to modern and almost, finally, postmodern societies. Parsons also published a couple of extensive articles on the evolution of societies. He finished the second book the same year that Habermas and Luhmann published their common metatheoretical book, and we must study later publications to find its repercussions for them.

Parsons is often criticized for his abstract way of theorizing (Hamilton 1992). In the studies just mentioned, however, he tried to establish a framework for empirical historical interpretation. The idea was to conceive a scheme capable of "matching" empirical findings (Parsons 1971, 138). Sociological theory should form the framework, and historians could use it and contest it. We find a whole range of important sociological concepts used by Parsons: above all, differentiation, institutional patterns, ideas of universality, structure, stratification, hierarchy, authority, centralization, effectiveness, inclusion, innovation, adaptation, integration, community, and so on. Many are so useful that the important German scholar Hauke Brunkhorst, situated somewhere between Habermas and Luhmann (a position perhaps slightly thought-provoking) in 2012 evaluated Parsons as "the most important sociologist of the twentieth century." In particular, Parsons demonstrates how important it was that the distinction between, on the one hand, cultural religious symbols and, on the other, institutions and worldly power was institutionalized and differentiated in the medieval era, at the same time that free cities were developing. This was what Brunkhorst admired.

Parsons established a context for Luhmann and Habermas to think above evolution and history beyond the classical traditions of Durkheim, Weber, and Marx. While Marx's explanation of capitalist evolution and dominance was quite convincing in several respects, Parsons's scheme of a whole range of differentiations opened the theoretical fantasy: In "Comparative Studies and Evolutionary Changes" from 1971, Parsons embarked on discussions beyond the too-common scheme of a democratic and an industrial revolution (e.g., Nisbet 1967). First, he rightly saw that "probably the most important process in the modern era was the development of legal systems" (Parsons 1971/1977, 299), but he also conceived of a "commercial revolution" and an "educational revolution" related to a "cultural revolution" (Brunkhorst 2014a, 87). Once the conceptual scheme is opened, it is also questioned. Parsons repeatedly conceived four functions in a framework, which can be contested philosophically as well as historically. Together with Shmuel Eisenstadt (1963), he rather impressively argued that the worldly power structures of empires of Antiquity got authority and legitimacy sustained by their differentiation from cultural systems; furthermore, powerful effectiveness was differentiated internally (as political and personal goal attainment) and as external adaptation (economy). Cultural systems were also differentiated in integrative institutions (churches) and latent structures (belief systems). Such an interpretation scheme should not simply be skipped when it is empirically underpinned. For Luhmann and Habermas, however, Parsons most of all displayed a lesson about how to build theories and how to work with them in the context of historical materials (Habermas *Construction*). In both dimensions, he failed. Let us take the basic idea of a "match" between theory and historical empirical studies and discuss what that research strategy means.

Habermas and Luhmann could have discussed Norbert Elias's later, rather famous *The Civilizing Process* as basic to their interpretation of the theme of evolution and history. First published in 1939, it was soon forgotten, although Luhmann sometimes refers to the original book. The Elias and Parsons contributions are comparable; both studied in Heidelberg in the 1920s and both analyze the history and evolution of functional differentiation. Elias's book was republished in 1976, at which time it developed a major reputation that demonstrated in many respects why Luhmann and Habermas could not be satisfied with the Parsonian solution. One main difference with Parsons is that Elias took "manner books" as empirical objects for analysis. They communicate and, in addition, they are symbols that stratify the structures of the emerging early modern society. However, neither Elias nor Parsons had any theory of communication and language better than those known from Durkheim and Weber.

One of Luhmann's first articles published after his joint venture with Habermas was the influential "Self-Thematizations" (in *Differentiation* 1982). Here, Luhmann clarifies a certain object for historical study, namely, the self-reflections of society as society: In social research, we cannot avoid observing evolution in such a manner that, throughout evolution, society developed in such ways that thematizations of society and its evolution emerged. Thucydides's *The Peloponnesian Wars* offers such an example of thematized military strategies as part of those wars. Yet his analysis was less methodologically reflected than Jean Bodin's or Hugo Grotius's studies of the international system from about 1600. Self-thematizations and self-reflections are already in history, and the question then becomes in which forms. On the one hand, self-reference is an indispensable fact; on the other, the different forms of self-thematizations are improbable results of evolution. Modern communication is an "improbable" fact (Luhmann *Self-Reference* 1990, 89; SA 3, 27).

We see such reflections in Elias's descriptions of books on manners and how they reflect and construct societal norms. Yet with the focus on communication in Luhmann and Habermas, the turning point is that meaningful communication emerged as a core topic for societal research, which is itself such a form of communication. Moreover, societal self-reflections must have been object and subject for a self-differentiation of society. Accordingly, from a methodological perspective, historical sociology should find and focus such self-reflections, self-observations, and self-descriptions. This means, however, that such self-descriptions crosscut the Parsonian distinction between the scheme of structures and a historical empirical material. The Bible, as probably the most famous of such self-descriptions, describes faith while at the same time is itself part of a construction of a religious system; the same, of course, can be said of the writings of St. Augustine, as well as Dun Scotus, Abelard, John of Salisbury, Machiavelli, Bodin, Hobbes, and so on. Self-reflections of law—whether as constitutions or legal theory—appeared constitutive and constructive to law itself. Society incessantly establishes speech acts about the construction of societal realities. Biographies form individualities. Legal, economic, theological, aesthetic, and sociological reflections are parts of the communication of society with itself.

In fact, Habermas repeatedly returns to a number of schemes elaborated in that article. First, society develops reflections. Second, those reflections become aware of their contingencies: other observations and reflections are possible, and the world develops as a horizon of other possibilities—certainly after the invention of the printing press (Brunkhorst 2000; *Theory* 2012, 174–80; 1997, 291–301). Third, the relations developed between the diverse reflections must become ever more abstract.[9] The development of reflection, the openness of contingencies, and increased abstraction are three decisive features in modern communication. These three aspects characterize the modern, functionally differentiated society, and Habermas and Luhmann use them in their *Zeitdiagnosis* of modernity. They both refer to Durkheim's *The Social Division of Labour* (1893/1930, 252–56) as one place to find the three themes developed in a theory of the evolution of the division of labor and more generally of the differentiation of society. Communication in a differentiated society cannot function and get any meaning, if it does not somehow turn reflective, contingent, and abstract. Durkheim's experience was that you could not arrive to the train station, Gare du Nord in Paris, and directly address to the first person you meet, "Where is aunt Odile?"

Before Habermas and Luhmann directly again interpelled each other concerning the theme of evolution and history, three other contributions should be mentioned: two from Luhmann and one from Habermas.

In direct opposition to German nationalism since Heinrich von Treitschke, which laid foundations for "realist theory" in international relations, and to Parsons's theme of societies *in pluralis*, Luhmann addressed society in an article (*World Society* 1971, 52–71). The polis tradition of society can no longer confine politics to a territorial circumscription and go into a world society blessed by a law of nations. The world as a contingent cognitive horizon is differentiated from normative expectations of what to do with it. In Antiquity, several worlds (and gods) were found, side by side, albeit together with the ideas of one God and, later, one global ocean, in which *il Nuovo Mondo* was found. There was only one world, which accordingly stayed outside the reach of any political system. Today, or at least since the Cold War, societal communication is worldwide, whether in peace and war, economy, science, mass media, art, sport, and several other fields. Nevertheless, normatively, politics and law often delimit systems more regionally. This theme of a world society and its con-federal or cosmopolitan orders became increasingly important for Habermas too, particularly after 1989.

At the core of the following exchanges about the research programs in this early phase of the 1970s, we find Luhmann's two articles from 1973 "World-Time and System History" (in SA 2; *Differentiation* 1982) and "Evolution and History" (*Evolution* 1975), and Habermas's articles "Können komplexe Gesellschaften eine vernünftige Identität ausbilden?" from 1974 (in *Rekonstruktion* 1976, 92–128) and "Geschichte und Evolution" (in *Rekonstruktion* 1976, 200–259). Furthermore, there is a shorter comment from Habermas made at the German sociology congress in 1974, "Zum Theorienvergleich in der Soziologie: Am Beispiel der Evolutionstheorie" (in *Rekonstruktion* 1976, 129–43). Finally, there are Luhmann's articles "The Future Cannot Begin" from 1976 (in *Differentiation*) and the book *Funktion der Religion* from 1977, which extensively analyzes the evolution of religion, which I will discuss in chapter 5, as well as "Geschichte als Prozess und die Theorie sozio-kultureller Evolution" from 1978 (in SA 3 1981, 178–97). While publications obviously do not always follow swiftly after the writing, this was often the case for more celebrated authors; nevertheless, a whole range of unpublished manuscripts for books and articles was still stocked in Luhmann's office when he died in 1998. In particular, Luhmann wrote the seminal *Systemtheorie der Gesellschaft* between 1973 and 1975, which was eventually published in 2017. Luhmann was probably not satisfied with his analysis of the answers he gave to the questions concerning history and evolution (*Systemtheorie* 1975/2017, 259–450)—and therefore did not publish what was to be the 1132-page book.

In the first article from 1973 (SA 2, 107), Luhmann's idea is that the attribution of meaning is conditioned by selections that establish their possibilities with reference to different social systems of communication. It is one thing that systems and, hence, system differentiation are a condition for meaning to stabilize; another is that systems reproduce meaning within their own selected history. For example, the history of legal dogmatics is differentiated from the history of theological dogmatics, each of them operating with their own differentiated temporal horizon. Precedence, memory, and expectations function in different ways in such systems, and they condition what is meant with temporalities outside these systems in the environment of world history. Hence, historical sociology must establish system histories and differentiate among them and how they establish their respective self-thematized histories. World history cannot unify differentiated system histories, since they tell opposed stories, which risk diverging. World history is not a history of consensus and unity; rather, it is one of difference, dissent, and conflict between different forms of system evolution. They operate with different temporal horizons or "temporal bindings," as Luhmann writes in a later formulation of *Soziologie des Risiko* (1991).

World history is often supposed to be increasingly complex, and that is possible; however, it is also (easily) possible for system histories to be simpler, as when one hundred thousand languages are reduced to five thousand languages. Or whenever thousands of legal traditions or calendars are homogenized, when units of length and weight are standardized, and so forth.

Hence, systemic historical sociology describes a history of time, of change, of presence, of memory; on a higher level, it is the history of the changes in the relation between change and stability, and, above all, how the past was different in the past—and the future too. For Luhmann's systems theory, different systems have their own history and temporal horizons. Thus, a more abstract temporal history is necessarily a measure to generalize coordination, and this might seduce observers to think about only one world history (and one God), as if a century counts in Iraq or China the same way it does in Nevada. Yet all system histories unfold at the same time, synchronically, though they have very different and opposed temporal horizons, which simultaneously also could be described as nonsimultaneous (*Ungleichzeitige*). Whereas Parsons found that culture controls other systems, according to Luhmann there is no control available between systems; on the contrary, we find bottlenecks. Some systems might continue as obstacles, as when soldiers must still march despite the invention of planes, trains, and automobiles. Temporalization does not simply mean increased speed and acceleration; there are also different histories of tempo. Long-term developments, change, and revolution are not about the same temporal horizons in finance, organization, science, education, politics, love, or war. They are unlikely synchronized and are "nonsimultaneous" (*Ungleichzeitige*).

In his article "Evolution and History" (SA 2, 150–70), which became so influential for the further debates, Luhmann comes to a first platform of devices for a (systems) theory of evolution, which we now know had already been so much more meticulously developed in the then-unpublished *Systemtheorie der Gesellschaft*. Theories of evolution must interpret how evolution can observe itself in terms of evolution theory; and while this result seems improbable from any idea of an origin or beginning, the result is indispensable. "In the beginning was the word," however, was declared in the first line of the Gospel of St. John and extremely well recapitulated by St. Augustine in his classic philosophy of temporality in *Confessions* (chap. 11). St. Augustine's analysis remains to this day one of the most basic texts for temporal theories and in particular those of Luhmann and his Bielefeld colleague Reinhart Koselleck. Thus, rather than looking for an origin, a first mover, a *causa finales*, or a God-ordained creation, Luhmann's primordial device is to search for transformations of the past/present distinction: that is, the bottleneck, the *Engpass*. When, how, and in which texts does this distinction appear different from what it seems to have been in the past?

Altogether, this means that systems emerge when they gain the ability to detach their own temporalities and time-horizons from other systems. They find their own storytelling devices, so to speak, and—in the case of legal evolution—this could be in the form of legalized expectations regarding the legal order of a future present moment; it could also be in the form of interests that bind future payments to today's payments and allow payments today. In both forms, a will is contracted so that greater payments will follow tomorrow. Will, indeed, is such a temporal device and binds today's intentions to later intentions; aesthetics is another, and therefore another form of temporal device.

After their coauthored book was published, Habermas was named director of the Max Planck Institute in Starnberg. Among the most important among Habermas's many young assistants was Klaus Eder, who later contributed extensively to analyses of evolution and history, including his state doctorate (habilitation dissertation), *History as Learning Process?: On Germany's Legal-Political Development, 1780–1945* (*Geschichte als Lernprozess?*, 1985). In 1976, he published a booklet about early antiquity's state-building that was based on an article from 1973 about evolution. Here, Eder reconceptualized Marx's theory of historical stages of production into a theory of evolutionary learning. This became important for Habermas's later contributions.

Habermas and Luhmann both try to combine sociological conditions with historical narratives. The structural conditions of possibilities and realities should not be confused. In the reconstructions of historical materialism, the French philosopher and structuralist Louis Althusser enjoyed considerable influence in the social sciences in the 1970s. He is a common target for criticism among both Frankfurters and Bielefelders. When Althusser writes about the "overdetermination" of structures to history in *Reading Capital* (*Lire le Capital*, 1965), Luhmann typically turns such an explanation upside-down, explaining that "underdetermination" is much more plausible. The point is not only that structures determine what should happen but that structures (e.g., legal systems, monetary systems, art systems) also open up possibilities for innovation, variation, contingencies, or what Habermas calls emancipation. In a functionally differentiated society, systemic structures cannot steer other systems and structures. Neither structural determination nor negating dialectics from Lenin to Georgy Lukács to Althusser can replace the lacunas of lacking temporal theory. Instead, historical sociology should explain contingencies, which means how history opens up for "constructions of historical situations by the participants themselves" (Luhmann *Evolution* 1975, 158).

As an example, Luhmann demonstrates how "the civil society" (Hegel's *bürgerliche Gesellschaft*) should find new forms, namely, after the specialization of functional systems differentiated from an overall, comprehensive whole once identified as a religious corpus. On the microlevel, people should find new forms of universal inclusion in their relations to the functional systems in education, in politics, in the military, in families, in the economy, and in religion. Religion was not only secularized; it also specialized and "sacralized" itself from a former hybrid legal cohesiveness with church organization. Individuals could no longer be identified as members and part of a coherent whole; they had to identify themselves on the brink of society as members and in distinction to such membership. A parallel explanation is offered by Habermas (in *Transformation*, 54), though in principle Habermas still conceived society as a collective macrosubject—a figure he later transformed. Nevertheless, in Habermas's response in the lengthy article "History and Evolution" (*Rekonstruktion* 1976, 236), he attacks this whole/part model of the universalized functional inclusion of subjects to systems for explaining nothing.

Whereas Marx wrote about the development in production relations (*Produktionsverhältnisse*), Habermas differentiates the development of economic systems from the development in legal rationalization and developments in individual and social moral reflection. His point is that historical materialism neglected to analyze the developments in the law and morality. Capitalism could only develop if those two parts are rationalized according to their own developmental logics. Of course, Durkheim and Weber already demonstrated how these preconditions developed. Habermas instead reconstructs the classic differentiation of developmental logics and dynamics in terms of communication. Norms and rules must follow communicative learning processes:

> Rationality structures are embodied not only in amplifications of purposive-rational action—that is, in technologies, strategies, organizations, and qualifications—but also in mediations of communicative action—in the mechanisms for regulating conflict, in world views, and in identity formations. I would even defend the thesis that the development of these normative structures is the pacemaker of social evolution.
> (Habermas, in *Evolution*, 120; *Rekonstruktion*, 35)

Habermas's reconstruction of historical materialism was generally read in the mid-1970s as a correction to the Marxist discussions among students and younger scholars that were extremely widespread in Europe at the time. For the many Marxist scholars, Habermas's "reconstruction of historical materialism" was indeed a tremendous provocation and established an internal critique in Marxism that, more than anything else (including Polish Solidarnosc and the disintegration of the Soviet Union), eventually led to the breakdown of intellectual Marxism and ended in a "deconstruction."

While Habermas and Luhmann both underline the importance of learning processes that link micro- and macroprocesses (Luhmann "Reflexive Mechanismen," in SA 1; "Evolution des Rechts," in *Ausdifferenzierung* 1981, 13; Habermas *Evolution*, 121; *Rekonstruktion*, 36), there is a difference. Habermas tackled the problem head-on and therefore had to stand on the shoulders of others. He took only a few years to investigate before producing publications diffusing his ideas; and several of his writings in *Rekonstruktion* appear to be first drafts of hypotheses that do not penetrate the analyses of historical materials. In fact, this publication strategy was fruitful in the context of the Marxist-reduced narratives that were flourishing at the time. Moreover, in the writings shortly after 1971, it is difficult to evaluate the extent of the historical reading in which Habermas and Luhmann have engaged. In 1971, Luhmann and Habermas would both appear to have some penetrating knowledge of historical narratives. The *Systemtheorie der Gesellschaft*, unpublished in 1975, occasionally reveals extraordinary amounts of references (e.g., on Chinese history, 1975/2017, 208). Then, beginning in the late 1970s, Luhmann began publishing about his extraordinarily extensive readings of all kinds of texts, an endeavor that impresses even those historians with very good knowledge of texts and periods.

In *Rekonstruktion* (1976) Habermas offers three articles in response to Luhmann's "Evolution and History." In 1974, he published two articles. The first, "Could Complex Societies Form a Reasonable Identity?,"[10] is among the most complicated articles Habermas has ever written, which says a lot (there is a much abbreviated, insufficient version available in English: "On Social Identity" in *Telos*, published in 1974). The second response to Luhmann is in "Comparing Theories in Sociology: The Example of Evolutionary Theory" and is simpler. The third article, "History and Evolution," is thematically much clearer in its lengthy elaborations on the meaning of narratives in historical research and evolutionary theory. None of them is translated.

In the first article, Habermas initially engages with Hegel (since the article was a speech given when Habermas received the Hegel Prize in

Stuttgart, a prize Luhmann received in 1989), then with German philosopher and Hegel specialist Dieter Heinrich (who received the prize in 2003), and finally with Luhmann. Habermas questions the point of conceiving of society as an identity, since "identity" is a formula for individual identity. Yet individuals are identified and recognized as included and excluded from the form of that recognition, since they must identify themselves in their difference to society and its forms of recognition. The individual is human (*ein Mensch*) because she is not only a subject and a citizen, but can sustain her identity by *not* simply being identical to what is recognized as her social role. The argument is somewhat similar to Luhmann's arguments about nonidentity among human beings and in their relation to society, which Luhmann argued at the time. In relation to Hegel, the argument certainly finds its basis in Adorno's *Negative Dialectics* (1966) and in his reception of Søren Kierkegaard's critique of Hegel. However, this all means that we can hardly accept an idea of a societal "identity." Habermas's central point is that Hegel's "means of thinking the system" ("Denkmittel des Systems," *Rekonstruktion*, 97) must be reconceptualized.

Accordingly, it would be too simple, as Durkheim does, to reconceptualize evolution in two stages: one where individuals are completely part of a whole and simply similar to one another, and the second where they are tolerated as different. We must enter the stages in between. Similar to the first vein, a Greek Aristotelian polis conceptualizes an identity between society and individuals. On a third level, theological dogmatics universalize themes and suggestions to describe relations between God and individuals and to redescribe how this is decisive for state organization, law, and so on. On a fourth and modern level, the question arises whether even a reformed religious interpretation can aim to comprehend ideas of a reconciliation of individuals with society. Note that this stage theory also turns into a question of the idea of counting discontinuities between stages. As Luhmann later explains in an article about époques (*Epochenbildung*, 1985), we could count to one (as Durkheim does), two, three, four; Luhmann usually uses three stages (two ruptures), but in his seminal publication, *Theory of Society*, from 1997, he uses four and is close to the three-stage evolution proposed by Habermas. This discussion is of course very similar to the scheme first proposed by Marx in *The German Ideology* (1845). There, Marx repeatedly stressed the importance of urban development and, furthermore, distinguished, first, the mode of production in Antiquity where the medium of work was based on slavery; second, the feudal mode, where work was exploited directly in serfdom; and, third, increasing forms of capitalism based on trade capital, industrial capital, and financial capital at the world-market level, which finally ended with no more unexploited environments to exploit. However, when Habermas then outlines stages for learning processes in normative communication, he uses the three-stage cognitive Piaget scheme (preconventional, conventional, and postconventional), which he transforms into a moral scheme, and, later, using Lawrence Kohlberg, he divides each of those three stages into two levels (*Rekonstruktion* 1976, 172ff.).

For Habermas, however, this originally Hegelian question about the place of subjectivity as a yardstick for measuring society remains with him. This is repeated in his lecture series from 1985 (*Discourse* 1987, 16–18; 1985, 27–29), where he still evaluates Luhmann's universal theory as a response to Hegel's "means of thinking." According to the article from 1974, Habermas sees the strength of Hegel's proposal as being that individuals cannot formulate their questions about their own self-identity without means proposed by societal formulations of this identity, which, basically, is one of monotheist religion. Social thought should try to reformulate contingency, differentiation, and nonidentity in its own ways. Habermas recognizes Marx's claim that reconciliation has no social reality as long as class structures remain, and class differences are now globalized. However, the communist parties proposed a reconciliation, with their communitarian reasoning as a solution, a story that never broke with their particularistic (and often bureaucratized) form. Others proposed nationalism as particular reasoning.

In this article, Habermas prefers to find an answer in Luhmann's conceptualization of a "world society," if not as a Kantian confederal form—which Habermas later engages with intensely—then as a reality. Habermas's Hegelian question regarding the form of unity in society is apparently dissolved with Luhmann's theory, according to Habermas. First, society cannot be comprehended as an interaction system with an intersubjective presence and adequate lifeworld expressed in norms to direct such a society. World society is, so to speak, exactly not a global village; if anything, it is a giant global metropolis. Thus, Habermas preferably finds it promising if no single self-steering functional system claims to steer the whole unity of a world society. The functional perspective about social systems is that systems overload the political and administrative steering capacities; and morality is overloaded with responsibility. There is no unity available in the functional systems perspective, nor does the capitalist system expose such unity. Administrative systems, too, can tend to reestablish governmental solutions to whatever comes up and to dissolve contingencies of the lifeworld into the form of environment in their systems. The problem is that a social system is based on a "deficit of reflection" (Habermas *Complex*, 113); it merely reflects its own solutions.

Habermas does not expose Luhmann's reconstruction in its radical form: First, there is no *single* system, but rather a "plurivers" of extremely differentiated systems. Thus, the lifeworld is not alienated toward a single all-encompassing system but is, rather, so to speak, alienated toward all social systems, including families, organizations, political systems, legal systems, art systems, and scientific systems. Luhmann is therefore preoccupied with passionate love on the grounds that it seems to be the single system that promises to keep a hope or at least a seductive narrative of reconciled nonalienation.

Second, Habermas still recapitulates systems as planning systems that bracket the present and steer the future from past experiences, and he sees this as a "perversion of progress." Thus, Habermas in 1974 has not really gotten the point that evolution temporalizes the present and does so in extremely functionally differentiated ways. Luhmann has not promised that a world society conceptualized with systems theory avoids risk; on the contrary, conflicts can take place everywhere, not only inside the systems but also between the opposed temporal horizons of differentiated systems. The question remains whether a "critique of functional reason neglects structures of intersubjectivity because of the self-orientation of system-structures" (114). Finally, Habermas sees possibilities for a new "communicative floating of traditions" in a world society that does not remain bound to given administrative solutions but opens the floor for participation in public and political debates. Two decades later, Habermas and several others brought Kant's draft of a range of postnational confederal republican forms into such debates. In the 1970s, it was rather the (then so-called) new social movements that could describe new communicative participation beyond conventions and traditions. Luhmann later (in *Exklusion* 1995) referred to social networks, such as Luc Boltanski's (1991, 1999), which was some kind of French recapitulation of Luhmann and Habermas's frame of analyses.

In 1974, Luhmann published an article with the long title "Preliminary Remarks Towards a Theory of Symbolically Generalized Media of Communication" (*Einführende*). This, certainly, is a—perhaps and probably—ironical repetition of Habermas's first chapter in their coauthored book, although Habermas there writes about "communicative competence."[11] In his article, Luhmann responds to Habermas's critique in *Legitimation Crisis*. Luhmann asks what it means that there could be "motivational limits to growth" (a parallel to the Rome Club that famously questioned the ecological limits to growth in 1972). In Luhmann's analysis, development in functional systems is one thing; the decision-making processes in organizational systems are another. In organizational systems, the decision-making capacities can become the bottleneck in power structures whenever the medium of truth and social research becomes evident. The problem is how systems react to one another and use reflections in dogmatics, in research, and in art, responding to them by building new codes into them. The early 1970s were characterized by what Luhmann calls "confused embarrassment" (*Verlegenheit*) and even "epidemically confused embarrassment," not only in social movements, but also in social research; it became a question whether this confused embarrassment became part of decision-making processes in organizational systems.

In Habermas's overall statement with historical materialism, in the article "Toward a Reconstruction of Historical Materialism" (in *Evolution* 1979), he briefly responds to Luhmann that learning processes cannot be observed simply as increasing complexities in functionally differentiated systems (*Rekonstruktion* 1976, 191; *Evolution* 1979, 174). The relations between linguistic use and acting in systems therefore have to be investigated. This theme turns into a major discussion with Habermas's response to Luhmann in the lengthy (but untranslated) article "History and Evolution."

"History and Evolution" represents a remarkable point in their debate. First, it is the only place where he considers temporality. We have seen how the temporalization of communication is extremely important to Luhmann. Here, however, Habermas intervenes preferably in reconsidering hermeneutical approaches from Hans-Georg Gadamer and Reinhart Koselleck. During their debate in the 1970s, Luhmann's Bielefelder colleague Koselleck published a very important series of articles (*Futures Past* 1979, translated in 2004). In this vein, Habermas's overall idea is that historical interpretations consist of historical research and historical narratives. Historical narratives are, basically, contemporary narratives about a past that has a beginning, a central event, and a result. This influences our account of history (i.e., what the past and future were about), and, hence, actual society. As impressively stated by Gadamer, with whom Habermas had several important discussions, we cannot avoid interpreting past events from the present perspective. In fact, Habermas does not refer to Gadamer in the article—he does not see the forest for the trees. Habermas's account is precise and accurate, demonstrating that he could very well take Luhmann's phenomenology of the present into account. However, Habermas's discussion remains in the hermeneutical context, though he, by way of introduction, refers to some sociological phenomenologists. This is a rather odd reference, since some of the authors referred to (e.g., Goffman and Garfinkel) are extremely ahistorical. Sociology could work with overall generalizations of historical data without turning to the narrative events told by historians. Yet according to Habermas, such a division of labor would be fruitful to neither historians nor sociologists.

Second, in Habermas's account, this point about historical research and historical narratives somehow pushes Luhmann to an extreme position, as if he would only establish a sociology of evolution based on aggregations. This is remarkable since Luhmann later innovates several decisively important new levels (or even transformations) in his research project. At that moment, Luhmann was already skipping the (inter) action theory as the fundament for his social theory in favor of a thorough communication theory. This is the first among three transformations undertaken by Luhmann in the years 1975 to 1977, which, I would assume, is the reason why he did not publish his seminal *Systemtheorie der Gesellschaft* (2017), which he had otherwise completed at the time.

If the focus is on communication, Luhmann's book on *Power*, published in 1975 (and translated in 1979), can be viewed as the first representation of his full but still unfinished theory, since there he finally abandons any idea of action or interaction theory as being basic to his social theory. This is also where he completes the distinction between the three main themes for his general theory: evolution, differentiation, and communication.

Equally important, however, was the fully completed turn toward the idea or, as he later states, "fact of self-reference" (*Teleologie* 1981, 31). In *Funktion der Religion*, the present moment for Luhmann is the indispensable self-reference.

For the theme of history and evolution (and along with Koselleck), however, a third important transformation followed: Luhmann began exposing his empirical undertakings about semantic history. He demonstrates how semantic variations opened for communication codes, which selected semantics and strengthened codes into guiding codes and forms that stabilized in systems, which in turn opened for variance. The first publications in this research project followed shortly after Habermas's "History and Evolution" with *Funktion der Religion* and the article "History as Process and the Theory of Sociocultural Evolution" (*Prozess*, in SA 3).

Altogether, however, the much more decisive transformation came with the multivolume *Societal Structure and Semantics* (*Gesellschaftsstruktur*, vols. 1–4, 1980; 1981; 1989; 1995), which also included *Love as Passion* and *Evolution of Ideas* (2008).

Luhmann was not at all interested in using historical research about semantic innovations and code innovation as the topic for broad historical narration in these volumes, or in *Economy as a Social System, Law as a Social System, Art as a Social System, Politics as a Social System, Religion as a Social System, Research as a Social System*, and so on. Luhmann, certainly, would not tell stories. The theme definitively concerned historical research linked directly to the sociological theory of evolution and structural transformations. Could this radically different undertaking from that which Habermas suggested was a dead end for Luhmann partly also be the result of Habermas's further argument in "History and Evolution"? Here, we must remember that, on the advice of Thomas McCarthy, Habermas broke off his own elaborations and restructured them over the next four years while writing *Theory of Communicative Action*.

Habermas appreciates a well-known exposition of Luhmann's other Bielefeld colleague, the historian Hans-Ulrich Wehler, in *The German Empire, 1871–1918* (1973/1985), with whom he took sides in the famous German "Historians Dispute" (*Historikerstreit*) in the later 1980s. Pupils of Luhmann, such as Hans-Ulrich Gumbrecht and Rudolf Stichweh, have written extensively about the history of literature and about the present moment, respectively, regarding the history of universities, whereas pupils of Luhmann twisted the Bielefeld school of historical sociology into longer and broader European narratives.[12]

Habermas's point is to find the narrative organization of the exposition, and he proposes the use of the rationalization of a cohesive coordinated action (*Handlungszusammenhang*). History and evolution can follow the post-Hegelian path of a rationalized learning and progression process. This could take the form of an objective spirit that learns through its conceptual real institutionalization and its ideal innovations of ideas, as in the history of church and religion, universities and research, or legal institutions and legal reflections. Indeed, if Habermas left that research project, it was not to oblivion; he reestablished it in the 2010s and it was ultimately accomplished with Habermas's seminal *Auch eine Geschichte der Philosophie* (2019).

For the German generation of Wehler and Habermas, the million-dollar question is obviously how Germany could fall into the "special path" (*Sonderweg*) of derationalization and political pathologies (*Rekonstruktion*, 220–21). For others, like Koselleck and (in particular) Luhmann, it is a trap to scrutinize German and European political history using an excessively narrow magnifying glass. Hence, developing a methodology to observe this trap is not only interesting; it is also urgent and demanding beyond what we can imagine from other traditions. This is one reason why neither Luhmann nor Habermas accepts Parsonian ideas of an "equilibrium" between systems and their environment. For Habermas, there is too much "anomie" (Durkheim) in the environment, too much alienation (Marx), and a lack of sense (Weber).[13] Norm development in the social integration of such an environment can be absorbed, colonized, or dissolved by wild-going systems, such as those demonstrated by Marx (capitalism) or Clausewitz (war).

Whereas Habermas and Luhmann both dismiss that causal explanations are useful in historical sociology, Habermas finds too much openness for contingencies and varieties that can be selected, and he fears that Luhmann will turn up with "historical fact finding." Frankly, Luhmann's point, as seen in his later analysis, is that there is no original state (for instance, as an origin of any legal or illegal state) that can explain later developments in law; instead, it is merely later evolution in law that can explain and judge past developments as legal or illegal (Luhmann *Gesellschaftsstruktur* 1989, 3:11–64; *Mittelalter* 1991).

Of course, it is difficult today to recapitulate Habermas's argumentation about the possibilities of Luhmann's conception without an eye to what Luhmann actually achieved over the following two decades. Habermas finds that Luhmann should "not be able to explain the emergence [*Entstehung*] of new structures" (*Rekonstruktion*, 228). Habermas will not, as in the 1960s with Eisenstadt (and later with Bourdieu), refer only to elites and counter-elites; in this manner, he returns to the obsolete idea of functions of reproduced system identities in analogy to the life/death of organic systems. This is not the path of Luhmann's systems theory. The interesting push Habermas gives to Luhmann is

Events—change—structures

Since the simple counterposition between events (*Ereignisse*) and societal structures is too abstract, the point is to find what *change* in communication is about. Habermas proposes learning, as Luhmann did in an earlier article, "Reflexive Mechanismen" (from 1966), whereas Luhmann there and in 1976 also proposed the use of the scheme varieties/selections/stabilizations, yet also "learning about learning." Habermas proposes that new levels of differentiation in transformed systems cannot emerge without the corresponding social integration of norms. Hence, the crisis criteria for transformation and change are new learning processes in the integration of norms. For instance, this could emerge as a public sphere between the legislative, executive, and judicial powers.

In a lengthy note in "History and Evolution" (in *Rekonstruktion*, 254–256n47), Habermas expresses his dissatisfaction with Luhmann's answer: "When the basic concepts are analyzed in a functionalist way, it does not explain anything about the emergence of temporal structures." Habermas does not really offer any argument for this accusation; on the other hand, in 1976, anything more than a description of transformations in Luhmann's text is not evident. When reading Luhmann's analysis with his later solution (*Gesellschaftsstruktur* 1:1980, 87–88, 89, 105, 215), however, the answer is already hidden in the conception of differentiation, since different temporal horizons (e.g., between present and future) paradoxically establish the difference between reproductive structures, which repeat and therefore establish involution as a difference to variety. Temporalization happens not only by variations but by the difference between variation and invariation (stabilization), and rest and restlessness (the classic example is Simmel's analysis in "Fashion," 1923). Stabilization gives new (!) meaning to variety and, hence, even to stability: that is, even new reflection about what newness is about. Accordingly, the invention of writing as stabilized communication invents new forms of speech, as is the case with the printing press, which strengthens the symbolic presence and innovation in love letters—and Luhmann later added the Internet as a machine for synchronizing operations. Obligatory binding and the freedom of will are conceptually united as difference (*Gesellschaftsstruktur* 1980, 1981, 1989, 1995, 1:218). Hence, evolution becomes "self-selective"; the point is not to explain variation as such, but variation because of stabilization, in the case that it represents a nontyrannical stabilization (1:226). Accordingly, in the aftermath of Habermas's critique, Luhmann replaces action analysis with time analysis (1:245–47). Differentiation establishes instantaneous nonsimultaneity (*Ungleichzeitigkeit*). Time acts. And this takes place in communication in between concepts and counterconcepts.

The real challenge in temporal theory came from Koselleck (1979, 2000). However, if Habermas perhaps provoked Luhmann to strengthen his analyses in favor of explaining temporal transformations, Habermas achieved success far beyond what he ever could have hoped, as Luhmann's explanations of time and change are historically underpinned by references and extensive analyses far beyond what any answer in social theory hitherto had established. It is difficult not to take Koselleck's merits and Paul Riceour's later three volumes *Temps et recit* into account. Nevertheless, as a text interpretation of temporalities, Luhmann's systems theory outmatched hermeneutics and offered an immense range of analyses about the semantic transformations in code development and, accordingly, in systems structures.

In line with the German Historians dispute, it seems as though Habermas, with his conception of the "History and Evolution" theme, will remain committed to a comprehensive political action of placing Germany and Europe in the modern world society, thereby aiming to criticize ideologies. Meanwhile, Luhmann will observe the social and political semantics from a distance in order to observe the risks and paradoxes, restraints, and possibilities of the semantic contribution and construction of the structures in modern world society. Therefore, he repeatedly criticizes obsolete old-European semantics that stick to ideas and dreams of an overintegrated medieval world.

Somewhat similarly, toward the end of "History and Evolution," Habermas warns against historical narratives that hide prejudices about *the* totality of history:

> When even the evolution theory itself becomes absorbed in a history of great survival, mixed forms of theory and narration arise with a problematic status.... So it seems that the totality of the history is turned into an object for an overstretch of evolution theory into narratives, as if the evolution passes through a macrosubject that has become the carrier of a continuous history of humankind. (*Rekonstruktion*, 246–47)

With this warning against "consensual preconditions" and even a restored consensus in Germany after 1945 with "transcendentally used limitations," Habermas delimits evolution theory from the "whole of history" and its "macroprocess," on the one hand, but also, on the other hand, from very narrow historical microprocesses. A historically informed evolution theory "should not delineate any linear sense or continuity, not necessities or irreversibility" (*Rekonstruktion*, 246–48, paraphrased by Luhmann's recapitulation of the debate in 1978 in SA 3, 183).

As against Habermas's warnings about grand totalizing narratives, in his many subsequent volumes about semantic history and structural differentiation, Luhmann clearly did not (at all) follow the path of any narrative history, and likewise warned against the abuse of naive evolution theory. The project definitively turned toward a combination of historical *research* and evolution theory. Luhmann indeed seldom used some of the trendsetting authors in historical sociology, such as Otto Hintze, Barrington Moore, Charles Tilly, Perry Anderson, Michael Mann, Hendrik Spruyt, and Brian Downing, who delineated basic explanations for state-building and often told narratives of one or another dominating functional system. Preferably, Luhmann occupies his research with more specialized historical analyses of particular countries or specific periods and specific semantics and system developments. Harold Berman's interpretation of the legal revolution in the long twelfth century or Ernst Kantorowicz's analysis of the king's two bodies was more decisive to Luhmann. Above all, his historical material was the self-descriptions in the original sources: the historical texts on law, love, money, politics, research, education, and so on.

Luhmann responds directly to Habermas's "History and Evolution" with an article from 1978, "History as Process and the Theory of Sociocultural Evolution" (republished in SA 3, 178–97). This is among the final articles in this second phase of the Habermas-Luhmann debate. At the time, overwhelmingly references started to be made back to former publications as well as to the intense debates in Germany. They concern historical materialism less than themes about conceptual history. Reading Habermas and Luhmann, accordingly, gives the impression of listening to Richard Wagner's opera *Niebelungenring* with themes, tunes, drums, violins, and annotations that refer and give associations to whole ranges of former themes. In fact, Wagner got that idea from Hegel's way of writing and structuring materials—and today, such storytelling-structuring narratives have penetrated movie history and their soundtracks, so we all know all about what this means. This allows for complexities extending beyond the surface line of argumentation. Yet Luhmann normally writes in clear, lucid prose. While he is much easier to translate than Habermas, the hidden references to the increasing range of arguments in the common debate are nevertheless obvious in the text. A great range of the themes from Kant and Hegel, to Weber, hermeneutics, Parsons, Koselleck, and the common debate since 1971 are reconstructed in the light prose of Luhmann's article from 1978. Basically, the ontology of history appears as it "is" and should be separated from what we know of it, yet it will not suffice to narrate, as if history could be told through the actors; Luhmann insists that we must establish a distance from which the "knowledge of evolution is itself a result of evolution" (Luhmann Prozess 1978, 181).

In the article, Luhmann thoroughly takes the notion of "event" (*Ereignis*) into his explanatory scheme. Thus, at that moment, Luhmann operates with an argumentative path of transformation:

> varieties of events—codes/media—duplicated codes—systems—structural differentiation

The point is not only to find communication media and codes that render communication in such media probable, since this was already debated in several forms, from which Parsons established his theory of symbolic media of exchange. This would not suffice to explain transformation. Taking varieties of events into consideration is obviously decisive; nonetheless, Luhmann then adds another theme: the duplications of codes as the self-reference of codes whenever they become able to codify themselves from within, as when law regulates the distinction between legal and illegal or when research is undertaken about research. As mentioned, early on (in 1966), Luhmann conceptualized the idea of "learning to learn." He establishes an "evolution of evolution" together with another form of explanation: Evolutionary learning takes the form of "preadaptive advances," since the differentiation of systems later lets them achieve new and more modern functions when further system differentiations follow, as when private law becomes useful to later commercial contracts centuries after its invention.

Probably the most influential comment on the Habermas-Luhmann debate about narratives of history and evolution came from a most unexpected observer: the French philosopher Jean-François Lyotard (1979). Again, a social thinker born in 1924 and one of the most German-oriented of the French philosophers, he was in some respects close to Adorno but adorned in the communicative turn, like almost everybody else in social thought. In 1979, he published a small occasional book that would become the most path-breaking book on "postmodernity": *The Postmodern Condition*. Amazingly, this booklet appears thoroughly as a comment to Habermas and Luhmann. It interprets their discussion and then introduces it to the French audience. First, he recognizes the importance of a social, political, and investment-based construction of knowledge, which asks for a stronger view on communication and speech acts. Yet there are no more valid "big narratives" (Christianity, communism, nationalism)—only small narratives in a confused, extreme differentiation between all kinds of small networks and subsystems. The strength of the book was less its accuracy (in the beginning it was severely criticized by the Habermasians) and more its freshness and sociological imagination looking forward.

In the turmoil of the 1970s, Luhmann's reconstruction of a theory of social evolution was, outside of Germany, observed as an extremely specialized undertaking in the higher circles of German university intellectuals. Once again, if we are to understand the intellectual pressure on scholars such as Habermas and Luhmann, we must understand the extreme confusion about where to go and what would happen, intellectually as well as in everyday life, especially for younger people. Would Western societies experience a revolution? A nuclear disaster? An ecological disaster? Or might bureaucratic technocracies continue with, for example, Vietnam-like wars in a unilinear progression, as if nothing happened after 1968? Accordingly, the questions in social theory were indeed cognitive as well as moral: How would society evolve, and what should be done about it? What *could* be done? Philosophers such as Richard Rorty (1979) relativize not merely the answers, but also the questions. Whereas Habermas engaged in debates about rationality and relativism, and liberalism or communitarianism, Luhmann (*Observations* 1993) pushed his observations to unprecedented heights to observe the observations. At the same time, both authors continued to elaborate on their theories of modernity.

Whereas communication for Luhmann is differentiated in interaction systems, organization systems, and a whole range of functional systems, Habermas observes numerous modalities in communicative rationalities according to a somewhat different range. Here, the problem becomes how similar and how opposed they are to each other. For Luhmann, there is no hierarchy between the three social systems or between the functional systems, although he does intensively argue that interaction systems developed the communication codes earlier than organization systems, and that functional systems have appeared relatively late. They first gained autonomy during the Enlightenment, for instance, with the separation of powers. Yet for Habermas, there is a hierarchy, or rather two: one led by the closeness of rationalizations to reasoning; the other—capacities to distort communication—establishes another hierarchy.

5

EVOLUTION AND HISTORY

The Harvest (1977–)

To some pragmatic readers, Habermas's and Luhmann's entire bodies of work probably seem at odds with the normal requirements of modern science and university research. After all, which young researcher would embark on a thirty-, forty-, or fifty-year plan to write sixty books and four hundred articles revealing how the modern world developed its form and meaning, its risks and lack of meaning? Do these authors presume to replace God? Or, more likely, Kant and Hegel? What does it mean to aim for such a project and to pose such questions, indeed making a serious claim to have answered them? Most researchers work with far more modesty and are satisfied, as are most readers. Alternatively, they would write about the issue in an essayistic style, perhaps more familiar to American readers and writers than to Germans. So what are the Grand Theorist megalomaniacs up to when they give an entire account of systems and meaning in the modern world?

Explaining what the whole world and its parts are about might be a European legacy (if not a disease) invented in the Old World. Certainly, theology in the twelfth to fourteenth centuries with the rediscovery of Aristotle took up such projects. This paved the way for more secular analyses from Thomas Hobbes and John Locke to Baruch de Spinoza and Gottfried Leibniz, Charles Montesquieu and Jean-Jacques Rousseau, who sometimes gave God the role of an ideal principle, while earthly life had to be explained by other means and interpreted by different principles.

When Immanuel Kant and Georg Wilhelm Friedrich Hegel entered the scene, they indeed transformed that heritage. Modernity was now the context, and the texts of philosophy and social thought became a professional, university-based endeavor in which questions, methods, and scopes were set free. Enlightenment was not merely a possibility inasmuch as a duty, to be addressed with valid, critical, and self-critical analyses. Every door should be opened, every stone should be turned—and every insight should be founded. This could be irritating for the reader who concentrates for years to understand Kant or Hegel (let alone both). Reading and understanding Kant and Hegel do not only require patience, long hours of reading, and a reasonably bright mind, but also a rather heavy bag of introductory textbooks and interpretations. It is tantamount to traveling a long road to the golden mountain, only to realize that the climb is steep, hard, and filled with sweat and toil, if not blood and tears. Still, at the summit, the sight is amazing; one acquires a perspective that is able to turn in all directions, and the air is fresh and clean.

Karl Marx and Max Weber were somewhat similar in scope and breadth, while Émile Durkheim was easier, more rationalist, and empirically simpler. Nevertheless, the question becomes whether such large and heavy theoretical constructions are necessary. There are three answers, the first having to do with the complex history of Europe, the modern world, and the Nazi experience. Yet the world society in which we live today is as complex and not easier.

The second answer is somewhat simpler, clearer, and more common: How often does one read texts and analyses and ask a simple question about the use of a concept or a distinction? Say an author writes, "Here is a model with two variables: the center and the periphery." Why should such a distinction occur—what are the reasons behind the concepts of "the center" or "the periphery"? Why use one distinction rather than five? Why care at all? Or, as Friedrich Nietzsche suggested in his *Genealogy of Morals*, what is the value of values? If we communicate about communication, how are we imprisoned by communication and how do we obtain insights from that prison? We must go behind our distinctions and beyond our intuitively given insights and questions. When a question arises, we must ask why that question arises. The difficult task when reading Kant, Hegel, Habermas, and Luhmann is less to turn the pages and more to begin questioning our prejudices and finding the genesis of our insights, to begin our archaeological endeavor on the ground on which we stand.

The third reason relates to the use of grand theories, which we came to know in social theory through, for instance, Weber's *The Protestant Ethic and the Spirit of Capitalism*. The problem for grand theories is to demonstrate how there are interconnections between work and religion, politics and law, one functional system and another, microquestions and macroquestions, or today's discussion of, say, shame, guilt, and honor for war veterans and the same categories in the twelfth-century Crusades. Such topics cannot be addressed by small theories or with blurry and weak concepts.

Within the theme of history and the evolution of modern society, we are forced to question the categories, concepts, and distinctions used in social thought. This is a far more complex undertaking than taking a given model and pressing it upon an external object, as material given to us. History is far more than an object; it is inside us, with ourselves as subjects, and, in particular, in our forms of communication. This part of the Luhmann-Habermas debate is thus about some of the major issues in society: How does it develop? Why did Western society come to be the birthplace of modern society? What do we mean by modernity? Or by development, evolution, and rationalization? Is modern Western society the best society (and why or why not)? In which ways do present and future developments in China pose challenges to Western society and culture? How far is Chinese evolution from Western evolution? Such questions can be discussed without simply turning to accounts of the number of refrigerators or hospital beds per inhabitant. Rather, the point is to get an idea of the structure of modern society and how that structure evolved, so as to imply basic features about reason: How does it become possible to reason about society—to construct systems that function and that allow us different forms of reasoning?

Whereas Habermas has certainly been influenced by American pragmatism as a scholarly development, Luhmann's approach to a theory of societal development is thoroughly pragmatic in another sense. In his toolbox, he compiled all kind of readings from a broad range of disciplines, from theological history, aesthetics, and philosophy to modern management (i.e., from what Habermas considers emancipative reflections to some of the most technocratic social sciences). For over thirty years, Luhmann's aim has been to develop what he calls an adequate social theory of modern society. The difference between this and normal sociologies of modern history and evolution is that Luhmann's toolbox reflects the scope of theoretical knowledge and the scale of empirical insights of an author who steadily compiled one hundred thousand pages of notes, the famous so-called *Zettelkasten* (since 2015 available on the website http://zettelkasten.danielluedecke.de/en/). Over the course of almost fifty years, Luhmann read with an incredible speed, accelerated by his toolbox of prior knowledge, telling him what to search for, with an aim to reconstitute categories and concepts far beyond what went wrong in the Western world from 1914 to 1945, in particular in Germany.

RATIONALITY, RATIONALIZATIONS, AND HISTORY

In social science, Max Weber (1922/1980) brought the concept of rationality to the fore in such a path-breaking manner that it soon became one of the most used, perhaps even celebrated concepts. Neoclassical economics and management sciences embraced it and idealized its potential to a level that would make Weber himself turn in his grave. Some, like Herbert Simon, as early as 1945 in *Administrative Behavior*, asked for some degree of moderation and formed concepts like "bounded rationality," to be followed a decade later by Charles Lindblom's descriptive idea of "the science of muddling through" and James March's "garbage can" model. This came as no surprise to Weberians.

Weber distinguished between goal rationality (goals/means) and value rationality, as well as between formal rationality and material rationality. In his many empirical undertakings, the material context of any formal idea was preponderant; the social world is—indeed very much so—about "muddling through." His (certainly penetrating) skepticism as to what concerned progress in the implementation of rationality hung on this historical notion of a decline in formal conditions. At the same time, however, as most clearly expressed in his foreword written in 1920 to *The Protestant Ethic and the Spirit of Capitalism*, he described a number of empirical forms of rationalizations in music, theology, economics, cities, transport, law, bureaucracy, war, science, politics, and so on. The idealized formal distinctions seemed at odds with the infinite empirical variance in rationalizations.

More stubbornly and more deeply penetrating than anyone before them, Habermas and Luhmann began wrestling in the late 1970s and early 1980s with the *problematique* of how to solve the question of ideal rationality and historical rationalizations. Of course, it is possible to investigate when and how "ratio," "rationality," and "reason" began to appear in society. The use of *raggio di stato*, *raison d'État*, and "reason of state" between 1580 and 1630 would probably form some initial leitmotif and guideline (Luhmann *Rationalität* 1981/2008, 189). Theoretical and philosophical analyses of reason and reasonability were widespread in the second half of the sixteenth century and early Enlightenment. Yet the great standard-setting outline was delivered by Kant, who developed his philosophy of reason with the question of what a priori forms of reason do in the world and have done throughout historical developments. Hegel and Nietzsche continued that debate. This was the scene into which Max Weber entered and "left a jungle of conceptions about rationality" (Luhmann *Rationalität* 1981/2008, 211).

To Habermas, very adequately,[1] the overall puzzle concerns three themes: (a) What is reason and rationality? (b) What represents rationality and rationalizations in the empirical historical world? (c) And what links (a) with (b), that is, how can this link be established methodologically, verified, and falsified (Habermas *Communicative Action*, 1:6)? To Luhmann, these questions have too easily, since Hegel, been answered with notions of *identity*, and he interprets Weber as questioning the systems or institutions that dominate the world. Since Marx, Kierkegaard, and Nietzsche, however, *difference* is more probable. Since Kant, critical theory has not simply been telling a story about a world that is not good enough for reason; rather, it is about a world that is not adapted to systems that develop their own (sometimes-irrational) rationalities. At the place of claiming reason as the center of a world with which to reconcile, the point is to observe how world history develops its own stories that differentiate from one another; and one of those stories is that of "reason" and "rationality." History is not only rational but also filled with irrationalities: How is this to be conceived? In Syria or the former

Yugoslavia, violence developed according to logics that do not reconcile reason with world society.

Around 1980, Habermas's answer was to develop conceptions of communicative rationality and strategic rationality, and accordingly to conceive a society of communication divided into two forms with an open horizon of communication in a lifeworld and a closed form of a calculable, steered form of communication in steering systems. To Luhmann, this did not sufficiently radically break with the Weberian dilemma of formal concepts and historical developments. The idea of reason and rationality is constitutively bound to its *self-implication*, namely, that rationality itself must be a rational concept: "The concept of rationality subjects itself to its own rules; it presupposes its own claim for justice, whereas the concept of bread does not have to be eatable, and the concept of beauty does not have to be beautiful" (Luhmann *Rationalität* 1981/2008, 187, cf. 228). This self-reference is inherent in a far wider form of communication that exposes self-reference in communication as an empirical historical concept *and* a philosophical concept.

After their initial interchanges in the early 1970s about the theme of history and evolution, Habermas and Luhmann began their sociological reconstructions of the history of worldviews (Habermas's term). The most famous result was probably Habermas's *The Theory of Communicative Action* (1981), in which especially the second part of chapter 6 deals with Habermas's own version of evolution. Communication establishes interpretations, which are preconditions for the division of labor envisaged by Durkheim as the motor of social evolution. More than anything, this concerned a communicative rationalization of forms of understanding. "Forms of understanding" are analogous to what the Hungarian Marxist Georgy Lukács (1923/1971), following Marx and Weber, called "forms of objectivizations." As useful was Habermas's distinction between, on the one hand, the horizon of a lifeworld open for communicative meaning and interpretation and, on the other, functional systems historically developed in a difference to the open-ended communication forms.

Several of the systems discussed by Habermas and Luhmann might initially seem similar, such as power and economy. In chapters 6–8, I analyze two of them, politics and law, in a more substantial way. And yet Luhmann and Habermas began their main mature investigations with analyses of religion. Of course, Durkheim and Weber early on made that theme famous in sociology. Later discussions revised those classical analyses here and there, and Parsons and Peter Berger took them together. What was there to be added?

Three possibilities were left: First, religion as a form of communication could be subject to investigations far beyond the elucidations established by Durkheim (1912/1960). There, he elaborated an indeed initial and path-breaking yet still rather simple form of communication analysis of religious rituals. Second, the form of the theory could be interpreted in new ways when religious evolution became subject to a critical theory (Habermas's style) or a systems theory (Luhmann's style). Third, with their discussions about the history-and-evolution theme in the early 1970s, they touched on the emergent conceptual history in Germany (and in France alongside Michel Foucault and others; and in England, J. G. A. Pocock and Quentin Skinner). A conceptual history has a wide range of interconnections with theological history. Luhmann's and Habermas's contributions could be measured with their capacities to involve all three levels. Luhmann, in *Function of Religion* (1977), was the first to embark upon a major substantial development, though it was not before 1980 that his systematic publications developed their final form in all three of the dimensions mentioned by Habermas.

EVOLUTION IN RELIGIOUS DOGMATICS

Luhmann's theory of the evolution of modern society developed in several stages. Apart from the initial writings in the early 1970s, Luhmann's first major publication on the subject came with the book on the sociology of religion, which he finished out of respect for his wife, in 1976, shortly before her death. For her, "religion always meant more than theory," as he wrote in the dedication. The three-hundred-page elucidation of a sociology of religion turns out to be a first-rate, substantial examination of the developments in religion that preconditioned what could be described as the limited function of religion in modern society. However, Luhmann's reconstruction of religion goes somewhat further than the analyses we know from Durkheim, Weber, Parsons, and a number of other important interpretations (e.g., Bellah, Luckmann, Berger). His analysis of religious communication does not merely "redescribe" the function of Durkheim's distinction between rituals and beliefs in communication. Aside from further elaborations in communication theory, the difference concerns time and temporalization.

In brief, rituals and beliefs are redescribed according to their paradoxes, as when belief is individualized, and when it is collectivized when rituals are communicated. In the first evolutionary stage, religion should establish meaning in a society, which experienced contingencies about what it did not know about the world or about an unforeseen future. In the second evolutionary stage, the point was not to control contingencies but to control the control over contingencies. Therefore, conflicts and discussions about the form of contingencies emerged. As a consequence of the communication about belief, the corresponding concept, communication about disbelief, became subject to the communication form (*Function* 1977, 136–39). Yet varieties of religion cannot find a unitary form of functional definition. "The function of religion concerns the determination of the world" (*Function* 1977, 79). Religion frames that which is determined and undetermined in a world; the medium of this framing is conceptions of sense and nonsense. The radical innovation in Luhmann's conception is that not only sense but also the binary opposite, nonsense, is included in what gives sense to religion. Contingency is therefore very important, probably the most important concept in Luhmann's theory of religion.

Moreover, Luhmann left an unpublicized manuscript from 1971, *Contingency and Law* (*Kontingenz und Recht*). This three-hundred-page book was printed in 2013 by Suhrkamp, the leading German publisher, used by both Luhmann and Habermas. This study also conceived the code "legal/illegal" and its redescriptions in law: that is, law also evolved as the control over the control of contingencies. As in law and organization, "dogmatic" is about a coupling between binding and freedom; rules enable changes to rules, form enables reform.

This is not the place to recapitulate Luhmann's entire theory of religious development; rather, the point is to depict its outline for his general theory of evolution. With his little masterpiece, Luhmann embarked on a tremendous empirical *and* theoretical project investigating the developments in society. He defined society as the system of communication.

The point of Luhmann's study of religion is to reconstruct how religion communicates. In short, in society, we find communication about, for example, God, prayer, and the Eucharist; another thing is whether the psychic system can connect or disconnect to it, as if individuals believe or not.

In this endeavor, his initial approach is, first, to look for binary codes in such communication; second, he observes how such codes were controlled in theological dogmatics. The history of dogmatics offers the analyses to be studied, which could pave the way for developments in monotheistic cultures—Jewish, Christian, and Islamic—before, during, and after the Roman Empire. "Church, diacony, and theology" certainly became important for modern religious developments (*Function* 1977, 267). However, the scope is larger. Luhmann includes a number of studies in Hinduism, Buddhism, Confucianism, and African religions to describe how to cope with contingencies. Moreover, the empirical scope became much wider with his posthumously published *A Systems Theory of Religion* (2013; originally published as *Die Religion der Gesellschaft* 2000).

Book-based religions owe their form to script and reflect this invention; they became authorized and canonized in the form of the Bible, the Quran, and Daodejing. Hence, theological dogmatics expanded in a number of descriptions about societal order. Order was religious in a number of ways; it was differentiated in whole and its parts; it gave meaning to collectivity and to individuals as parts of such a collectivity; it communicated about communication and excommunicated unauthorized forms of communication. Orthodoxy and heresy were described. Luhmann, accordingly, embarked on a discussion of every kind of historical description of dogmatics and of course of recent theology in order to investigate communication codes. Above all else, this concerns developments from, broadly spoken, medieval discussions in the eleventh century to the late Enlightenment, covering the long transition from a society with stratified social orders to a functionally differentiated modern society. In comparison to Habermas's much later *Auch* (2019), however, he rarely discusses a certain author (e.g., Luther), instead investigating dogmatics as a form of "intertextuality," which strives for coherence in theological self-descriptions, as the agenda of theology (Luhmann *Religion* 2000, 332–40, 353).

This approach offers two devices for social theories about the emergence of modernity. First, it is possible to search for binary codes and the emergence of such dualities (*Function* 1977, 122, 124, 190). Second, self-reference in dogmatic communication becomes crucial: "In social systems self-reference is that everything communicated also has to communicate about the communication itself and oneself and one's partners that are forced to self-description, and to its problems" (*Function* 1977, 31).

In *The System of Modern Societies* (1971), Parsons also addresses the emergence of modernity as a process of differentiation. So did Durkheim, according to the idea that differentiated societies presupposed moral integration (or disintegration as anomie), whereas Weber's account of differentiation concerned rationalization. Luhmann criticizes Parsons for a much-too-overloaded conceptualization of inclusion (*Function* 1977, 233ff.). In the Christian church, inclusion was central to medieval Catholicism yet became subject to citizens' inclusion after the bourgeois revolutions. Inclusion into clerical and noble orders was replaced by inclusion into work and welfare states. However, sense is only offered with the exclusion of nonsense; the sense of God is to exclude the nonsense of the devil, as symbols of inclusion are to be distinguished from the diabolic exclusion. With this criticism, symbolic codifications double their communication codes into theological dogmatics. Whether in theology or law, dogmatic self-descriptions code communication about communication codes. Stratified hierarchies and organizational systems of membership and nonmemberships have thereby been authorized and have taken power over society.

Between 1976 and 1980, Luhmann and Habermas undertook the task of a major reconstruction of social theory that could replace the social theories of Marx, Durkheim, Weber, and Parsons and offer a more coherent analysis of communication as the medium of societal sense-formation. Whereas the Frenchmen, Foucault and Bourdieu, were about to undertake a similar de- and reconstruction, the German reconstruction certainly had the much broader ambition of a competing reconstruction of Grand Theory formation. After these reconstructions, debates across the Rhine border between Germany and France began to appear. For Habermas and Luhmann, the task was different. I return to these similarities and differences in chapter 9.

THE HEIDELBERG DISCUSSIONS
WITH PARSONS (1979)

In 1979, Heidelberg University invited Parsons to celebrate the fiftieth anniversary of his doctoral habilitation, received in April 1929. By that time, Parsons had turned into a straw man for criticism in the United States, and his theory was refuted as conservative, consensus-theoretical, and even ahistorical (Gouldner 1970; Hamilton 1992). The Heidelberg meeting ended more dramatically than anyone could have imagined: Parsons met the two major social theoreticians in Germany and experienced that they indeed took his thoughts from the 1930s to the 1970s so seriously that they used them as standard-setting for their own ambitious Grand Theories.

Paradoxically, Luhmann targeted the framework of action established by Parsons's social thought and reconstructed what, to Luhmann, should be framed as acts, whereas Habermas's aim was to reconstruct the systems theory of media. That is, Luhmann almost used the starting point that could have been expected from Habermas, and vice versa. The result was published by the leading German publisher Suhrkamp Editions in 1980 and edited by the Heidelberg professor and Weber specialist Wolfgang Schluchter, *Verhalten, Handeln und System* (*Behavior, Act, and System*).

Luhmann's contribution was about acts and temporality (*Temporalstrukturen* 1980). Only if a theory of acts concerns the temporal meaning of acts will it be possible to construct a historically oriented sociology, which is a theory about social development and the formation of modern society. The differentiation of systems and system developments are about differences in time. Acts produce such differences, yet acts can merely be understood as forms, which should give meaning to the relations between past, present, and future. To give meaning to acts is to tell the story about a connection established in a moment about some processes that stretch from a past to a later moment. The evident point is that communication establishes the relation of past, present, and future. A far more complex issue is that communication in the form of an interchange (*Wechselwirkung*) establishes simultaneity or that which Parsons (and later Luhmann) calls double contingency. Causality brackets simultaneity in favor of past and future; however, Luhmann's aim is to reconstruct the social form of simultaneity. Only with a notion of simultaneity will it be possible to communicate about present moments of the past and how futures were subject to communication or intentions in the past. The double construction of the presence as moment and, simultaneously, enduring long presence (represence or even eternity) is a historically communicative achievement of first rate, compared to anything offered since Antiquity (e.g., Saint Augustine). Yet the firm idea of a unity in that story broke. This happened with the Reformation.[2] Today, in a more secular way, we may see this rupture in the Belgian city of Bruges, where the belfry of the town hall, with its clocks, competes with the tower of the church, which had an upper stage added in the 1480s. Hitherto, eternity was corporally present at the very moment, simultaneously with a distinction between past and future; it broke, however, whether because of the printing press revolution of stabilized textual reproduction of sense or because watches objectified time. The self-reference of time turns the present into the subject simultaneously given with eternity. Time thus binds the present moment to different futures and to modalities about risky differences between temporal horizons of differentiated systems: time binding is not the same in theology as in law, economy, art, or politics. Luhmann, in this text and in several analyses, offers an immense range of models about such temporal complexities. Even a superficial recapitulation of the stories told in theology, art, law, politics, or organization provides evidence that temporality is constitutive of any idea about acts or systems. Finally, Luhmann refers to Habermas's recapitulation of Parsons's systems theory of money as exchange medium.

Luhmann's interpretation about temporalities is undoubtedly crucial—even decisive—for any account of payments, money, and credit. Even more than money, credit presupposes stabilized temporal structures and speculates about communicative inclusive and exclusive accesses to innovation. The world's first bourse was established in Bruges, and a new measure of time-binding outside of the church had arrived.

In his article, Habermas discussed Parsons's theory of money as exchange medium (Parsons and Smelser 1958). Acts institutionalize the possibilities for such exchanges. For Habermas, language presupposes rules of exchange. Money is a special form of language. Yet to him, a culturalist account, as established by Parsons, is insufficient. It is necessary to reconstruct what in language as a communicative act constitutes the specialized medium of money as well as any other specialized, systemically formed medium. "Money replaces linguistic communication in special situations and in certain respects" (Habermas *Handeln*, 77). Media such as money do not specify language but relieve language. Language can therefore become more specialized; in everyday life, you know the price and therefore you can engage in dialogue with the trader about different issues, at the place of a longer price negotiation, as in an Arab marketplace. Money is uncoupled from consensual communication of intersubjective communication, yet money also relieves the pressure for coordination. Habermas argues that the linguistic medium has an asymmetric and constitutive relation to the money medium. The uncoupling is based on a possible back-coupling to language. Hence, contracts and credits should be possible to explain, for example, in big trade.

Habermas briefly states how he will not reconstruct the historical emergence of capitalist money markets; rather, he seeks to compare money with power as medium. According to Parsons, power too is an exchange medium that is symbolically generalized. Power organizes law and organization. Thereby, authority is generalized, though it still constitutes solutions to conflict by means of entrusted legitimacy and thereby presupposes the possible reconstitution of consensual motivation. Here, Habermas uses Luhmann's previously developed concepts of systemic trust, formed in Luhmann's *Trust* (1968). It is not easy to see how power as violence (in the medium of war) presupposes consensus, and Habermas does not delimit that form of violent, enforced power. Power is restricted to acceptable coordination by means of generalized organization and law.

While Habermas's arguments about uncoupling and relief became important to his seminal *The Theory of Communicative Action*, he did not embark on any substantial elucidation about the historical emergence of money codes. Therefore, an evaluation of the historical signification of the uncoupling and relief argument is still left to Luhmann's theory about system evolution—or to Parsons, Weber, or Marx.

The little meeting in Heidelberg passed unnoticed in wider circles; more famous was its immediate aftermath: Diabetes-stricken Parsons left for Munich and died three days later, and it is possible to speculate on strange stories about the moment and the experiences in Parsons's last week.

THE FACT OF SELF-REFERENCE

Luhmann's analyses about the development of modern society took a turning point in these years. We have already seen that his turn toward a communicative foundation of social theory was completed with his booklet on *Power* (1975). The publication *Funktion der Religion* introduced a new concept into his framework: the notion of self-reference, though already in the then still unpublished *Systemtheorie der Gesellschaft* (1975/2017, 1001) Luhmann had embarked on the concept. However, this concept actually corresponded to longer discussions in systems theory about self-organization (von Foerster 1961), self-referential systems (Deutsch 1963/1967), and autopoiesis (Maturana and Varela 1979), not to mention Kant in *Critique of Judgment* (1790, §65). And, as mentioned earlier, Habermas for several years somewhat pragmatically had already used the concept of "self-regulative systems" to describe what Luhmann was up to, though Luhmann had not himself used any such "self-" concepts.

Moreover, Luhmann's turn toward self-reference went far deeper and broader; in the 1980s, however, it still seemed as though the Chilean biologists Humberto Maturana and Francisco Varela's poetic term *autopoiesis* took the front page. The notion of self-reference is important for Luhmann's historical sociology at philosophical and indeed methodological levels; and at those levels, it is important, too, in a comparison with the Frankfurt idea of critical theory. The point is simply that historical sociology must solve an amazing paradox, one that has triggered philosophy and social theory since Kant and Hegel, since Marx and Nietzsche, and that has been demonized as overly idealistic as well as self- or Eurocentric. One might argue that the basis is the simple idea that we do reason, we do make philosophy, and we do make science. That also means that doing such things is a fact before anything else is a fact. The very self-reference of communication and, in particular, communicating about research as communication does take place beforehand and a priori to anything else about which we have objective knowledge.[3] Yet this does indeed imply that history must have evolved in such a way that the very form of that self-referential communication is established in the course of societal history. Communication about historical developments is self-referential in the sense that the present stage of communication is a fact as an a priori "fact of reason" (Kant) to any analysis.

How could communication evolve into such self-referential forms? This is, of course, an empirical and historical question. Yet the other side displays a paradox, which is that this present stage historically has been what Luhmann with a peculiar term calls "improbable" in the sense that, say, one hundred thousand years ago it was by no means evident that modern society, modern states, research-oriented universities, and so on would develop. Even a mere three thousand years ago, it was indeed improbable. Many more forms and systems in modern society are unlikely and "improbable." Generally speaking, "communication is improbable," but is, a priori, a fact (*Self-Reference* 1990, 86–98). We can think about a range of unlikely communication forms, such as sophisticated payments of credit across oceans, love affairs across social distinctions, or simply two different people meeting in a café. That evolution emerged and developed to the present stage of civilization is an unlikely achievement—but also an unavoidable fact! Hence, historical sociology must combine these two statements, the fact of present self-reference and the question of how this became possible rather than improbable. Hegel tried to state this paradox in terms of his famous phrase, which resumed Kant's philosophy of history: "What is real is rational, and what is rational is real" in the introduction to *The Philosophy of Right* (Hegel 1821/1972). It means that historical reality has—unavoidably—implied some kind of rationality, and that rationality has some kind of reality. Since Kierkegaard, Marx, and Nietzsche, however, reality has admittedly been also more or less irrational. Exactly with this point, in order to elucidate these paradoxes, sociology, history of ideas, and empirical history come to the stage.

This combination paves the way for empirical hypotheses and the analysis of archives. Luhmann therefore moved social theory from a philosophical endeavor to solve problems of philosophy pertaining to history into sociological investigations about historical self-descriptions. In so doing, he solved the paradox that Parsons's systems theory, according to Gouldner, was unable to solve.

Frankly speaking, the supposition is that there are Luhmannian, Habermasian, and Kantian positions: in short, obvious communications and sophisticated arguments before Luhmann, Habermas, or Kant. Systems theory began long ago, even before the Enlightenment. Discourse ethics can be found in conversation well formulated already early in the Enlightenment, a point on which Habermas also touches in *The Structural Transformation of the Public Sphere* (chap. 2).

Beforehand, still indebted to philosophy of history, Habermas's friend and colleague Karl-Otto Apel, in his seminal *Transformation of Philosophy*,[4] exposed the argument about an "a priori of a communication community" based on an "unavoidable" and "indispensable" "community of argumentation." Critical theory, broadly described, from Kant to Habermas/Apel to Luhmann, is constitutively based upon this rather teleological fact of (almost-tautological) self-implication: We a priori know about the, at the moment, final stage of history, the telos of evolution, as the present stage. This is actually what Germans calls a (post)rationalization (*Nachrationalisierung*): We cannot, in any possible way, avoid the self-reference of the present state, or the fact that theory formulation is established in the medium of communication. We are where we are, but how come? This is what Luhmann, in his introductory chapters to his seminal series in the historical sociology of knowledge, *Societal Structure and Semantics*, mentions as "the fact of self-reference" (*Gesellschaftsstruktur* 1980, 1981, 1989, 1995, 2:31, cf. 2:63, 191).

To be sure, the point is far simpler than it sounds. Most social researchers feel fear when hearing names such as Kant and Hegel, not to mention references to hardcore academic disciplines such as philosophy, history, and sociology. Yet the point is almost incredibly simple (as important and sophistically pronounced statements often are): In studies of language development, we cannot state that it was impossible for such a thing as a meaningful language to develop! Should we state so, we deny our own communicatively founded possibilities of denying.

This somewhat philosophical contribution, "Self-Reference and Teleology in Perspective of Social Theory," corresponds to the first chapter in the second volume of *Gesellschaftsstruktur* (1981). Here, Luhmann exposed a philosophy of history that begins with Kant's famous thesis in *Critique of Practical Reason* (§7) of how a "fact of reason" must embark on a historical sociology.

Confronted with the background of still logically unsolved problems of a self-referential reasoning, the following theses get significance. (1) In reality there are self-referential systems.... (2) ... the reflection of systems demands self-implication.... (3) Observing and knowing systems are, on their side, self-referential systems with specialized functions.... (4) Self-referential systems do presuppose an infrastructure of a variance of processes.... (5) In the systems, there are ambivalences, indeterminacies, redundancies that simultaneously serve as turning points for communication and as a place keeper for possibilities.... (6) From here, meaning can be reformulated in correspondence with phenomenological analysis, namely, for some parts among self-referential systems, i.e., the personal and the social systems.... From this background, research can begin that departs from the *fact of self-reference*; and as uncomfortable for logics as this fact may be, therein it can observe a *problem*, which is not only that of logics. (*Gesellschaftsstruktur* 1980, 1981, 1989, 1995, 29–31, Luhmann's italics)

METHODOLOGICAL DEVICES: ANALYSIS OF SEMANTICS, CODES, AND SELF-DESCRIPTIONS

We have seen how Luhmann analyzed the history of theological dogmatics. Yet an important and even crucial problem, as discussed by Parsons, Habermas, and Luhmann, and previously by Weber and Durkheim, addressed the following: What kind of autonomy was inherent in those spheres, fields, or functional systems that are usually described as those of religion, economy, law, art, science, war, mass media, love, organization, and so on? Did they have similar structures and autonomies? How many such spheres or functional systems are to be found? When did they emerge in history? Furthermore, what are the characteristic forms, codes, and self-descriptions that are not only inherent in such systems but also constitutive for their construction and formation?

Initially, the answer is that research must examine semantic variations, selecting the communication codes that were stabilized and that received their final form when they began to monopolize certain forms of self-reference in the form of authoritatively referred texts or self-descriptions.

Hence, there are three devices: self-descriptions, codes, and semantics. Moreover, questions are also raised as to how the self-descriptions are to be separated and differentiated from one another.

The investigation follows almost obviously from the notion of self-reference. Since self-reference is to be found in history, each of those spheres, fields, or functional systems probably has a number of so-called self-descriptions. They are often written by authors who depend on the functioning of the subsystems, and who turn their scriptures into more or less authoritative dogmatics or, at least, references and milestones for further communication. In the evolution of law, self-descriptions in the form of constitutions or interpretations of law are obvious texts to study. Similarly, we find the political treatises of Machiavelli, Bodin, Hobbes, Montesquieu, and so on, which are familiar to anyone who works seriously with the history of political thought. Accordingly, here in the textual self-descriptions, we find a first useful limitation of the otherwise-overwhelming task undertaken by Luhmann. In a delimitation of Hauke Brunkhorst's important "reconciliation" of Luhmann's and Habermas's theories, Habermas initially exposed some doubts of this task (Brunkhorst 2014a; Habermas *Construction* 2014).

Second, as explained in *Funktion der Religion*, Luhmann focused on the search for binary codes of communication together with the duplication of codes that control codes. Precisely such self-descriptive codes about codes constitute the object of investigation. They often reinforce certain central codes that are used to codify which communication codes are put to use and included in a specified communication system, and which are excluded as corrupt, abuse, prostitution, heresy, dope, and so on. Systems theory renders it possible to observe how communication codes become objects for their own metacommunication: for example, with love as passion of love, law about valid law, research about research, credit to pay for money, aesthetics about art that comments art, and so on. Indeed, a simplified device here is to search for such codes of codes in order to find what historians use to explain the revolutionary take-off in, for example, systems evolution in law, war, finance, organization, education, or politics.[5]

Third, and perhaps most importantly, Luhmann needed an even more empirical device to target variances of communication. This came with the concept of semantics. Semantic variance is found in words, which could be objects for codification, for binary meanings. They are the empirical substance with which to work; the micromedium of codified forms of communication. Semantics is the raw material, which finds forms when submitted to codification. When his influential Bielefeld colleague, the historian Reinhardt Koselleck, established conceptual history with the immense multivolume, coauthored publication *Geschichtliche Grundbegriffe* (Basic historical concepts), Luhmann was not satisfied with the sociological lack of intertextual coherence among the 140 political concepts analyzed in all kinds of detail in the coauthored publication. He aimed to establish the complex coherence of connections and disconnections with systems theory. Yet the target is not deductively to press coherence upon an incoherent infinite variance of semantics; rather, the point is to find those semantics that connected and paved the way for binary—asymmetric—oppositions between, for example, inclusion/exclusion, payment/not payment, and legal/illegal. In historical texts, we can find millions of words and an infinite variance of semantics. The point is to analyze how selections in this variance occur and appear in the form of stabilized codes. When Luhmann writes that "complexity itself works as a factor for selection," this means that paradoxes, contrasts, and binary schemes are in focus. The investigations focus in particular on the years 1500 to 1800. This leaves two questions: What acts? What is acting?

PARADOXES AS THE DRIVER OF HISTORY

Hegel saw the dialectics of oppositions as the motor driving universal history. Following him, but turning the point to empirical history, Marx saw class conflicts as this driver. The simultaneity between opposed, dissenting, and conflicting parts does—as already before in Hegel's writings and as underlined by Kant—close the doors for causal simple linear explanation. For Luhmann, paradoxes in communication therefore become a central focus.

The acts of individuals who are acting with certain intentions to create certain effects are less in focus than the form of their communications, which establishes paradoxes to be solved. Regardless, intentions and motivations are unstable outside communication. Paradoxes create innovations and change in a different form than do individualized and privatized intentions. Motivations may be shrouded in privacy and remain excluded from communication, while communication works. Communication is even able to communicate about privacy and to talk about unspoken secrecies.

This seems to be a major point of conflict between Luhmann and Habermas, since, for Habermas, individuals speak: language systems do not speak, but humans do. Upon closer examination, however, the difference becomes less obvious. On the one hand, Luhmann does not claim that communication takes place without human bodies, emotions, and thoughts; on the other, Habermas claims that language is not private but that it unavoidably follows public forms (*Communicative Action*, 2:15–22; 1981, 2:30–39).

Hence, in this manner, Luhmann offered a solution to the classic sociological dichotomy of agency and structure. This was a puzzle for sociological textbooks such as George Ritzer's widely used *Sociological Theory* (2014), and has been known in work from Weber and Durkheim all the way to Bourdieu's *Le sense pratique* (1980) and Anthony Giddens's structuration theory in *The Constitution of Society* (1984). In Luhmann's explanation, anyway, the medium for change is time and communication. Thus, semantics, codes, and systems replace agency and structure.

In 1980 and 1981, Luhmann published two volumes of *Gesellschaftsstruktur*. Unlike the third study about historical semantics and social structure, *Love as Passion*, published in 1982, they are a difficult read. The series is based on an extremely wide use of historical texts, from law and education to interactions among nobles and a history of taste and political theory. At the same time, Luhmann puts his entire theory to use and presupposes a well-established knowledge of history. They may be compared with Foucault's writings about the very same texts, and Luhmann seems to have worked with a similarly large compilation of texts.

In this sense, compared to Habermas, Luhmann is closer to his object: his archives (similar to Foucault). While we rarely hear the single authors speak as individuals behind the text cited—as is sometimes displayed in Foucault's analyses—we are certainly caught in the communication form and the paradoxes of their period. History—its themes more than its authors—speaks through the writings of Luhmann and Foucault. In Habermas's *Auch* (2019), the succession of great philosophers is the main frame, yet without the hundreds of writers filling the gaps between those thinkers.

The title of Luhmann's book series indicates that *semantics* are *condensed* into *codes* with *forms* that pave the way for *structures*. Those condensations and structures are differentiated from one another, as when love affairs begin to be differentiated from heritage structures as described by law and capital accumulation in the eighteenth century. Early on, law began to belong to communication in courts and chanceleries, whereas war became subject to military communication about territories, borders, and the reason of state. Such complexities did not only follow a binary distinction between traditional society and modern society. Codes emerged and stabilized a stratified society in which communication about the social order dominated the principles that were accounted as valid.

To detect how Luhmann uses paradoxes to explain change and evolution, there is an illustrative example, which is very close to the "figurations" and "social forms" already explained by Elias and Simmel, respectively (as in Simmel's articles about "Fashion"). Luhmann explains the example in his first substantial article in the first volume of the series, "Interaction in the Upper Layers: On Transformations of Their Semantics in the Seventeenth and Eighteenth Centuries" (*Gesellschaftsstruktur* 1980, 1981, 1989, 1995, 1:72–161, esp. 96ff.). Here, paradoxically, *evolution* emerges through *involution*, since manner codes about phenomena such as honor became increasingly stabilized with forms, sophisticated rituals, duels, reply-techniques, dress codes (are flowers accepted in the ladies' hats? are birds?), and everything that belongs to courtesan communication. This meant that even very small changes became significant and loaded with meaning. Communicative involution deflated *innovations*, which became extremely precious. Hence, innovations became loaded with ever more importance and meaning, a form similar to fashion for Simmel (1908). The result was that *evolution* occurred because of this peculiar combination of *involution* and *innovation*.

Luhmann uses this temporal scheme of paradoxes in many of his analyses, and he interprets it as a temporal scenario that loads communication with meaning in a *text* as opposed to *context*. The present moment becomes a significant difference to past and future events. It obtains a certain form of meaning, as in passionate love, in decision-making in law, organization, or politics, or in art. The "guiding difference" (*Leitdifferenz*) is not who does it with which intention, but rather that it is done or even that it is observed in communication as difference. In art, the presence of a situation with the artist that offers a certain form to the work of art forwards ideas of aura, originality, and individuality in distinction to the object of creativity. Originality becomes a decisive deed: Art is to be new and not a repetition, especially since the printing press revolution in the late fifteenth century (Luhmann *Theory* 1997, 291–302, 531).[6] Because of stabilizations in the formation of positive, formal, and homogeneous law, laws open for changes; these changes can be identified, submitted to alternative proposals and variations, discussed, and democratized. Selections of variation lead to stable forms, which in turn allow for new variation; thus, forms condition reforms (*Law* 1993, 230–73, in particular 259; *Theory* 1997, 1001–4). As mentioned earlier about the Heidelberg debates, time acts. Obviously, acting is a temporal form, and Luhmann therefore investigates how temporal forms have been transformed (also in time) and transform time. Hence, self-reference does not exclusively belong to the subjective consciousness of the psychic system, but also to the communication systems. Communication changes, communication acts.

Stability and change are interdependent, and society can maintain an accelerated pace of change exactly because of stabilized structures delimited in differentiated systems. Since the Second World War, modern societal structures have been extremely stable in the modern Western World, but this paved the way for innumerable inventions and an ever more accelerated and meaning-loaded focus on innovation. Hence, we cannot observe a zero-sum game between stability and change, but a plus sum.

HABERMAS'S THEORY OF EVOLUTION AS DIFFERENTIATION FROM SYSTEM AND LIFEWORLD

In the same period, Habermas established his conception of modern development with a distinction between preconventional, conventional, and postconventional knowledge and moral rule-following. The distinction stems from Jean Piaget's studies about learning processes among children and was further developed with Lawrence Kohlberg's analyses of moral learning processes. The problem for Habermas, of course, was to establish a transition from the microlevel of individual, ontogenetic learning processes to social, phylogenetic learning processes. Even more difficult was any claim that antique or medieval authors did not follow postconventional rules or were limited in their reflections. Likewise, when Anthony Giddens and Ulrich Beck declare posttraditional society to be a "reflexive modernity," this stands in striking contrast to the reflections found in a great range of texts from the fifteenth and sixteenth centuries. As readers who are acquainted with Luhmann's semantic history or Foucault's writings know well, reflections were not merely to be found among a few authors, say, Machiavelli, Luther, Hobbes, and Spinoza, but also among wide circles of those who constituted the upper social orders and who organized societal order. Society became organized with communication and learned to organize economic transactions, marriage, contracts, fortifications, travel, and organization itself through the medium of communication.

On a somewhat superficial level, we may compare Habermas's triple concepts of preconventional, conventional, and postconventional learning processes with Luhmann's distinction between segmentary society, stratified society, and functionally differentiated society. This triple conceptualization corresponds to Luhmann's triple notions of interaction systems, organization systems, and functional systems.

To Luhmann and Habermas, the basic question for a sociological theory of modernity is how functional and organizational systems could become detached from whatever was meant by the interaction systems. Interaction systems take place in the presence of actors communicating with one another in a manner in which communication is only possible if there is some kind of trust and credibility invested in the interactions among these persons. Valid claims of truth and justice are not strongly differentiated from those of trustful speech, and vice versa. Luhmann's analysis in *Trust* (1968) described the lifeworld of meaningful communication in such interaction systems; yet he did also describe how trusted systems could have a constitution differentiated from such a trusted and confident world. In this sociological sense, Luhmann's early booklet *Trust* is quite comparable to the endeavor established by Habermas thirteen years later in *The Theory of Communicative Action*. Like Luhmann, Habermas departs from Max Weber and Émile Durkheim as well as Georg Herbert Mead. "I would therefore like to propose (1) that we conceive of societies *simultaneously* as systems and lifeworlds. This concept proves itself in (2) a theory of social evolution that separates the rationalization of the lifeworld from the growing complexity of social systems" (*Communicative Action* 1987, 2:117). Habermas does not merely conceive one transition in evolution from natural history to societal history; he also aims to conceptualize how system integration evolves through the system differentiation of symbols beyond the level of actors' consciousness. Biological systems have nothing to do with the construction of meaning in social systems, yet in the societal history of social systems, there is another evolutionary take-off when functional systems become detached from interaction systems (Brunkhorst 2014a, 13–15). DNA cannot understand meaning.

His perspective is that religion is mediatized by communication, and communication uncouples law from magical ethics, ethics from law, and, at a later (third) stage, conviction from responsibility. This double differentiation of uncoupled morality from institutionalization runs along with another uncoupling. Hence, in *Communicative Action* (172), Habermas quotes Luhmann from *Zweckbegriff* (1968, 339): "We shall designate as 'formally organized' . . . those social systems which make recognizing certain expectations of behavior a condition of membership in the system. Only those who accept certain specifically marked out expectations can become and remain members of formally organized social systems." In a first evolutionary stage, internal interconnections of meaning are mixed with external relations of things (*Communicative Action* 2:159). Habermas proceeds along a line in which he focuses on how the "coordination of action can be transferred over to delinguistified media of communication only when contexts of strategic action get differentiated out" (*Communicative Action* 2:180). The perspective is to get to an analysis: "Where reputation or moral authority enters in, action coordination has to be brought about by means of resources familiar from consensus formation in language" (2:183). Whereas this is an evident form of rationalization from Habermas's perspective, it is not evident how his focus on discursivation should cope with an idea of "delinguistified media of communication" rather than some methodologically driven study of narratives[7] of conceptual or semantic history by means of "linguistified media of communication." If the linguistic media of communication are too focused on a rational coordination of consensus, they underestimate the aesthetical, semantic, and conceptual narratives that condition what Habermas could have called strategic self-regulative systems. Before such systems become stabilized and codified as strategic, they contain far wider variations in their semantic range.

With this strategy, Habermas before *Auch* (2019) jumped from Antiquity to the distorted, uncoupled communicative systems of the eighteenth century. From an American (somewhat nationalist) angle, this does not appear as a reduced view on evolution; from European and Chinese perspectives, however, most of the evolutionary (un)learning processes are thrown out with the bathwater. This perspective becomes obvious as "linguistification" or "discoursivication" (compare the somewhat more beautiful German term *Versprachlichung*), which Habermas so meticulously developed in his brilliant comment on Durkheim's sociology of religion in *Communicative Action* (2:77–111). Fruitful as it was, it had not been developed methodologically as useful for further investigations into conceptual and evolutionary history.[8]

Habermas exposes a framework for analysis; yet in the almost nine-hundred-page, two-volume seminal book, his exposition of social evolution and history only occupied forty-three pages. Compared to Luhmann's (at that moment) three volumes on the historical evolution of communication systems (the two volumes of *Societal Structure and Semantics* and the volume on the *Function of Religion*), Habermas merely offered a framework and, before *Auch* (2019), he was not even close to the textual and semantic density of Luhmann's studies.

The problem for both authors is to conceptualize how social communication developed in the aftermath of these segmentary tribal forms of communication, which Durkheim described in his study about tribal religion. They were obviously also described by later anthropologists, whether functionalists, structuralists, or hermeneuticians. In fact, Habermas and Luhmann hardly diverge in their descriptions and frameworks for studies on segmentary societies: "The social structures do not transcend the horizon of simple interactions interwoven over comprehensible social spaces and relatively short spaces" (Habermas *Communicative Action* 2:156). Regardless, their knowledge about such societies is mostly secondhand, albeit well informed by authors such as the early Egypt historian Jan Assmann—who is discussed by Luhmann and also intensely by Habermas in *Auch* (2019)—and Klaus Eder's study of state-formation in early Antiquity.

The problems relating to how to cope with conceptual strategies of lifeworld-oriented communication and communication in self-regulating systems do indeed involve historical analyses of transformation in communication from early antiquity to stratified societal transformation to early modernity and state-organized, functionally differentiated world society. How does communication assume form and transform itself, reform itself, and become modern?

Habermas probably felt himself squeezed between two bases for analyzing the problem: The one, basic analysis was a close follow-up on more or less mythological and philosophical ideas about societal communication founded on lifeworld experiences and linked to basic interaction systems, as if such communication forms could be conceived in a constitutional form in segmentary societies. The other basis for analysis would be modern society:

> Modern societies attain a level of system differentiation at which increasingly autonomous organizations are connected with one another via delinguistified media of communication: these systemic mechanisms—for example, money—steer a social intercourse that has been largely disconnected from norms and values, above all in those subsystems of purposive rational and administrative action that, on Weber's diagnosis, have become independent of their moral-political foundations. (*Communicative Action* 2:154)

Like the French philosopher Jacques Derrida (1989), Luhmann is certainly more unhappy with any idea that there should be some kind of original basic form of communication that we could lay as the foundation before we have texts. Texts transform the meaning of speech and communication. Nevertheless, the self-description of communication in texts, accordingly, is our most important entrance to the past, probably in preference or comparison to archaeology and paintings. The idea of a foundational origin is an idealized latecomer, described in the forms of myths and later constituted as mythologies:

> I have already indicated how mythical worldviews blur the categorical distinctions between the objective, social, and subjective worlds, and how they do not even draw a clear line between interpretations and the interpreted reality. Internal relations among meanings are fused with external relations among things. There is no concept of the non-empirical validity we describe to symbolic expressions. Concepts of validity such as morality and truth are merged with empirical concepts such as causality and health. To the extent that the mythical understanding of the world actually steers action orientation, action oriented to mutual understanding and action oriented to success cannot yet be separated, and a participant's "no" cannot yet signify the critical rejection of a validity claim. Myth binds the critical potential of communicative action, stops up, so to speak, the source of inner contingencies springing from communication itself. (*Communication Action* 2:159 [German: TKH 2:237–38])

Such a description would meet little opposition from Luhmann, but his sociology of religion explains how such mythology is indebted to later theological semantics about origins.

Nonetheless, it is anything but obvious that Habermas, in *The Theory of Communicative Action*, is less concerned with Luhmann's theory and more with Parsons's systems theory: *A Critique of Functionalist Reason* and *Lifeworld and System* serve as the double subtitles to the second volume of the book. Indeed, the starting point for his framework is revealed in a recapitulation of Luhmann:

> Niklas Luhmann distinguishes three levels of integration or of system differentiation: the level of simple interactions between present actors; the level of organizations constituted through voluntary and disposable memberships; and finally the level of society in general, encompassing all the interactions reachable, or potentially accessible, in social spaces and historical times. [Here, Habermas refers to Luhmann's article "Interaction, Organization, Society" from 1973, reprinted

in *The Differentiation of Society* in 1982.] Simple interactions, organizations that have become autonomous and are linked with media, and society form an evolutionary developed hierarchy of action systems nesting inside one another; this replaces Parsons' conception of a general system of action. (*Communicative Action* 2:155)

Habermas accepts those three layers, which have been described in sociology since Tönnies and even Hegel as community (*Gemeinschaft*), republic (*Gemeinwesen*), and society (*Gesellschaft*). However, Habermas's evolutionary theory jumps extremely quickly from the first level to the third. He extensively describes the kinship lines and communities in archaic societies as shortly or even suddenly jumping into modern society:

> Systemic mechanisms remain tightly intermeshed with mechanisms of social integration only so long as they attach to pregiven social structures, that is, to the kinship system. With the formation of genuinely political power that no longer derives its authority from the prestige of leading descent groups, but from disposition over juridical means of sanction, the power mechanism detaches itself from kinship structures. Organizational complexity constituted at the level of political domination becomes the crystallizing nucleus, of a new institution: the state. (2:165)

The problem for an evolutionary theory about history is that Habermas, here in 1981, leaves what he calls "hierarchized tribal societies" after a few remarks about antic empires. Immediately, he begins mixing descriptions of communication systems, such as economic, legal, and military systems, into those two-thousand-year-old semantics with descriptions of functions in capitalist states, as they developed late in the Enlightenment. For historical research such as communication history and conceptual history, this avoids the real task of what empirical rationalizations should search for: namely, how the modern world became possible, as conditioned by differentiations from Antiquity to modern society. When Habermas, in 1981, refers to stratified society, he does so with very brief ontological descriptions of a group in early antiquity, when, for instance, law, possessions, judges, and warriors came in positions. This concerns the transition from preconventional morality to conventional morality. From there, he passes to a next level, where postconventional morals supersede conventional morals. In so doing, he is jumping from Moses to Montesquieu, or, in America, from Indian tribes to the founding fathers, as if no communicative developments took place in stratified society, as if late antiquity, the long Medieval period (especially high Medieval centuries), the Renaissance, and Absolutism did not transform communication, authorized the slave trade and its world system, and so on.

In Luhmann's conception, as briefly referred to by Habermas in the earlier citation (*Communicative Action* 2:155), the developments of organizational systems are described in analyses of hundreds of semantic variations about communicative forms, concepts, and codes, such as inclusion/excommunication, delegation, presence/re-presentation, dogmatics in theology and law, *corpus spiritus* to *esprit de corps*, and so on. The first problem in Habermas's description is that it was exactly those narratives and conceptual transformations he asked for in his comment on Luhmann in "History and Evolution" (in *Rekonstruktion* 1976, 244–300), as discussed above in chapter 5. He doubted that Luhmann could satisfy that requirement as a criterion for sociology (and philosophy) to get in touch with historical research.

The second problem is that the linguistic or communicative turn in a theory about the development of modern society must obviously embark on the inner hermeneutics of communication: of dialogues—namely, about, for example, concepts such as mutuality, reciprocity, noble duels, and court arguments, in the fourteenth or sixteenth or eighteenth centuries, and so on. The aim is simply to find the predecessors and operations, which pave the way and offer path dependencies in an emergence of modern communication forms before the public sphere in the eighteenth century. However, before *Auch* (2019), Habermas had not gone deeper into communication history than he did in the first chapters of *The Transformation of the Public Sphere*, from 1962. Did nothing happen between Plato and Kant? From the laws of Solon to legal positivism, are there no transformations? Or did nothing of what Harold Berman names "Revolutions in Law" take place? Before Brunkhorst made him aware of these long-term evolutionary achievements, Habermas (*Construction*) had hardly distinguished between posttribal law and Roman law. Furthermore, he had not analyzed what Christianity did to law (which was so important for Weber and Parsons) in the lengthy twelfth-century "legal revolution" (Berman) or in the Reformation. This lack is a task somewhat mitigated in Habermas's final *Auch eine Geschichte der Philosophie*, centrally occupied with the learning processes more in academic history of philosophy than in societal communication, broadly speaking.

Yet to Luhmann, the Reformation and Renaissance were a major undertaking in a detachment from the hitherto-interaction-based (Eucharist) descriptions of communication forms toward those more abstract forms, which followed with the printing press revolution. This transformation did not merely pave the way for Erasmus, Luther, Zwingli, Calvin, and many others, but also for a great number of inventions. They took place in almost all communication forms, from novels, to the reproduction of art in the era of technical reproduction (Walter Benjamin), to law books, travel (atlases, maps), science, military manuals, political theories, and decisively, as described by Jean Bodin (1583) in this framework, organization systems, which became detached from interaction forms among present persons.

This implies that Habermas, in *The Theory of Communicative Action*, did not argue why merely "money and power" emerged as generalized forms of communication. How did the concept of power actually take power over itself and its own definition? What became exposed and visible, and what became invisible? The problem is not that such analyses could not find their way into Habermas's framework, as brilliantly exposed by a number of French historians (in Boucheron and Offenstaedt 2011).

Rather, the problem is that Habermas does not examine what Luhmann calls the "improbability" of communication, that is, the contingencies in history: Why was it not different? And why were some communication forms stabilized to the extent that organization systems and functional systems emerged? When theological communication conditions ideas of office, commission, membership, and discipline, which were semantics reformed in the late sixteenth century, this certainly cannot be answered by making references to positions achieved among officials in the empires of early antiquity. Montesquieu and Kant were grandsons to neither Plato, nor Aristotle, nor Cicero. In this sense, the *sociological* history of linguistification should be reconstructed after Habermas's *Auch* (2019), if it should be depicted according to any story other than that told by Luhmann or Foucault.

In order not to make the discussion too abstract, a couple of historical examples could clarify what is meant. Since Habermas, also in the view of his followers, aims to reconstruct Marx's view on the evolution of capitalism, we may take a look at the transition of interaction systems. We observe transformations from the network society of entrusted people, which had some ideas of being mutually creditworthy, say, between major European fourteenth-century cities, to an advanced stock-market-based capitalist credit system in seventeenth-century Amsterdam. Credibility in the Amsterdam stock market developed from personal interactions that were entrusted into impersonal objective systems of risk calculations, which tried to trade with trust and time in the form of generalized and neutralized (and therefore lower) interest levels. This is a well-known story told by authors as different as Fernand Braudel, Charles Kindleberger, Isser Woloch, Randall Germain, and Niall Ferguson, as well as by Luhmann's followers, such as Dirk Baecker in *Womit Handeln Banken?* (1991) and Elena Esposito in *The Future of Futures* (2011).

The overall idea of the exposed conceptions has been subject to some discussion within the Habermas School. It is important to illuminate if that criticism elaborated on critical theory in a direction that opened the door for clarifications about Habermas's use of systems theory and about which kind of systems theory, eventually Luhmann's, was on the other side of that door—or if the door closed?

McCARTHY'S CRITICISM OF SYSTEMS THEORY

Habermas's undertaking is discussed and criticized in a special issue on Jürgen Habermas of *New German Critique* (NGC) from 1985 by a number of North American professors, including Peter Hohendahl, Thomas McCarthy, Dieter Misgeld, and David Rasmussen; they are all Habermas's followers, so to speak. Their papers were presented at a conference held in Dubrovnik (InterUniversity Centre, IUC) in 1984, while Hans-Ulrich Gumbrecht organized another conference with Luhmann in a neighboring room at the little conference center (see Gumbrecht and Link-Heer 1985; Gumbrecht and Pfeiffer 1988; Gumbrecht 2004, 3–15).

Peter Hohendahl (1985, 21) takes up a story somewhat different from those found in religion, economy, law, and organization. He discusses the differentiation of art as a medium for communication. For Kant, an object of art is conceived *as if* it is an object for judgments, though the object is in the reflection of the observer (Kant, *Critique of Judgment* 1790, §6; Böhme 1996). According to Hohendahl, Habermas aims to "relink system and lifeworld" and the judgment of art into the lifeworld instead of a detached communication fused into the functional institution of art. Yet according to Luhmann's seminal analysis of art in *Art as a Social System* (*Art* 2000; *Schriften* 2008), the printing press revolution generalized art in the form of books. Names were signed on the oeuvres exactly because they became detached, printed, and objects for repetition in concert halls, theatres, and cinemas, not to mention CDs, YouTube, art books, and so on. (cf. Benjamin's *Art in the Age of Mechanical Reproduction*). It seems as though there is no zero-sum game between the individualized aura and the meaning of the lifeworld in relation to the generalized medium of art.[9]

This highlights another problem in a too-distinctive differentiation between functional systems and lifeworld. One aspect is that it is not evident that money and power, as proposed by Habermas, are to be described as the only systems—remember that Habermas's claim was to establish an empirical program for historical rationalizations. How many self-regulative systems evolve in the course of history might indeed be an empirically open question. But what about mass media systems, law, politics, research, war, education, religion, and so on?

To this point, Thomas McCarthy's article, with the somewhat provocative title "Complexity and Democracy, or The Seductions of Systems Theory" (in *New German Critique*, 1985) is revealing about how at least some part of the debate received Habermas's use of systems theory. This also answers the question as to whether the door opened toward Luhmann's systems theory.

The title indicates that the article intervenes in the debate on "complexity and democracy," which began between Luhmann and Habermas in the late 1960s (a theme I elucidate much further in chapter 6). McCarthy begins with a dramatic claim, rephrasing Marx, since in his very first phrase he declares that "There is a spectre haunting Habermas' *Theory of Communicative Action*, a close relation to the totally reified world that haunted Western Marxism,... the spectre of a cybernetically self-regulated organization of society, a 'negative utopia of technical control over history.' ... His strategy is to enter into a pact of sorts with social systems theory" (McCarthy 1985, 27–28). One may wonder if McCarthy begins with this statement as a premise and prejudice or as a conclusion of the argument to follow. He offers a kind of romantic Tönnies-like defense of Durkheim's analyses of social differentiation (division of labor) and moral social integration, where "the inevitable result was anomie" (29). To be sure, this is not adequate as a review of Durkheim, nor does it give justice to the much more nuanced review of Habermas. Durkheim and Habermas argued that moral social integration is possible with the conditions posed by a social form of differentiation that demanded moral communication on a more reflexive, abstract, and contingent level. On this point, Habermas completely agrees with Luhmann in their respective readings of Durkheim, in particular, as previously mentioned, with Luhmann's description of reflexive, abstract, and contingent communication (in *Self-Thematization* 1972/1975, 324–27). Because of this misreading, McCarthy established an analogy between Durkheim's criticism of Spencer and Habermas's criticism of Luhmann, and "the role of Spencer is played for Habermas by Niklas Luhmann" (McCarthy 1985, 29–30). He claimed Luhmann's systems theory to be a theory of systems adaption to their environment, whereas for Luhmann the departure was exactly the opposite: the distinction between systems and environments.

Habermas headed toward a social theory capable of understanding and explaining what social and political coordination is about. When, for Luhmann, power is about synchronization of coordination, McCarthy pushes Habermas to find a third road between the roads of lifeworld integration and systemic steering. Nevertheless, remember that, in Luhmann's systems theory, systems are not about steering but about observation. Luhmann was concerned about how to observe consequences and risks when society attempts to synchronize communication according to codes.

These dilemmas led Habermas, in 1985, to reconceptualize his social theory and to develop a tripartition of social integration, political integration, and system integration. This is revealed in his articles and books from 1986 onward, yet it was never reconceptualized at the level of social theory, only in political and legal theory, and this tripartition is merely found in the concluding article in *Between Facts and Norms*.

Durkheim and John Rawls (1993) distinguished between simple coordination, on the one hand, and cooperation as a kind of coordination of coordination, on the other. Luhmann described such a distinction in terms of first-order and second-order coordination. This concerns less the fact that coordination goes on in society and more that coordination is coordinated, reorganized, and reestablished; and it is this reorganization and reform that is politicized.

The somewhat amusing paradox is that McCarthy strove to draw Habermas away from Luhmann's systems theory but ended up pushing him toward such a second-order occupation with political, organizational, and legal coordination.[10] For Habermas, this coordinative integration system became a question of embracing the legacy of the separation of powers and, behind that form of differentiation, a much wider functional differentiation, which emerged during the Enlightenment (Charles Montesquieu et al.). Whereas this is completely acceptable to Luhmann, the issue about coordination concerns politics as a medium for the synchronization of a disunified, nonsynchronic society, divided in conflicting functional systems. For Habermas, coordination still concerns mutual understanding, whereas for Luhmann it is mainly about synchronization, its risks, and its blind spots.

ABDUCTIVE SOCIAL THEORIES

Luhmann's *X of Society* series concerned the early modern semantic variations from the point of view of modern functional differentiation. The result, hitherto, with modern society is known, and the question becomes how self-descriptions established a closed monopoly for the internal communication in those functionally differentiated systems. To read and use those studies is a much easier read than are the four volumes of *Societal Structure and Semantics*. His seminal *Social Systems* from 1984 could give the impression of a deductively constructed theory, and the *X of Society* series could then superficially or initially offer such an interpretation. As already discussed with Habermas and Parsons in Heidelberg, however, the point is precisely how those different functional systems have a number of divergent forms, codes, evolutionary histories, and semantics. A basic reason for this divergence is quite simple: They did not emerge at the same time, and since religion was the first to develop semantics, codes, and self-descriptions, religion also established an entire vocabulary of wholes and parts.

Carl Schmitt (1922/1996, 43) once famously forwarded the idea that "all important political concepts originate in secularized theological concepts." Whereas Luhmann could have written this too, his take, indeed his paradigm, is in contrast to Schmitt: that is, that those concepts do not integrate into a united whole but developed with differences. Semantic codes and forms develop systems precisely because of internal complexities of differences: Codes are invented in order to solve paradoxes and innovate meaning, and they only attain meaning because of differences. In that sense, Luhmann developed neither a Hegelian nor a Parsonian system, which would unite differences (Gouldner 1970, 210); rather, he aimed to describe a disunited system based on dissent, conflict, and paradox. Theological dogmatics developed to expand an ever more complex solution to dissent, with a variety of determined and undetermined concepts. This is what fundamentalists do not like. For some Islamic thinkers, it is too sophisticated that God is divided into three with the Son and Holy Spirit, yet divisions are crucial for those paradoxes embedded in ever more complex self-descriptions.

Such frameworks of evolutionary forms based on internal complexities were decisive in legal evolution as well as evolution in research, credit evolution, evolution in war, politics, organization, art, education, and so on.

Societal Structure and Semantics is indeed an inductive series of analysis of semantic variation in forms. Often, those forms are too loosely coupled to emerge into more stabilized and determined forms of structural couplings. Luhmann wrote the series while at the same time writing *Social Systems* (1984), which he began immediately after finishing the first two volumes in the series and the volume on *Love as Passion* (1982). The many topics offered occasion to write more abductive analyses in a kind of synthesis between the deductive, strictly theoretical elucidation of concepts in *Social Systems* and the more inductive, complex analyses in *Social Structure and Semantics*. While abductive methodology is central, Luhmann seldom used the concepts of induction, deduction, and abduction. Abduction is a concept developed by Charles Sanders Peirce to coin what Kant conceptualized as "reflective judgement" (Kaag 2005), which is to find the form of rules and concepts that adapt to a certain given situation, which in this case is the transition to modernity. This transition took a long time, accelerating during the Enlightenment. It took off in the early eighteenth century and culminated between 1750 and 1850, the so-called "saddle time" (*Sattelzeit*, Koselleck's concept).

Finally, Luhmann combined all of his insights. Initially, he did so in the short English article "The Differentiation of Society" (in *Differentiation* 1982, 229ff.) and in a number of short articles in *Soziologische Aufklärung* as well as in a four-hundred-page Italian publication, *Teoria della Società* (1992). This was followed posthumously by a two-volume manuscript with introductory lectures (delivered from 1991 to 1993). Yet among his major publications, his magnum opus is *Theory of Society*, vols. 1–2 (2012, 2013) (*Die Gesellschaft der Gesellschaft*, vols. 1–2, 1997), which combines the deductive, inductive, and abductive analyses into a coherent framework. This for decades will undoubtedly stand as one of the most coherent analyses in sociology in the grand theoretical line from Karl Marx's unfinished *Capital*, to Durkheim's (almost-premature) *Division of Labor*, to Weber's unfinished, posthumously published *Economy and Society*. Whereas Durkheim's masterpiece, his first book, was too simple, too deductively framed as the work of a young rationalist philosopher who embarked on empirical analysis, Weber's was too complex and disordered and a mess of insights, which opens the door for infinite, extremely fruitful discussions, *as if* society could be analyzed in a rational manner. Norbert Elias's *The Civilizing Process* is a standard-setting publication, between the Durkheimian clarity and the Weberian historical complexity.

METATHEORETICAL DEBATES IN THE 1980S

After the publications in the first half of the 1980s, new international discussions accelerated. Discussions about modernity vs. postmodernity and communitarianism vs. liberalism took place, both becoming immensely popular.

Jean-François Lyotard's booklet *La condition postmoderne* from 1979 came to enjoy widespread popularity and was interpreted as a provocation against the modernist strain. His argument concerned the conditions for research and universities in a society where commercialized investments led to true stories and narratives about what was to be held as valid and legitimate in a society. Yet he continued the critical examination of scientific knowledge observed in its societal conditions, in this sense taking up motives from Max Horkheimer's *Critical and Traditional Theory* (1937) and Habermas's *Technics and Science as "Ideology"* (1968), but turning his arguments in favor of a Luhmannian decomposition of grand narratives. Narratives about valid and legitimate knowledge were to be authorized, each in their own subsystem and with their own small narratives. Like Habermas, Lyotard started with discussions of Wittgenstein on rule-following, life forms, and speech acts. Nevertheless, he ended up in a position close to Luhmann's, and his little book could be regarded as a French interpretation and up-to-date actualization of the Luhmann-Habermas debate.

Habermas explicitly entered both debates. So did Luhmann, albeit in a far more distant position, since his distinction between psychic systems and communication leads to a strong anticommunitarian view, whereas he published the booklet *Observations of Modernity* in 1993. In 1985, Habermas concluded his series of lectures about social thinkers in modernity in *The Philosophical Discourse of Modernity*, which included a twenty-page comment on Luhmann and, in particular, on Luhmann's *Social Systems* published the year before. The book represented an attack against (mainly French) positions and a defense of modernity. It was in favor of rational claims to valid communication about truth and justice. Derrida and Foucault were the main targets, whereas Habermas interpreted Luhmann's systems theory from a different perspective; Habermas's idea was to take the initial thread from his twelve lectures and discuss Hegel's idea of subjectivity as the principle of modernity and then use it as an admittedly particular and extreme yardstick for an evaluation of Luhmann's *Social Systems* (1984). Particularly with the last two chapters from *Social Systems* in mind, "Self-Reference and Rationality" and "Consequences for Epistemology," Habermas questions if Luhmann has established a social philosophy capable of replacing the entire German intellectual tradition since Kant and Hegel! His answer is that Luhmann's project should be interpreted at that level but may miss some decisive features.

Habermas and Luhmann both wrote a few longer mutual comments on each other's publications. Luhmann, in 1986, wrote an article that is a comment on Habermas's *The Philosophical Discourse of Modernity* more than it is a review on *Communicative Action*, which Habermas published in December 1981. However, in fact Luhmann published two other major comments on Habermas in 1986.

IS LUHMANN'S SYSTEMS THEORY METABIOLOGICAL?

Habermas's *The Philosophical Discourse of Modernity* is an indeed theory-laden work. It is a tour de force of two hundred years of philosophy, established in a twelve-lecture series about different authors, from Hegel to Luhmann. Habermas initially establishes five points in his comment on Luhmann's *Social Systems*. To Habermas, they should enlighten and show what Luhmann is up to.

The first point is that Luhmann's system/environment distinction is a repetition of German idealism and its notion of a philosophy of consciousness. Hence, the world is reduced to an unknown world-in-itself, on the one hand, and the system corresponds to a transcendental subject. The subject/object distinction reappears as a system/environment distinction. Luhmann replaces Kant's (and Leibniz's) distinction between perception and apperception with a reflexivity of first- and second-order observation; accordingly, it is founded on difference and not on the unity of the identical subject, which cannot escape its identity with its thoughts—as is claimed in the usual interpretation of Kant. According to Habermas, Luhmann's achievement is introducing Husserl's notion of meaning. Consequently, we find ourselves with an empirical series of different meaning systems.

Second, meaning-based systems also replace Hegel's idea of spirit (*Geist*). Psychic systems and social communication systems replace Hegel's distinction between subjective spirit and objective spirit. One may add that at least Hegel becomes much easier to read with this invention in mind. Hegel's difficult notion of "in and for itself" is easy to translate into "internal to systems" and "external to systems." Here, Habermas does not discuss the fact that Luhmann makes the same point toward Hegel as Habermas's Frankfurt School predecessor Theodor Adorno (in *Negative Dialectics*, 1966), namely, that there is no reconciled unity between different dialectical oppositions, only difference and nonidentity.

Third, Marx's conceptuality of a self-(re)producing society is enlarged with a more general notion of autopoietic social systems: that is, systems that produce themselves with their own elements. For Marx, labor forms the interchange between society and nature, whereas for Luhmann a far more general notion of operations establishes the differences between system and nature without any possibility of a dialectical upheaval. Marx's exposition is merely a special case of this general form.

Fourth, systems are no longer ontological, yet systems-theoretical observations of social systems are themselves to be observed as part of those social systems, and the epistemological shift therefore does reestablish its position, although not as metaphysics but rather as "metabiology": "Then we can use the term 'metabiological' for a thinking that starts from the 'for itself' of organic life and goes behind it—the cybernetically described, basic phenomenon of the self-maintenance of self-relating systems in the face of hyper-complex environments" (Habermas *Discourse* 1987, 372; 1985, 430).

At the end of his concluding review article, Habermas returns to the idea of what he calls "metabiology," which obviously challenges the term *metaphysics*. Biology and life replace physics, causality, and materialist mechanics. Habermas appraises this replacement. However, we can read Habermas's use of the term in two different ways.

One is that Habermas finds systems theory in general—including Luhmann's more cultural way of doing systems theory—too inspired by biologists such as Humberto Maturana, in the same way that earlier open-systems theory was inspired by Ludwig von Bertalanffy's biologically based input-output-feedback idea.

The other is a more Kantian interpretation based on Kant's philosophy of history and its idea of a so-called "teleology of nature," with the form of reason as the (already-mentioned) indispensable telos of natural and cultural evolution and history. Here, "metabiology" refers to the distance and distinction between natural evolution and reasoned research about the evolutionary systems that have been established in the course of natural and cultural history: We are always and unavoidably not merely part of natural evolution, but are also culturally and with our research projects at a "meta-"distance or in a second-order observation. This is definitely a far more accurate way of reading, closer to Habermas. Anyway, both Habermas and Luhmann depart from an a priori of metacommunication implied in the fact of communication. Certainly in *Critique of Judgment*, Kant also departs from this implication of communication (*Mitteilung*). Remember that more recent systems theories of self-organization and autopoiesis, established by Heinz von Foerster and Humberto Maturana, respectively, departed from Kant's evolution theory. The entire systems theory movement, as it escaped from Germany in the 1930s (including attempts by Parsons 1978, 352–433, and Bertalanffy 1968, 186ff.), worked to replace neo-Kantianism and its culture/nature duality with the later Kantian philosophy of history.

Such a metabiology is therefore exactly what Kant spoke of in his historical teleological theory of self-organizational systems in *Critique of Judgment* (1790). Luhmann's theory of self-reference certainly does replace Kant's idea of a transcendent reason a priori with the form of self-reference, which Kant himself described as the position that, first, natural systems and then cultural systems are supposed to have in the evolution of mankind from natural history to civilizational and cultural history. In other words, a form of Kantian a priori reasoning must have been historically possible before Kant arrived on the scene (Harste 1996).

Fifth, to Luhmann, the idea of society's reason promises too much. System-rationality and self-reference decompose an old-European (theological) idea of society's unity with itself. It is therefore not the task of philosophical speculation but a matter for sociology to find what is possible to reconcile and what is risky. Habermas nevertheless insists on dealing with an idea of the "reasoned identity of complex societies": "If functionally differentiated societies have no identity available to them, they also cannot form a rational identity" (*Discourse* 1987, 375; 1985, 435). Here, Habermas deplores that society has no "center," and he proposes the establishment of a conception of the "self-representation of society" in the form of "public spheres" (in the plural). Luhmann's nonreconciliation thesis is cognitively based: it is simply considered as a fact that reason and evolutionary systems will not unite; on the contrary, such hopes are even risky and "dedifferentiate" society. When Habermas therefore declares that Luhmann's position is an "anti-humanism" (1987, 378; 1985, 436), it is not because Luhmann, according to Habermas, declares that social systems should attack or subsume humans; rather, humans have escaped total subsumption.

In a second section of his review, Habermas therefore turns his attention to another level of discussion: that of lifeworld and intersubjectivity. Luhmann responds to all three themes. His response to the metabiological theme is the most spectacular and will be discussed more substantially in chapter 7. Luhmann published an answer with the book *Ecological Communication* (1986), which represents an application of *Social Systems* toward systems/environment problems. Together with Ulrich Beck's *Risk Society*, published the same year, these two books established the theoretical core of an ever more important, critical sociology of environmental risks.

Communcative Action, Habermas's seminal sociological chef d'oeuvre, consists mainly of that which Luhmann calls third-order observations of other authors: Stephen Toulmin, Gadamer, Weber, John Searle and J. L. Austin, Georgy Lukács, Max Horkheimer and Theodor Adorno, Ludwig Wittgenstein, George Herbert Mead, Émile Durkheim, Peter Berger, Thomas Luckmann, Alfred Schütz, and Parsons. As usual, Habermas develops his theory in the medium of comments on and arguments with other authors, most his contemporaries. In this book, Luhmann is somewhat hidden between the lines. Habermas knew that Luhmann was about to develop a major theory, and it is therefore possible to argue that Habermas's third-order analysis of the sociological discourse of modernity came either too late or too early to include Luhmann's theory in this impressive line of theoretical comments.

Another perspective is that Habermas's greatest impact with the book was to get rid of obsolete Marxist discussions about theories of society. While Habermas in many respects subscribed to Marxist analysis and intentions, it was time in the late 1970s to lift one's head above the somewhat still uninformed student discussions about Marx and neo-Marxism that had been taking place for a decade. Habermas managed to shift his focus toward communication and to describe how societal rationalization and differentiation took place in the medium of communicative modalities. Yet the deductive philosophical bias of a theory that steadily embarked on discussions about modalities of speech acts was remote from sociology and social research. It was actually necessary to read Searle, Austin, Wittgenstein, and others in order to grasp Habermas's points. This was very informative, for sure, for younger university teachers, who should have found some ideas about what was important to read and not to read. In this sense, Habermas offered extremely useful guidelines about the theoretical agenda and tour de force through the landscape of philosophy and social science.

Yet when we look for a theory of the development of modern society in *The Theory of Communicative Action*, we fall astray with a much-too-simple framework about the stages in modern development. In the German editions, Habermas's two-volume book contains 1166 pages in the first German Suhrkamp edition, and Luhmann's own two-volume book contains 1164 pages. This similarity in itself almost appears to be one of Luhmann's usual, extremely dry jokes. Luhmann's book is actually about the advent of modern society, whereas Habermas's is about how to discuss modern society. Luhmann's posthumously published *Systemtheorie der Gesellschaft* (2017) contains 1131 pages.

This statement is certainly not meant to underestimate Habermas's achievements. An adequate proposition is to see Luhmann's theory of modern society and its historical development as adequate for a sociological answer to a question about how to observe what modern society "is," and Habermas's contribution as an answer to a question about "what to do" with it. Neither Habermas nor Luhmann narrated any "European Interpretation of History," or a Whig interpretation in Herbert Butterfield's sense, and they certainly did not narrate a German interpretation to replace the infamous *Sonderweg* after 1945. Only they are constitutively aware that the blind spots of such interpretations are unavoidable and even indispensable. Butterfield (1931/1965) warned against excessively simple teleologies, such as a British parliamentary road to a modern "utopia," which certainly have been dismissed since the Brexit negotiations. The Kantian teleology was more about a confederal world history, and it is still constituted by risky systems. The two chapters to follow display this narrative.

IV
THE DEBATE ON LEGITIMACY

6

COMPLEXITY AND DEMOCRACY (1968-71)

Today, in social theory, we think about power and critique in a much more comprehensive way than most social science did in the 1960s. Yet those were the years when a lot of reconceptualizations had to take place. Concepts and visions had to be revised if not revolutionized. For some, especially the students, reinterpretation was not only about theory and philosophy but also about practice.

In hindsight, it is a safe bet to say that it is barely a coincidence that the debate grew in these directions during the years that followed May 1968 and the student revolt. The student movement had been a kind of cultural crisis as well as a flowering period with a wholly new creation of new possibilities and has given rise to a new and wholly different way of looking at social norms. It went far beyond the earlier sociological self-limiting to the study of institutions and norms determining what to do and how to communicate. In France, for instance, poststructuralist ideas flourished and accelerated during these years, as documented by authors such as Jacques Derrida, Michel Foucault, Pierre Bourdieu, Jean Baudrillard, and Jean-François Lyotard. What Émile Durkheim had called the "precontractual layer of morals" turned into a complex blend of "anomie," alienation, and efforts to reconstruct trust and motivation. The new social movements and communication codes born during these years were openly at odds with long and immemorial traditions of conformity. Among the first of these innovative moves was a radically widened scope of social research. In the late 1960s and the 1970s sociology transformed into a laboratory charged especially with the in-depth analysis of the philosophical preconditions for social communication. Likewise appeared ambitious tasks such as the creation of a new hermeneutics of the meaning of means and ends and new theories of norms, of individualization, and so on. The range of the agenda corresponded to a reborn universalist drive; yet, at the same time, it was fueled by a specifically modernist vocation, suggesting that once again "everything solid melted into air," as Karl Marx had pointed out in connection to the year 1848 and the years preceding (Berman 1983; Marx 1848/1964, 465.). Every theme opened for discussion. In addition, society, again, took a globalist turn to world society.

THE BACKGROUND IN THE 1960S: THE POWER CIRCUIT

In section 19 in *The Structural Transformation of the Public Sphere* (1962) Habermas depicts, empirically, how the circuit of power unofficially obstructs the officially beauty-painted circuit due to neofeudal corporate organization. This unofficially reversed, however real, power-circuit framed the analyses of both Habermas and Luhmann in the years following the publication of *Transformation*.

On Luhmann's side, the 1960s saw a diversified range of important books, *Folgen* (1964), *Grundrechte* (1965), *Politische* (completed in 1966–67, yet published only posthumously in 2010), and *Macht* (completed in 1966–67, published in 2012). Together, they all provide the in-depth background of his treatise *Legitimation Through Procedure* (1969). Two studies about somehow broader topics—one (*Zweckbegriff*, 1968) dealing with what might be seen as a philosophy of systems theory, the other (*Trust*, 1968) devoted to the sociology of everyday life—displayed a more general concern about social theory and social explanation. Surprisingly enough, the study devoted to procedure as source of legitimacy features—apart from its introductory section and its concluding chapter—a structure that is borrowed from the traditional public-law tripartition between separated powers: judicial, legislative, and organizational powers. Moreover, this depicts generally those studies Luhmann finished during the years 1964 to 1967.

Contrary to Parsons, Luhmann was never a friend of the foundationalist language widespread in value-driven social and especially political science. It is difficult to speak of his article "Complexity and Democracy" (*Komplexität* 1969) otherwise than in terms of its founding importance for the ensuing legitimacy debate between Habermas and Luhmann. This study of the irreducible complexities of separated powers offered a first approach to what constitutes the very puzzle that has been so suggestive to the long and almost never-ending debate between the two sociologists, the intimate core of their lifelong disagreement. The constraints of the historical situation are constituted in Luhmann's title "Complexity and Democracy." This duality effectively couples the two problematics that originate in diametrically opposed spheres of sociological interest. The debate has largely sparked from here. Yet, of course, this was not intended in 1969. Nevertheless, to slightly exaggerate, the duality corresponds to a controversy between a Montesquieuian complexity and a Rousseauian democracy.

In a very broad framework, we can say that the Habermas-Luhmann debate on legitimacy is about social theory orientated either toward conflict or toward consensus. While Habermas describes repression and power from the point of view of critical theory, Luhmann is, in more than one sense, far more "critical" in this instance. His concern was preferentially with matters of real conflict, or dissent; Habermas's unwavering and primordial interest lies with possible consensus and its conditions.[1]

The basic issue here is that Habermas's basic political commitment to the dialogical consensus dimension springs from his understanding of the mission of the sociologist as a chooser and defender of "causes" deemed to be politically worthy to be defended, while Luhmann, on the contrary, sticks to a more rigorous method without getting sidetracked by matters of judgment or value-driven choices. He remains entirely focused on the conditions that effectively define and structure communication. Here, real dissent takes an important leading role. Today (after its recent publication) we can trace the emergence of these views to Luhmann's early theory of power, in *Macht im System* (1967/2012), developed few years before the debate.

In this study, Luhmann refers to Habermas's celebrated study *Theory and Practice* from 1963,[2] suggesting a new notion of power according to which power ultimately is the differentiation between reason and decision. Some of the insights featured in *Macht im System* were saved from a half-century of hibernating in a rarely read book by the fact that part of this argument was taken up in an article by Luhmann written in 1969 (in *Klassische* 1969). For the young Luhmann, the challenge that power is about and has to master is located at the borderline between the form of communication and its limits. Power, in a word, goes beyond the mere possession of means of enforcement. It is essentially in need of consensus: "Power remains exposed as long as it is only supported by physical power, and not also by consensus" (*Macht* 1967/2012, 70; cf. *Politische* 1967/2010, 95).

All too often, power is described according to the priority given to the possession of a material dimension. This material dimension relates, in fact, to the social dimension of domination alone. Yet power is a form that reduces complexity in a third dimension as well, a dimension located beyond consensus and enforcement and, to be sure, a temporal dimension.

Accordingly, power reduces insecurity and can secure a future situation (*Macht* 1967/2012, 63). And yet, in these early writings, Luhmann, though already polarized toward the question of the future, has not yet elaborated a self-referential conception of power (Harste 2017). Rather, in 1967, he sticks closer to what can be identified as a certain Hobbesian inheritance to be found in Montesquieu, namely, the doctrine according to which power and freedom are mutually reinforced. Power, according to this doctrine, stands in need of freedom, otherwise its main operations, such as decision, delegation, and differentiation, cannot be performed. This might at first look surprising, considering that what power, any power, is clearly and principally about is always a problem of limiting or binding some freedom. Deprived of freedom, power itself necessarily retracts, implodes, suffocates, being prevented from its vital proximity or access to action. Power in the modern age is about acting, about matters of doing things and getting things done. In this respect, language or common parlance reveals something essential, at least in French, where the concept of power carries the name *pouvoir*, which, depending on the context, can also mean simply "to do" (however, not—this time—in English, where the entire sphere of potential action is entrusted to a separate noun). The German is also instructive here, if in quite a different way. The German noun for power, *Macht*, implies a direct proximity to the verb *machen* (doing, making), giving rise to the tempting possibility of combining verbal and substantive forms, in order to show how both really are pointing to one identical question. (The implication is indeed so clear that it is not part of what native language-users pay attention to, and most German-speaking people are effectively astonished to learn about it.) Indeed, "Macht macht Macht" (power empowers power). This strange self-reference, or perhaps self-preference, of power has given more inspiration to French thinkers like Foucault and Bourdieu. German discussions of the matter were, by and large, commanded by a superior preparedness to trust diverse theoretical elaborations of power differentiation and weigh their relative validity claims.

Eventually, Luhmann did not really succeed in developing a theory of power as self-referential system. But this theory alluded to the fact that power always implies, and includes as well, the power to define power, to communicate about power, and to develop semantics about power, and indeed, as he will say later on, the power to "invisibilize" power. All of these concerns will be much more obvious for the later Luhmann, who only first developed his strictly communicative turn in his later *Power*, published in 1975, and then his theory of self-reference. For the early Luhmann, the word *power* referred to power and the circulation of power in political decision-making by means of law. Now Habermas had urged, starting with *The Structural Transformation of the Public Sphere* (*Transformation* 1989, §19, 176), that we need to take into account that, in modern, complexity-ridden welfare states, power would obviously not be present under the simple and moving features that Jean-Jacques Rousseau had painted portraying the form of a "circuit of power" from the people to the people ("quand tout le peuple statue sur tout le peuple," Rousseau 1762/1971, 530). Rather, neocorporatist forms embodied in processes of state administration, the co-optation of pressure groups, the bureaucratization of mass media, and the like lead, as Max Weber had already observed in "Politics as Vocation" (1919), to some less-official yet very real circuit of power in the opposite direction. This image of circulation that, unofficially but powerfully, doubled and more than outweighed the official and opposite circuit of power was used by Luhmann too. He devoted to it some extremely detailed examinations, starting with his long unpublished treatise *Politische Soziologie* from 1967. The theme continued to keep his attention, in *Political Theory in the Welfare State* from 1981 (which included a collection of smaller articles translated from *Soziologische Aufklärung*, volume 4, in 1987) and up to his final contribution to the topic, *Politik der Gesellschaft*, published posthumously in 2000.

In Habermas's *Between Facts and Norms* (Facts BFN 1996, 328–30, 341–59; 1992, 398–400), we see the same concern with the realities of power that do not lend themselves to Rousseau's lofty description: "Here the administration does not just consist in the complex with the highest organizational density. It also sets in motion a circulation running counter to the 'official' circuit of power" (1996, 335; 1992, 406). Hence, Habermas and Luhmann all along agreed upon the description of the unofficial power circuit. Therefore a question appears: *Is there anything left in this description that offers orientations about whatever could and should be done under those conditions?* According to Luhmann, "Everything is possible, and there is nothing I can do" ("Komplexität" 1969, 43; cf. Cohen and Arato 1994, 316; Habermas, *Faltering* 2009, 138–83).

The two influential authors who need to be considered under this heading are the Canadian-American political scientist David Easton (1965), who suggested an input-output-oriented feedback circulation of public power in political decision-making processes, and Karl Deutsch (1963/1967), an émigré from Prague and a specialist on matters of government, who pioneered applying a form of systems theory to politics. After Parsons, they, more than anyone, took systems theory to established political science. Since Rousseau, people's sovereignty has been thought of as the power that a people exercises over "itself," the people, by *making use* of the law as an instrument for implementing policy preferences. Deutsch and Easton did not naively simply describe the hope of a circular decision-making, in which the will-formation of the people decided upon governmental processes; they described overloaded political systems unable to respond to all demands and therefore in need of reduced complexity.

"Power founded on competence and exercised as law is named authority" (*Macht* 1967/2012, 64). The medieval idea was that eternal authority should synchronize with temporal power and therein be present, which is re-present. In modern political systems, authority derives from people's sovereignty, and should synchronize with organized power. In *Macht im System*, Luhmann formulates this power circuit in a way informed by Easton, in the view that in "democratic political systems the public strives for power over politics and politics likewise for administrative power over the public" (35). Yet "power is conditioned by higher forms of organization" (47). Hence, power entails a conception of the "organization of reflexive power that is formed and increased by division of labor and development of communication" (96). Communication is not only about circulation of power vertically from top to bottom, or the other way round, but also horizontally. In the late 1960s, political scientists launched a discourse of neocorporatist moderation. Easton's open-systems theory was in a sense reduced in its towering ambitions, first by Deutsch's suggestion that circulation in social systems was, as soon as it was to be implemented in reality, necessarily subject to restrictions and diminutions that were generated in the process by unforeseen events. These notions of reductions, even of self-reference, were to loom large in the reconstructed approach to social systems theory that Luhmann was working on throughout these years.

The decisive move here was a move out of the political overdetermination or predefinition of the systems paradigm, or in other words a move toward a pure systems theory in which the themes of systems closure, self-reference, self-organization, and autopoiesis could play a more important role than in the "power-infested" zones of politics. Yet, while some of those terms, in particular "autopoiesis," were not used by Luhmann at this point, others were, such as "self-organization." Yet in this case, they were used as much by Habermas as by Luhmann, indeed in certain cases, such as that of self-regulative systems, the term was suggested by Habermas.

This proximity to short-term antecedents, especially within the U.S. social and political sciences, should, however, not cover up the important extent to which both Luhmann and Habermas find, over the long term, a common ground in Émile Durkheim's political theory about deliberative democracy (Durkheim 1908/1969). Many of the elements of what could be termed the classical understanding of how communication functions as a precondition for the evolution of power can be traced to a Durkheimian model. In his relevant writing, or rather lectures, Durkheim also stated that political theory has been concerned for far too long with forms of government defined in political terms (aristocracy, monarchy, democracy), thereby losing contact with the realities of state organization and how it communicates, negotiates, and "makes up its mind" in bodies of societal decision-making and deliberation.

To state that the complex matter of a separation of powers is constitutive to democracy refers not only to Jean-Jacques Rousseau's *Du contrat social* (1762), yet also to Charles de Montesquieu's *L'esprit de loix* (1749). The latter was even more fundamental to at least Durkheim, who had devoted his Latin-written academic thesis to Montesquieu. The prominent and fundamental character of Montesquieu's separation-of-power thesis had been widely endorsed during those years. Carl J. Friedrich reedited his *Constitutional Government and Democracy* (1941/1949/1968), written during Nazism, in which he delivers a strong argument in favor of Montesquieu's doctrine. Earlier power-oriented, largely military-lead nation-states had provided the effective foundations to become, one day, democracies. In the case of the United States as well, the War of Independenc, the Civil War, and the two World Wars operated as a catalyzer to establish the two-agenda road map of federal government plus democratic principles (Porter 1994). The construction of power was a forerunner to democracy (Poggi 1978). It was important, however, that this didn't concern power in any contingent form. What was at stake was a certain form of balanced and separated powers that alone could be considered as harbingers of a rule of law to be established. This balancing was established within a much wider functional differentiation that also distinguished between those powers that were excluded from the first-level powers that he considered alone: religious power, military power, economic power, educational power, science as power, and the norms and virtues of a civil society.

COMPLEXITY AS SEPARATION OF POWER

For all those who agree with this conception, the basic problem of modern democracy is a product of the institutionalization of the separation of powers. Luhmann's article from 1969 "Complexity and Democracy" tries to deal with the problem, and Habermas struggles with it as well

(*Legitimation Crisis* 1989, 130–42). It is the foundational problem of politics in modernity, what one might well identify as the constitutive paradox built into modern society even before its democratization began. The basic problem that even constitutes modern politics at the same time as it creates the crisis of modern politics is double. Many aspects of the historical constitutionalization have been well known for informed European scholars since the days of Max Weber and the German historical school, with authors such as Gustav Schmoller or later Otto Hintze. Gianfranco Poggi who, influenced by both Luhmann and Habermas, published *The Development of the Modern State* in 1978 provides an excellent short overview of the basic problem at stake in this connection.

Alexis de Tocqueville had already presented the first aspect of this *problematique* when his reports as an observer of the political situation of the United States were published in *Democracy in America* in 1835. *Ancient Regime and the Revolution* (1856/1988) made it clear that "an administrative revolution preceded the political revolution." Jean-Baptiste Colbert's contributions to central administration had lastingly revolutionized the relation between government and state at the end of the seventeenth century. Thus, democratic decision-making is conditioned by an administrative machinery capable of implementing political decisions top-down.

Accordingly, this means that the organizational form of modern society in itself is decided *before* and in a way *external* to democratic decisions. At the time of the French Revolution, not to mention the Revolution of the Weimar Republic, the relevant decisions were already made. Thus, in a sense, the rails, on which the trains of any further political and administrative history will roll, were built—as unintended consequences. That means that the form of bureaucracies, their hierarchy, their departmentalization, the individualized white-collar work based in offices full of professional staff, their salaries, their budgets, their careers, their education—all of this has been long in place as a matter of perfectly consolidated preparatory arrangements. Those bureaucratic bodies and hierarchies developed and became indispensable for political decision-makers well in advance of the time in which any concerted proposals were initiated.

When the so-called absolutist rulers found themselves in a situation that moved them to make use of these "dispositives," their decisions smoothly fitted into what had already been initiated. Tocqueville, Max Weber, and Émile Durkheim were well aware of the fact that this administrative autonomy never stopped developing. Only extremist dictators could conceivably alter the agenda-setting power of central administration. If they wanted to do so, they would use no other "method" than that of dissolving or "dedifferentiating" (Luhmann) the distinction between politics and administration.

PARADOXES OF DEMOCRACY

Therefore, what is really at stake in Luhmann's and Habermas's democratic paradox lies in the fact that only when a rather important number of constraints had emerged did the democratic autonomy of a political sovereignty reach the threshold of self-determination. They were in the meantime firmly in place, for reasons, or as a consequence of actions, that lay well beyond the reach or the control of politics. Habermas himself recognized, in chapter 4 of *The Structural Transformation of the Public Sphere*, the uncomfortable and paradoxical fact that representative republicanism, and the doctrine of the separation of powers that had imposed it, had been solidly in place well before it had come up with its own, much more acceptable and harmonious raisons d'être, and that already Immanuel Kant, in his later years, had perfectly recognized this.

Yet, equally clearly, the new *interstate community* constituted by international treaties had been at least equally codetermined by compromises and dispositives for balancing power, which had been in place well before any effective political self-determination of sovereign polities, thus imposing their constraints on the political sector, much more than the other way round.

In "Complexity and Democracy," Luhmann, fully aware of these limitations and conditions, declares it obsolete to insist on democracy as an ideal of citizens' identification with a polity, according to the old-European tradition, as if any kind of full participation in a societal whole political body could be an answer to the problems of modern society. This whole/part idea had its origin in Aristotle's *Politics* before it was entirely redeveloped during the twelfth and thirteenth centuries under the aegis of the Catholic idea of a fully integrated community constituted under the sign of salvation. More than on most other themes, Habermas and Luhmann can agree upon the inadequacy of such communitarian ideals for modern society. Yet, Luhmann points, already in his article from 1969, to another, much more consequential sequel of recent social evolution, namely, the notion that "human beings should not be conceived as part of social systems, but as their environments [*Umwelt*] and as such as some in a problematic relation to systems" (Luhmann *Komplexität* 1969, 36). Referring to Erving Goffman, Luhmann writes, only "total systems" such as psychiatric asylums provide an example of a social system today that *defines* the individual person.

It should not be forgotten that the interest in ideas of nonidentity, present in Luhmann, was, at this point (1966), chiefly promoted by Habermas's Frankfurt *Doktorvater*, Theodor Adorno, who devoted to them *Negative Dialectics*, his philosophical magnum opus. Moreover, this idea of a human identity separated from society and existing outside and even beyond its outskirts had already been recognized since Jean-Jacques Rousseau and up to Søren Kierkegaard—the Danish theologian-philosopher to whose work Adorno, forty years earlier, had devoted his senior dissertation (*Habilitationsschrift*) and who is praised still more by Habermas. In Rousseau's words, the human being, conceived as man (*homme*), is indeed different from the individual conceived as a subject to the government (*sujet*, in the political sense of the word) or as citizen (*citoyen*). It is noteworthy that in 1972—at a time when Habermas devoted a nonnegligible part of his attention to sociological theories of roles—Luhmann inquired repeatedly into the idea of nonidentity. In the 1980s, on the other hand, the list of Habermas's own main themes included individuality, assigning the topic a place close to the center of a whole series of studies (Habermas *Individuierung*); Luhmann, at the same time, came up with a major analysis of the complex semantics of individuality and individualization. Accordingly, there was some common ground on that subject between both thinkers.

Yet, before that, we need to have a closer look at the potential identification with a social system. Can the individual, today, be thought of as being part of a social whole, in the sense in which this was generally admitted since Aristotle? Does, in other words, "the part participate[] in the whole" still today?

With the achievements of the Enlightenment, politics emerged as a kind of thing hitherto unheard of, a new praxis—a self-determination that wouldn't at all be sufficiently described as the replacement of one "court" by another (parliamentary) "court," a replacement of one Versailles for another great building and meeting hall.

Whereas religion, the court, the daily life of the noble elites, the higher lawyers in the king's councils, the higher administration, and even finance and military decision-making were all rather intermixed, the new form strictly separated the juridical courts and its educated professions from an at least equally professionalized administrative elite. While financial circles appeared in banks and stock markets, public debates emerged at this time everywhere in town life, outside the courts, in cafés, in discussion salons in the forecourts to operas, in theaters, and in courtrooms. Politics took over roles and territories that it had never before occupied; it provided new shapeless, or only "council"-shaped, fora for deliberation, clubbism, decision-making.

What was new was not the form of the council in itself, which had been institutionalized for centuries, but rather the new forms of separation and differentiation it involved. Durkheim coined a term, *deliberative democracy*, for the new forms and uses of councils.

Habermas, in *Legitimation Crisis*, quotes Luhmann about what is at stake: "Politics can no longer presuppose its decision basis, but must itself create it. It must accomplish its own legitimation in a situation that is defined as open and structurally indeterminate with respect to the chances of consensus and to the results striven for" (Luhmann *Komplexität* 1969; Habermas *Legitimation Crisis*, 132). In Habermas's understanding, the new achievement here is that we are confronted not only with a differentiation between the administrative system and the legitimation system, but with a new form of decision-making process, distinguished from other forms of "generalized motivations, values and interests" (Habermas *Legitimation Crisis*). In Luhmann's understanding of this same process, on the other hand, the term *democracy* is something like a pious "understatement" of a much wider transformation, in contrast to Habermas, who (in *Structuration* 1962/1989) described the construction of the public sphere as a general precondition for what we today describe as democracy. Luhmann also inquired into the meaning of the word *public*, in an article of the title "Public Opinion" (*Planung* 1970), yet above all he focused upon the organizational and legal specialization, professionalization, and differentiation as general preconditions of democracy as they were at work in the political system.

For Luhmann, in other words, the main and most structuring move consisted in the fact that administration and law had specialized. Each in its way and direction and with its own results withdraw from the circles of "high society." In other words, they escaped—or emancipated themselves—from the vertical or hierarchical anchoring of older societal models. It was this transformation that resulted in the transformation of the public sphere into a political system specialized in a certain political form of decision processes—a form that was separated from law and from administration (Luhmann *Widerstandsrecht* 1984).

It is in the course of this process that, Luhmann suggests, a certain form of "self-steering [is induced] in political calculation" (Luhmann *Komplexität* 1969, 39). What is new is that we find a "reentry" or "repetition [*Wiederholung*] of the political into the political system" (39). Luhmann equipped himself, over the next twenty years, with a whole vocabulary and conceptual arsenal to make sense of these process forms. Casting them in the terms and procedures presented by George Spencer Brown's *Laws of Form* (1969), he will interpret them as "reentry." At the end of the 1960s Luhmann neither used nor knew of Spencer Brown or, indeed, of any theories of self-reference.[3] The point he is making is nonetheless the same, already at this stage. For Luhmann, what has been important throughout is understanding politics neither as the material decision-making processes happening within the specialized administration systems and their results, nor by reducing it to the social dimension of collective will-formation that replaced the sovereign prince with the people. Luhmann is unhappy with these current ideas, such as the idea that politics imposes widely shared ideas; he is unhappy even with defining democracy as the majority's participation in decision-making, since

> Decision processes are in charge of selection, of the elimination of other possibilities. They produce more *no-s* than *yes-es*, and the "no"-share increases the more rationally they proceed, the more attentively they consider other possible ways to go about things. Asking for decision processes to be a matter of fully fledged engagement and participation of all people is to expose them to a principle of frustration. True, those

for whom this is what democracy consists in are bound to come to the conclusion that it is incompatible with rationality. (Luhmann *Komplexität* 1969, 39; quoted in Habermas *Legitimation Crisis*, 132–33, translation modified)

In reading these lines, we could think back to the so-called "democratic deficit" debate that began around 1979 with the first elections to the European Parliament and all the *no's* (or, with Brexit, "nays") that were at the time directed against the European Community's then still more complex decisions. Effectively, this debate later became central to Habermas's interventions claiming that what this was about was, rather, a *Verfassungsdefizit* (constitution deficit). A "democratic deficit" was constitutive to democracy in states, since, as we have seen, the state, its form, its basic structuring architecture (especially the separation of powers, the division between departments, and so on) had developed not through democratic processes, but before modern democracy was on the horizon. Political and organizational decisions were due to wars and to elite decisions among noblemen and princes. Already at this point, the democratic input/output feedback power circuit of decisions processes in European matters was only reforming things that had been already established. Accordingly, dissatisfaction with formal democracy (representation etc.) became widespread when the popular and almost populist ideal was about participation of the parts in the whole of decision-making. From this perspective an obvious discussion would be whether or not a "democratic surplus" could be described in European integration and global cooperation (Harste 2015; MacCormick 2009, 289).

Among the motives fueling their discussion during the years 1969 to 1973, the questions at stake between Luhmann and Habermas were, however, still of an altogether different sort. The main issue was, could new social movements claim to bring new ways of democratic participation into the political system? Though Luhmann did not leave a doubt that such innovative moves were clearly a realistic option at the time, at the top of his list of questions was the weighing of the intended and unintended consequences of such radically "emancipatory" moves. In the eyes of some observers they were looked upon with a certain skepticism. Habermas, on the other hand, was rather more sanguine about action, if not outright optimistic; this at least can be easily deciphered from his discussions in *The Structural Transformation of the Public Sphere*, which were largely critical.

Yet, it was Luhmann who, since his seminal book on organizational sociology (*Folgen* 1964), displayed a major critical impetus against traditional hierarchies and formal bureaucracies. In this study, he encapsulated a staunch defense of higher communicative rationality, more elastic structures in the build-up of organizations, arguing that the motivations that fuel the work done in organization increases when procedures are smoother, orders and rules bend, and negotiation is the normal way of doing things. Clearly, what Luhmann is arguing for, here, should not be confused with democratic participation. Furthermore, in another organizational analysis ("Lob der Routine," published in *Planung* 1971) Luhmann praises the virtues of strongly pattern-dependent ways of proceeding, since rational change is conditioned by some stability and routine. In the same way, Luhmann also thought that democratic reforms are conditioned by the presence and resiliency of stabilized forms.

In the present, Luhmann observes, "politics is just as much exposed to contingency" and "instability" (Luhmann *Komplexität* 1969) as is the case in such systems as science, economy, or art, which are known to be innovation-dependent and constitutively volatile. Politics is no longer authorized by its princely connection with eternity, but with its connections with the present moment of the popular vote, news, in the worst case populism, and in the best case a central, well-informed judgment of the present situation and its necessities and its "reason of state." Within politics, the principal form in which contingency, volatility, and instability make themselves known, the main expression of this new unrest, is precisely democracy. The word *democracy* offers the marker by means of which a situation makes itself recognizable as a political situation.

Here Luhmann points toward what German intellectuals call "Zeitdiagnose," the momentary state of the political question, in particular the awareness in the present situation *about* the present situation, with the trends that draw a line and indicate what is politically to be done. The problem comes up at this point, as for Luhmann the question is almost never to be cast in the terms "What is to be done?," followed by some normative answer; rather, it is a question of how to establish an adequate description of the present state.

> Reduced to a brief formula, [this] has to do with the fact that the political system can no longer derive its identity from the society if it is required by the society precisely as a contingent system which could possibly be otherwise. It must, then, identify itself through structural selection in a situation of consciousness no longer comprehensible with old European concepts. (Luhmann quoted by Habermas *Legitimation Crisis*, 132)

For the inexperienced Luhmann reader, who has just familiarized herself with Luhmann's uncompromisingly cold-blooded, even level-headed accounts of complexity and contingency, Luhmann somewhat unexpectedly shows a serious awareness of what might be called the other, "human" side of complexity. "Democracy has its rationality and humanity: its Reason, in this option. For this is what distinguishes the human way of relating to the world. It relies upon sense-making procedures. It is based upon life, thus continuously confronted with the necessity of decision-making and 'choice-acting,' at every moment anew" (Luhmann *Komplexität* 1969, 40). At the same time that this makes it quite obvious that Luhmann's detachedness allows for some understanding of political passion, the observation here is precisely the argument that such a thing as political life exists, that it is about the possibility of change—for instance, the change from one government to another one.

In 1968, Luhmann published the short but important treatise, *Trust*. In the case of democratic political systems, trust is present precisely in the fact that the party out of which the government is made up trusts that the present opposition will be allowed to compose the next government if it wins the next elections. Hence if the party runs in the next election and is victorious once again, the government will act in the same way. This mutual trust is basic to democracy. In this sense, political change is effectively at the core of modern democracy; and—for Luhmann—this story is more modern and more central to democracy than the often-repeated but barely sustainable narrative about participation within a social whole. An earth-shattering example occurred when Donald Trump declared that he might not trust the presidential election if he lost—the opposite of Al Gore's run for the presidency in 2000, which he supposedly lost, albeit with more votes than George W. Bush, like Hillary Clinton. And unlike the distrust of Trump and his followers at the 2020 elections.

In a case similar to Michel Foucault's so-called "antihumanism" during the same years, for instance, in *The Order of Things* (*Les mots et les choses*, 1966), Luhmann found himself confronted with an impossibility of using the idea of seeing the whole modern world society as a "whole," capable of integrating every individual into, as it were, one extended human family. This supposed an extended adolescence, and a strength of faith capable of short-circuiting the fact of modern alienation (*Komplexität* 1969, 44). In order for any change to happen, politics needs to make sure, first, that it provides for the conditions of change to be in place. Before any decision is made, politics has to select the form of "changeability." Changes in time need to become possible and legitimate. This is why modern politics is, primarily, about temporalization.

Thus, unambiguously, Luhmann's account of modern politics is in itself a "modernist" account. Yet the heated argument begins at the point at which the advocates of politics as candidates for a societal leadership role choose the obsolete orientation in favor of reduced complexities, and prefer *confidentiality* of interaction over the *trust in the working of functional systems*. The narrative of confidentiality would clearly best suit people's will, as happens every time they rebrand modern politics as a personal exercise, or when politicians are selected according to their qualities as practitioners of archaic storytelling in their mediatic versions (41). This explains in part the political career of people like Silvio Berlusconi, Ronald Reagan, George W. Bush, and in particular Donald Trump. Charisma and communitarian ideals about identification become indistinguishable in modern mass media. Luhmann does not underrate this moment, to be sure; "technocratic calculability" is not, for him, a rational answer to this form of irrationality. Neither do populism, communitarianism, or charisma answer technocratic inflation. One might argue that Luhmann, then, underestimates the later development of spin-doctors; his reply would arguably be more accurate: that spin-doctors rarely follow overly calculable guidelines; instead, they reduce the complexities of unstable politics to voting measures (*Politische* 1967/2010, 397).

In an overall perspective, the political system consists of three parts, the public, politics, and administration. It seems conceptually odd that something called "politics" is supposed to reenter the political system, but the point here is the necessity of observing *politics* in its autonomy from both the public input into the political system and the administrative output from the political system. Politics "as such" is located by Luhmann in the short space inhabited by the decision-making itself, a time-space that is located in an artificially aggrandized short-term interval between past input and future output and constitutively exaggerates it, creating a present time in which the present, the presence, the re-presentation of the decision-yet-to-be-made, virtually constitutes the reality of politics. Luhmann, suggesting his theory of the constitutive preference of the now for the now, sticks to this tripartition of the political system in his later analyses, especially in *The Political Theory of the Welfare State* (1981/1990).

THE SYNCHRONIZATION OF SOCIETY WITH ITSELF

From today's perspective, almost half a century later, one of the easiest entrances to Luhmann's theory of society is to read his booklet with the ambivalent and ironic title *The Reality of the Mass Media* (1996/2000). As is the case with the mass media in one respect and organization systems in another, politics *synchronizes society with itself*. Politics re-presents society within the present time and redistributes not only material goods, but also what the present time as such is about—what will eventually appear as its profile in historical observation—and what "counts" within its being, its time-internal, time-bound operations. According to Luhmann's analysis in *Legitimation* (1969), modern political life has to decide how to handle contemporary decision-making under special conditions— the conditions of a society with separated powers and functional differentiation. The simultaneity of the political system and the social system, to which Luhmann's "synchronizing" interpretation of society alerts his reader, is constitutively simultaneous and contemporary with several other, parallel simultaneities, or rather synchronizations. This takes place not merely in the coexistence between politics and society, but between each single one of the functionally differentiated systems and society. Importantly, however, these processes, though happening at the same time, are in one important sense not synchronic among themselves, as they do not follow the same rhythm, the same form of processes. Time in politics is not the same time as in economy, in law, in research, in education, in art, or in organizational systems. Communication about time leads to dissent and not to consensus. What this opens up is the necessity of a time management in society, a necessity of establishing synchronization, as a condition of coordination and consensus.

This gives rise, among other issues, to the question of what it means to coordinate long term with short term. A whole range of themes and conflicts could emerge, yet in democratic decision-making one form of handling the medium of decision processes is to distinguish the temporality of *decision-making* processes from the temporalities of the process of *deliberation* and of the giving and taking of advice. Choices to be made and decisions to be taken—this is very much the daily bread of societal routines. The ways in which this is dealt with happen in view of mastering these necessities, in courts, in politics, and in administration, are far from following similar temporal procedures. Past, present, and future diverge, and decisions are differentiated—so much, it can be said, is generally the case for all functionally differentiated systems. Yet it is not only that argumentation, proofs, and conclusions are established according to different criteria; their time horizons diverge. While "the buck stops in the court" (and deliberation therefore takes time), organization may still decide to revise later on; politics may come up with the idea of deciding on a plan, or of not deciding on it, according to the question of whether it is going to be implemented before or after the next elections and so on. Politics doesn't prioritize matters as much as time, and it often prioritizes short horizons to long horizons.

In order to summarize these themes and bring them within our general horizon, the point is that, while, toward the end of the 1960s, Luhmann and Habermas were both concerned about conflict and consensus, the divergence between them was located within a competition between time and society. To Luhmann, the entire matter of appropriately understanding and handling conflict and consensus was essentially a "question of time"—though obviously not in the sense in which this formula is most customarily used, as an expression only of urgency or of the competition for priority, but rather in the sense of the inherent time-exposure of everything that happens in society, in the sense that social structures are always and inexorably event-dependent, that all societal happening is time-bound. For Habermas, on the other hand, the importance of consensus draws on a wholly different resource of motivational energy: consensus is a problem of, and an appeal for, social forces. Consensus is relevant, or indeed indispensable, to the extent to which social motives need to be socially and politically coordinated. To leave matters in their insolvable nonsimultaneity is as important for Luhmann as are the difficulties of coordinating a consensual drive for Habermas.

7

PARADOXES OF LEGITIMACY

Crises and Risks (1973–91)

LEGITIMATION CRISIS AS A TOPIC

In the moment at which Jürgen Habermas's study *Legitimation Crisis* (1973), with its strong political message, appeared in the windows of the bookstores of the Western part of the then-divided Germany, Europe—Western Europe—was living through the heyday of the post–World War II period, and the German Federal Republic through its economic miracle after the war. Let me shortly recapitulate the situation. Public opinion was unanimously and firmly convinced that unemployment was about to disappear. More than a decade of unprecedented growth rates had led to unprecedented widespread wealth. Due to the success and importance of the very politically moderate social democratic parties, social equality and social welfare were more prevalent and consequential than ever before—or since. In the United States, welfare and growth expectations probably peaked before, in 1967. The strange kind of Cultural Revolution brought about by the new consciousness of the late 1960s and heralded by its student movement further added to this environment. It succeeded where comparable movements had failed. Most spectacularly, the post–World War II Weimar Republic had tried to definitively break the back of the last remnants of authoritarian society, as well as of a still more remote aristocratic society, until it was halted by Hitler's ascent to power. The student movement of the 1960s finally did away with these remnants—and in its Marxist élan abolished some of the aspects of "class society" as well.

For the first time in its history, Germany had gotten to a point where an observer could reasonably conclude that privileges could no longer be upheld without reason. Power needed to be justified, and could and should be exposed to the question of its legitimacy. To this end, the critique of institutions was justified. It was also omnipresent. In very diverse forms, the doctrine that dominated German and European universities was Western Marxism. The idea of a breakthrough to a new and better society on Marxist foundations led the student movement and showed the way toward what they saw as an emerging new society. Frankfurt and the Frankfurt School of critical theory was one of the centers for the student revolt in Germany. However, on the one hand, in retrospect, it is easy to see today that the worldview of those involved in this movement and much of the certainty that underpinned the convictions of its protagonists were based in part on shaky foundations. On the other, posthierarchical politics got a new tune.

The dialogical approach to political reasoning was the trend of the day. The young Habermas, teaching students who were only ten to twenty years younger than he was, limited himself largely to confronting them with the question of whether the trend they embodied was indeed as widely shared as they themselves believed. Yet he also challenged Marxism with what he—probably overly adapted to student language—named "a reconstruction of historical materialism" (*Rekonstruktion*). The Vietnam War was more remote for Europeans, of course, than for those on U.S. campuses; even so, as a secondary trauma the Vietnam disaster fit into the horizon of that generation of German students, whose conflict with the generation that preceded them—the generation that was tainted with the national-socialist regime—made them ready to revolt more radically. Simultaneously, a kind of metaphysically experienced fact—in particular in Germany—was that the Cold War suddenly could end the history of mankind.

In this situation, there was almost an obsession with political theory in far wider circles than intellectual academic groups. Beyond this particular period, the lasting questions were still those that had fueled the Enlightenment: How can society be described adequately? How can the social order be transformed? How can the potential of the political order be used in order to provide it with justified claims to legitimacy? Finally, which of the linkages between political theory and social theory are possible?

It was a moment at which almost everyone, including the majority of social researchers across the board, tended to perceive no possible future outside of one that assured endless growth. When the first dark clouds gathered on the horizon, they were first seen by Habermas and some of his collaborators at the Starnberg Center of Research into the Conditions of Life in the Scientific-Technical World, headed by Habermas as director since 1971. There, among others, James O'Connor wrote his analysis *The Fiscal Crisis of the State* (1973), Claus Offe (1972) described the structural problems of the welfare state, Klaus Eder analyzed the evolutionary logics of social movements, and, in their opus *Die neue internationale Arbeitsteilung* (1977), Folker Fröbel, Jürgen Heinrichs, and Otto Kreve offered a pioneering description of the consequences of a new international partition of work with new industrial zones in South East Asia. Together, they all began to work with the hypothesis of a major economic crisis and whatever it might bring in its wake. In fact, the tipping point was reached with the so-called oil crisis in October 1973, and in the following years, the West experienced a major economic setback. This experience was what Luhmann outlined in a small article from the 1980s, a comment on Habermas and an Italian professor, Danilo Zolo (1992), in terms of disappointments and hopes (Luhmann SA 4, 133–41).

In *Legitimation Crisis*, Habermas had analyzed the political and motivational consequences of economic crises. Only a few years later, Luhmann, in *Welfare* (1981), *Ecological* (1986), and *Risk* (1991), founded his analysis of the severe limitations of political systems in responding to real societal problems, generally located *outside* politics, and also continued to highlight the framework of risks inherent in a functionally differentiated society. Poul Kjaer, Gunther Teubner, and Alberto Febbrajo (2011) use both Habermas's and Luhmann's positions to show the connections as well as the different perspectives and consequences that follow from their analyses. More recently, if not conclusively, Hauke Brunkhorst, centrally placed in between Habermas's and Luhmann's positions, published a penetrating analysis, about *Legitimation Crises—Constitutional Problems of the World Society* (2012), discussing problems, crises, and risks afresh.[1] Many of those signs of crisis accelerated, but as a crisis in the political systems' capacities to respond, with the Brexit and Trump's procedural victory; however, Macron's "revolution" in 2016–17 was opposed to this. In 2017, Habermas discussed the future of Europe with Macron, only to see Macron overloaded with the Yellow Vests from November 2018—half a century after the complexity debate appeared!

Such crisis scenarios suddenly struck the entire world society with the pandemic in spring 2020. The thousand-dollar question is how ecological virus contamination was to be structurally coupled and eventually contained by organizational health systems and by research systems, by economic systems, legal systems, mass media systems, political systems, motivational systems, even systems of inclusion, exclusion, and racism, eventually to be framed by either moral panics or restructured and reconstituted moral discourses of solidarity. The last possibility to Habermas' satisfaction eventually partly survived in the frame of post-Keynesian negotiations in the European Union in July 2020, whereas Great Britain, United States, and Latin America experienced breakdowns of all those systems, one after another. Yet the U.S. too embarked on the post-Keynesian ship after Biden became president. If such systems disrupt the expectations and entitlements posed as legitimacy claims of the population, mistrust appears and systemic crises might escalate to entire catastrophes—as in the 1930s. The problem is that if at least three such systems refer to one another and turn self-referential and reinforce lacunae in their otherwise structural couplings, the crisis will deepen in chaotic ways. This is why the Habermas-Luhmann debate about legitimation crisis and risk systems is more actual than ever before.

What I want to offer is a way of understanding how Habermas and Luhmann elaborated analyses capable of dealing with the questions that emerged with the crises and, more generally, with those risks in modern society that Luhmann characteristically designates as "paradoxical." This, of course, is what the Habermas-Luhmann debate was about, at least since it was displaced from its initial level.

LEGITIMATION CRISIS (1973)—THE FOUNDATIONS

A large part of the surprise provoked by Habermas's book *Legitimation Crisis* in the German academic audience is owed less to its claims than to the level at which it stages its discussion. Habermas's *Legitimation Crisis* is a concentrated, small book, which can be read as a coherent comment on or rejoinder to Luhmann's lengthy elucidation of some of Habermas's earlier arguments about and against systems theory, arguments that can be found in H/L (1971). The year before *Legitimation Crisis*, Luhmann published the two-volume systems-theoretical *Theory of Law*. In retrospect it is easy to see that Habermas's *Legitimation Crisis* and Luhmann's *Theory of Law* have had a greater impact than most other works by either of the two: the pressure exerted by the exchange on both of them made their writing more readable than most of their other texts. Habermas's *Legitimation Crisis* is less about law than about politics; it also does not seem to directly address, let alone respond to, Luhmann's works preceding *Theory of Law* (1972) or *Legitimation durch Verfahren* (1969). Be that as it may, it is remarkable that this early stage of the debate ends with a discussion of law.

It is, however, equally noteworthy that no such law-indebted conception was, or could have been, part of Habermas's analysis in 1973; for Habermas, law played at this point a different sort of role, and was a matter to be discussed alongside morality, strategically distorted by power.

Indeed, it is systems theory that provides the theme of the first of three parts of *Legitimation Crisis*. Habermas here presents his well-known distinction between system and the "lifeworld" as a basis for sociopolitical analysis. However, this phenomenological twist first appeared in Habermas's article from 1966 "Technical Progress and the Social Lifeworld" (in *Technik* 1968). In this article, systems are self-steering cybernetic machines technically interpreted from a systems perspective, one indeed opposite to the steering-critical perspective forwarded by Luhmann in these years, yet probably unknown to Habermas at that time.

The second part of *Legitimation Crisis* describes a dynamic of crisis transformation that, passing from the economic system to the administrative system and the political system, finds its final laboratory in what is called the "motivational system." This is quite obviously not understood as a system in Luhmannian terms; but for Habermas it has the virtue of eventually "integrating" the entire strategy of transforming the crisis, in the medium of norms that are to be justified. The third part analyzes the conditions for such a moral form of justification in the medium of "domination-free" discourses. The book ends with a kind of concluding ten-page reply to Luhmann.

AN INTERLUDE: CRITIQUE, CRISIS, AND THE TRIBUNAL OF REASONING

In 1959, Reinhart Koselleck published his important study *Critique and Crisis*, now regarded as a classic. It was devoted to the simultaneous and historically innovative emergence, in the decades preceding the French Revolution, of the double diagnosis of a threatening crisis (of the ways and institutions in charge of politics and public power) *and* the emergence of a critique. This reached out far beyond any simple reform suggestions, and drove its way well onto the level of what reasoning was about and how reasoning paved the way for a crisis in traditional institutions.

If we subject this connection between critique and crisis—the influence of which is perspicuous throughout the first part of *Legitimation Crisis*—to even the most cursory of examinations, we find that it provides us with some precious indications regarding the stakes and strategies involved in political critique during times of crisis. The intimate mutual connections between financial crisis, political crisis, and the critique of solutions and reforms are not a novelty of more recent crises—for example, after 2008 or 2020. Their role was obvious in the 1970s and in the 1930s, and was equally undeniable throughout the decades before 1789. Both Habermas and Luhmann are quite aware of this historical dimension. Yet in order to take stock of these interconnections, the purely political level of analysis had to be supplemented by a normative level, more exactly a level related to the legal system. In this respect, Luhmann's ways of dealing with the issues opened up for him direct means of access to the crisis-sensitive issues, from his groundbreaking *Legitimation* (1969, esp. pp. 46, 70ff.) onward.

Habermas was, at this time, still operating confidently on the grounds of the classically modernist assumptions that a political system was ultimately taken to be in charge of everything that happens in society besides a self-integrating lifeworld. There are some innuendos that go in the right direction, but in general, the decisive momentum of the legal system for society was not very apparent in *Legitimation Crisis*, especially compared to Habermas's later studies (after 1986). Indeed, it looks almost as if the legal form lacked, not only in *Legitimation Crisis* but also in his previous analysis of these matters, *The Structural Transformation of the Public Sphere* (1962). In these books, the model for political reasoning is quite obviously formulated in opposition to reasoning that one finds in courtroom proceedings. It rather appears to be a kind of reasoning about aesthetical themes of reception—later investigated by German scholars such as Christa and Peter Bürger.

One of the many interlinking discoveries that feature in Luhmann's reconstruction of modernity is epitomized in the notion of a procedure (*Verfahren*). This comes accompanied by the explicit claim to be rediscoveries of discoveries and inventions located in the making of modern society. For Luhmann, this title covered what he would also call "negotiations in interaction systems." What is a "procedure" according to Luhmann's *Legitimation durch Verfahren*? The history of the term and in particular its genesis are obviously borrowed from law. In sociological terms, however, the historical evolution and evolutionary success of procedure are that of a mode of cooperation: not only a matter of reciprocal role-setting, but a formula by means of which one could approach successful ways of assigning pace and time used for purposes of discussion, their "finalization," and their sequencing. Procedures are about apportioning questions and answers in such a way that they follow each other in a rhythm that is neither too fast to allow for finding alternatives or variations, nor too slow to enable the decision-making process within the system to respond to, and compete with, the actual challenges of its environment. There is a limited margin of tempo in which decisions and criticism need to be practiced in order to come up with minimal systemic efficiency. In that sense, procedures are about synchronization.

The point here is that any reform is bound to take time (though not too much time!); it is precisely in order to be substantially adequate that reforms need to stick to precise timing. Luhmann's procedural model unifies matters of content and matters of time with the social form of legal argumentation. It has its definite origins in the realm of legal actions and court procedures. Yet the initial episodes of the twenty-first century have made abundantly clear that financial regulations and reforms in times of crisis follow "double standards." Substance and time, or, in other words, the care for the right decision at the right time, are both assigned a central role that current routines and currently available models assign through the banking-system only to *either* substantial adequacy *or* procedural time.

SYSTEM CRISIS AS IDENTITY CRISIS

Habermas's interest in theory was (and is) located at the opposite end of such efforts; where Luhmann refers to process or procedure, Habermas tries to explain the social constitution of a political crisis. Thus, while Habermas also uses what he refers to as "system analysis," his use, which forestages the structure of systemic solutions to imbalances, ruptures, and steering problems, privileges the political system—even if it is the coupling between the steering problems of systems that leads to critical limits that lie at the heart of his questioning. Habermas's agenda also includes the issue of how to create the ambitions of restructuring the medium of critical debates. It is clear that such an approach requires that crisis and critique first have to be dissociated from each other and treated as independent, if not diametrically opposed, factors or potentials. It is with these tasks in mind that Habermas tries to find a conception of system crisis.

This bipolar understanding of crisis and critique underlying Habermas's analysis becomes manifest if one looks to Émile Durkheim. Indeed, in Habermas's eyes, Durkheim's analysis becomes itself readable as functionalist, even "systems-theoretic," considering that it describes how normative systems—systems made of norms—establish themselves by means of the distinction between deviance and normality. This of course supposes that the system can describe an environment, simply by interpreting its environment as being a part of itself. Seen from Habermas's angle, this is perfectly sufficient. If crises can be cured by critique, one is indeed referred to the question that underlies his argument: Why should a social system be in need of any nonsystemic form of reflection? "According to this systems approach, crises arise when the structure of a social system allows fewer possibilities for problem solving than are necessary to the continued existence of the system. In this sense, crises are seen as persistent disturbances of system integration" (*Legitimation Crisis*, 2). We may simply think about crisis and conflict in the most banal Marxian terms, as when production relations (e.g., property rights) do not allow for developments in productive forces. Yet the form of the argument is more general than Marx's model. Nevertheless, Habermas finds the classical (Marxian) model useful in looking for the internal contradictions in social systems (such as a capitalist system):

> It can be objected against the social-scientific usefulness of this concept that it does not take into account the internal causes of a "systematic" overloading of control capacities (or of a "structural" insolubility of control problems). Crises in social systems are not produced through accidental changes in the environment, but through structurally inherent system-imperatives that are incompatible and cannot be hierarchically integrated. (2).

Now, almost half a century later, it is clear that Habermas's interrogations anticipated a major issue today: that known as a system's sustainability.[2] For Luhmann, systems reproduce and sustain themselves by their own elements. Yet, what if a system fails at this task? Here the answers diverge. For Habermas, such a system is confronted with "steering problems": "Crisis occurrences owe their objectivity to the fact that they issue from unresolved steering problems. Identity crises are connected with steering problems" (4). At several different points in his life, Habermas links these problems to a wide range of examples, which include Russia, forced to turn into the Soviet Union (or, later on, from the Soviet Union back into Russia again); or France, turning from its ancien régime to its revolutionary embodiment, and from this into Napoleonic France, then into Restoration France, and so on. The issue here is that of the identity of a social system and its limits. What constitutes and identifies a system such as Russia in the moment, in which one asserts that it can, or needs to, be reconstituted as the Soviet Union? An entity X "corresponds" to the legal constitution A, before suddenly being resurrected corresponding to a different legal constitution, B. Habermas's point here is about sameness. Even if entity X does not stay integrally the same—not the same territory, not the same capital, not quite the same population—there is something that remains the same, which keeps its identity.

If a society, understood as a system, is not able to describe its own limits and its own identity, then another form should be found that is capable of reflecting the continuity and its transformation. It is this "other form" that Habermas describes as a society's social integration. Habermas conceives of society with the help of two terms, "system integration" and "social integration."

Biological systems receive their identity from the limit or threshold values (in terms of temperature, need of water, and so on) that define their conditions of living and thriving; there are well-defined criteria determining whether a biological system is alive or dead. We can conclude that the identity of a biological system coincides with its sustainability, that preserving its conditions of continuation at once means preserving its identity.

This issue of "systems steering" appears only at the moment at which a system leaves its "preconceived" identity behind and moves away from "itself," totally or partially. Thus the idea of identical systems that can be steered and keep crises at a distance presupposes some kind of narrative about systems evolution and systems change. Nothing, no transcendent ontological warranty or preestablished harmony, prevents the social system from falling into crisis and, what is worse, from not finding an issue from the crisis other than at the price of changing—of "replacing"—its identity.

> The political system of a highly differentiated society can no longer be understood as a means to an end and can no longer be regulated by rigid external guidance. In order to pursue its functions, it has become so differentiated from the rest of society, so autonomous and complex, that it can no longer base its stability on fixed foundations, practices, or values. It can become stable only by creating possibilities for change. In this way, variability has become a condition of stability. (Luhmann *Political* 1971 in *Differentiation* 1982, 158)

For Luhmann, a social system's identity involves no essence. The social system involves no preexistent differential aspect in which it would reside and which could be identified and upheld as its substance. It is nothing apart from the performances that allow its own continuation. Something is and remains identical, but this identity is that of the successive operations themselves; it is wrong to conceive of a social system as if its identity were enshrined, once and for all, in some ontological core, "substantial" element, or essential feature. No one will deny that the identity of a social system thus conceived barely corresponds to what most people would come up with when asked what they associate with the word *identity*. To use the notion of social systems in connection with the problems involved in "steering" some pre-existing identity means misunderstanding what is most fundamentally at stake in the conception of a social system. Preexisting ontological characters have no standing in a social system, as Luhmann conceives it (*Systems* 1984; Thornhill 2007b, 336–39; Backhouse-Barber 2017). Moreover, seen from Luhmann's vantage point, causally or instrumentally steered input/output systems belong, as it were, to the dinosaur age of social-systems theory, which Luhmann sets out to leave behind (as early as *Zweckbegriff* 1968).

Luhmann has persisting problems with the very notion of a "crisis." In his text, the notion most frequently occurs in quotation marks, and this is why Luhmann preferred to establish a theory of risks, of systems blindness, and of lacking or deficient structural couplings, and remained reluctant about the more drama-inducing or emotionally charged term *crisis* throughout.[3] By 1968, he had already offered the active and decision-inducing concept of "risk" as more adequate than the excessive reliance upon an invariable set of circumstances and the resulting fixation with notions such as that of "security" (*Zweckbegriff*, 156–61).

Biological systems run into crises if they are contaminated with parts of their environment impossible to integrate. If we go back in the long history of epidemic crises, if not to the biblical descriptions of plague then to the tremendous plague that struck the European-Asiatic world in 1347–51, there were no modern scientific understanding of its causes and remedies. Yet theological interpretations of theodicies were at hand. The diabolic interference caused a breakdown in the orthodox interpretation of a cosmic worldview ordered by God. The obvious response was to strengthen orthodoxy and to judge heterodox heretics as outlaws. This response, however, radicalized heresies and thereby invoked the coming Reformation and its ensuing confessional wars. Still, with absolutism, power became even more powerful. Yet power was in need of complex measures. It still more differentiated in its organizational build-up. Whereas plagues and cholera, in the aftermaths of the wars, continued to create immense crises, power needed devices, research, law, and eventually mass media and the public sphere. Moreover, it was in need of learning processes.

Hence, the heterodox contamination was to be integrated into systems, biological and social. Vaccine systems developed immunity as described in Kant's *Critique of Judgment* (1790, §§63–65). As we all know, the modern systems spread and disseminated worldwide. Less room was left over to viruses, which subsequently enter human habitats. Research systems try to find vaccines—and sometimes fail or react too late. As is well described by Michel Foucault, since the late medieval diseases we have tended to react to external contamination with walls around cities and later nations. However, they will not do in the case of pandemics.

TRUST AND CRISIS OF THE LIFEWORLD

There cannot be, however, any question, whether for Luhmann, Habermas, or anyone else, that we need to always remain conscious of the fact that, in everyday life, we do speak about crisis, and increasingly so since 2007 and even more 2020. Whenever we are confronted with questioned norms, or with identities whose survival are at risk, we are at least prepared to have these states referred to under the category of "crisis." Habermas, introducing Edmund Husserl's already-famous notion of lifeworld (*Lebenswelt*) from *Die Krisis der europäischen Wissenschaften* (1937/1962), refers in this sense to a "prescientific" notion of crisis, a notion familiar from pathological medicine or from Husserl's phenomenology, and tries to turn it into a social-scientific category.

For Luhmann, on the other hand, in *Trust*, the reference to an intersubjective lifeworld as a general framework runs the risk of exposing its communications to a possible spiral of both mistrust and risk:

> Men live from day to day in this intermediate zone without specific problems of trust or distrust. . . . Insofar as the need for complexity grows, and insofar as the other person enters the picture both as alter ego and as fellow contributor to this complexity and its reduction, trust has to be extended, and the original unquestionable familiarity with the world suppressed, although it cannot be eliminated completely. As a result, it becomes a new form of system-trust, which, as a conscious risk, implies renouncing some possible future. (*Trust* 1968, 23; 1979, 21, 22, translation modified)

To Luhmann, the confidentiality and familiarity of personal systems must be distinguished from the trust, which operates in communication systems. Trust is neither imposed nor allowed by the world into which we are born; trust is a venture that is more or less risky according to as-yet-unforeseeable later events. The divergence between the two approaches is clear: Habermas's argumentation operates at the two levels of system integration and social integration, or in other words at the level of problems met by the agencies that he identifies with systems (political and administrative, economic, sociocultural) for steering purposes on the one hand, and the level of encounters based on the intersubjective reproduction of the individual's attempts at relating to meaning in the lifeworld on the other.

Of course, as sociologists, Luhmann and Habermas are both preoccupied with the great sociology of interaction and encounters in the "lifeworld" as they were studied by scholars from Alfred Schütz and Erving Goffman to Peter Berger and Thomas Luckmann. Yet their ambitions are also philosophical in the tradition of Husserl and Maurice Merleau-Ponty.

By 1973, when Luhmann had already offered a thorough analysis of the stakes in his book *Trust*, Habermas in fact had not said much about what he wanted to describe with the notion of a lifeworld. Habermas's more ambitious analysis was to follow in the second volume of *Communicative Action* (140–48). Here, we find an effort to come up with an adequate description of crisis, such as anomie, reification, alienation, loss of meaning, loss of freedom. In 1973, Habermas was still satisfied with a concept of the lifeworld that would allow him to claim that lifeworld experiences are an important factor in reasoning precisely about the motivations and norms that determine a socially integrated society. This is why Habermas distinguishes between system integration and social integration: only if preexisting norms or identities determine their reality can systems be controllable and remain subject to steering.

THE QUESTIONABLE PROBLEM OF "STEERING"

We can now see that Habermas's notion of a system is narrower than Luhmann's in the sense and to the extent that it stipulates the presence of "integration," or of an encompassing mastery that the system exercises about itself. "We speak of system integration with a view to the specific steering performances of a self-regulated system.... From the system perspective, we thematize a society's steering mechanisms and the extension of the scope of contingency" (*Legitimation Crisis*, 4, 5). This epitomizes a systems approach of a particular kind, one that has been boiled down to the level of a somewhat reductive idea of a system's "power" that allows it to "steer" society or a specific part of its current agenda. One could argue that this covers, to some extent, what Luhmann's conception of political power attributes to formalized organization systems. In fact, Luhmann maintained throughout, from his early major study on organizations (*Folgen* 1964) to his posthumously published *Organization and Decision* (2000), that complex organizations are characterized by the fact that, far from being simply objects of decision-making, they decide themselves whether or not to follow a decision and to what extent, rather than the object. Like Pence's decision not to follow Trump on January 6, 2021. Luhmann only adds an insistent claim that social and political theory needs to provide an adequate account of organization no less than for law. Thus, a question comes up when Habermas contends that

> In the analytic framework of systems theory, social evolution (which takes place in three dimensions: development of productive forces; increase in system autonomy [= power]; and change in normative structures) is projected onto the single level of the expansion of power by means of reducing the complexity of the environment. This projection is seen in Niklas Luhmann's reformulation of fundamental concepts. (*Legitimation Crisis*, 5, translation modified)

The question is obviously whether the words "expansion of power," which Habermas chooses, deliver a correct description of the relevant passages in Luhmann or whether they must instead be qualified as a misleading presentation. If one looks into Luhmann's theory construction at its later and ever more developed stages, the shortcomings of Habermas's rendering seem undeniable. But even with only Luhmann's *Trust* (1968) in mind, the limits of this description are clear. As an illustration of how far "power expansion" misses the point here, after all, the remit of "social systems" at this stage already included, for Luhmann, love, which figured as one social system among the interaction systems.

Meanwhile, Habermas's use of the vocabulary confronts its reader with only three "systems": an economic system, an administrative and political system, and a sociocultural system. His acclaimed analysis in *Legitimation Crisis* starts off, in the second part of the book, with a painstaking account of the dynamics of crisis transformation, where he links the conceptual discussion both to empirical analyses of what happens when systems overstretch their capacities to handle control by self-regulation, and to philosophical reasoning about norm reproduction and argumentation. The brilliance and usefulness of Habermas's crisis transitions analysis, which we shall see in detail later, should, however, not too hastily be mixed up with an acceptance of a conception of steering systems, in the sense of a description of what is taking place in systems, which narrows down the perspective on systems to that of steering performances.

Most characteristically for Habermas, system integration, social integration, and a subjective sense of becoming embedded in a crisis situation form a unity: "Although the subjects are not generally conscious of them, these steering problems create secondary problems that do affect consciousness in a specific way—especially in a way as to endanger social integration" (*Legitimation Crisis*, 4, translation modified). Concretely, during a severe crisis such as the pandemic crisis, organizational managers might create moral panics since they try to handle power and steer, as if organizational systems might be possible to integrate socially, which they according to Luhmann cannot—and therefore create unintended exclusion in order to include their communication effort into themselves. This might lead to unjustified and even illegal measures.

Even at the point of the initial and concept-formative level of *Legitimation Crisis*, there is no doubt that Habermas had still not really received the central message of Luhmann's conception of systems as noninstrumental autonomous systems; yet, in those days, it was Habermas who used the term *self-regulative systems* more than Luhmann did.

According to Luhmann, systems typically cannot be used for steering, as steering is an activity solely reserved for mechanical power. As mentioned, furthermore, Luhmann had already shown (in *Folgen* 1964) that organizational systems are constituted as routines of informal and uncontrollable communications. Following on the quotation earlier (from *Legitimation Crisis*, 5), Habermas claims that

> Systems theory can allow only empirical events and states into its object domain and must transform questions of validity into questions of behavior. Thus Luhmann always initiates the reconceptualization of such notions as knowledge and discourse, action and norm, domination and ideological justification, below the threshold of a possible differentiation between the performances of organic systems and of social systems.... The advantages of a comprehensive conceptual strategy turn into weaknesses of conceptual imperialism as soon as the *steering* aspect is rendered independent and the social-scientific object domain is narrowed to potentials for selection. (5–6, emphasis added)

The passage suggests that Habermas continued to believe until 1973 that Luhmann's systems theory was essentially a theory of "steering" and "control." If this is the case, then it is difficult to avoid the conclusion that Habermas's interpretation presents a rather exceptional performance of the art—or, perhaps, the power—of reading into an author what one would like to find there. This is especially evident given Luhmann's continuing insistence that *no* position within modern society allowed its incumbent to "steer" society, or to "control" its evolution. "Modern society is impossible to steer" (Willke 1997, 82; cf. Willke 1992, 207, about Habermas; Willke 2001). Luhmann's Bielefeld colleague Helmut Willke became quite successful with his later elaboration of systems as self-steering systems.

On the other hand, it is clear that Habermas, too, has a point—even if it is not quite the one he wanted to make. It is in the logic of these systems to use strong couplings and strong second-order codifications in order to give rise to evolutionary take-offs. Clearly, Habermas tried to defend a much more loosely coupled form of communication in the medium of discursive reasoning to find the form in which reforms and transformation can take place and become formative for new systems.

At the end of this part of the debate, we see that both Habermas and Luhmann recognized the paradox of this initial conceptual formation: namely, discursive reconstitution can be established only in a certain type of society—in a society that is constitutively operating under favorable conditions, which includes Montesquieu's classic principle known as "separation of powers" as part of a much wider functional differentiation. As long as, from a systemic viewpoint, things work out optimally or at least manageably, there is at least a minimal chance for the domination-free discourse hoped for by Habermas to have some impact. This favorable situation is conditioned by a great number of functionally differentiated social systems. Such systems stabilize functions not to be questioned and debated simultaneously. By way of images one is tempted to think of the way in which a situation of the kind is subtly expounded in the movie *Lawrence of Arabia*, and the book where T. E. Lawrence (in *Seven Pillars of Wisdom* 1935/1997) makes clear that all existing discussions and any contribution to any possible theme are emptied of its promises and becomes futile as soon as the electric plant (in Damascus) ceases to function—like so many other things in Damascus since 2011.

LIMITATIONS TO CRISIS OR CONTINGENCY ABSORPTION

Indeed, several of the social systems Habermas discusses provide an "open door" for any normative structures conditioning them; sociocultural systems, political systems, and economic systems are specifically mentioned. Later on, Habermas became more concerned with legal systems; systems of science/research are, of course, also subject to analysis (though they normally are of lesser relevance to a theory of legitimation crisis). Quoting Max Weber, Habermas summarizes the stakes in the following fashion:

> The basis of legitimacy reveals "the ultimate grounds of the 'validity' of a domination, in other words . . . those grounds upon which there are based the claims of obedience made by the master against the 'officials' and against the ruled." Because the reproduction of class societies is based on the privileged appropriation of socially produced wealth, all such societies must resolve the problem of distributing the surplus social product inequitably and yet legitimately. (*Legitimation Crisis*, 95–96)

Habermas, no less than Weber, lets himself be guided by the idea of a society capable of "steering" itself—"all societies must resolve the problem of . . .," as if societies had been self-governing from the time of their creation. This competes with the capacity of successfully and deliberately steering and governing their course through the sea of other possibilities. He also contends that social systems operate at a wider range, and therefore imply media in a broader sense. In this context, Luhmann proposed that law, for example, operates as a form in the medium of expectations, and economy as a form in the medium of payments.

Yet Habermas's remarks on the broader medium come close to what Luhmann had described earlier on, in his book *Trust*, when dealing with the distinction between trust and confidence/confidentiality. Habermas insists that the point is how social systems stand not only in need of integration externally, but also, and more decisively, in need of an "integration of inner nature through the medium of norms that have a need for justification. These imply, again, a validity claim that can only be redeemed discursively" (*Legitimation Crisis*, 10).

In order to grasp the distance between the views, Luhmann criticizes steering ideas of integration, which cannot allow for delegation of power and decision: that is, in Habermas's view, the realm of discursively redeemable validity claims to all paths in society, whether socially integrated or systemically integrated. Second, in Habermas's conception, we are dealing with the matter as if the place of systems in society is limited to the context of what is acceptable according to the standards of human intersubjective communication.

Since Habermas's own discussion is highly abstract, it is easier to turn to later applications in order to understand what is at stake. One such example is to be found in the long-standing discussion of the French Revolution that starts with Alexis Tocqueville's *Ancient Regime and the Revolution* from 1856. The political revolution had been successful because it was preceded by an administrative revolution. Because of wars, administrative systems developed, yet were accompanied by a growing need for new taxes. The aristocracy refused to pay taxes, but their refusal could not be sustained and defended in the ever more public debates about tax reforms. French citizens instead claimed that a new institutional and political order about "what rights were about"—in all senses—had to be imposed. Applied to an analysis of the French

Revolution, Habermas's argument has led to a series of quite convincing results (Hinrichs 1989).

For other specialists in the French Revolution, while the evolution of French society accelerated for several decades around 1800, the important observation is that it was not the transformation of the French political regime that pushed France into the modern age. Rather, the advancement of modernity came from the evolution of the decisive mutual reliance and dependency relationships (which systems theory conceives under the name of "structural couplings") that are located between the various systems: the military system, tax system, administrative system, legal system, educational system, health system, research system, traffic system, and so on, all of which were evolving in directions reflecting their own innovative slants.[4] It was not until a hundred years later that Émile Durkheim, in the series of lectures called *Civic Morals and Professional Ethic*, could describe the French political system in terms that brought their description into close proximity to the basic democratic ideal of deliberative democracies. Luhmann, Foucault, and Bourdieu offered various other evolutionary interpretations: Though the head of King Louis XVI was cut off by the revolutionaries (Foucault 1976, 117), in political theory the idea of the king has not been subject to political revolution; nor do we have to wait for Napoleonic administrative practice in order to bring about the changes. Rather, what we have to keep in mind is that, although functional and organizational systems build up massive transformations over the long run, they rarely come up with noticeable changes overnight. To a Luhmannian systems theory, the remarkable (r)evolution and enlightened reform of functionally differentiated systems are their synchronization of delegated and functionally differentiated competences—in this particular case, reinforced by Napoleon's dictatorship as organizational system and its aftermath.

The student movement of the 1960s offers a further, no less obvious example. Here, changes were brought about in the sphere of the semiauthoritarian conventions that then determined political, organizational, and educational life. Bureaucratic rules and routines were forced into more flexible structures. Yet what happened to them? Habermas certainly made an important contribution to the history of politics with his general postulate that rules and norms needed to be justified. One needs to understand this as part of a political practice. In those years,

Habermas indeed argued in public debates that justification *had* to have a say in a political order, for example, about organizational systems and their decisions. In retrospect, it is easy to see today that organizations have found a way out of formally bureaucratic structures, which they have succeeded in making more flexible, and that the justifiability of processes and procedures has become very widely contingent on linguistic or, in fact, media performance.

Yet, within or outside of the context of the student movement, it is questionable whether this "flexibilization" should be counted as a solution to the problem. Habermas's idea was to establish awareness of hypocritical forms of strategic communications (such as managerial soft talk about "mutual concern," "corporate spirit," and "organizational culture") and their distance from the much sharper conditions posed by what he calls "dialogue." Management communication is seldom ethical. It is strategic, or rather, it is a simple continuation of other means, of hierarchical privileges; more often than not, it is part of a strategy with the unique goal of extorting a "yes"—a "green light" for some course of action that a board of management wishes to push forward. In turn, Habermas's "free from domination" (*herrschaftsfrei*) clause proves its indispensability. Only dialogue operating under domination-free conditions makes a "no" answer to a managerial suggestion as possible as a "yes" answer.

One of the most urgent problems on Habermas's list in 1973 had been that of revising the then-current analyses of legitimacy in a way that responded to the advanced capitalism by then in structured social and economic realities. By the end of the 1960s, the traditional sources of legitimacy problems had been exhausted and replaced. In particular, the more trivial criticisms of capitalist repression, still faithful to critical Marxist or neo-Marxist ideas of contradictions between productive forces and relations of production, fell prey to the new internal developments of social theory. We are confronted with a different situation whenever the norms structuring a lifeworld are submitted to a cultural change of an intensity that prevents functional systems from maintaining stable relations required by life in such a floating world.

> Only when members of a society experience structural alterations as critical for sustained reproduction and feel their social identity

threatened can we speak of crisis. Disturbances of system integration endanger sustained reproduction only to the extent that social integration is at stake, that is, when the consensual foundations of normative structures are so much impaired that the society becomes anomic. (*Legitimation Crisis*, 3)

Underlying Habermas's idea that normative structures have "consensual foundations" is a certain notion of what is—or should be—called a "crisis." According to this idea, to speak of a crisis makes sense when a society's integrity, its *wholeness*, is at risk, when in other words social integration no longer performs its function. We may refer to Greece or Iceland[5] after 2008, Detroit since the 1980s, certainly to Iraq and Syria, and in particular to the pandemic-torn nations after 2020. Yet the questions remain: When and according to which criteria would the notion "crisis" apply and for what purpose? Certainly, anomie develops, but not in Iceland. Crisis is less than apocalypse and far more than needs for adjustment. The bottom line for Habermas is that "crisis" becomes a name for changed self-naming.

Note the distance from Luhmann. Luhmann downplays the notion of "crisis" to the point of ironically questioning what difference—if any—there is between "crisis" and "society" (Luhmann *Theory* 1997, 2:327).[6] Habermas, on the other hand, places the term *consensus* at the summit of modern society. Unlike Niklas Luhmann, and more like Carl Schmitt, Habermas *does* know of a "summit" of modern society, which he situates in the *political* institutions that are in charge of its overall condition of possibility—that is, its political integration, in Habermas's shorthand. The difference between the Macron-Merkel leadership of European political integration in summer 2020 and Trump's disintegration of the United States is remarkable. Thus, the continuing process of discursive exposure to acceptation or rejection, or in other words the permanent search for consensus (Biden), determines the entire normative structure that serves as the source of all legitimacy. This includes the question of if procedural change of leadership is accepted.

Yet we should be aware that whenever Habermas finds a need for consensus, it is only as to matters of cooperation, the word being understood in the sense of "coordinated coordination." Habermas does not postulate consensus on every societal matter. The "when" clause ("when the consensual foundations of normative structures are so impaired that society becomes anomic") of Habermas's most programmatic phrase is significant in this respect. The decisive point, stated by the first word of the sentence, "when," triggers Luhmann's question: "What happens then?" When and under which form do "anomia," "lack of motivation," "lack of meaning," and so on make a difference that makes a difference? Does "anomia" here only play the part of a negative foil, a triggering device for the moral idea of consensus? Is its mission that of bestowing a specific urgency upon the claim to consensus?

In contemporary Europe and North America, a broad conservative consensus finds support in the view that there is no consensus, and that refugees and immigration pose normative challenges that are comparable, if not worse, than any form of unemployment, stress, or despair among young people. Luhmann, at any rate, follows just the opposite strategy. For him, consensus and dissent are needed in the sense that every dissent *supposes* a consent. But dissent is more essential than consensus insofar as (1) it forcibly generates communication rather than merely providing for acceptation and (2) dissent between differentiated systems also entails the capacity to say "no" ("*Nein-sagen-können*") which is the obvious consequence of a society capable of both evolution and tolerance, as is the case of modern society, born out of the escape from the moralistic and anti-individualist claims of premodernity (cf. Habermas *Communicative Action* 2:74; TKH 2:115).

The essential aspect of the difference between Habermas's and Luhmann's analyses in 1973 is not, as is often thought, the fact that Habermas added lifeworld and intersubjectivity as forms of social integration to the systemic model. Luhmann himself had already operated with a distinction between functional systems and an environment (*Umwelt*) experienced (*erlebt*) as lifeworld. The difference consisted in the fact that Habermas, faithful perhaps to the early modern opposition of persons (or "bodies") and systems, was sticking to the idea that social systems were essentially steering systems.

To sum up, primarily, a *discourse theory of normative justification* had to be developed and then connected to the societal importance of justifiable norms that claim legitimacy. What is at stake here is the notion that a democratic critique of legitimacy is only possible in a functionally differentiated society that detaches democratic deliberation from functional reductions of complexities. Above all, issues of democratization of externalized foreign policy and world affairs need to be part of the analysis. Luhmann started this analysis (in *World Society* 1971), and Habermas entered this discussion, which was to become of increasing importance for him, at the end of the 1980s, for example, in *The Crisis of the European Union* (2012).

THE MODEL OF CRISIS TRANSITION—THE APPLICATIONS

Many may wonder why Habermas and Luhmann have to be so Goddamned complicated in their writing, each in their way. They remind so much of their German ancestors, Kant and Hegel. To many they seem almost impenetrable and life is too short to enter such elaborate and even sophisticated analysis. Yet if we enter into econometrics or elucidations in law, we are not much better off. Worse is the fact that econometric logarithms and sophisticated legal argumentation are often used to derange people's life and expectations in impenetrable ways and beyond any accountable idea about what is going on and why. Nevertheless, Habermas and Luhmann demonstrate that good reasons and sophisticated forms of problem-solving mechanisms are also embedded into our everyday lifeworld and our normal social institutions and communication forms. Accordingly, we should not bend ourselves too much when faced with instrumental rationality; there are other rationalities, and they are not less developed.

It was in response to this point, and in this situation, that Habermas established his dynamic of crisis transition (*Legitimation Crisis*, 40–41).

Since Habermas conceived systems as steering systems, he believed that they were able to cope with the problems of economy (or international politics or ecology): "The continuing tendency toward disturbance of capitalist growth can be administratively processed and transferred" (41). The serious question, however, was this: If, after everything, the administrative steering capacities are not up to the task, what happens then? How, for instance, would one have to imagine the spreading of the disturbance?

Habermas conceived of three additional conditions or factors that could imperil the presuppositions of a balanced society. In 1973, the possibility of ecological disaster had, for the first time, appeared on the horizon. Environmental politics and solutions became necessary and even urgent on the governmental agenda. Second, since the international balance was ready to blow up under the Cold War, the military-industrial complex had and has a huge capitalist interest in surplus value production and therefore in armament and international conflict. Somewhat closer to Habermas's problem of a "motivational crisis" was the third factor: the question of whether limits to growth can be found in the inner anthropological nature of modern human beings. "While organizational rationality spreads, cultural traditions are undermined and weakened" (47). Administrative reforms and needs for flexible working hours cannot proceed at a speed that neutralizes the increasing problems linked to the fact of raising children.

In order to take into account both organizational and cultural challenges, Habermas worked with a classification of possible crisis tendencies specific to systems that he summed up in the following table 7.1.

In addition, there is, for Habermas, typically a transition dynamic. A crisis often starts as an economic one (or an ecological one or a military one). As such, it might be open to successful resolution strategies—or not. What happens if it fails to be resolved, or if residues of the crisis enter the circuit of administrative procedures? Then the administrative systems should solve the remaining problems according to their rationalities. What, however, if the problems are not fully solved on this level either? Then crisis dynamics are displaced to the problems of identity and social integration. This is the point at which we encounter an example of what Habermas calls a legitimation crisis. Yet the point

TABLE 7.1 The Crisis Transition Process

Point of Origin	*System Crisis*	*Identity Crisis*
Economic System	Economic Crisis	-
Political System	Rationality Crisis	Legitimation Crisis
Sociocultural System	-	Motivation Crisis

is whether the problems, of which the notion of crisis is one, are resolved. For in the case that they are not, according to Habermas, a motivation crisis is in store. When crisis plus the lack of crisis-solving mechanisms reaches that level, the moment of a real crisis—a constitutional crisis—has arrived. It did arrive several times over, first in Iraq, and then in Syria. Certainly, the pandemic crisis in 2020 induced such a crisis scenario of transitions, from the pandemic coupling between environment and social systems to the health system and its organization system, to the research system, the economic system, the political system, the system of mass media, and the moral panic of motivational systems. This too includes the world society and its international systems (Harste 2020). Hence, a realistic account has to adapt to Luhmann's far more differentiated account of the complexity of structurally coupled systems.

How does Luhmann relate to Habermas's account of crisis? On the one hand, he increases the number of systems. From the tripartite system distribution that we find on Habermas's menu, featuring, as it does, the economic, the political, and the sociocultural systems, Luhmann takes away the sociocultural, which, owing to its inherent lack of functional specificity, could not be correctly described as a system in his sense; nevertheless, as early as *Trust* (1968) he referred to the risk of mistrust. Yet at the same time, he adds the functionally well-defined systems: the health system, research system, educational system, legal system, mass media system, art system, religious system, ecological systems, and others.[7] He later discussed problems of similar characteristics (under the category of "risk displacement"). Habermas, as previously shown in this chapter, investigated the same range of facts under the heading of the question of whether displacements are normatively (legally and ethically) acceptable.

According to Luhmann's systems theory, a full analysis of all the respects in which one of the functionally differentiated systems relied upon the services or performances of another, or "structural couplings," would involve a very high number of relationships—say, a hundred or hundreds, if one assumes the existence of ten or twenty functional systems (including their organizational support). On this point, Habermas selected only a few; however, in more substantial and extremely concentrated analyses, he involved a rather broad spectrum of interrelations. Basically, either

- the economic system does not produce the requisite quantity of consumable values; or
- the administrative system does not produce the requisite quantity of rational decisions; or
- the legitimation system does not provide the requisite quantity of generalized motivations; or
- the sociocultural system does not generate the requisite quantity of action-motivating meaning. (*Legitimation Crisis*, 49)

AN ECONOMIC CRISIS?

Habermas analyzed the economic system with the most recent Marxist theories available in the early 1970s. Today, Thomas Piketty's *Capital in the Twenty-First Century* (2013) and *Capital and Ideology* (2020) would probably be the reference for Habermas's concern about inequalities and imbalanced economic systems. Yet, Luhmann later on developed his own systems theory of economy, labor, capital, money, finance, and credit (in *Wirtschaft* 1988). The conclusion Luhmann made in this respect (published as "Limits of Steering" 1997) succeeded in unleashing the much-discussed thesis of the impossibility of guaranteed steering across the difference between two functional systems. A system can control itself by its own means, yet it cannot control the communicative distinctions that operate in another system and another medium with forms other than its own. Political economy, the term understood as a general science of how to handle a system in charge of controlling the self-reproduction of a society, does not open doors to a modern political control of economy. Rather, political economy is about a difference displayed between two systems. Here, Luhmann would probably agree with Foucault's claim in *Naissance de la biopolitique* (2004) that politics is constituted by that difference between traditional political power and society/population, yet Luhmann's thesis is much sharper.

Luhmann's younger colleagues Dirk Baecker (1991), Michael Hutter (1993), Elena Esposito (2011), and John Paterson (2013) later pushed systems analyses further, in a way that in particular allowed them to especially take up the former line, from Marx to Weber and Simmel's *Philosophy of Money* (1900), that money and credit are about time, about handling time, and about synchronization and synchronizing the present trade with future possibilities in the recently added medium of communication. Banks trade with trust and time in the medium of communication. This conception allows Luhmann's pupils to study the extreme growth of derivatives and the bubble economy that resulted in the credit crisis starting in 2008. Elena Esposito's *The Future of Futures* (2011) represents perhaps the most advanced piece in this series.

AN ADMINISTRATIVE CRISIS?

The next step in the transition mechanism relates to the administrative rationality necessary to mitigate what is known as the boom-bust cycle of capitalism. Unemployment, pensions, health problems, education, and so on all become more difficult to finance in times of crises; the point of a crisis-solving economy, if one looks at it in a Keynesian way, is to not fear increases in expenditures.

Administrative development has to be legitimized just like taxes on public investments. This happens under the threat of a deficit in legitimacy if this condition of administrative rationality is not satisfied. The paradox lies in the simple fact, repeatedly observed by Luhmann, that governments must intervene yet must also avoid interventions; in fact, governments must intervene in order to avoid intervention. This is not a hopelessly insoluble contradiction; it is the paradox that ensues from the fact that governments can do both. They can declare interventions in principle, and suspend them for the time being. Or intervene now, and not later.

However, unemployment may prove impossible to alleviate, schools may prove incapable of being improved, hospitals may prove incapable of performing better when simultaneously, for example, lifestyle-related diseases such as obesity, diabetes, or stress-induced pathologies spread or are on the rise. There is such a thing as a tendency for governments to become overloaded with demands and tasks—a risk that David Easton was aware of as early as 1965 and that seems to be a common denominator for all systems analyses, including Luhmann's.

Habermas is aware of this and goes along with its claim. He explains that "precisely this normality becomes problematic to the extent that the state lays claim to the role of a responsible planning authority that those affected can burden with their losses and they can confront with demands for compensation and prevention" (*Legitimation Crisis*, 65). Luhmann (in *Welfare* 1981) deepens a similar argument discussing the singular problem of "compensations-for-compensations." Without going into the temporal problematic, Habermas does not buy Luhmann's reference to time as a crisis-avoidance strategy that can alleviate contradictions and turn them into paradoxes: "These problems can become so concentrated that in the end even recourse to the resource of time no longer offers a way out" (*Legitimation Crisis*, 65). However, Luhmann had a major empirical point when, some years later, he unfolded all implications of the everyday saying that "time can solve every problem" into a sophisticated theory of temporal risks. A government just as well as an opposition may sell hopes or implement programs as if they were functional equivalents (*Risk* 1991, chap. 7). To Habermas, the "rationality deficit of an overloaded administration" does not in itself dissolve the possibilities of an incrementalism (*Legitimation Crisis*, 65); in this sense, Habermas is a leftist social-democratic reformist, not an advocate for revolution. Yet there may be limits to compromises caused by more universalist claims for justification.

According to Habermas's Marxism-inspired analysis from 1973, economic parameters exert a "dominating" effect over all the others. If the economy can in fact be described as the dominant function system according to Luhmann's account as well, this is not because of a superior power in its hand. The opposite is the case. It is because of its superior powerlessness: not because it would "dominate" (that is, rule or impose its will on) the others, but—astonishingly enough—because it generates the highest "failure rate" or "quota of carelessness [*Versagensquote*]" (Luhmann *Theory* 1997, 769; 2013, 104). Other systems can threaten to stall as well (one might think of religion or law); and surely the quota of failures is impressive for the history of capitalism as a whole. The *problematique* of war as a social system also comes up at this point since war by definition is the most careless system (Harste 2004, 2016b).

In spring 2020, the pandemic crisis displayed how the health system, quite surprisingly, discharged the economic system to a secondary position, yet because of the moral solidarity normatively held to defend the lives of people who were the unproductive old and the unhealthy. In most countries, this happened because the organization of hospitals was not fit to take care of the overloaded system of treatment with respiration machines and even face masks. This organization failure was less obvious in Germany, Norway, and Finland than in United States, United Kingdom, Italy, Spain, and France.

An important common point between Habermas and Luhmann lies in the fact that both welcome the efforts to "compromise" (Habermas) or "compatibilize" (Luhmann) the divergent requirements involved in the enterprise of modern society, by means of administrative or organizational practices. "The possibility that the administrative system might open a compromise between claims that would allow a sufficient amount of organizational rationality cannot be excluded from the start on logical grounds" (*Legitimation Crisis*, 64). Organizational systems coordinate functional systems and establish structural couplings and compromises between competing risks and diverging or conflicting functional systems. Organizational systems "absorb contingencies," as Luhmann says in a reference to Herbert Simon and James March's *Organizations*.[8]

The temptation, for Luhmann, or for a Luhmannian thinker today, might be that of saying: "elementary, my dear Watson." First point: Complex organizational systems are simply not constituted as machines to be piloted by first-order decisions or "commands," according to some ruling decision-maker's sovereign will. Organizational systems coordinate and communicate in the medium of coded decisions, each of which is always occasioned by a specific "situation" and each of which contributes to the creation of further such "situations" and, thereby, to further such decisions. Power in organizational systems emerges because of delegation, and delegation is always relinquished control (*Folgen* 1964, 268ff.). This is why Luhmann, contrary to what the young Chris Thornhill claimed (2000, 205ff.), is indeed in the position opposite to Carl Schmitt's decisionism, though there is a range of superficial similarities. There is no unity of decision, only difference. Decentralization is the condition of centralization, not the other way around.

Second, organizational systems neither exhaust nor control functional systems. Schools are not education, university organization is not research, churches are not religion, galleries and theatres are not art, the military is not war. This is why, in a complex and functionally differentiated society, such as the one in which you are probably reading these lines, "steering" is an inappropriate concept and an inadequate story, which becomes possible when the distance between the observer and the observed is recognized as founding an asymmetrical and irreversible difference.

LEGITIMATION CRISIS AS POLITICAL CRISIS?

On this topic, Luhmann's first answer to Habermas seems to be his theory about power in the book *Power* (1975), yet for the ten years following publication of the book, Luhmann was at work trying to further improve his theory in the context of risks and paradoxes inherent in modern society. In 1991 (in *Ende*), he stated that the double idea of critique and crisis, which underlies the conceptions of the era he calls "bourgeois," should be dismissed in favor of a conception based upon paradoxes, risks, and second-order observation. In these years, Luhmann's popularity in European social research began to surpass Habermas's—despite a range of attempts to avoid this, especially Gerhard Wagner's (1997) response to Luhmann's "At the End of Critical Sociology" (*Ende* 1991) and Max Miller's article "Intersystemic Discourse and Co-Ordinated Dissent: A Critique of Luhmann's Ecological Communication" (1994). Nevertheless, for us, instead of discussing these debates, it is more fruitful to return to Habermas's theory of crisis transition, since several themes there are still unresolved, and only resolving these themes will allow us to leave the level of what Habermas called "system integration" and to enter the level of "social integration."

If organizational reforms by themselves cannot solve crises in the economic system—or the health system—then the political system will be burdened with claims for a change of laws and decisions: higher or lower taxes, transfer of responsibilities, universal health organization, better welfare, lower education costs, and so on. Political systems are often overburdened with contradictory claims such as lower taxes and better welfare systems. Hence, Luhmann states than political systems paradoxically decide to solve the problems—yet at a later moment. The classical logical criterion that logic forbids self-contradiction does not hold and turns into a paradox when time is involved and it is decided to establish better health care, yet mainly to do it later. This is why debt and credit often become solutions: that is, to offer more in the present situation—and to postpone payments of debts, money that the state via national banks borrowed to pay and then pay back with inflated repayments.

In order to approach legitimation crisis and motivation crisis, Habermas first passed through the Marxian problem of the form of abstract commodities, as analyzed in the first chapters in Marx's *Capital*. Commodification, spanning the entire gamut of labor for use-value to labor for commodity-value (and further configurations), offers the current answer to the quest of system integration, in both economic and strategic terms, which tends to dominate increasing parts of our everyday life. According to this conception, each and every aspect of life includes a vocation to undergo a strategic rationality. Strategic rationality has received a discursive form in management culture with discourses about flexibility, vision, corporate culture and identity, motivation, sense-making, and broader forms of procurements of management communication. In Luhmann's temporal terms, the solution is to promise to do better in the future. Anyway present values are inflated, if not forgotten, in the future and the solution is—by means of institutionalized systemic differentiation—to create trust in futures. Habermas's claim, however, is that "There is no administrative production of meaning. Commercial production and administrative planning of symbols exhausts the normative force of counterfactual validity claims. The procurement of legitimation is self-defeating as soon as the mode of procurement is seen through. Cultural traditions have their own, vulnerable, conditions of reproduction" (*Legitimation Crisis*, 70). The problem for Habermas stems precisely from the fact that private life is increasingly subjected to politicized public administration and has to defend arrangements intervening in the hermeneutics of understanding daily life experiences about anything from socialization in schools, to families, to elders and relations between parents and children. Cultural socialization into everyday life is transformed into a productive life that will serve as an input to an economic system that would otherwise experience imbalances.

A MOTIVATIONAL CRISIS?

For Habermas in 1973, his own allegation that capitalist cyclical fluctuations can lead to crisis is ultimately a question of motivational developments in modern social life. What does a comparison with Luhmann yield on this precise point? In *Trust* (1968) Luhmann makes a more sociological (and less psychological) suggestion than that of his "motivation"-riven colleague Habermas. The study concerns an abstract trust, just enough to enable the everyday operations of banks and firms, public administration, and the political reproduction of the conditions of legitimacy in whose absence those systems cannot either come into being or remain in being. Nothing more or less than such abstractions is the condition of modern society. If we go back to Habermas's exposition in *The Structural Transformation of the Public Sphere* from 1962, we can see what takes up the role of trust in his account—namely, a number of basic modern life conditions embedded in the civil society of bourgeois privatized families and a privatized economy, cultural taste, and the aggregation of private yet standardized and generally accepted values. The response to such modern conditions is not communitarianism, not for Habermas and certainly not for Luhmann.

Most prominently, these conditions are outlined in the chapter on motivation crisis in Habermas's *Legitimation Crisis*. They include some fundamentally middle-of-the-road positions. In short, some form of acceptance and passivity is the condition for crisis avoidance. All of this is obviously directly contrary to the student movement mentality of the 1970s, which determined the point of view from which *Legitimation Crisis* is written, which suggested rather that every norm was contested. "The times they are a-changin," in Bob Dylan's words. Since then, just about everything has changed, yet nothing has been transformed in Western modernity. One who saw coming what these orientations were going to lead to was Luhmann. In his previously discussed article "Complexity and Democracy," he wrote with painful accuracy: "almost everything could be possible, and I can change almost nothing" (*Komplexität* 1969, 44; quoted in Habermas *Legitimation Crisis*, 131). To Habermas, "this sentence expresses Luhmann's fundamental experience." Today, this is clearly developed in their common German successor sociologist Hartmut Rosa's *Social Acceleration* (2005/2015). Habermas, in his own view, aims to participate and transform; Luhmann on the contrary, to observe; this is not to be passive, but to keep distance. The effective relationship must of course be a bit more complex, as can be seen from the fact that participation *presupposes* observation (and observation *presupposes* participation).

Habermas claimed that genuinely bourgeois ideologies, which live only from their own substance, cannot

- offer support to interpretations that overcome contingency in the face of the basic risks of existence (guilt, sickness, death),
- satisfy individual needs for wholeness [*Heilsbedürfnisse*],
- provide the possibility for human relations with a (fundamentally objectivated) nature, i.e. with either outer nature or one's own body,
- permit intuitive access to relations of solidarity within groups or between individuals;
- allow an effective political ethic in political and social life, accommodating an objectivistic self-interpretation of acting subjects. (*Legitimation Crisis*, 78)

Favored by an age of rather incomparable wealth, the so-called "economic miracle" of the post–World War II decades in the Bundesrepublik during the third quarter of the twentieth century, the reaction of younger generations was directed at a different target. It was directed precisely at the opportunism of the older German generations, those who had allowed the National Socialist regime access to power, lived through it, as if it were "innocent," and were now "trying to forget and to look forward, rather than backward." To the U.S. ex-serviceman returning from Vietnam, haunted by posttraumatic stress disorder (PTSD), no reconciliation was open, in a society that neglected all forms of suffering and discomfort under the weight of its standardized norms and its dutiful pursuit of happiness. It gives rise to a will to leave behind all that is nice, neat, or simply formal. The world of the university and the world of art refuse to merely mirror, reprocess, and reproduce the residuals of the economic and political systems. They became militant, radical sites of development of antiestablishment languages. Yet today, facing Trump's populism, they may favor another more constitutional establishment. A rationalized form of establishment becomes popular, and the question is what Habermas and Luhmann have to offer to this form of problem-solving.

A NORMATIVE RECONSTRUCTION?

Habermas saw himself confronted, in the situation between 1960 and 1970, with the question of how, and for how long, the politico-economic compromise that he sees building up all around him can last. He starts with an analysis of capitalism and its conditions, and he arrives at a sociological inquiry into individual motivations for action and their sustainability. Habermas points out that the popular culture of individual egoism typical of the Germany that has been economically successful since at least 1960 is a successor of the conformist norms, which puts itself in the position of the normative traditions. In addition, facts become subject to strategic communication and to rhetorical manipulation as fake or fictive facts, or what Habermas already in 1962 called "faction."

In Habermas's version, the core analysis revolves around a reality that is easy to spot in Luhmann as well, if under slightly different names, for instance, in his later booklet *The Reality of Mass-Media* from 1996. In Luhmann's analysis, the social systems, in terms of which he analyzes modern society, are *operatively closed*. The ensuing and turbulently increasing emergence of insides and outsides, of mutually inaccessible zones and levels, where, only a few generations earlier, society was experienced as a continuum, has introduced a pattern of hurdles in the midst of humankind's universal accessibility to itself. Modern society according to Luhmann is no longer master in its own house. This is so for two reasons: (a) Its structure is determined by an uncountable and ever-increasing number of inside/outside or system/environment borders rather than encompassing integrity or "wholeness." And (b), there is no space for "mastery" left in it: there is no "ruling" top or center in it; if anything, it is not power but powerlessness, not "rule" but "crisis," that enables a system to impose its imperatives. In his last work, Luhmann formulates: "operative closure brings disturbance, and disturbance brings operational closure" (*Theory* 1997, 770; 2013 2, 105). He is led to diagnose that in modern times, especially recent modern times, "growing complexity resulted in control problems that required that the alteration of social norms be speeded up beyond the tempo intrinsic to the nature-like cultural traditions" (Habermas *Legitimation Crisis*, 86). Too much change, at a pace that cannot but provoke traumatisms of upheaval.

If there are no moral limits to growth, the cultural reproduction and development of norms set close limits to the administrative rationalities that determine law reforms.

Habermas's decisive point is that "the validity of *all* norms is tied to discursive will-formation" (*Legitimation Crisis*, 87). With this conception in 1973, Habermas describes legal evolution according to a logic that is *not* the logics of systems evolution. Habermas does not consider the problem of moral reasoning as if he with it understands society's struggle of how to get over the crisis, but as a problem that is first of all mediatized by economy (or war) to administration and politics through the medium of law, *before* it actually reaches the level of moral reasoning. For Habermas in 1973, law and its development depend entirely on moral reasoning—a position he completely changed in the 1980s.

WAS THERE A LEGITIMATION CRISIS?

In 1973, Habermas, however, did not approach his topic on the basis of the preconception that a crisis will, let alone must follow. Economic fluctuations could, first of all, be absorbed by administration, passivity, and motivational adjustments. If this failed, consumerism could eventually alleviate disappointed expectations to a sufficient level. Mind that on this particular point, Habermas's prediction was unusually successful. For this is exactly what happened over the next fifty years. This, however, became a courtesy to massive commodity offers from Southeast Asia. These articles were cheap enough for the economic system to continue and reproduce its promises, and this even in front of unequal distribution. It is obvious that inequality empirically increased, especially in Great Britain and the United States. Yet, thanks to cheap commodities imported mostly from the Southeast, the miracle accomplished that the lower-salaried received cheap-enough commodities in large-enough quantity for the structural coupling between the economic system, the political system, and the motivational system not to be exposed to dissatisfaction, failing entitlements, and an immediate crisis cycle. Residual dissatisfaction existed, but revealed itself to be manageable through the usual means of passivity, spectacular reform, and procrastination.

Gunther Teubner stated 2006, before the crisis of 2008, that in *Legitimation Crisis*

> Habermas diagnosed a conspicuous trend in the crisis of late capitalism: explosive social conflicts have been moved from the private markets to the welfare state institutions. Today we can observe a reversal of this trend: explosive political conflicts that were formerly absorbed within the diverse regimes of the welfare state do not vanish after privatization; rather, after the take-over by the market, these conflicting energies move back from welfare state institutions to private markets and re-emerge there in new forms. It is now the new private regimes of governance that have to cope with them, but they cannot be resolved by market mechanisms. As a result, privatized activities will be driven into a new politicization. (2006, 185)

Today, the crisis transition process exposed in table 7.1 is reversed: Private motivations are in crisis, but they are reconciled by political outsourcing to free markets, as if they solve problems of anomie, alienation, and identity. As result, Southeast Asia came to power, and political systems have to negotiate or fight about whose consumers they prefer to deal with.

MOTIVATION CRISIS AS COMMUNICATION CRISIS

In the first, conceptual part of *Legitimation Crisis*, Habermas elaborated a neo-Marxist conception of economic conflicts between a depoliticized labor market system and its unspoken power relations. This discussion was, more than other parts of Habermas's analysis, embedded in the popular debates of the time. Yet, there was another point in his conception that was at least equally central. This is the idea that conflict structures (between motivations in the labor movements and the crisis cycle of capitalism) are not about hidden structures, but about conflicts that are expressed and take place in forms of communications. The point here is that only linguistic sentences, not, for instance, things, images, drives, or even motives, can be subject to logical contradiction.

Habermas, who was very conscious of this, nonetheless insisted that the contradiction "realized" in the space of the sentences should be transformed in a pragmatic analysis of propositions and normative utterances that could pronounce capitalist expectations and normative claims by citizens. Here, a key to the situation is offered by the observation that only participants who venture an utterance can become able to speak about, and discover, contradictions in sentences that are claimed to be valid by the political power and suffused discourse of an administration.

Habermas's contention is that individual motives need to be taken as valid whenever they occur in speech acts that can question or contest communications by governmental agencies. Normative statements of any sort, however, especially when they are offering a proposition about what to propose in cooperation and coordination, cannot avoid claiming (and thus also "discursively redeeming") the motives behind utterances in order to determine their weight and defensibility. In that sense, all utterances about what other people should do "bind" motivations, thereby nominating them as candidates to further discursive examination, checking to what extent the principles underlying them can be consensually justified. The central point of this central argument of Habermas is that thoughts and suggestions about coordination and cooperation cannot follow simple subjective wishes: they have to obey norms that in principle can be universalized and made valid for others. In our context, the decisive point here is that Habermas cannot accept the sharp distinction established by Luhmann between societal communication and the sphere of consciousness—individual experience, thoughts, and feelings. Communicated motives—which obviously send their roots deep down into consciousness, and are in no way compatible with a neat separation in systems of the psyche and systems of society—allow for a limitation for valid thoughts about society. That such particularistic and egoistic opinions do exist does not create doubt. However, Habermas's suggestion goes further than this. His suggestion is civilizational: A procedure of normative filtering of publicly held motives should perfect democratic politics. The realm of society, via its central agency, the political system, is brought into position to undergo a never-ending process of civilized learning.

DEMOCRACY AND COMPLEXITY

Habermas finally ended *Legitimation Crisis* with a ten-page discussion on Luhmann and the theme "Democracy and Complexity." Luhmann could not accept, as an adequate account of systems theory, Habermas's description of the systems theory of law, least of all his allegation of a theory of systems endowed with the capacity of steering. Habermas repeatedly maintained that Luhmann's systems theory was an—inadequate—theory of steering, planning, and control (*Legitimation Crisis*, 130, 131, 132). Habermas writes about "Luhmann's assumption of an (in principle) unlimited extension of administrative steering" (138); "in his opinion ... only steering capacity decides the level of development of a society" (139). Yet, there is no evidence of such an allegation in Luhmann's writings. On the contrary! In the book with the (somehow ironical!) title *Political Planning* (*Planung* 1971, 69), Luhmann even declares the causal and hierarchical control idea "theoretically ruined."

There is no denying that such a misapprehension is in clear violation of the ambitious standards of Habermas's own suggestion for the procedural conditions of claims to validity and the informal dialogic tribunal that has vocation to decide over them. Habermas entrusted a large part of his critique of Luhmann upon the erroneous presupposition that Luhmann's systems theory was all about an exaggerated optimism that systems can "control" their environment. Moreover, the misinterpretation that systems theory is mainly devoted to "steering" has constituted a decisive obstacle to the learning process that would finally, at least outside Germany, Italy, Scandinavia, and more recently Great Britain, Chile, Brazil, and perhaps even China, succeed in making Luhmannian systems theory part of the social-scientific canon. The fact is that Luhmann not only did not suggest a theory of the sort: starting from the most fundamental conceptual level, his work is a discussion of the reasons why the old-European assumptions of governability and rule can no longer be relied on. He reacted to Habermas's mistaken criticism with a threefold analysis: *Kontingenz und Recht* from 1974; *Power* from 1975, and *Function der Religion* from 1977. In their wake, he published, in addition, a range of studies on the impossibility of educational steering and, finally, a number of smaller articles and the booklet *Political Theory of the Welfare System*—following the same theme of overstated steering optimism through the regions of post–World War II political theory. None of these is solely answers to Habermas's allegations. Rather, I refer to them because they throw a clear light on Luhmann's position and exclude many misunderstandings. Luhmann's idea of self-steering is developed in 1972 in the following way:

> The administration's possession of its own structure means that it has its own possibilities, which need not be identical with the expectation of the environment; and non-identity with the environment even at the level of possibilities gives the opportunity for self-steering. At the same time, with this separation, even of the constitution of possibilities, the risk must be assumed that the problems that the political system solves are not the problems of society.... Only the administration itself can investigate itself. (Luhmann *Politikbegriffe* 1972, 224; quoted by Habermas *Legitimation Crisis*, 135–36)

Habermas, who quotes the passage in *Legitimation Crisis*, claims that here we touch the "end of the individual" doctrine in its Luhmannian form. However, Luhmann once again is misunderstood if one supposes that his heroes include "the individual" or "the subject." He asks, "The subject is not object, so what is it doing in our theories?" (*Differentiation* 1982, 325). The argument is that Luhmann aims to establish a sharp distinction between the subjectivity of individual experience (thought, feelings) and—as did Frankfurt School father Adorno—a nonidentical communicative society in which acts are embedded. This, of course, implies some form of societal autonomy and correspondingly some form of emancipated individual autonomy of the psychic system. The individual cannot entirely be imagined as subject to, or submitted to, a social system.

In a nutshell, this summarizes the results of a number of Luhmann's elaborations on legitimacy risks and paradoxes in the following years. Basically, Habermas maintains that individual participation in political systems is the criterion and fundamental requirement that link political legitimacy to individual motivation. Individual consciousness is then, eventually, a functional necessity for societal systems.

LUHMANN'S THEORY OF CONFLICT, RISKS, AND DISSENT

POWER AS COMMUNICATION

In the book *Power* (1975), Luhmann follows the analytics of communication, pointing out that the social dimension needs time, as communication cannot communicate about every matter in one sole moment. Hence, the complexities of communication have to be reduced in order to produce meaning. Reductions, accordingly, have to select among communications in dimensions that can be material, social, and temporal. These selections code whatever is relevant for communication in a binary schematic difference from what is excluded. Power is such a binary code and distinguishes the powerful from the powerless.

This triple scheme of material, social, and temporal dimensions he eventually continued to follow in his seminal opus magnum *Theory of Society* (1997). There he distinguished power as a form of communication, a form developed in evolution, and a form developed due to differentiation. Those three aspects were maintained as the overall framework for theory exposition.

In *Power*, Luhmann's theory finally turned fully into a theory of communication systems. Furthermore, he established his code theory of binary distinctions. This theory, in that respect, seems very close to Michel Foucault's genealogy of power and to Pierre Bourdieu's field theory published the same years. Yet Luhmann only made few references to them, and none at all in *Power*. Since Bourdieu has selected the impact of symbolic practice on the habitus of individuals as his topic, it would seem that he was indeed less capable than Habermas of distinguishing between the thought and taste of psychic systems and those of communicative practice. Closer come Foucault's distinctions between a genealogy of discourses and what such discourses communicated about individuals. Keep in mind that, different from Foucault, Luhmann did not conceptualize power as a self-referential and self-descriptive system of communication. A radical, or Nietzschean, interpretation of power would suggest that power *has the power* to define itself and communicate about its own forms, codes, and differentiations. Luhmann could not go that far before his theory of self-reference was fully elaborated. Yet, "the conditions for forming a dichotomy between 'ruling conditions' and 'critique' are part of the theory itself. This treats such disjunctions as elements of a communication code and asks about their genetic preconditions, their functions, their results, their complementary mechanisms, their chances of development" (*Power* 1975, 118). Somewhat more to Habermas's possible irritation Luhmann added that "such a theory can also be characterized, as Gouldner would have it, as moralistic and conservative, if one assumes that it conforms with the characteristics it has unearthed" (118).

According to Luhmann, power is basically a symbolically generalized medium of communication. Hence, physical violence is merely a very reduced and inflated form of power, whose application is generally limited to situations, in which threats and symbolically coded remarks fail to deliver the expected goods. Power is improbable and therefore in need of codifications and differentiations in order to unfold any effect. Power is in this sense a speech act; it is located in communicative and symbolic realities. Like money, truth, and love, power can communicate about power and thereby establish more power. Power leads to power; power empowers power, while lack of power excludes the possibility of using power, with many consequences for organizational power and persons in power. Power also organizes itself in hierarchies, thus giving rise to delegation and differentiation (Harste 2017).

One could think that Luhmann arrives a bit too fast at the paradoxes of delegation and differentiation. His insights on these points are revealing: First, power is only in power to the extent that power can be delegated and therefore be bracketed to the extent of dissolving itself in decisions about decisions. Second, power needs differentiation between organization, law, politics, military violence, mass media, economy, and so on. If power is characterized by its tendency to communicate about itself, to define itself, and to describe itself, then theories of power are already historically and obviously there to be found, and their semantics can be visible or invisible. Luhmann enters late into the discussions about the invisibility and secrecy of power; yet *Politics as a Social System* (2000), his seminal book on the matter, edited only after his death, did not really resolve the problem of the self-description of power and its history, a problem whose roots bring us back to twelfth-century Europe (Quillet 1972).

Since Luhmann's primary aim is to focus on power as a site of the differentiation between code and function, he apparently does not share the radical criticism and moral dismissal of power in favor of argumentative discourses led by Habermas:

> I differ from much current opinion in seeing the problem of legitimacy neither as one of establishing a sufficient (even a logically valid) *argumentation* for the power-code nor solely as *factually accepting* it on the basis of a mixture of consensus and force, but as structure and processes which can control it as it becomes contingent. Argumentation and acceptance are only aspects of this general problem of contingency control. (*Power* 1975, 145)

The most original contribution of Luhmann's theory of power consists in the display of the idea of temporalized power. Power is to synchronize. Whereas Habermas focuses on the social dimension of power as coordination and cooperation, Luhmann develops a theory of power as a communicative form that allows the handling of synchronicity and actualization, the postponing of decisions, and, above all, coping with the copresence of different functional systems at the same time. Simultaneity allows for higher complexity: "Here too, symptoms of overloading become evident. Tempo, synchronization, and timeliness become problems in the exercise of power and distort its preferences." The problem is "control[ling] the synchronization" (163).

This brings us to Luhmann's next level of theoretical elaboration, exposed as the self-reference in political systems.

THE OVERLOADED POLITICAL SYSTEM

Between 1979 and 1981, Luhmann wrote a series of introductory analyses on political systems and self-referentiality. As Luhmann's most incisive and certainly most conflictual suggestions about how social thought about modern society is related to his conceptions of politics, we shall take a bit more time for this particular topic.

Political systems, Luhmann claimed, are systems in charge of doubling or copying politics into themselves. Operating with a differentiation between rulers and the ruled, the political system "buys itself into" this same differentiation, thereby marking itself out within functional differentiation at large. Over the long term, political systems distinguish political professionals ("rulers") on the inside from political subjects or consumers ("ruled") on the outside. However, more importantly than this is the fact that they distinguish themselves over the short term according to a political code that differentiates the political professionals, those on the inside, into government and opposition.

However, of course, functionally differentiated social systems according to Niklas Luhmann have a specific feature: they include their outside—in other words, those we have just called the consumers of subjects of politics are still part of the political system. This is why the political system combines (a) politics in the strict sense, (b) the public, and (c) its own administration. Politics in the strict sense determines: it provides the political system at large with its identity as self-reference. And this self-determination receives its code by the differentiation into government and opposition within the broader differentiation of rulers and ruled. However, the two other components—that which is communicated within the larger public, and that which is subject to a complex organizational system of administrative decisions about decisions—are, if less manifest and especially less manifestly political, equally indispensable for the continuation of the political system.

On the one hand, the state of the political system constitutes and addresses. This most currently is referred to simply as a capacity of "the state." The state happens incidentally to be the strange monopoly that is thereby awarded to the political system, as if there were not also a state of the economy, science, of the defense forces, of religion, and so on. Yet it is the estate of the political system that makes the political system stable and provides it with an address, whenever it has to refer to itself, to describe itself, and so on. It is only this stabilization of the "state" (of politics!) that has made it possible for the political system to continue, subject to permanent short-term variations or oscillations between government and opposition. And it is only the public, as the constructive collective decision-maker over politics, that provides the internal distribution of roles with the required legitimacy. Through the elements of its threefold structure, the political system can make sure that its variations correspond synchronically to the conditions in society.

There, however, is an illusion that imperils the political system at large, and that Luhmann has drawn attention to since his first encounter with Habermas. The state of the political system has been universally understood to be a territorially defined so-called "nation-state." Luhmann's influential analysis of "world society" (1971) exposes this choice as unfounded or as founded only upon the contingent conditions that have historically presided only over a few formative years and centuries of modern society. The effective splitting-up of humanity into territorially divided parcels, each of which is complete with its political order, sovereignty, government, procedures, and so on, seems to be inadequate in an age in which political systems are claimed to be responsible for what happens at a world-society level and are thereby easily overloaded with demands (*Politik* 2000, 222, 334). In fact, states copy from one another: How could they then be sovereign? Their organizations use similar reforms, innovations, decisions, and programs—and they always have done so.

A second form of overload is due to the demand that political systems with their decisions about forms of welfare programs should compensate for societal risks. Luhmann's point here is neither about encouraging nor about discouraging such risk-compensating decisions. That citizens' rights and political rights are taken to entail social rights is for Luhmann part of the situation to be analyzed—including the political tendencies involved there. Generally, such "compensatory" motivations are not, from Luhmann's point of view, something that should be discredited. Rather, the problem is at a later point down the pipeline: it is the problem of how to compensate for such compensations. Damage control can spread unintended effects—these have to be dealt with (and compensated) separately.

Political systems claim that they can determine control, decisions, delegations, coordination. This is then the third form of an excess, or overload, of the system by what is attributed to them. This differentiation of the political systems is due to the fact that self-determination is conditioned by the self-reference of law, the closure of complex organizational systems, i.e., taken together the rule of law or separation of powers in legislative, judiciary, and executive powers—and the self-reference of mass media, economy, education, research, war, art, health, and so on. The suggestions for political systems are that they can make authoritative collective decisions to bind the whole of society, but according to Luhmann, the whole is not, as Aristotle believed, more than the sum of its parts. For Luhmann (*Differentiation* 1982, 238), the whole is less than the sum of its parts—in other words, making decisions for the whole exposes the system to far more contingency than making decisions for the system itself. Each subsystem has a picture of itself and of its relations to every other ingredient of its societal environment. Therefore, each subsystem establishes a total description on its own account: every communication code and even code time, as if the political system was sovereign; yet this famous classical term only means that it establishes a self-reference to itself.

If God was believed to create the world (and in only seven days), the political system cannot replace such an imaginary (Castoriadis 1975; Taylor 2007). In its current shape, the political system seems to occupy the "top" or the "center" of a social pyramid—but society is no longer formed according to center and periphery or according to top and ground. In this sense, the political system seems to have simply continued the role of the sovereign prince, at the price of putting the sovereign people in his place and putting the feedback cycle with public participation as input and administration as output instead of monarchical legitimacy. Yet, nothing could fit less well to current trends and realities than such a cryptoconservative model. Habermas and especially Luhmann were the first to explain what it meant in political theory. Habermas (in *Unübersichtlichkeit* 1985, 141–66) described the intransparency of corporatist and neocorporatist governance embedded into a comitology of organs, in which dedifferentiated communication codes and validity claims found their ways. In the 1970s such descriptions became common knowledge in Western political science (Heisler 1974).

All together, thus, overload is the fact that the political system is differentiated territorially and organized in more or less functioning states, even in collapsed states such as Syria, Somalia, or Iraq and Afghanistan. This does not fit into the world society. In the case of the ecological world order in which all of society and all societal communication take place, it is hopeless to isolate ecological awareness into an isolated political system. Donald Trump's vision of ecological sovereignty is simply an obsolete dream outside any social or natural reality. A great deal of Luhmann's adherents, such as Rudolf Stichweh (2000), Mathias Albert (2000, 2016; Albert, Kessler, and Stetter 2008), Gunther Teubner (2006), and Stephen Stetter (2007), have argued for still more advanced analyses about such a world society. These have been adopted by Hauke Brunkhorst, who in *Legitimacy Crises* (2012) places his analyses in between Luhmann's observation of world society and Habermas's more normative challenges about what to do about it (*Faltering* 2009, 109–30; *European* 2012). Fragmentation and collisions in international law may rule (Koskenniemi 2006b; Teubner/Fischer-Lascano 2007). In fact, among the earliest preparations to the COP 21 Paris Agreement rejected by Trump in May 2017, and readopted by Biden in 2021, was a combination of Luhmann's analysis of risky systems in a world society and Habermas's deliberative ideas of international diplomacy, led by French diplomats and headed by the former EU Commissar president Jacques Delors: The differentiation of functional systems leads to dissent; the organizational system of diplomacy strives for consensus; yet the informal interaction systems may obtain some dialogue and discursive argumentation (Harste 1997).

ECOLOGICAL COMMUNICATION AND THE BLIND SPOTS OF SYSTEMS

Connected to the neocorporatist problematic is the ecological one. Luhmann opened it up shortly after the publication of *Social Systems* in 1984. He took the consequence of its vision of the sharp distinction between system and environment and displayed its idea in terms of ecology. There is an astonishing coincidence here, in relation to the term *environment*. What have social systems to do with environments? Differentiated systems such as law, economy, politics, science, religion, and the like are defined as systems in reference to their environment. Can systems observe their own limitations and observe themselves? And what happens when the environment can only be observed by systems, considering their own environments, and not on "the" environment's own premises? In Immanuel Kant we find the expression "the world in itself" ("Welt an sich")—is there today anything that would correspond to the idea of an "environment in itself"? We do not communicate with viruses, but about viruses. Systems have so-called tipping points in their resonance with environments; a major subject to investigate is how tipping points in nature's environmental systems are structurally coupled with tipping points in social systems. The pandemic crisis in 2020 is an example. Not for epidemiologists, but for most social systems, the pandemic was an unforeseen blind spot. The extreme urban growth in China (Wuhan) tipped the viruses of bats, which found new habitats in human bodies. From there the pandemic spread and intervened in all kinds of global social function systems, several of which created tipping points in political economy, and the balance between market and state transformed.

A system—the implication of this specific finding is what Luhmann's entire oeuvre tries to unfold—communicates exclusively with itself and not with its environment. It communicates by means of its own codes: for example, it communicates about environment with environmental law, or about environment protection with reference to codes of industrial property law. Nature as such communicates no law of its own, yet, as soon as its hour comes, law develop laws of protection, of precaution, of prevention, of sustainability, and so on. Still, such environmental law is coded in terms of legal systems and not in terms of the environment as such. The system can only observe what it can observe. And the system "cannot observe that it cannot observe what it cannot observe" (*Ecological* 1989, 23, 26; 1986, 52, 59; *Theory* 1997, 1110; 2013, 2:323). In this sense, whereas Habermas in *Theory of Communicative Action*, with a much discussed phrase, wrote about the "system's colonization of the lifeworld," Luhmann demonstrates a much larger theory about what Habermas calls colonization.

Several times, Luhmann remarks what classical critical theory did on such occasions; it criticized the realities for their lack of rationality and at the same time presupposed that theory was rational itself and that its proposals were *more* rational than the realities, only to increase the criticism whenever realities misbehaved and refused to take the critical proposals into account. Bourgeois principles of humanity, freedom, and reason were used as standards for such criticism (*Ecological* 1986, 16). Moreover, Luhmann distinguishes what Habermas does in such circumstances: namely, communicate about realities and presuppose that rationality is inherent in the communicative form. Therefore, Habermas, according to Luhmann, does not fall into the trap of presupposing a single center or a hierarchically ordered solution to crisis. Rather, he adheres to the opposite conception—loosely coupled intersubjective communication is the displaced center, for transformation (*Ecological* 1989, 36, 113, 133–36; 1986, 75, 214–15, 249–54; *Theory* 2013, 2:327–28; 1997, 1116–17).

With *Ecological Communication*, Luhmann established what some sociologists may call a critical systems theory. The same year, in 1986, the German Ulrich Beck published another famous and much discussed study, *Risk Society* (*Risikogesellschaft*). Beck's exposure seems at first sight closer to classical critical theory; but he is—probably wittingly—closer to Horkheimer's version of critical theory than to Habermas's, less because systems theory is only used as a marginal problem-setting and more because he fails to use communication theory: ecological risks are what is perceived, consciously or due to myths or moral panics, but not due to discourses or communication.

Keep in mind that systems do communicate about environmental issues in their own terms and codes. This is why they dissent about observations, about what is to be seen, about what is important and urgent, about what standards and thresholds have which implications. Many such well-organized functional systems use experts, but those whom they choose more often than not disagree, as they disagree also with the governmental agencies, firms, and mass media to whom they have recourse. Several studies have been undertaken to test Habermas's and Luhmann's theories about what happens at small or major conferences that should lead to consensus about, for instance, environmental measures (Harste 1997). Examples are legion, and COP 15, 16 . . . 21, 22, 23 in the United Nations Framework Convention on Climate Change are excellent examples. One model for doing so is the so-called consensus conferences; another is the record of diplomacy. With Luhmann's theory in mind, the prediction of disagreement among experts, governments, and systems is ready at hand—a clash about what the problems are, about which standards and codes are to be used for observation, for application, and for future investments. Environmental politics, negotiations, collective decision-making, and cooperative coordination are about essentially contested concepts, codes, and definitions.

However, the analysis of such consensus/dissension analyses of conferences should not end with the conclusion that at the end everything turns into a complex mess and a conflict. The clash between *functional systems* is organized in frames of *organizational systems* that convene the meetings. Since some negotiation experience and diplomatic memory most often are used by experienced organizers, official meetings and expositions are interrupted by long breaks, coffee breaks, dinners, walk-and-talk possibilities (including at such choice places as Camp David), and long hours when systems representatives meet in *interaction systems* where other agendas easily turn into metacommunicative forms of themes with other perspectives (restaurants, coffee quality, hotels, holidays, skiing, children, and the like). Therefore, Luhmann's sociology of formal organization orients attention to the informality of material situations of decision-making (*Folgen* 1964). Therein, other communication codes can emerge, new semantics can turn up, and new possibilities can emerge whether this takes place in the intersubjectivity of dialogue or silence as metacommunication. Exactly herein we observe a meeting place between Luhmann and Habermas, without a Carl Schmitt or Donald Trump as a state of exception.

THE RISKY SYSTEMS

In *Risk*, Luhmann quickly mentions that Habermas lacks analyses of temporal codes for discourses: How much time does a discussion take, and what is the *speed* of a domination-free discourse (*Risk* 1991/1993, 52/44). Today, most people have forgotten it, but the context of risks changed immensely when the Cold War dissolved after Gorbachev's rise to power in 1985. From *Ecological Communication* (1986) to *Risk* (1991), the future was reinvented after it almost apocalyptically ended in September and November 1983 when the world was an inch from a nuclear catastrophe. Long-term scenarios were lost, but regained.

In his book on risk, Luhmann focuses on the temporal codes of systems. Diverse functionally differentiated systems do not bind time in the same way. Some systems, like family systems, have temporal bonds that last long into the future, say, a 100 or 120 years, if you consider an elderly person's relation with their grandparents; others, like the mass media, function on the contrary with very short time bonds, as later described in Luhmann's booklet *The Reality of Mass Media* (1996/2000). Twitter and Facebook may have temporal resonance inside a few minutes. Investment and interest rates in economic systems may observe five to seven years for some investments and fifteen to thirty years for a mortgage for house loans. Political elections operate with, say, two to six years. When Trump dismissed COP21 (the Paris Agreement) to push America last, a number of commenters immediately began to discuss how long time this dismissal endures. Law, with its codes of expectations, its rules about precedence and about law reforms, is about binding time too: for example, with the Twenty-Fifth amendment in the United States; with the construction of an environmental law system such as what the European Union took on, and with the initial directives that were invented in the mid-1970s, and about twenty years later led to a coherent system of environmental law, with a number of holes, which, in the so-called *acquis communautaire*, were to be filled over the next twenty years—altogether twenty to forty years. However, to build a complete new form of environmental law in the EU would first demand a dismantling of the former and then the construction of a new one, which would take, say, fifty years. This much time is not available according to observations of present climate problems, and *this* is a risk too: We have the systems we have, and we have to operate with them and to operate reforms of them and with them. Luhmann and Habermas are both extremely aware of this modern condition, and its critical risks.

Accordingly, the two books *Ecological Communication* and *Risk* expose a response to Habermas's theory of legitimacy crises. The double perspective from the two books can be resumed in the following scheme (table 7.2).

To Luhmann, the law system serves as "the immune system of societal conflicts" (Luhmann *Law* 1993, 161, 565; 2004, 171, 475). This short formula contains a much wider description of a system that brackets the transition of perceived conflicts and crisis in social systems of economy, international imbalances, and ecology—to take Habermas's s themes from *Legitimation Crisis*. It is quite enlightening to see how Luhmann combined his theory of law with his theory of risks. The legal reorientation of problems does not only transfer conflicts about matters into a legal reinterpretation about substitutions or guilt (entitlements and repayments of unfairly distributed scarcities); it also redistributes suffering in time. Social inequalities may get substituted for economic rights, as Habermas contended in *Legitimation Crisis*. However, they also get another form when some can retire, others cannot, and the rest complains. Luhmann defines *risks* according to the asymmetry of those who

TABLE 7.2 The Six Risks of Systems—in General and in Particular

General theory about system risks Cf. Luhmann: *Systems*, 1984.	Risks in a functionally differentiated system (law, education, research, economy, war, politics, and so on), e.g., environmental politics
1. The risk not to observe the environment.	The political system observes the environment only in terms of the political code (what serves the government? what serves the opposition?)
2. The blind spot of the system and its limits to self-correction: it "cannot observe that it cannot observe what it cannot observe."	The political system cannot react otherwise: it can correct itself, but there are limitations in its corrections of its corrections; its self-perceptions entail misperceptions.
3. Conflicts between the different temporal horizons of functional systems.	The political system is temporally bound to the next elections that also offer the temporal horizon that limits its long-term view. Other functional and organizational systems operate with other time spans that are not the same; they conflict.
4. Dissent in communication between functional systems: functional systems do not communicate with one another.	Accordingly, communication abets matter and time, conflict and dissent. Consensus conferences about environment appear to be dissent conferences using new sayings of broad formulas as oil in troubled waters as an invisibility strategy for "communication" as a phatic gesture in communication.
5. There is no recursive entrance to a system of total vision that morally transcends and visualizes everything. The whole is less than the sum of its parts.	Neither morality, religion, public media, nor everyday life can reconcile and visualize *all* aspects. The Whole is less than the sum of its parts and appears to be only an aspect.
6. In modern society, there are only those systems that operate and none other. All observations and possible reforms only establish meaning by and through the systems; exclusion of different observations occurs, and that is a risk.	Calls for other systems of environmental treatment (law, waste, economy) take decades to implement and then things happen too late. They can only be invented on the shoulders of already-existing systems, at the condition of being indebted to their codes, and form dependencies.

decide, and *danger* according to those who become affected by those decisions.

This distinction leads to a double form of conflict dissolution. One dissolution takes place in the form of law, and the second in the form of politics.

> The function of law is solely to bring about certainty of expectation, especially in anticipation of unavoidable disappointment. But this change of direction goes only part of the way to solving the problem. Certainty of expectation is also at risk when conduct, which conforms to expectations supported by law, cannot be assured and when there is not even the slightest chance that expectations can be fulfilled. Law cannot always say: you are right, but unfortunately we cannot help you. Law must at least be able to offer substitutes (punishment, damages, etc.) and to enforce them. And even then law cannot guarantee that the guilty party is solvent; and the political system will not assume that it is its task to step in and pay in lieu of the guilty party just in order to lead law to victory. (*Law* 1993, 153; 2004, 164–65)

Law may soften despair and establish expectations for future solutions at the same time as the complainers get used to lower expectations and demands. When Davis Easton and Karl Deutsch wrote about the overloaded aggregation of demands, Luhmann quickly saw how law became inflated as an immune system that should compensate with legal substitutions for the absence of available or "affordable" political solutions. In their analysis of risks in *Niklas Luhmann's Theory of Politics and Law*, Michael King and Chris Thornhill describe this situation:

> To give affected parties legal rights or to introduce legal regulations to protect their interests may satisfy pressure groups for a time, but it merely passes the problem over to law without offering any political solution to the conflict between decision-makers and those affected. Luhmann concedes that juridifying risk problems might help to—break down complex issues into partial decisions—and "provide each side with opportunities to attain its goals," but in depoliticizing the problem by transferring it to the legal system, there is no guarantee that the legal system will accept the political view. Politics runs the inevitable risk,

therefore, that the most expedient solution might not be the lawful one. Law cannot be relied upon to carry out political objectives. Transferring risks to law is, therefore, itself a risky business for politics—the risk being the delegitimization of the political system through its failure to manage, or give impression that it is able to manage, risks. (2003, 190–91)

System communication functions in a medium between decision-makers and those affected—roles that may change, but most often, they still leave one part as the included part and the other as the excluded part (Luhmann *Exklusion* 1995, in SA 6; *Law* 1993, 580–84; 2004, 487–90).

8

"BEFORE THE LAW" (1992-)

From the mid-1980s, the Habermas-Luhmann controversy took a distinctive turn toward the sociology of law. Yet Luhmann's continued endeavors were much larger and still concerned a wider scope of social theories and analyses, whereas Habermas limited his range to the philosophy of law and debates about European integration. In the first part, I discuss the transformation; in the second part, I talk about the overall reconstruction in the seminal works on legal theory from the early 1990s; in the third part, I develop eight comments as point of comparison to the controversy; in the fourth part, focus on the more specialized discussion on legal argumentation. In 1996, the debate continued in the *Cardozo Law Review*, the last mutual comments before Luhmann's death in 1998. This debate is discussed in the final part.

HABERMAS'S RECOGNITION OF LUHMANN'S "LEGITIMACY THROUGH PROCEDURE"

After Habermas's series of lectures *The Philosophical Discourse of Modernity* (1985), his occupation with social theory took a legal and political turn. Social theory was not solely about the social integration of a community (*Gemeinschaft*) or a system integration of a society (*Gesellschaft*), but also about the political, organizational, and legal integration of a republic (a *res publicae* or *Gemeinwesen*). The first of Habermas's publications to bear witness to this transformation is the sixty-page article "Law and Morality," presented as the Tanner Lectures at Harvard University in December 1988 (available online).

We should note that this happened in the direct aftermath of Habermas's review of Luhmann's—some would say—first principal work, *Social Systems*, and of Luhmann's series of comments on that review. With Luhmann's *Ecological Communication* (1986), Habermas probably saw not only the critical potential of Luhmann's systems theory, but also its potential for applied studies of social problems far beyond the problems of ecology and pollution.

In any case, a much further reach came from the political transformations after Mikhail Gorbachev took power in the USSR in 1985. An opening for the constitutional problems of future world society became visible. New agendas suddenly appeared, and Habermas—as usual—very quickly looked through these open windows. It was not *Between Facts and Norms*, published in 1992, but the earlier *Law and Morality* that displayed these new opportunities. Yet of course, the fall of the Berlin Wall, the reunification of Germany, the fall of the Soviet Empire, and the Yugoslavian Civil War gave an immense impulse for Habermas to push and even hasten a new framework for a political theory of societal constitution, even if it—as many commentators have argued—could be claimed that *Between Facts and Norms* eventually was unfinished and too hastily given final form. Indeed, Habermas himself decided that a later English edition should have another afterword added.

This short history of publications also explains why *Between Facts and Norms* stimulated so many comments and discussions in the 1990s despite being almost unbearably difficult and complex. Most readers in the 1990s had to go to conferences about the book in order to find their way through it, only to find other readers who also had difficulties in reaching an adequate interpretation. But *Law and Morality* (1988) is far clearer, in spite of the difficult but classical theme of the constellation between law and morality.

The headline of law and morality has penetrated legal philosophy ever since Sophocles's *Antigone*. It developed as a core since the high medieval distinction between positive law and natural law. With the

Enlightenment's legal reforms, followed by Rousseau and Kant, the philosophical construction of the form of legal and moral reasoning was clarified. Yet the challenge was still to demonstrate what it meant for law empirically—meaning not only for a sociology of law, but also for a theory of political constitution.

Law and Morality consists of two parts. The first concerns Max Weber's unfinished sociology of law (from 1913) and his distinction between a principle of formal rationality and a reality of material rationality. The second part in Habermas's text is followed by a short reappraisal of three interpretations of this deformalization.

Previously, in his *Theory of Communicative Action*, Habermas displayed his dissatisfaction with Weber's double distinction between goal-rationality and value-rationality on the one hand, and formal rationality and material rationality on the other. Communicative rationality comes in between those kinds of dual rationalities, in between the strategic goal-rationality and the value-rationality, and in between formal rationality and material rationality. Yet for Weber a broad outline about cultural sense (*Kulturbedeutung*) and interconnected meanings (*Sinnzusammenhänge*), in fact, also comes in between, as well as Weber's empirical developments of a whole range of rationalizations. However, in *Law and Morality*, the scope investigated is much narrower. The focus is on the interconnected or rather entangled procedures between moral communication, legal argumentation, and political argumentation. Whenever law pragmatically functions, it is because of procedures that argumentatively could be justified. This allows for an analysis beyond the contract theories, from Thomas Hobbes to Immanuel Kant.

To Habermas (the philosopher), the idea of a contract leads to a model for discussion, whereas for Luhmann (the lawyer), contracts basically reduce material, social, and temporal complexity: What is the subject? Who is involved? And for how long?

Justification concerns what could be valid and what is morally justified. This is the result of Habermas's elucidation of the Weberian analysis of still-increasing modern law, and it somewhat follows Émile Durkheim's famous discussion of a deliberative relation between contracts and precontractual social norms. The point concerns procedures; following the influential British legal scholar H. L. A. Hart, he says that they have two levels. These two levels of first-order rules and second-order rules are not identical to Luhmann's concern for a distinction between first-order observation and second-order observation, though the second order in particular concerns sociological conditions. In Habermas's reconstruction:

> For the purposes of this wider analysis, the concept [of a legal institutionalization of *procedures* is central]. It must be broadly conceived and not connected from the outset to a specific form of law. H. L. A. Hart and others have shown that modern legal systems include not only legal precepts, permissions, prohibitions, and penal norms but also secondary norms, rules of empowerment, and rules of organization that serve to institutionalize processes of legislation, adjudication, and administration. (*Law* 1988, 229; translation modified)

With this, Habermas reminds the reader of Luhmann's earlier book *Legitimacy Through Procedures* from 1969. Not only a legal system but also a polity and a society constituted as a society of procedures (*Verfahrensgemeinschaft*) are crucial for Habermas's reconceptualization of a theory of social, legal, and political society. The German term *Verfahren* reconciles process with procedure as a kind of "way to go on."

> In this way the production of legal norms is itself regulated by legal norms. Legally binding decisions in due time are made possible by procedurally defined but otherwise indeterminate processes. Furthermore, it must be borne in mind that these processes connect decisions with obligations to justify or burdens of proof. What is institutionalized in this manner are legal discourses that operate not only under the external constraints of legal procedure but also under the internal constraints of a logic of argumentation for producing good reasons. (*Law* 1988, 229)

Habermas here initially uses Hart to relaunch the concept of procedural rules and those procedures used in legal forms of reasoning not only in courts but also in daily life. Yet from this background, he reintroduces Luhmann to his Harvard audience in the Tanner Lectures. The self-production of norms regulated by norms are close to Luhmann's and Gunther Teubner's self-referential, self-organizational, and autopoietic conceptions of reflexive law (Teubner 1986/2011, 1989/1993). Yet for Habermas, the value of morality is added to legal argumentation and thereby leads to legitimacy: "Legitimacy is possible on the basis of legality insofar as the procedures for the production and application of legal norms are also conducted reasonably, in the moral-practical sense of procedural rationality. The legitimacy of legality is due to the interlocking of two types of procedures, namely, of legal processes with processes of moral argumentation that obey a procedural rationality of their own" (*Law* 1988, 230). Apart from the distinction between law and morality, Habermas here operates with two central themes, that of procedure and that of *interlocking* (*Verschränkung*). There is an interconnected and entangled form between legal procedures in argumentation and moral procedures. Morality learns from law and law from morality. Habermas forwards

> the thesis that proceduralized law and the moral justification of principles mutually implicate one another. Legality can produce legitimacy only to the extent that the legal order reflexively responds to the need for justification that originates from the positivization of law and responds in such a manner that legal discourses are institutionalized in ways made pervious to moral argumentation. (243–44)

This argument is somewhat similar to what Luhmann calls structural coupling. In Luhmann's theory, law and morality are structurally coupled, but not similar. The difference from Habermas is that Luhmann, in an almost Nietzschean way, does not claim that a moral theory about the good will is also a priori a good theory. Such a coincidence might empirically be the case, but the opposite could also be possible. To Luhmann, a modern ethical reflection of morality is conditioned by a functional differentiation. The Kantian pure ethics of will-formation was conditioned by the reforms in positive law that have taken place since the early Enlightenment. Since his early publications, Luhmann repeatedly has forwarded a theory of separation of powers, including in the dissertation *Grundrechte als Institution* (1965) and *Legitimation durch Verfahren* (1969), throughout the 1980s, and finally with *Law as Social System* (1993). Any discourse-based revision of ethics undertaken by Habermas is founded on such functional differentiation, and this is also a reason, if not *the* reason, why Habermas's discourse theory ethics is not a transcendental universalistic theory, but a historically embedded pragmatic theory.

For instance, rape is morally completely inacceptable; politically too. However, legally and extremely paradoxically, in the courts experiences of rape are acceptable *if* they cannot (!) be proven by hard observable evidence beyond doubt and often—at least if the offender is rich, has good lawyers, and has a good public reputation—beyond explanations offered by psychologists that rape was the case rather than a normal affair. Hence, hard, proven evidence is subject to argumentation, but courts do argue differently than everyday argumentation and everyday expectations of even sophisticated principles of attention, respect, and care do. This legal carelessness in favor of proven evidence is what Luhmann observes as a fact—and, as we know with the Me Too criticism, a risk.[1]

In *The Philosophical Discourse of Modernity*, Habermas—albeit very briefly—also claimed that such a notion of legal autonomy was necessary to embed Foucault's criticism. Since this critique of Foucault's method of criticism was a major concern for Habermas in these years, this too may have led him toward a recognition of Luhmann's theory of functional differentiation. According to Luhmann, modern morality is successively conditioned by such functional differentiation and is not acceptable as a dedifferentiated moralizing culture. Habermas subscribes to such a defense of differentiation; however, he forwards the idea of an enlightened added value because dedifferentiation dissolves argumentative procedures and the entangled learning processes, from legal procedures to moral procedures. Certainly all three—Habermas, Foucault, and Luhmann—could reconcile in a criticism of communitarian moralization tendencies, though with very different reasons. Accordingly, it seemed to be crucial to Habermas not to reduce law to morality nor to reduce politics to the combination of law and morals. This entanglement is illuminated "by the fact that in constitutional systems the means of positive law are also reflexively utilized in order to distribute burdens of proof and to institutionalize modes of justification open to moral argumentation. Morality no longer lies suspended above the law as a layer of suprapositive norms.... Thus a procedural law and a proceduralized morality can mutually check one another" (*Law* 1988, 246, 247). The point was to keep law and morality separate while nevertheless allowing for learning processes or structural couplings. Here Habermas and Luhmann's point of *relief* (*Entlastung*) seems to be a common denominator: "Moreover, the professional administration of written, public, and systematically elaborated law relieves *legal* subjects of the effort that is demanded from *moral* persons when they have to resolve their conflicts on their own" (246).

The problem, however, is that functional differentiation is not formal differentiation. Differentiation has to be observed sociologically, according to what Weber called material rationalities. One of the main analysts of law and political theory situated between Habermas and Luhmann is the Frankfurt professor Ingeborg Maus. She too urged Habermas to take up Luhmann's analyses of procedures in jurisprudence and how they related to institutional differentiations (Maus 1986a, 1986b, 1992). Though "Maus shares the liberal concern for well-defined legal propositions that narrowly circumscribe the scope of discretion for courts and administrations, she no longer sees the rationality of the Rule of Law as residing in the semantic form of the abstract and general norm. Legitimating force is exclusively attributed to the democratic *process* of legislation" (*Law*, 236–37; referring to Maus 1986b). The point is not simply to trust democracy as the people's will or to trust a revitalization of formal procedures. The idea is to focus on democratic procedures as an ongoing process that, in Luhmann's terms, continues the interchange between government and opposition that may lead the governing and the governed to have trust in their form of rule (Luhmann *Politische* 1967/2010; *Legitimation* 1969; SA 4; *Politik* 2000). "The conditions of legitimacy for democratic law must be sought in the rationality of the legislative process itself. Thus, from our discussion there emerges the interesting desideratum of investigating whether the grounds for the legitimacy of legality can be found in the procedural rationality [*Verfahrensrationalität*] built into the democratic legislative process" (*Law*, 237). There is no automatic mechanism or legal formalism that ensures how procedures of democratic processes should become identical with the procedures of administration. So what is left? As already demonstrated by Weber, "of course, family, labor, and social law also confront the courts with material that cannot be treated according to the classical model of civil law procedures for subsuming individual cases under well-defined general laws" (238).

In contrast to Luhmann, Habermas aims to describe some kind of morality in the procedure of law: "Political power exercised in the form of a positive law that is in need of justification owes its legitimacy instead—at least in part—to the implicit moral content of the formal properties of law" (241–42). Luhmann's point is simply that this may be the case, or not, and in any case is not a priori secured. The idea of justification in the settlement of law simply does not expose a moral point of view, even if such a moral point could be inherent in what Habermas calls linguistic performances. To settle law is to establish meaning. This does not mean justified and morally reasoned meaning; it merely concerns what has meaning in the courts. Whereas, according to Habermas, the 'idea of impartiality forms the core of practical reason' (241–42), the realities may be far removed from such hopes. Often we may search in vain for administrative implementation of such ideas, although it is true that in reality such principles do rule in some institutions at some places.

A wide range of examples could demonstrate this point with regard to which principles are put into use, for example, in Scandinavian public administrative practice (Eriksen 2001; Eriksen and Weigaard 2003). A typically Habermasian short example could show that participation in George W. Bush's illegal Iraq War was not hindered in Denmark, but was in Sweden and Norway. In most places, what has legitimating force are the procedures that distribute burdens of proof, define the requirements of justification, and set the path of argumentative vindication. Famous here is the German foreign minister Joschka Fischer's oral reply to the U.S. secretary of defense Donald Rumsfeld: "You have to make the case and to make a case in a democracy is to be convinced, and excuse me, I am not convinced; that is my problem, and I cannot go to the public and say, 'well, let us go to war and there are the reasons and all that,' and I don't believe in that" (*The Telegraph*, February 11, 2003). Reasons have to follow a certain procedure to be recognized as valid, depending, of course, on context, and the context of military invasion is strictly institutionalized, according to a number of criteria. The case of the Iraq invasion is notable, because formal criteria were so clear and recognized, but nevertheless were broken. Therefore, in daily administrative routine and derogations from law we would expect even looser interconnections between legal procedures and morality.

Habermas, first, correctly sees that Luhmann leaves the legacy of constating or settled norms and rules, and that means the normative implications of such an agenda. However, Habermas does not recognize the full extent of the way Luhmann (like Bourdieu and Foucault) replaces norms with symbolic codes. Code theory is more easily symbolically described and is binary in its description of forms. Whereas legal norms thereby quit the idea of normativity, Habermas proposes to reconstruct a firmer foundation of normativity. Second, Habermas recognizes how Luhmann forms positive law as a form that, because of its stability, paradoxically can be transformed. Third, the procedures in a legal system bracket conflicts and replace them in another medium (cf. Luhmann *Systems* 1984, chap. 9). Legitimation through procedures does not constitute consensus, but displaces dissent and conflict. Habermas recognizes this with a reference to Luhmann's *Legitimation durch Verfahren* (1969):

> At this point Luhmann gives an interesting interpretation to the idea of legitimation through procedure. With regard to the addressees, institutionalized legal processes serve to check the readiness for conflict of defeated clients in that they absorb disappointments. In the course of a procedure, positions are specified in relation to open outcomes of this sort. Conflict themes are stripped of their everyday relevance and are painstakingly reduced to merely subjective claims to such an extent "that the opponent is isolated as an individual and depoliticized." Thus, it is not a matter of producing consensus but, rather, only of promoting the mere appearance of general acceptance, or the likelihood of its being assumed. (*Law*, 253–54)

In *Between Facts and Norms*, Habermas accordingly speaks about "the paradoxical emergence of legitimacy out of legality" (*Facts BFN* 1996, 83, cf. 130; 1992, 110, cf. 165).

In previous chapters, we have seen that Luhmann replaces norms with temporal bindings in the form of communication about stabilized expectations. Expectations are not to be reduced to psychological descriptions, but are forms that operate in communication. They are the medium of bounded communication in law, for example, continued as conflict or diplomacy, war or love. In this temporal sense, Luhmann's description of law fulfills more of what Habermas demands, which he himself does not fully describe.

Luhmann's basic point, however, is that decisions always follow even if no decision is made—a classical theme in organizational decision-making theory ever since political scientists Peter Bachrach and Morton Baratz invented the theory of nondecision. Yet in Luhmann's temporal theory of decisions, expectations and law bind one situation to past and future situations. This is much larger in scope. The temporal solutions to problems often take place in commissions, where a decision is embedded in ongoing discussions that are prolonged in infinite procedural debates and includes new information, if not changes in members and staff. It may be ethical to open for such universalistic engagement with still other viewpoints, but eternally extended discussions also likely result in displacements of focus and theme. Time—whether as extended time or as a form of impending time pressure—replaces the idea of a Hercules judge as well as an idea of moral universalism embedded in procedures (*Law* 1993, 339). In this sense, procedures also legitimize, and may legitimize nondecisions, for example, in ecological communications about pressing problems that are still far from being resolved.

Here, Habermas's moral point of view is not that there is a morality in the court; however, that morality follows alongside the court, in the forecourt, and in the corridors, in the comments to court, and in the arguments about what could have taken place in the court or whether administrative decisions should be taken to court. Everyday decisions anticipate what could appear and be considered valid arguments. Therefore, Habermas can follow Luhmann's analysis for some distance along the road:

> The concept of the systemic autonomy of law also has a critical value. Luhmann sees in the tendencies toward deformalization a danger of law's being mediated by politics; in his framework, "overpoliticization" appears as the danger that de-differentiation would take place if the formalism of law were weakened and finally absorbed by calculations of power and utility. The autonomy of the legal system depends upon its capacity to steer itself reflexively and to delimit itself from politics as well as from morality. (*Law*, 255)

However, in the end, Habermas is not satisfied with what he observes as Luhmann's theory of law from 1986. Habermas asked for a more complete analysis, a request Luhmann acknowledged in a discussion in Copenhagen in 1992 and of course shortly after responded to more fully with *Law as a Social System* (1993):

> In the meantime, however, Luhmann can no longer play down substantive and reflexive law as mere deviations. Therefore, he now sharply distinguishes between the legal code and legal programs, so that the autonomy of the legal system need only depend upon the maintenance of a differentiated legal code. About this code, however, he has nothing to say but that it permits the binary distinction between justice and injustice. From this tautological formula, no further specifications of the internal structure of law can be gained. It is no accident that Luhmann fills in with a question mark the place where the unity of the code should be explained. (*Law*, 256)

Here Habermas refers to the problem of the excluded third position in binary codes as it is discussed in Luhmann's *Ecological Communication* (1986, 73); this discussion reappears in their *Cardozo Law Review* discussion from 1996.

Habermas does recognize the pragmatic references Luhmann uses for his functional description of how juridical processes normally operate. However, with Klaus Günther, Habermas claims that in the very pragmatism of juridical argumentation, critical standards about, for instance, universalism, equality, fairness, and so on can find some application (*Law*, 258; Günther 1986/2011). Habermas recognizes that Luhmann's functional theory of law is no legal positivism (about what simply appears as settled law), since law is never already completely settled, and accordingly, normative criticism does not apply to a functional theory in the same way that classical natural law supplemented positive law with a framework of critical measures. A code theory of law pragmatically and operationally lets material as well as moral arguments re-enter, as long as they function (less for the purpose of and more) inside the very reproduction of justice in legal reasoning (Günther 1986/2011, 425). Legal reasoning is about preserving a legal right to communication about legality and illegality. This implies that moral standards can infiltrate legal reasoning as long as the legal form is preserved and reproduced self-referentially as autopoietic law. According to Habermas, this form of opening through closure also opens for politics and power (*Law*, 259). Law is not completely apolitical or above power. As in theological dogmatics, the idea of law originated with politics, such as King Solomon's paradoxical interpretation and application of the Ten Commandments as if they came from God, that is, as if unity, consistency, and coherence could be preserved and expected in the future.

A well-argued discussion about this position has been very influential in discussions on the European Court of Justice. The important Luhmann-inspired scholar Gunther Teubner paved the way for such analyses with his general *Law as an Autopoietic System* (1989/1993). This was the background for the theory of EU justice as a self-referential spiral of *acquis communitaire*, explained by Joseph Weiler's path-breaking article from 1991 "The Transformation of Europe" (in Weiler 1999). There is no doubt that Habermas's view and Luhmann's analysis in these debates fused together with authors such as Poul Kjaer (2006, 2010), John MacCormick (2009), Menendez and Fossum (2011), Chris Thornhill (2008, 2011), Hauke Brunkhorst (2012), and Christian Joerges (1996; Joerges, Kjaer, and Ralli 2011), not to mention Gunther Teubner (1987, 1997, 2007; Teubner and Fischer-Lascaeno 2007). The system of law no longer operates inside a sovereign nation-state, but in a world society. Legal systems operate in a way that is posthierarchical and postsovereign, yet they are not dissolved. Simply because laws cannot be less than deficient, the observation rather is that legal argumentation develops settlements of law as if courts could be legislative, for instance, in the European Court of Justice.

Legal systems still codify how legal expectations operate in communication. Moral arguments occur, for instance, about whether the United States should subscribe to an international court of justice for war crimes, whether refugees should have limited or enhanced possibilities for lawful trial, and so on. Above all, arguments are accepted as valid according to criteria of whether they operate in similar legal systems; if EU law operates with an extended liability for (pollution) emissions, this could turn into an argument in U.S. law to do likewise. On such points, Habermas shares with Luhmann the idea that the legal system can only accept arguments that appear in the legal form; yet this does not mean that political or moral reasons cannot motivate whether an issue is brought to court.

As a preliminary conclusion, it is obvious that Habermas oriented his position with reference to Luhmann's from the mid-1980s. Still, however, Habermas did not observe the importance of Luhmann's temporal theory, a crucial theme discussed in Richard Nobles and David Schiff's *Observing Law Through Systems Theory* (2013, 131–63). Furthermore, Habermas suggested that Luhmann should develop his theory of legal argumentation. This Luhmann did in chapter 8 of *Law as a Social System*.

After Habermas's direct reappraisal of Luhmann in the first part of the second lecture "On the Idea of the Rule of Law" of his Tanner Lectures, *Law and Morality*, Habermas embarked on an eleven-page historical sociology of "reason and positivity: on the interpretation of law, politics, and morality." This, basically, concerns the interconnection of what Habermas describes as the "indisponibility" of moral arguments for instrumental reasons in legal reasoning: they are not available for instrumental disposition. Historical analysis demonstrates that sacral divine law was not replaced by the pure contingency of a functionally equivalent resource that could legitimize law through natural law, the law of reason, or simply public support.

Accordingly, there is no way other than a reconstruction of the interconnected or structurally coupled legal reasoning and moral reasoning that were established from the long twelfth century of legal reforms to the Enlightenment of Montesquieu, Rousseau, and Kant. A group of French historians has demonstrated this (Boucheron and Offenstadt 2011). In late-medieval cities in Europe, associations, corporations, city halls, and courts very often experienced how quarrels and decision-making processes took place similarly to how they experienced procedures with forms of argumentations *pro et contra*; the *disputatio* of canonical law entered other forums that were also central to powerful disputes. The canonists tried to ensure a coherent *corpus juris* that monopolized the views of the pope, whereas the *glossatores* cemented the huge compilation of Roman law known as the *Digest* and reassembled it into the first coherent corpus by the Bologna monk Gratian. A third, more academic group followed the pedagogical concept of a university professor posing a question that should be the subject of a dispute, often focused on contradictions. With the *jus statuendi*, such procedures entered city life after the Peace of Constance in 1183.

Today, in particular the (somewhat) Habermas-influenced scholar Hauke Brunkhorst (2014a) and the (somewhat) Luhmann-influenced scholar Chris Thornhill (2008, 2010, 2011) agree on the importance of this long institutional path-dependency. A first and superficial view of such confrontations of texts and discussions reveals the differences between Habermas's reconstruction of legal history and Luhmann's reconstruction. The Habermasian reading of such deliberations would tend toward interpretations that concern possibilities of consensus, whereas Luhmann tends to look for dissent. However, in fact both Habermas and Luhmann observe the procedures of such debates, disputes, and contradictions.

The problem is to observe what constituted duties and obligations in moral discussions as well as in courtly procedures throughout those centuries of early modernity. In some sense, this task is easier than it may appear, although Habermas did not elucidate empirical investigations comparable to Luhmann's.[2] Moral duties and legal obligations underwent a clarification, purification, and communicative coding that finally separated legal argumentation from moral argumentation over a period from the 1690s to the mid-eighteenth century. This happened alongside a separation of powers philosophically sustained far beyond what we know from Montesquieu. Kant's "tribunal of justice" was very real as a philosophical endeavor in the courts of France (Behrens 1985; Harste 2016a). Lawyers had to follow procedures in the courts, yet they entered the courtyards and later the associations, the salons, and the cafés and continued to discuss, argue, and reason, embedded in these procedures and principles of explanation, expressibility, and listening. Hence, in court they could claim that moral reasoning and norms developed outside the court, in reflections about what took place inside the court.

To Pierre Bourdieu, such analyses are important touchstones and yardsticks (Bourdieu 1989/1996, 377–82). Habermas's, Luhmann's, Bourdieu's, and by some measures also Foucault's descriptions of the formation of rule of law, "der Rechtsstaat" or "l'État de justice," are worth comparing against that background (Harste 2016a). Habermas, in *The Structural Transformation of the Public Sphere*, invoked such empirical and philosophical investigations but limited them to literary criticism. In the Tanner Lectures, he offers only a few hints, such as the development of contract theory between Hobbes and Kant, that is, as a medium of power and a medium of will-formation. Yet Luhmann discussed what legal argumentation was about from the twelfth century to Kant.

A DISCOURSE THEORY OF LAW OR A SYSTEMS THEORY OF LAW?

It is tempting to compare Habermas's seminal work on political and legal theory, *Between Facts and Norms* (1992), with Luhmann's somewhat similar seminal work, *Law as Social System* (1993), which eventually was supplemented with his posthumous *Politics as Social System*. The two books on law have almost identical length—as, in addition, do their seminal sociological books, Habermas's *Communicative Action* (1981) and Luhmann's *Theory of Society* (1997), or his *Gesellschaftstheorie*, published posthumously in 2017, but written in 1975.

In a discussion in Copenhagen in 1992, Luhmann recognized Habermas's work, which he at that moment had read in manuscript. He did not pose any opposition to it, stating simply that it had a rather complex form and represented a discontinuity with Habermas's former writings. Once again, as in 1981, when Habermas published his general *Theory of Communicative Action* ahead of Luhmann's publication of a general theory in *Social Systems* (1984), he published *Between Facts and Norms* ahead of Luhmann's *Law as a Social System*. Whereas this strategy of finishing major books first, perhaps pressed by public circumstances, may have seemed quite wise at the time, in the long run it may have been less wise, since Habermas increasingly used Luhmann's theory as the standard model to comment on, revise, and adjust. This certainly is the case with *Between Facts and Norms*.

What made Habermas's extremely discussed six-hundred-page book from 1992 so overwhelmingly complex was its character as a commentary on those tremendous challenges faced by Germany, Eastern Europe, and European integration, not to mention the former Yugoslavia, written *as if* those changes could find an adequate theoretical redescription. In fact, transformations began in 1985 when Gorbachev became general secretary of the Soviet Union and new signals came that the Soviet superpower would no longer intervene with military forces in Eastern European countries.

Habermas at that point, although much more theoretically and formally, embarked on a redescription similar to what Max Weber, seventy-five years before, had developed in his legal sociology in 1913, in which transformations of the formal rule of law (or *Rechtsstaat*) developed material rationalities that resulted in a certain German type of professionalized "social state" (*Sozialstaat*). When we remember the consequences of World War I in Germany, and the indeed fatal consequences that the top-down specialized professionalism had on the more universalistic (formally rationalized) expectations that war veterans and their relatives had, we understand the accuracy of Weber's warnings about missed opportunities for human rights and about an ice cold winter that could arrive (cf. Cohen 2001). We also see the hypercomplexity of Habermas's endeavor in the period when he wrote, and somewhat rewrote, *Between Facts and Norms* from 1989 to 1992.

Moreover, we could draw parallels to the transformations witnessed by Immanuel Kant from 1788 to 1797, when he developed his standard-setting historical, social, cultural, and legal philosophy, setting to the task *as if* such a philosophy were possible to form. There is no doubt that Kant's measure presented a yardstick for the idea that such a painstaking task could be useful, both for research and for pragmatic reasons.[3] Habermas was the worried and concerned participant in the transformations in Europe around 1990, whereas Luhmann was the observer. This distinction between participation and observation is fundamental to understanding the differences between Habermas and Luhmann, and indeed to understanding what it means to reason about social transformation (*Auch*, 1:35).

This also reveals why the Habermasian form of analysis is far more in need of the Luhmannian form of analysis than the reverse. Nevertheless, the important contribution of the book is that it admittedly displayed the overcomplexity of the situation when the Cold War ended. This ran together with new forms of globalization, with the Internet, with renewed long-term ideas about future history, with an endless opening of new conflicts in Eastern Europe, Africa, and the Middle East, and with new forms of immigration and social integration. What form could Europe, European integration, and the European Union take at that moment, and what was the form of the political, legal, and social theory that could describe it? This also appeared to be extremely relevant elsewhere for setting an agenda, for instance, the Pacific integration of China began in the 1990s after the turbulence identified with the Tiananmen Square protests in 1989.

These problems are endemic to the theme of finding the particular "structural coupling" (Luhmann) or "co-originality" (*Gleichursprünglichkeit*, Habermas) of morality, law, and politics in a particular context and situation. Often, in German Idealism, the point is presented as if the general is in the particular and the particular in the general. In the early 1990s law and separation of powers were in transition in Europe, the nation-state had became exposed to wide-ranging transformations of the political integration between and above states, and former models were rendered obsolete, whereas new forms were not yet constituted. It is no wonder that it was difficult, if not impossible, to posit a clear and consistent theory about law, politics, and morality.

For Luhmann the task was much clearer. In fact, he was not greatly concerned with what happened during political Europe's transformation around 1990. His very important pupil and follower Gunther Teubner (in Frankfurt and London) was much closer to the transitions in European and international law, as were a number of others, such as Christian Joerges (at the European University in Florence) and Professor Inger-Johanne Sand (in Oslo), and we have to look to their writings to find a Luhmannian theory of European law. Luhmann's task was the same as it had been since the mid-1960s: to expose a theory of law, including the conditions for the evolution of law, from tribes, stratified societies, and empires to states and beyond. Law as a form of communication has been transformed many times over. Hence, new forms of structural couplings develop between law, politics, justice, morality, public spheres, individuals, religion, finance, war, and so on, all along with internal evolutions in the subsystems themselves. The subsystems may become more or less functionally differentiated, and eventually new forms of networks and governance may emerge. Thus, we see developments in important post-Luhmannian positions, such as Poul Kjaer (2014). Yet

Luhmann's point is less what we (we!) shall (shall!) do about it (about what!); Luhmann's aim is certainly not to embark on any strategic or moral discourse about tasks to be fulfilled. Rather, his aim is to describe and thereby defend differentiation forms and hence to protect individuals and other systems from the interpenetrating or "colonizing" (Habermas) codifications forwarded by other systems.

EIGHT COMMENTS

At first glance, a number of topics seem similar between Habermas and Luhmann's analyses of law. First, they are both thoroughly sociologies of law, indebted in particular to Weber's and Durkheim's sociologies (Günther 1986/2011), as well as to Kant's and Hegel's philosophies of law.

Second, constitutively, law is a form of communication and has to have communicative meaning. Law does not exist and has no validity outside communication. In *Between Facts and Norms*, Habermas seems to use Luhmann's description of what Habermas calls "subject-free communication" (*Facts BFN*, 170, 362, 365). To Luhmann more than Habermas, the transformations were and are worldwide and due to communication processes and related to electronic media changes, which are similar to previous innovations in writing and with the printing press. Indeed, Luhmann's overall transition to a communication theory, first in the booklet on *Power* from 1975, then in *Social Systems* in 1984, and finally in *Theory of Society* from 1997, was remarkably ahead of the global transformations heralded by the Internet, satellites, mobile phones and smartphones, tablets, and whatever else is yet to come long after Luhmann's death. Previously, Daniel Bell in his influential *The Coming of Post-Industrial Society* (1973) ascribed aspects of those early transformations in communication to productive forces described in Habermas's *Technology and Science as "Ideology"* from 1968.

Third, the same concerns power. However, Habermas's point in *Between Facts and Norms* is that there are still, realistically observed, some normative dimensions to be added. He adds them with the Luhmann scholar Helmut Willke:

A systems theory that has banned everything normative from its basic problems remains insensitive to the inhibiting normative constraints imposed on a constitutionally channeled circulation of power. Through its keen observations of how the democratic process is hollowed out under the pressure of functional imperatives, systems theory certainly makes a contribution to the theory of democracy. But it offers no framework for its *own* theory of democracy, because it divides politics and law into different, recursively closed systems and analyzes the political process essentially from the perspective of a self-programming administration. The "realism" that systems theory gains with this selective approach comes at the cost of a disturbing problem. According to systems theory, all functional systems achieve their autonomy by developing their own codes and their own semantics, which no longer admit of mutual translation. They thereby forfeit the ability to communicate directly with another and as a result can only "observe" each other. This autism especially affects the political system, which also self-referentially closes itself off from its environment. In the face of this autopoietic encapsulation, one can scarcely explain how the political system should be able to integrate society as a whole, even though it is specialized for regulatory activities that are meant not only to rectify disturbances in functional systems but also to achieve an "environment friendly" coordination among systems drifting apart. It is not clear how one should reconcile the autonomy of the different functional systems and the political system's task of holding them together: "The heart of the problem lies in the improbability of successful communication among autonomous, self-referentially operating unities." (Habermas *Facts BFN*, 335–36; 1992, 406–7; citing Willke 1992, 345.

Habermas's problem is that Luhmann and his followers very well could be right. Yet it may also be correct that some form of what Luhmann calls the "loose coupling" of normative reasoning could enter into the political, legal, and organizational circulation of power and create transformations. This, however, is not sufficient to conclude, as Habermas does, that Luhmann is not able to describe the constitution of power as a self-referential system. Luhmann's approach "operate(s) with concepts of power that are insensitive to the empirical relevance of the constitution of power under the rule of law, because (they) screen out the internal relation between law and power" (*Facts BFN* 1996, 336; 1992, 407). It is correct that Luhmann's conceptions, especially in the enlightened perspective of Foucault and Bourdieu before his seminal publication *Theory of Society*, never developed a stronger theory of power than the one expressed in *Trust and Power*. Yet we, in particular in politics and mass media, tend to explain law according to a positive dogmatic of coherent law whereas law proceeds with far more pragmatic procedures of speed, costs, lack of information, skill, and what have you as metaphors, context and environment (Wiethölter 1986/2011, 1989).

Fourth, the forms of separated powers, rule of law, balance of power, *Rechtsstaat*, and the conditions for such forms are central to a sociology of law. Yet such a separation is constitutive not only of a legal description of the separation, but also of a political description, an organizational and a publicly mediatized description, a theory of military systems, and so on. Those different forms of descriptions are *as such* not identical. This is why those forms should be primarily conceptualized and compared in sociology if they are to have any meaning in law studies, political science, moral philosophy, and so on. The sociology of law, political sociology, organization sociology, the sociology of mass media, and others have to be conceptualized in order to conceive of adequate comparisons and to observe and reflect their forms of power, symmetrical or asymmetrical.

Fifth, the peculiar paradox already discussed in chapter 6 is that any conception of political self-determination, such as Rousseau-style people's sovereignty, is conditioned by the autonomy and self-reference of law, including the separate autonomies of other social subsystems. The paradox, hence, concerns the fact that political steering is constituted by the differentiation of the political subsystem from other subsystems: political steering is conditioned by the inability to steer those other subsystems. This means that political systems are overloaded with demands that are impossible to reconcile.

Sixth, human rights, and previously natural law, emerged as a reflection of the development of positive law. Habermas and Luhmann certainly do not offer the same or even similar descriptions of this emergence. Whereas Habermas in *Auch* (2019) later analyzed philosophical learning processes in history, Luhmann goes far deeper into the conceptual and semantic history of natural law, that is, the foundational premodern history of the conceptions of human rights that flourished in the prerevolutionary period before Rousseau and the founding fathers, the Federalist Papers, and the French First Constitution. A major discussion theme for Luhmann is the problem of structural couplings, or the simultaneous origins of legal positivism and human rights. To Habermas, there is a strict cosimultaneity or copresence of positive law and its transcendence through human rights—human rights as a legal form that also has a moral and public form that transcends law. In a way very similar to Luhmann's conception of "structural coupling," Habermas repeatedly uses concepts of "interconnection" and "entanglement" (*Verschränkung*) and concepts like "wheelwork" (*Verzahnung*). In spite of the mechanical connotations, the point in common for our two authors is less about causality than about time and copresent developments.

The transition from natural law to human rights, however, was a major transformation, and in *Law as Social System* (chapters 6–11) Luhmann describes how it took place in French, German, and English courts from the sixteenth to the early eighteenth centuries; the early Enlightenment is especially important. The common topic is what society and its subsystems can learn, and what they have learned, from court procedures (Harste 2001, 2016a).

Seventh, in itself it is worthwhile to pinpoint the themes of cooriginality, copresence, and simultaneity or synchronicity of private spheres and public spheres, and of human rights together with subjectivity and objectified public roles. As stated in previous chapters, Luhmann penetratingly, and especially in his *Risk* (1991), develops a theory of enforced synchronization compared to evolutions of nonsimultaneities (*Ungleichzeitigkeiten*), such as the risk of differentiations in time-binding norms among differentiated functional systems. In short, Habermas's foundational idea in this respect came from the apparently simultaneous, if not synchronic, publication of Rousseau's *The Social Contract* and *Émile*, both in 1762. Moreover, *The Social Contract*, in an important conceptualization, argues that the so-called "general will" is binding to everybody. The main point is that it obliges everyone to accept and tolerate deviances and disagreements, and no one can disagree with the principle that disagreements should be allowed. Accordingly, every human—"human" in contrast to citizen or subject of power—must recognize the human right of particular differences. *Émile, or On Education* is simply the narrative of such an autonomous will-formation.

Habermas, to be sure, already elegantly developed this conception of synchronicity of objectivization/subjectivization, generalization/particularization, and nomothetic law development/ideographic exception in chapter 2 of *The Structural Transformation of the Public Sphere*. Yet, to the legal historian Niklas Luhmann, as he argued in the long article "Subjective Rights" (1981), this is not sufficient to establish the point. The reason is that subjective rights of shame, honor, lust, guilt, punishment, accountability, and so on were developed semantically—if not eventually codified—far earlier, in the twelfth century, and have since transformed several times over. For instance, in the Reformation, a number of virtues developed, such as piety, grace, discipline, asceticism, charity, forgiveness, and so on. For example, shame and later piety took forms in texts yet also in bodily communication, such as lifted eyebrows.

Eighth, private law and administrative law are subject to materially specified programs. Law and political ideas developed according to specified material needs, situations, and contexts, which reveal pragmatic expectations about how communication will operate. Habermas may, from the bottom up, be inclined to develop abductive reasoning about what is done and, ethically, should be done in such situations, whereas Luhmann tends to observe new semantics and innovations that become stabilized, only to see if they provoke paradoxes, conflicts, or solutions to former problems.

Many discussions that appeared in the aftermath of Habermas's *Between Facts and Norms* preoccupied themselves with controversies about whether Habermas's discussion of one or another position (of John Rawls, Ronald Dworkin, Weber, Aristotle, Kant, Hobbes, Rousseau, and so on) was correct with respect to this or that, and whether the topics were discussed adequately. Since Habermas often develops his theories in discussion with others, this makes his theoretical constructions vulnerable to debates and criticism—and difficult to follow if the reader has not read the same books as Habermas. Some find misunderstandings, purposeful or not, and these debates sometimes tend to forget the subject at hand in favor of ad hominem disrespect and misperception. To Luhmann, such quarrels are misleading, since communication has its own autonomies distant from ideas about how people, authors, and readers identify with positions, which could be taken or not taken.

LEGAL ARGUMENTATION

In a strict and very legal sense, it could be claimed that the most central topic in the debate in 1992–93 between Habermas and Luhmann was about "legal argumentation." This concerns chapter 8 in Luhmann's *Law as Social System* and especially part 3, chapter 5, in Habermas's *Between Facts and Norms*.

Habermas's question is whether it is possible to fulfill the task of establishing an abstract principle of discourse, which at its core can account, on the one hand, for simple interactions among people copresent in an interaction system and, on the other hand, for interactions among those who might have rights and claims (Habermas *Facts BFN* 1996, 233; 1992, 286–87). This, too, is the starting point for Luhmann in his exposition of the role of courts and procedural history (in *Law* 2004, 274; 1993, 297). In *Legitimation durch Verfahren*, he begins his analysis displaying the historical fact that courts, in order to have any authority, have to have some place and scope in which communications are free to decide upon and determine matters that are not already decided and determined (*Legitimation* 1969, 21, 59–68). Courts are based on a principle of indeterminacy. The court was set, on chairs, in a confined setting in which deliberation could take place: it may have been in the middle of a village or in a setting similar to the Lord's Supper—both arrangements could serve as functional equivalents that authorized the setting. Because of this historical differentiation between court communication and everyday interaction, we may ask whether this is still adequate in modern society. In other words, is there some form of abstract discourse principle that covers both, as Habermas suggests, or do we only have the form of meaningful communication in its most general form, as claimed by Luhmann? Neither of them, in any case, would claim that legal argumentation is only a subset of moral reasoning.

Of course, there is a tension between the reasonable legitimacy of applied law and positive law as to what should be considered in connection with just decisions. Either valid law could apply to moral reasons, or moral reasoning could be used in law if such principles were allowed to be used directly in a legal argument. Yet Habermas tends to seek a third position, where new settled law copes with former laws and practices but also reasons with validity claims in order to cope with hard difficult cases and new issues and topics. Here Habermas tends, for empirical reasons, to let the institutional reasons rule: "Procedural law does not regulate normative-legal discourse as such but secures, in the temporal, social, and substantive dimensions, the institutional framework that *clears the way* for processes of communication governed by the logic of application discourses" (Habermas *Facts BFN* 1996, 235; 1992, 288; emphasis in original). This form has obvious similarities to Luhmann's conception of reduced complexities. The modalities of communication are differentiated into certain forms that code the reduction of temporal, material, and social complexity:

> In such situations the urgent generalization of perspectives has a temporal, a material, and a social aspect. Temporally, the acceptable horizon for events becomes postponed into the future; the relevant span of time becomes wider. Materially, more themes come into consideration. Possibilities of action, which do not "as such" coincide, become settled through motives, revenge, and gratitude. Socially observed, the forms of encounters are simplified through a typically expected denominator, which should not always appear as new, for example, as cooperation or as conflict. (Luhmann *Legitimation* 1969, 76)

At the end of the day, Habermas uses Luhmann's tripartition of a temporal, social, and material reduction of complexities involved in courtly procedures: the temporal rules against delays, the social rules of exchanges between *pro et contra*, and the material production of what become accepted as proof and facts. The organizational form becomes decisive for the functional form and its procedures become decisive for communicating a discursive principle.

If it is not clear in reading *Between Facts and Norms*, Habermas's stronghold is to discuss what social, political, pragmatic, and ethical reasoning has learned from court procedures. His analysis of pragmatic discourses is apparently still bound to follow instrumental ideas of goals and means (*Facts BFN* 1996, 159–60, 164–65; 1992, 197–98, 203). This becomes clearer when Luhmann's analysis of legal argumentation in chapter 8 of *Law as a Social System* is taken into account. Habermas, to be sure, uses Luhmann's description of procedure, and Luhmann directly addresses Habermas's endeavors several times in the chapter. In the chapter's first note he recognizes that "Habermas formulates the important contention that we must ensure that juridical argumentation is able to respond to other than just moral premises" (Luhmann *Law* 2004, 305, note 1; 1993, 338, note 1).

Yet he also addresses a certain difference from Habermas's topic, since Luhmann insists that we have to be aware of the self-understanding and self-description of law and legal procedures as they have developed in modern society. In a note, Luhmann coins the decisive difference from Habermas:

> In his [Habermas's] view, which follows on from Max Weber, texts with the validity of positive law initially replace reasoning. "The special achievement of the positivization of law consists of shifting problems of stating reasons; that is, largely relieving the technical operation of law of the *problems of stating reasons*, but it does not consist of the removal of these problems" [*Communicative Action*, 1:354]. Habermas takes a different turn after that. A lawyer sees the deficiency of reasons necessitating an *interpretation of texts*, which in turn requires further reasons. Habermas, however, sees the problem in the fact that the *"textuality" itself needs a reason*—neither a formal one nor a functional one (this is not possible without texts) but a substantial one in relation to postconventional criteria which are yet to be agreed upon. Clearly Habermas is demanding more than is and can be practiced as law in view of the responsibility courts have to arrive at (quick) decisions. (*Law* 2004, 307, note 7; 1993, 340, note 7)

In Luhmann's *Law as a Social System* (2004), chapter 8 and parts of chapter 11 are concerned with analyses of legal argumentation. However, the historical interpretations of legal evolution are the subjects of chapters 6, 9, 10, and 11, and are the concern of a number of Luhmann's previous elaborations of a theory of legal evolution.

Law is primarily about the production of texts (laws, verdicts) with texts. Argumentation as such is not valid law, and only transforms into legality by means of written procedures. Memory is not representative as such, but is only so in the form of writing. This battle of orally customary law against a still stronger and more positive written law developed from about 1100 to 1500 in Europe; written law was primarily a legacy from the Roman Empire, whereas somewhat north to Lyon customary law was more important. Starting in early-modern law, oral argumentation does not, as such, change legality in the same way as written documents, though there is a structural coupling between writing and speech: "Through texts, the system is able to coordinate itself by its own structures without being committed to indicate in advance how many and which operations, such as quoting certain texts, will trigger or change the reuse of certain structures" (*Law* 2004, 305).

Today, interpretation in law is not about an oral performance entangled with fixed written texts. "Interpretation is about producing new text with old texts" (*Law* 2004, 306, translation modified; see 1993, 340). In a longer note, Luhmann adds an important point, emphasized by Habermas in his comment to Weber in *Communicative Action* (TKH 1:354): law in the form of legal texts relieves reasoning and offers some form of argumentative deficit that calls for further interpretation. For example, an application questions whether a law is also valid in a certain other case, and an interpretation has to follow. Invoking the jurisprudence of Jean Domat, Luhmann adds that law therefore does not take place as a first-order observation, but instead only as a second-order observation: "Texts are not to be understood verbally but analogously according to what gives meaning" (*Law* 2004, 307; translation modified). The point is that the legal text was made in order to give meaning to future situations, and hence to bind law, to establish an improbable situation, and to ensure that a certain use of law also binds expectations for future situations, that is, brackets contingencies. Texts are established in the (counterfactual) sense of not leaving much to be added in the future.

Therefore, legal reasoning develops in order to establish meaning—for valid law and not (or only accidentally) for the environments of the legal system. This takes place through a combination of redundancies and variations. Legal procedures do not cite past settled law as if it is a covering law that forever has to be followed in its given precedence. They cite examples, not analogies. Yet examples offer variety and each new case can offer variety. Hence, to develop, law has to cope with variety or even invent variation to clarify how new laws can establish valid law.

In this way, Luhmann's elucidations describe how legal argumentation establishes a kind of interconnected complex of meaning (Weber's

Sinnzusammenhang) in between formal law and material substantive law. This is established not in the intersubjective dialogue of speech acts and linguistic performance, but in an intertextuality that makes use of spoken language, but the point is the self-production of texts as valid law.

Law has to exist. The raison d'être of law and legal argumentation is not to be moral or political or to make society function as a whole, but only to leave law to law and to make law function. And therefore morality and politics, public debates and scientific argumentation are all relieved and emancipated to establish their own form of argumentation.

Argumentation concerns whether arguments are good or bad and whether they should be accepted or not, and it argues therefore about arguments. Hence ideas of procedural argumentation may seem to be similar for Habermas and Luhmann, but

> theories of ethics, of any kind or the currently fashionable economic analyses are equally inadequate explanations of legal reasoning in practice. Legal reasoning often uses relatively general terms such as fault, liability, contract, or unjust enrichment. But these terms feed off their repeated use in countless different contexts. Therefore it is possible to use them as the basis for a decision within a familiar meta-context, although they are not readily applicable without a concrete explanation. By doing so, conclusion by analogy builds a bridge between dissimilar cases. (*Law* 2004, 311)

Analogies of matter tend toward observing new things as they once were and thereby stick to conservatism. Both Habermas and in particular Luhmann defend the autonomy of law, which—from another angle and similar to Foucault's (2004, 86–87)—displays a criticism of the ordoliberal German-Austrian idea of an economic constitution of law (Joerges and Everson 2020). This problem of the structural (de)coupling and desynchronization of law with the economy, politics, or morality goes back to Weber's sociology of law.[4] To be "guilty in the court" is a completely different phenomenon from being, for example, taken as "politically guilty" and responsible to the mass media. Courts developed historically to avoid violent conflicts, and if trial leads away from vendettas and the use of mafia methods, then courts have fulfilled their function of immunizing society against escalating conflicts. Thus to Luhmann, legal argumentation developed not from God or the good, but on a path away from the devil, away from conflict and escalated dissent.

Everything is not available but why should certain "good" concepts be able to enter legal argumentation better than "bad" or "less good" concepts?

> Someone who does understand reasoning as a reference to reasons will find the necessity to find reasons for the reasons as well. Someone who must find reasons for reasons needs tenable principles. Someone who refers to principles ultimately refers to acknowledged principles in the environment of the system. This is especially the case when such principles carry the additional signature of "moral," "ethical," or "reasonable" principles. (*Law* 2004, 312)

The courts do not have natural or divine law to their disposition; in our everyday lifeworld we may be inclined to claim that we could dispose of this indisposition and bring those claims with us into the courts as participants or witnesses. We may even claim our interests to be presented in courts by lawyers; but the intertextual development of law in courts primarily defends the interests of producing and reproducing law as a sustainable system.

What seems obvious in the environment of the legal system does not necessarily appear to be reasonable for the legal system and its legal argumentation. Legal argumentation and reasoning are not the same as argumentation and reasoning in other systems such as the family system, the art system, the mass media, the economy, the political system, or the war system. "Can principles do away with the requirement of their having to distinguish themselves from each other? And if not: who does the distinguishing, if not the legal system itself?" (*Law* 2004, 312).

Law always has to operate with particularities, as if something more general could be said. Hence, there are good or bad arguments and law weights such arguments, but it does not discuss the weight of the weight: it does not argue why argumentation takes place; it simply takes place and so it has been since the Roman institutionalization of court procedure, and it has also been the case outside the post-Roman legacies.

The paradox is invisible, and we cannot turn it completely visible. "The theory of argumentation is brought into the operation of argumentation" (*Law* 1993, 343). Accordingly, Luhmann's redescription is close to

Habermas's and he admits that procedure, in law's pursuit and judicial inquiry, often is described as reasonable. Especially in early Enlightenment France (d'Aguesseau 1759) this became common and part of positive law.

Habermas and Luhmann agree that in law we find a "surplus of procedures" and a deficit of cognition and motivation. Whereas Luhmann tends to dismiss any moral idea that good or bad motivations could be forwarded in legal operations, Habermas tends to lean on the implicit moral motivations of procedures.

Accordingly, the focal point for Habermas is what can be learned, morally, from legal procedures. If Luhmann's

> official use of law is not to destroy the belief in its legitimacy, the initiated must interpret legal procedures differently from the way clients do—namely, as an institutionalization of obligations to bear the burden of proof and to provide good reasons for any decisions. Arguments exist so that lawyers can indulge in the illusion of not making decisions according to whim: "Every argument diminishes the surprise value of further arguments and finally the surprise value of decisions" [Luhmann, *Betrachtung* 1986, 35]. Certainly, from a functionalist perspective argumentation may be described in this way; but Luhmann considers this the whole truth, since he attributes no rationally motivating power to reasons at all. In his interpretation, there are no good arguments for why bad arguments are bad; fortunately, however, through argumentation the appearance is created "as if reasons justify the decisions, rather than (the necessity to come to) decisions justifying the reasons" [33].
> (Habermas *Law*, 254)

Luhmann's point is not to indulge Ronald Dworkin's Hercules judge as the foundation for legal decisions, but simply to state that legal systems strive to follow their obligation to determine or retain an interdiction against undecidability. The buck stops in the court. More specifically, the buck stops, so to speak, at the best narrative in the court; or it stops in the administrative process that displays the best narrative simply because such process allows for further arguments without surprises and with a discretion that does not foster hypocrisy but allows for some honesty. As Richard Nobles and David Schiff claim in *Observing Law Through Systems Theory* (2013, 50–57),

To be effective, the legislature needs the judges to carry out operations that it cannot expressly authorize. Judges must make the law, in the sense of dealing with the inevitable contingency within a system that cannot provide in advance for all situations, by using communications that do not admit that law, in this sense being made. These particular examples of "hypocritical" communication facilitate a workable version of what is commonly referred to, within the legal and political systems, as the doctrine of "separation of powers." Whilst the need for judges to make law is inescapable, their ability to proclaim that this is what they are doing, as they do it, leads to different forms of law making than would occur if judges could use communications that confessed to their law-making role as they were doing so. (Nobles and Schiff 2013, 54)

Of course, this is lawmaking as incrementalism. In EU law, it is called law by *acquis communautaire*. Law has to be coherent and holes have to be filled, at the same time as the world changes, new complexities occur, contexts, words, and concepts change, and new holes appear. This is not the personal wish of a judge held by his own political commitment. It is his job to reestablish the law to fill the gaps, which reappears repeatedly with still more variance. To distinguish between finding the law and making the law is part of routine operations, yet the discretion used in this operation is precarious.

Hence, Nobles and Schiff can conclude with some poorly hidden reference to Habermas that

> Debates which are informed by ordinary language philosophy, speech act theory and other forms of linguistic philosophy, and focus on language and not systems, fail to identify the constraints placed by systems on actors' use of language. Arguments about the construction of meaning which limit themselves to language and its use, but ignore the restraints which arise from law's existence as a separate system of communication (with its own redundancies) have produced a series of irresolvable disputes about what truly occurs within legal systems. (Nobles and Schiff 2013, 56)

Since Max Weber's *Sociology of Law* (written 1913), a number of discussions have tried to find their way between formal jurisprudence and material jurisprudence, often in United States called substantial law. Luhmann does not accept the simplified model, in which British Common Law should be more material and continental European law more formal. Rather, the conceptual development of legal dogmatics and the empirical reference to interests do not follow a simple distinction between internal law and external environment, or between rationalist ideas and empiricism. Law concepts and interests, if anything, are developed in a mutual occupation that offers concepts to interests, such as obligations to take children into consideration or national security. "National security" is a political and military concept, yet if it should be used in law, jurisprudence has to develop its legal conceptualization, or to neglect it and exclude it from law.

Law is not a linear trivial machine used to predictions. Law does not predict; it interprets in an ongoing cognitive openness of new knowledge and new civil norms, which enter into law only if legal reasoning is able to reenter them in its operations. "The system cannot guarantee . . . a rational state. . . . Any discourse theory (such as Jürgen Habermas') that ignores this neither does justice to the highly developed peculiarity of the legal methods of persuasion nor achieves its goal" (Luhmann *Law* 2004, 353; 1993, 402).

The point is which interests are accepted in jurisprudence, that is, which interests can be conceptualized in law and which ones cannot. Exclusion is at least as important as inclusion, as in famous examples: Are capital-owner interests to be preferred to consumer interests? Production interests preferred to ecology protection? Property rights to slavery preferred to formal rights of human universalism? (Luhmann *Law* 2004, 350; 1993, 399). To expose such preferences, the legal system, paradoxically, constitutes observations and remembrance about other possibilities and other interests that could be decided as legal.

Even lawgiving does not control how laws are interpreted. Once the law is given, settled law may offer another validity, as the consequences may become different than supposed. Yet, Habermas cannot avoid this thesis of lacking governmentality (as Foucauldian scholars couldn't either). Thus, Habermas has to make recurrences to a third strategy: If communication procedures, in general, in politics, and in administration, have learned from law procedure, they may get a form that is acceptable to legal argumentation—jurisprudence does not have to bend the material argumentation in order to refer to reasonable discourses. Indirectly, public reasoning is not simply any environment external to law. This concerns Hegel's "Cunning of Reason" (*List der Vernunft*) and is discussed in German jurisprudence and sociology of law, conceptualized as rationalized legalization and juridification, or *Verrechtlichung* (Maus 1986a; Böckenförde 1991; Frankenberg 1986/2011, 309).

LUHMANN ON INDISPENSABLE NORMS

On one important topic, Luhmann's argument has shortcomings compared to Habermas's discourse ethics. Luhmann continues the classical story about the natural fallacy, that it is not possible to infer from facts to norms: "An inference about norms cannot be made from facts" (Luhmann *Law* 2004, 352; 1993, 401).

Hume and Kant are the classical references. Yet, even for the later Kant, the famous neo-Kantian distinction between facts and norms does not hold and neither does it in the quite accurate analysis by Émile Durkheim. We cannot describe the world and the facts of the world if we are not able to infer from descriptions to normativity: "if this is bread, then it should be possible to eat it," "if this is a text, then it should offer some meaning," "if this is a society then some norms should be valid in it." To Durkheim (1895/1937), rules and norms are the facts and the data to observe with sociological method. Luhmann, immediately, revised his position in another article, "Are There Still Indispensable Norms in Our Society?":

[T]he legal system seeks the foundation for its own method of observing the world in the *distinction* between norms and facts. In contrast, sociology is free to deal with norms as facts as well—obviously as facts of a particular kind. A possible construction is to understand norms as formulas for *contra-factual expectations*, for expectations of behavior, that is, that do not allow themselves to be irritated by factual behavior, but which are adhered to even when they are frustrated. The guiding distinction here is not fact/norm but learning/not-learning. The usual manner of speaking, which is calibrated to "ought" and talks of "validity," is then conceived as an expression for the right to refuse learning and the right to maintain expectations, even when they are frustrated. (*Norms* 2008, 20–21)

Trump's post-factual politics toward environmental issues is an example about how not to learn from facts—and it is a fact that even futures are ignored. Modalities as will-formation are parts of social communication. The future is part of the present, in the form of expectations. Social communication cannot be dispensed from references toward what might be expected from a contingent future. Hence, there is no simple distinction between necessity and contingency. From the point of view of sociology, Luhmann's theme could seem obvious.

However, even if this solution seems easy to handle, Luhmann's initial question in the article became extremely important in political, moral, and legal discussions in the decade after his death, in 1998. He raises the question of if it is possible to constitute rules for a state of exception. If a terrorist, as a fact, has a weapon of mass destruction, ought we to torture? Or ought we not to torture? Luhmann begins his analysis with this dilemma:

> Following good legal custom, presenting a case might help attune us to the topic of this talk. Imagine: You are a high-level law-enforcement officer. In your country—it could be Germany in the not-too-distant future—there are many left- and right-wing terrorists—every day there are murders, fire-bombings, the killing and injury of countless innocent people. You have captured the leader of such a group. Presumably, if you tortured him, you could save many lives—10, 100, 1000—we can vary the situation. Would you do it? In Germany the matter seems simple. One consults constitutional law. Article 1 (Human Dignity) provides for no exception. Indeed, the layman is at first astounded that the norm is formulated as fact. Is it therefore possible for torture not to violate human dignity? The jurist will let him know better. So far, so good. If not in terms of justice, then at least in terms of the legality. For common law, which doesn't operate in such legal-positivist terms, there is an extensive discussion that is relevant here. (18)

Formal positive law is opposed to pragmatism, and neither has no risks. Luhmann poses the question of whether human dignity, honor, virtue, or natural law as recognized in noble stratified societies offers answers to solve the dilemma. Human rights have evolved as to describe the form of individualized individualities that began in the eighteenth century, as if individuals with chances of careers and futures should have chances to escape. Yet, he does not really find solutions in classical moral and legal philosophy, from Kant to Hegel:

> For *Kant* "eternal peace" can only be guaranteed through states that grant citizens legal protection. *Habermas* adds this desideratum of the affected persons' to the democratic participation in constitutional procedures. Both suggestions are modern insofar as they avoid a dogmatic (metaphysical, religious, indisputable) anticipation of correct decisions that would sort the rams from the sheep in advance. But both suggestions are also characterized by other-worldliness and ignorance of the law. Neither *Kant* nor *Habermas* poses himself the problem of the right to break the law. For both the problem's solution lies in arrangements that enable access to the insights of reason. For its part, reason is handled like a tribunal or like a source of insight that, under conditions of uncoerced communication, enables precisely that which it presupposes, namely, understanding without coercion. (31)

If reasoning about law and justice is possible as some form of domination-free dialogue with the terrorist, then solutions could be found. This, however, is not obviously the case in this somewhat famous, if not outright nonrealist, hard case that never adapts to the real world, but has been used in political fantasies about the invented real world so often that it almost constituted the social reality (Barry 2015).

> However, if negation actually exists, then there is not only positive self-reference, but negative self-reference as well. The state of today's world guides the gaze more to the problem of a decision between justice and injustice that is made not in accordance with the law—for example, as mentioned at the beginning, the case of torture, or cases of international intervention, or cases of the retroactive condemnation of "crimes" that were covered by positive law (but ostensibly not through "supra-positive" law) at the time of their commission. (Luhmann *Norms* 2008, 31)

The "state of exception" and its necessities stating "extraordinary" exemptions to law refer to the so-called "reason of state" and its absolutist rule in the early seventeenth century. According to Luhmann, human rights will not do to make exceptions to such a state of exception. Rather, as a surprise to those who follow his cognitivist position, Luhmann proposes a notion of "human duties":

> In this situation one could replace the semantics of human *rights* with one of human *duties*. That would mean holding state governments responsible, at least in the sense of keeping order within their territory. And it would correspond to a mounting tendency that also structures the global societal system more strongly for politics, and that understands the state organization not only as an expression of the will of the "people" but also, and perhaps first and foremost, as the international address for questions about the provision of order. (34)

This, in fact, was what two years later became proposed under the auspices of United Nation as the "Responsibility to Protect" (R2P), adopted in 2005. In this form, human duties are addressed less to the legal system and more to some form of cooperation between the organizational system, the political system, and the legal system.

THE *CARDOZO LAW REVIEW* DEBATE (1996)

Habermas's German edition of *Between Facts and Norms* was published in 1992 with the somewhat untranslatable title *Faktizität und Geltung*. Immediately debates began to find which themes in it were to be selected as the most important. Ten thousand copies were sold already before publication, at the same time as political debates flourished about how to conceive the world situation after the Cold War. This was one of the books expected to tell how to analyze the social, political, legal, and perhaps economic and international situation beyond the level of more normal political science, and was so discussed along with easier books like Francis Fukuyama's *The End of History and the Last Man* and Samuel Huntington's *The Clash of Civilisations*, both of them already discussed as articles. China was about to have its unprecedented rise; and the Internet globalized. The Balkan Wars escalated in Yugoslavia and the European Union appeared with the Maastricht Treaty on January 1, 1993; Bill Clinton moved into office and the Soviet Union dissolved. Theory was on its move, critical social theory certainly, and widely influential intellectual groups expected that it could take a, if not the, lead. In Germany, for sure, it was contested by Luhmann's social systems theory and in France by Pierre Bourdieu and the remnants of Michel Foucault, but it was contested less by the still spectacular, however loose, ideas of postmodernism. In United States, John Rawls's *Political Liberalism* (1993) was already debated in discussions with various strands of more or less liberal communitarianism (from Charles Taylor and Michael Walzer to Amitai Etzioni and Alasdair McIntyre).

On September 20 and 21, 1992, *Cardozo Law Review* established a conference with thirty-two scholars, many from Europe, and debated Habermas's book. This was published as vol. 13 in 1996 (a double volume), with the title *Habermas on Law and Democracy: Critical Exchanges*. Among the scholars were Niklas Luhmann and his close collaborate Gunther Teubner. At the same time, *Cardozo Law Review* also published a major volume: *Luhmann's Legal Theory, Closed Systems and Open Justice: The Legal Sociology of Niklas Luhmann* (Vol. 13 [1992]). Here, in the present chapter, the theme is only about Luhmann's contribution and Habermas's reply, which also ends or is the conclusion of his eighty-page "A Reply to My Critics" to the preceding twenty-four articles commenting on him.

In the debate, the problem is about the reality of law and the hope that interferes. In short, Luhmann seeks to analyze how law functions, and Habermas how people, discourses, or systems outside law hope it functions. Luhmann's article bears the very classical Latin title from Roman law *quod omnes tangit* (which means "what concerns everyone," and is normally followed by "everyone should have a say in it"). The tradition says that those who are affected by a legal decision should be heard about it, and that is what makes it a political decision. Decisions are paradoxes insofar they decide about the uncertainty of future decisions.

So much is clear: Habermas and Luhmann agree that the distinction between legality and legitimacy is not sufficient. Therefore, Luhmann also rescues Habermas from his painstaking problems of translation: The title *Between Facts and Norms* might mislead: "For the foundation of the theory of legal discourse discussed here, it is decisive that Habermas sets aside the customary distinction used in the law itself, between facts and norms, instead employing his own concept-titles facticity and validity" (*Omnes* 1996, 887).

Initially, the point is simple and is first about accurate translation, since in continental European languages (for example, German or French) this duality has a triangular form of legality (*Legalität*), rational legitimacy (*Legitimität*), and popular legitimacy (*Legitimation*). For instance, Rousseau constitutes his argument in *The Social Contract* upon this triangular form. This, of course, is extremely well known and important to German scholars, since Hitler's regime seemingly had "legitimation" as popular legitimacy, but not any rational legitimacy. To German intellectuals from Luhmann and Habermas's generation, this triangularity is certainly far more important and dialectically sharpened than we outside Germany might understand. Explained in Luhmann's words: "The distinction between legality and legitimacy is copied into legality and is expressed as a legal fiction. Legitimacy is legality in a form determined by this distinction" (892). Hence, Luhmann explains the triangularity, as well as the topic of the debate, with his methodology of distinction, form analysis, and reentry of a distinction into the two sides of the form of a distinction between legality and legitimacy. On the one hand, with legal observations, law could reinforce, if law were not only law but also admittedly recognized as law with legitimacy, yet of course legal argumentation could pass even if it had no popular or rational legitimacy. On the other hand, rational legitimacy could argue better about decisions to cope with as acceptable decisions if they easily could be transformed into law—and perhaps even better were inspired by law. So much the worse for decisions, which would have a painful way into legal forms, for instance, because of privileges, lacking universality, admitted corruption, lacking rule of law, and so on. In the United States' sometimes exceptional decisions too, the importance of such distinctions is enlightening.

Hence, this constitutive form is not the point of departure for Luhmann's questions to Habermas. In fact, Luhmann and Habermas do agree on so much concerning the basic analysis here that they hardly have any mutual criticism that bears upon this part of the debate. "Habermas argues consistently" (*Omnes* 1996, 889).

Yet nevertheless, they enter the problem from two different angles. According to Luhmann, the problem is about time. "More important for the overall construction of the [Habermasian] theory is the fact that at this point Habermas concentrates on the social dimension and *time stands still*" (887–88, Luhmann's italics). The hope, or rather counterfactual hope, for Habermas's discourse theory is that law refers to, or initiates, some forms and procedures of argumentation that will or should or could invent some future hopes, for instance, about universality. Luhmann agrees that this often could lead to nice or good innovations; however, "good" is, then, only good as a distinction from "bad," and any argumentation about good or bad in any future daily life would then again be different than whatever might occur as legally acceptable law. To say it differently, the hopes we may hope for in our discursive daily communication are still constituted outside the communication form of law. Paradoxically, Luhmann, the lawyer, is more skeptical about what law can bring about than about whatever Habermas could hope for and what law could inform us about. Luhmann stands in the court and says "sorry, this is not what you hoped for," whereas Habermas stands in the hearing of parliament or congress and says, "we will, should, and could." Accordingly, Luhmann concludes his comment with the problem of "could!" as his last word (899). Yet, in fact, this is a bit bizarre, because Luhmann tries to explain that Habermas might have good reasons to hope for more than law can offer; but Habermas also, according to Luhmann, has so much trust in learnings from law that he cannot avoid getting disappointed or disappointing others. Law is not very rational; perhaps law is just not irrational or is at least seldom directly irrational, and still differentiates better than the mafia, revenge, or violence.

Habermas does not uphold any transcendental hope about legal reason; Luhmann admits that Habermas seeks elsewhere than in past traditions for a unity, which is neither in religion nor in transcendental philosophy nor in politics: Habermas's "theory forced itself to become concrete" (898). Habermas's point, as well as his hope, is in the pragmatics of everyday cooperation and collaborative work and its reflexive power of diplomacies, respect, politeness, and capacities for expression and listening. This, of course, can be observed as nice; but this is not exactly what has constituted law. Courts are busy and most often far more busy than commoners believe. They have to improvise. Empirical sociology of law has to admit that, whereas legal scholars sometimes clarify their arguments with overly beautiful cases of well-ordered argumentation. Therefore time is a less-planned or less-steerable issue than logical procedures of discourse ethics might admit, or "could" admit.

At the end, Habermas reformulates Luhmann's questioning of traditional promises from Roman and medieval legal revolutions. The dualities between nominalism and universalism cannot be sustained when "contingent temporal particulars provide the basis by which universals can be understood as equally floating constructions" (Habermas *Cardozo*, 1554). It seems that Habermas accepts Luhmann's conceptual history of law. Luhmann's temporal argumentation follows the tradition of the medieval philosopher Duns Scotus. With this tradition, he tries to let Habermas stay alongside pragmatic traditions: law only exists in its operations and not due to any nominal or universal form of entity.

This, too, is argued in Teubner's comment on Habermas, which is the next article in the issue of the *Cardozo Law Review*. His title of this article is also in Latin: "De Collisione Discursum—Communicative Rationalities in Law, Morality, and Politics." Teubner's argument is a bit more about pragmatic incommensurabilities of fragmented discourses. This follows because Teubner addresses international laws and legal systems. If we talk about a legal system in China, how could we even identify it as legal—and not as sport, war, or family—if it was too different? Debates about (de)fragmentation of transnational or global law are ongoing among legal scholars such as Teubner, Hauke Brunkhorst, and Martti Koskenniemi. Among those followers of Habermas and Luhmann, there are no more paradigmatic struggles. Rather they tend to oppose proponents of sovereign nationalism, though adherents of Habermas's positions are certainly concerned with participation and are actively engaged in political reforms of, for example, the European Union or the United Nations more than adherents of Luhmann's positions, which have more ironic concerns about observation and distance. Yet it is possible and even obligatory to participate in distanced observation, and to observe inescapable participation.

Paradoxically, Habermas's critical discourse theory is somewhat rescued by Trump since his so-called "post-truth" fake argumentation neglects validity claims and argumentative procedures so obviously that Habermas's position is reinforced as the communicative facticity and its empirical reality in which we are all embedded, or at least all research is.

V

FURTHER DEBATES

9

BROADER PERSPECTIVES—LUHMANN, HABERMAS, FOUCAULT, AND BOURDIEU

In cafés and classrooms, at dinner tables or in the mass media, grand discussions are always taking place. Coffee, beer, and wine are consumed in large quantities, as arguments and opinions are exchanged, and often, passionate stands are defended or attacked. These discussions concern truth and the meaning of life (or even eternal life), the future of society, and the foundation of its problems. Such debates can be dramatic, but they are also engaging and sometimes fun, and often they seem to be nothing more than discussions for the sake of discussion. Among intellectuals these debates may be about the day's leading positions and grand theories, and they are, in part, a form of intellectual entertainment.

The big names in social philosophy sometimes find audiences of many hundreds, if not thousands, looking for keys to unlock the mysteries of modern society. Certainly, there are intellectual stars, and discussions about who will replace Karl Marx or Jean-Paul Sartre as the next pope or emperor—or about who will unmask the power of emperors and expose their irrationalities. Some of their arguments follow pathways of logic or ethics; some follow empirical evidence. Yet it is not easy to find philosophical measures and criteria for evaluating valid positions when the positions in question are about what counts as measures and criteria, argument and reasonability. Should Habermas's ideas be measured with Luhmannian systems theory, or the other way around? Should French social thought live up to American standards, or is German thought—from Kant and Hegel to Weber—the gold standard in social theory? Such ambiguities lead philosophical discussions to become that much more passionate: the criteria to follow are internal and even self-referential.

Followers may instead look to charisma or personality, or simply personal preference for one author or another. One could rely on a preference for a particular style, theoretical process, or method of analysis, or for grounding every position in the depths of philosophical history and sophisticated elucidations. Some are instead more persuaded by the simple telling of inspiring stories and narratives, whereas others are extremely well informed. Indeed, questions concerning the validity of reason and reasonability likely have a smaller audience than the more popular telling of beautiful and eloquent narratives. Some authors and schools write in extremely dry and analytical ways; others with a sense of aesthetics and cultural glamour; others with intellectually sophisticated, conceptually heavy ideas; and still others in a straightforward and pragmatic style. Some authors exhibit all four characteristics. Stereotypical narrative styles are well known: the British analytical, the French flair, the German sophistication, and the American pragmatism. However, typical of great authors is that they more or less master all those writing styles. The problem is identifying what determines and defines the themes and the debates.

I will dwell a bit on this intellectual context before I enter the more substantial theoretical questions in this chapter. Probably, the discussions that surrounded the "new classics" in social theory are more substantial than they appear to be. They may, at a distance, appear superficial. But they are not. They are about the relations between power and reason, communication and consciousness, social life and individual life; and they are less about fast fashions than about war and sorrow. The main aim of the present chapter is to discuss if different views could be fruitful for understanding the debacles in modern social theory.

It has been much discussed whether Habermas's and Luhmann's grand theories are elaborations on Marx's, Durkheim's, Simmel's, and Weber's social theories and practices (Günther 1986/2011). Yet currently, and even more frequently, it is debated whether French social analyses offer completely different views. Some may prefer to include *auteurs* like

Luc Boltanski, Bruno Latour, or older authors like Edgar Morin and Réné Girard in such a discussion. This would broaden the perspective beyond any possibility of ending the book for the present purposes; nevertheless I suggest a number of other entrances for discussions. As we will see, Pierre Bourdieu and Michel Foucault have some major questions in common with Luhmann and Habermas, in addition to a common scope and scale.

THEMES AS FASHION OR AS CHALLENGES

With a certain regularity, it appears as if each decade has its intellectual fashion, telling us what should be our greatest concern, our yardstick for measuring whatever happens in society. In 1962, Theodor Adorno wrote that the idea of progress made headlines everywhere, and in his typical way, he exposed its dark sides and paradoxes—yet he admitted that he certainly would not return to the first half of the twentieth century. In the 1970s, the big debate was about left and right, Marxism or positivism. This debate spread everywhere—in Europe more than in America, to be sure, but even nonintellectuals knew about this opposition. It entered into daily life and was discussed in all social circles and groupings.

During the 1980s, not less than two debates framed the concerns over whatever was at stake: the first was the debate between modernism and postmodernism or, in terms less about aesthetics and more concerned with social theory, modernity and postmodernity. Charles Jencks's book *The Language of Post-Modern Architecture*, published in 1977, and Jean-François Lyotard's booklet *The Postmodern Condition* from 1979 laid the groundwork for the very confused debates that followed (Luhmann *Post-Modernism* 1995). Often, the controversy seemed to be about German positions against French positions; compromises or interpretations of one tradition translated into the other were at the center of the debate, such as the Geneva professor Manfred Frank's *What Is Neo-Structuralism?* (1983/1989) about French social thought, but published in German. Another, this time French, explanation was offered by Vincent Descombes in *Modern French Philosophy* (1980), which exposed how

French debates emerged from a German heritage among refugees in the 1930s. This was especially the case with the Russian Heidegger scholar Alexandre Kojève, whose lectures on Hegel in Paris influenced a whole generation, including Jean-Paul Sartre, Simone de Beauvoir, Maurice Merleau-Ponty, Louis Althusser, and many others.

In France, as in Germany, much concern was about what was to follow the neo-Kantian strand in philosophy and its dualism between subjectivity and objectivity, which had dissolved into more sophisticated views. Postmodern views were especially skeptical toward the heritage of concepts regarding objectivist truth. After the Second World War, the German Friedrich Nietzsche's penetrating critique of power appeared more influential in France than in Germany. Indeed, French philosophy was deeply concerned with a heavily German legacy, from Kant and Hegel to Nietzsche and Heidegger. Reason and power interfered with each other and sat on a balance like two children on a see-saw, one heavier than the other, but the other—the critique of power—more radically distant from the middle. Somehow, Richard Rorty's *Philosophy and the Mirror of Nature* from 1979 seemed to take an American pragmatist position in between those two apparently very opposed intellectual currents.

The other debate in the 1980s was somewhat more American, but also very important in Europe. It was about communitarianism versus liberalism or individualism. In Europe, mainly conservative, nationalist, and, not least of all, Christian Catholics found new ways to express the idea of community: one example is the relatively unusual yet seriously discussed Scot Alasdair MacIntyre, who in *After Virtue?* (1981) took the peculiar position of a Trotskian Marxist fond of Catholicism. In America, even slightly leftist philosophers like the "Europeanized" Hegel specialist Charles Taylor took a somewhat communitarian position, for example, in his debate with Habermas on multiculturalism; this was close to another liberal communitarian position, namely, that of Michael Walzer (*Spheres of Justice*, 1983). It is not wrong to say that close to everything in that debate had already been settled by the young Émile Durkheim in his dissertation *Division of Labor* from 1893. Modern solidarity had to be solidarity among strangers or at least people with different specializations. Yet with John Rawls on the mid-liberal side, and Michael Walzer and Michael Sandel on the mid-communitarian side, the debate continued well into the 1990s. Many other names and positions could be mentioned in this regard as well.

In Europe, that debate took a new turn after the fall of the Berlin Wall in 1989 and became a far more political and dangerous quarrel between communitarian nationalism and liberal cosmopolitanism. In fact, for those of the (especially German and American) somewhat trendsetting intellectuals who, nearly every spring, met with Eastern European social thinkers at the International University Center in Dubrovnik, the quarrel began earlier on. This group included Habermas and Luhmann. Against the background of the young Marx, who authored *The German Ideology* in 1845, some of the Serbian Marxist Praxis-School social philosophers, such as Mihailo Marković, began to criticize globalist trends as early as 1981. This was not only about global capitalism, but concerned everything cultural that was at all cosmopolitan. The quarrel exploded between the still more cosmopolitan Habermasians and the communitarian nationalists in April 1986—shortly after Gorbachev's assumption of power. Of course, Luhmann held himself at the periphery, observing that quarrel from the outside, whereas Habermas was in the eye of the storm. His former doctorate student Zoran Dindić, closely connected to the Konstanz professor and Habermas associate Albrecht Wellmer, became mayor of Belgrade and prime minister of Serbia, but was assassinated in March 2003. Habermas forwarded European integration as a political constitutional process, thus favoring a kind of political community that stopped short of all-inclusive community ideas, whereas Luhmann simply claimed that society is no longer national anyway, but rather is a world society.

Back in 1979, Lyotard said that the great narratives were dead. There would be no more great Christian narrative to believe in as an overarching framework, no nationalism, and no socialism; not even a liberalism of individualist actors would survive. But in fact, globalization itself became *the* narrative during the 1990s, as if there were only one form and one trend in globalization, rather than many very different, even opposed, forms of it. There was considered to be One World and not a first, second, and third world, and one system of signs: the Internet with Hollywood as its cultural defense, backed by the U.S. army, navy, and air force; and one MacWorld power.

Of course, after 9/11, the globalization narrative twisted, and a new decade began. On the one hand, the so-called "War on Terrorism" was a global war. On the other hand, 9/11 was an attack on the McWorld version of whatever was meant metaphysically as well as concretely by globalization. Even before the end of the 1990s, Francis Fukuyama's "End of History" was replaced by Samuel Huntington's "Clash of Civilizations." Later, especially from 2003 onward, the neoconservative version of a preventive war against America's enemies appeared to be a nationalist idea based on "the American way of warfare" and was ultimately lost in every possible sense: strategically, tactically, financially, and in humanitarian terms. But during the Bush reign from 2001 to 2009, the political questions posed a classical intellectual problem to those at the center of political philosophy: Was it possible to put the necessities of a certain reason of state (*raison d'État*) at the center of every social measure and claim a so-called "state of exception"? This debate was launched with questions very similar to those that concerned the infamous German lawyer and Cologne professor Carl Schmitt's claim that the decision about such a state of exception was about the basic political claim to determine who was friend and who was foe (Agamben 2005). This was what George W. Bush did with proclamations such as "either you are with us, or you are with the terrorists" (2001); the doctrine was inspired by Paul Wolfowitz, who, for his part, through the German immigrant Leo Strauss, was inspired by Schmitt, who was probably the most learned Nazi thinker, or perhaps simply the most extreme opportunist. The decisions about war were to command the rule of law and the tradition of just war (*jus ad bellum*) and justice in war (*jus in bello*). Indeed this was the Nazi position, but it was the neoconservative position as well.

Of course, such positions could be reflected by not only Habermas's and Luhmann's defense of a rule of law, but in particular their descriptions and analyses of the relation between the rule of law and the modern social constitution, or the build-up and construction of modern society. If modern society is functionally differentiated, it has to be concerned with the rule of law, separation of powers, international agreements, contracts, human rights, and so on. Luhmann and Habermas certainly offer different descriptions of such a state of society, but they are indeed anti-Schmittians at their cores. Society can never use exclusion to find its way to a clean society.

THE DEBATES ABOUT SOCIAL THEORY

Yet if we broaden the debates a bit, the French concerns are also very interesting. To Foucault, one of the main tendencies ever since his first analyses in the 1950s has been to oppose the idea of a clean society that is able to include itself in society through politics of exclusion, as if such a goal could be obtained and as if such a nightmarish state is desirable at all. Foucault is perhaps the most widely recognized social analyst since Max Weber. There are many reasons for this recognition, not least that Foucault is relatively easy to read and his concrete genealogies of different themes of power and exclusion are stimulating for many disciplines, are well written, and are sometimes entertaining even at the level of novels. Most of his books, and also those lectures that have been published since 1997, concern historical analyses of the archeology or genealogy of one or another particular group exposed to exclusion, whether due to psychiatric diagnoses, illness, imprisonment, sexual stigmatization, the power politics of emergent welfare states, or cynical economic theories. Comparable to Max Weber's work, those histories are often delineated *as if* they themselves could be interpreted by a more general theory. Yet Foucault is indeed opposed to such a general theory. The reasons may come from his admiration of Nietzsche, in the sense that a strong and radical exposition of the genealogy of power also describes how power formed a discourse on truth and science. Accordingly, we may question the truth claims of an analysis that is itself the product of a history of power! Once, in a debate in an April 1982 between Habermas, Anthony Giddens, and the French social philosopher Cornelius Castoriadis about Foucault, Habermas eloquently described Foucault's position with these words: "Foucault enlightens as if he makes Grand Theory by not making Grand Theory." Foucault's position can hardly be described better, or with higher appraisal.

Whether we look at society with Habermas, Foucault, Luhmann, or Bourdieu, concerns about totalitarian inclusion and the neglect of differences appear repeatedly. The Germans Habermas and Luhmann can be compared to Foucault and Bourdieu, and many introductory textbooks in sociology and social philosophy increasingly do so. As was briefly mentioned in the introductory chapters of this book, those four authors belong to the same generation, born at the end of the 1920s, a generation that was young during the Nazi sweep of Europe. They therefore may have similar concerns with questions that somehow foundationally aim to elucidate problems that were evident in their youth. Yet in all four cases, neither Nazism nor totalitarianism is even close to being a major concern in their many chef d'oeuvres. Their developments of social theory and criticism are far wider and more far-reaching, looking back in history as well as forward to the constituents of modern society and sometimes—apart from some smaller texts by Habermas—*as if* Nazism and totalitarianism were easy to escape and overcome. However, this impression is surely a misperception.

POWER AND RATIONALITY

The problem of power, inclusion, and exclusion may find its elucidation at a deeper level. The counterposition of power and reason certainly captures some important, if not decisive, issues surrounding what is at stake. Reason has some power and power needs reason to endure. Foucault and Bourdieu invested their formidable energies in dismantling French power and thereby offered views, methodologies, and analyses that are useful far beyond the borders of France. Of course, France once was the superpower of modernity; codes, discourses, fashions, and social forms, not to mention state-building and the law of nations, emanated from Paris for hundreds of years. After all, where would the founding fathers and the Federalist Papers have been if it had not been for the French Enlightenment? And what would the modern economy have been had it not been for French Physiocrats? What would modern medicine have become without Louis Pasteur, not to mention rationality without Descartes, or democracy without Montesquieu and Rousseau? The French militarily led absolutism, which in time led to Enlightenment, and this counterintuitive fact gave rise to many important questions in social and political theory. Yet far closer to Foucault's and Bourdieu's own lifetime and experiences were suspicions about the form of power that could have led to a French form of antienlightenment if France had lost the First World War and fascism had come to rule in France.

When the German special path or so-called "Sonderweg" was discussed so intensely after the Second World War, the challenge was always to go back into German history and detect when Nazism began. What were the seeds, and what were the limits to German or Prussian enlightenment? To be sure, German philosophical enlightenment had its heyday with giants like Kant and even composers like Bach and Beethoven, a wealth of authors, novelists, universities, and schools, as well as, since the last decades of the nineteenth century, a strength in capitalist industrialism, armaments, and military power second to none. Did not Max Weber expose the weaknesses of what he called formal rationality in favor of the so-called material rationalities? Indeed, Weber described the many pluralist rationalities of modern society, such as theology-guided living; economic calculation; legal formalization; composition in music, painting, and drama; formally conceptualized theoretical science and research; the infrastructure of cities and other rationalization forms—most of them reconceptualized and studied by Luhmann and Bourdieu. Weber also described how those forms were endangered by domination and how domination became integrated into an institutional structure of capitalism, industrialism, and a certain discipline that fused into one inescapable "iron house"—and he did so even before 1914. Were not France and other states subject to the same tendencies? Especially in the 1950s, some German historians described the long road to fascism in the early beginnings closely interlinked with the eighteenth-century Enlightenment. Pietism, disciplined living, and military armament all came along with the separation of powers, flourishing universities, and advanced cultural life. But then again, it also did in France, and certainly in Great Britain and other modern countries as well. Herbert Butterfield's classic criticism in *The Whig Interpretation of History* (1931/1965), after Brexit, throws British political rationality back into European constitutionalism, if it is interpreted as parliamentary rationalization.

If we follow the course of Foucault's and Bourdieu's writings, they seem to work under the suspicion that modernity never escaped the despotism of a state rationale that transformed an aristocratic régime into a military state bent on the control of its population through more or less hidden discipline (Bourdieu 1994, 2004, 2012). Somehow all kinds of rationalities are still anchored in early modern fusion of powerful forms of control and self-control. "Politics is the continuation of war by other means," as Foucault tells us several times over in a reversal of Carl von Clausewitz's famous thesis from the early nineteenth century (Foucault 1975, 170; 1976, 177–81; 1997, 41). Military exercises developed practices that entered school discipline and even scholarly exercises at universities and intellectual life, as if every matter of life was subsumed into a total struggle for power.

It is difficult to state definitively whether Bourdieu's or Foucault's writings espouse the highest forms of pessimism, surpassed only by the even more dark pessimism of Weber. This comparison has prompted research examining its validity. Yet at least Foucault let individual self-understanding escape the formal, disciplined, and homogenized codes and discourses that categorize the life of subjects as objects, and therefore asked if those categorizations and classifications—as tax contributor, draftee, or social client—also concern the subject addressed.

Bourdieu might be more skeptical. His description of modern life exposes how all human beings are embedded in a kind of human habitus that incorporates discursive practices without the slightest possibility of escape or of reasoning free from those societally instituted codes of communication and reasoning learned in families, schools, public life, and workplaces. Even academic elites, the *Homo Academicus*, are embedded in these symbolic forms of power (Bourdieu 1984). In that sense, society—still—is close to totalitarian. Bourdieu also enlightens as if Grand Theory is made by expositions of the difficulties of emancipation from the powers inherent in modern symbolic practices.

Most of Foucault's and Bourdieu's writings are easier to follow than Luhmann's and especially Habermas's. They are more empirical and more concrete. The reader does not herself have to find examples that demonstrate the topic or theme under discussion. Yet their pessimism is sometimes unbearable. However, since Foucault, more than Bourdieu, almost exclusively demonstrates how power operated historically (in the seventeenth and eighteenth centuries)—with the second half of his lecture series *Naissance de la biopolitique* (2004) as the sole major exception—he seems to admit that modern life could have escaped the historical forms of power so accurately described in his books.

Nonetheless, of course Luhmann and Habermas experienced power—and not just any kind of soft power, but the Wehrmacht form, whether in the Hitler Jugend or as a soldier in the Wehrmacht. And after all, even the harshest and most disciplinary French classroom does not use power in any way comparable to the Auschwitz way of using power. To Luhmann and Habermas, rationalities in a reasonable form escape totalitarian power by far. They do not analyze the construction of totalitarian power in penetrating studies of linkages between the world wars, as if Germany or Russia could have escaped in ways similar to France, England, or America. Hannah Arendt did so—and quite remarkably did not drown in such nearly all-embracing elucidations.

This resistance to examining a recent past that still hit too close to home was likely what held Luhmann and Habermas at a distance and, in Luhmann's term, in a second-order observation of modern society. Like Parsons, they both aimed for a Grand and General Theory that could analyze and argue beyond the navel-gazing immediate findings about the society in which they grew up. Whatever is meant by systems and communication, they are forms that reach far beyond those organized in the totalitarian societies of the early twentieth century. Totalitarian political societies use and abuse modern systems and communication. Social theory can analyze how, when, where, and with whom, but should not forward those aims, questions, and analyses so much that they cannot see beyond them to other political societies or even to reasonable constituents and methods used in social research and political thought.

Foucault in *History of Sexuality* devoted much energy to dismantling the idea of a juridical repressive power that could be escaped by those critical means that linked the tribunal model of law, morals, and procedural reasoning (1976, 115–17). This criticism of the critical legacy is closer to Luhmann's criticism than may be disclosed at first sight. Luhmann is skeptical about the interlocking idea of legal reason and rationality, but displaces his critics of absolutist and even totalitarian repressive power to the form of power. He escapes the juridical-moral critique of power in favor of a more cognitive critique, since absolutist power development deconstructs itself by its own need for differentiation. Foucault dismisses the juridical legacy of power and power critique, whereas Luhmann embraces that form of functional differentiation that was the vehicle for Enlightenment and included the legal reforms of positive law and natural law. The point is not to be trapped into a tribunal of reasoning that is interlocked with the historical legacy of a power state that constructs itself with the medium of law; the point is to observe the evolution in the differentiation and separation of powers and in this sense to observe the many pluralist forms of rationalization.

COMMUNICATION AT THE CORE

Foucault, Bourdieu, Luhmann, and Habermas were all born within a short period of time, between 1926 and 1930, in continental Europe, and experienced related yet different histories. They also all embrace the turn away from positivism, or, even more broadly stated, away from all kinds of objectivism, whether rationalism or structuralism, neo-Kantianism, empiricism, or communitarianism. But their commonalities are not captured merely by describing what they did not do. They also engage in a certain preoccupation with language, discourses, communication, and symbolic practice. All things that research is able to constitute as sense, meaning, or truth are constructed in the rules and codes of speech acts and communicative discourses.

Those roots of logic and validity claims may be found in the 1920s and 1930s with Ludwig Wittgenstein, Karl Bühler, and Ernst Cassirer. These seeds flowered during the 1950s and 1960s and became known to some as the linguistic or communicative turn in the philosophy of the twentieth century, only to spread to social theory and research in the 1970s and become recognized everywhere in the 1980s. Not least in Great Britain, they were known by terms like "Oxford philosophy of language" and "speech acts theory" under an especially Wittgensteinian influence. At the same time, poststructuralism went beyond Ferdinand Saussure and Louis Hjemslev's or Roman Jakobson's elaborations of basic linguistic structures. Whenever we do research, we do it in terms of communication and language; Weber's iron cage may not be in the institutions but rather in discursive communication. Yet perhaps it is not a prison, but an oasis of hope and meaning.

Existentialism—in the quite different forms of Heidegger's existential ontology about being-in-the-world and Sartre's more individualist description of freedom, angst, loneliness, and individualism—certainly influenced all of them, but it was also something to escape from. Life is more social than postwar existentialism described. Communication and the inescapable linguistic embeddedness of thoughts and modern life show why modern life is not as absurdly lonely as existentialism claimed. Nor is it as egoistic or instrumentalist as rational choice ideas postulated.

For instance, Bourdieu, in his *Sens pratique* from 1980, describes how his development of methods to investigate symbolic practices goes in between a subjectivist existentialism and an objectivist structuralism. Social life is not rooted in individual actors acting freely outside society, nor is it simply reduced to an instrumental surface for deeper structures. Symbols are never only determined, but always operate distinct from given established forms and routines, at new places with new persons and in unforeseen situations.

Foucault and especially Luhmann might be closer to existentialist philosophy. Luhmann's philosophy sharply distinguishes activities of psychic systems, such as thoughts and feeling (dreams, images), from communication. He describes not only a difference between meaning in the form of social communication and meaning in the form of consciousness, but especially and decisively the different forms of temporality, for instance, between what is achievable in speech and the much faster speed of synchronized thought. Concerns with temporality (*Zeitlichkeit*) especially link Luhmann to Sartre, Heidegger, and even Nietzsche, whose philosophy of eternities reentering into the present was so important to Nietzsche as well as to Luhmann.

This great generation of Foucault, Luhmann, Habermas, and Bourdieu was undoubtedly so occupied with speech and discourses in order to focus communication beyond the surface level of propaganda and empty, meaningless talk. They do not subscribe to Theodor Adorno's view that modern television is a form of cultural fascism, but they do expose power and paradoxes as inherent constituents of modern communication. Bourdieu's and Luhmann's analyses of fields of symbolic practice and functional communication systems expose quite a number of similarities. They, like Foucault, observe and describe complex arrays of binary codes of communication and symbolic practices; and often they focus on the same forms of binary codes, such as exams passed or not passed, art or not art, research about truth or false research, and so on. Indeed, they try to find conflicts and paradoxes behind the doxa of official dogmas, illusions, and old-European visions. Communication codes established in Luhmann's theory as self-referential are, according to Bourdieu's conceptualizations, exposed as visions of so-called *illusio*. To Luhmann as well as to Bourdieu, there is an undeniable struggle for hegemony and domination of systems and fields: What is to count in the interpretation and observation of a certain complex situation, be it economic codes, legal codes, educational codes, scientific codes, or codes of art or politics? In social research we can observe this struggle in texts and interviews, or compare historical eras as well as states, organizations, or simple interactions according to such dominations or structural couplings of codes.

Therefore it is important to get a clear and well-researched analysis of the very form of differentiation between systems or "fields," as Bourdieu describes them. Bourdieu's concept of fields, each with their doxa, vision, and illusion, seems pretty close to Luhmann's concept of self-referential functional systems. However, one theme is rather obvious and accepted by most readers:

a. Luhmann defines functional systems through their second-order observations that not only code communication but also select and establish second-order codes about first-order codes. This allows for a very strict description of separated functional systems and therefore also separated powers. Luhmann, so to speak, describes the form of modern society that is preferable to Bourdieu's, but Bourdieu does hesitate toward such a strict second-order coding. Bourdieu's idea of fields describes fields in a much less differentiated and rather an overly integrated form. For example, students pass oral examinations not only because they know about matters, but because they behave well and look nice and could adapt as sons in law for the professor; politeness is dedifferentiated from knowledge, normativity, and cognition intersect. To Bourdieu, modern society never became fully modern in Luhmann's sense, for instance, when we compare their analyses of state power (Bourdieu 1994, 2004, 2012; Luhmann *Staatsräson* 1989, *Self-Reference* 1990:161–174, *Politik* 2000). At the same time, Bourdieu argues as if Luhmann's theory is well known, and should be standard-setting for a separation of powers. This especially is the case if we leave French ideas of politeness and courtly behavior as a supercode, which is and has to be standard-setting too, for all kinds of communication, even abroad in a world society that is not any more closely linked to the ancien régime legacy of prerevolutionary France.

b. When Habermas in their coauthored book from 1971 criticized Luhmann for having a philosophically defective concept of world, Luhmann responded with a conception that distinguished between "world" and "environment" (*Umwelt*). The *Umwelt* appears as a closed environment to systems. Yet it seems that Bourdieu's conception of fields embraces this closed horizon. A field takes a certain closed world as preunderstood and evidently understood natural horizon for the codes, doxa, and illusion inside that closed vision. In his elucidation "The Intellectual Field: A World Apart," the field is not simply a context or a milieu. The field constrains the agents to a certain symbolical practice and offers means to acknowledge a particularity inside a generality, as well as the general in the particular. In short and perhaps too briefly discussed, Bourdieu's point is that the environment, the *Umwelt*, enters into the system—the system as a unity of a system/environment difference. Therefore, Bourdieu argues that symbolical practice does operate with distinctions, but is overly irritated with a reintegration and reproduction of codes from the external side. "The field constitutes an exceptional world" (Bourdieu 1987a, 169). A field is not a functional system, but is a loosely coupled functional system in its environmental world. To Luhmann the closure of functional systems corresponds to an opened world horizon external to the closed horizon of the environmental world (*Umwelt*).[1] Luhmann's position is that any transgression and especially a revolution in art, law, education, research, or politics is in need of a difference to be reconstituted and "restabilized" (Luhmann *Theory* 1997, 2:292–97). To both Luhmann and Bourdieu this is indeed a historical phenomenon.

INCLUSION AND EXCLUSION

Luhmann, Habermas, Bourdieu, and Foucault can be said to have found their way in a complex historical context with certain tools they tried to combine and elaborate into still better analytical strategies. In quite a number of respects they expose similar yet different combinations, concepts, and strategies: for instance, Luhmann and Habermas's discussions in their co-authored book can be compared with Foucault's *Archeology of Knowledge*, published in 1969, or *L'ordre du discours* from 1970. Bourdieu's and Luhmann's early studies on the sociology of religion can certainly be compared to one another in many respects, as well as with Weber's studies of the religious imprint on modern society.

Inclusion and exclusion are a theme common to all four social researchers. To Bourdieu, inclusion reproduces itself. Inclusion seems to accumulate on the inner side of society's recognized symbolic codes, and codes established on the excluded side are not recognized; codes of inclusion (eloquence, originality, autonomy, self-discipline, and so on) seem to overintegrate different fields through social networks and social capital, exercising dominance and enjoying preferred status over certain symbolic actions. To Luhmann, individuals subject to communication in one or more systems may stumble when differentiated functional systems are not structurally coupled. Exclusion then integrates those on the external side of a functionally differentiated society, leaving the excluded to live a life squeezed in between functionally differentiated systems. This Kafka-like effect leads Habermas to strive for the inclusion or "reintegration of the others" through rights to nonexclusion. None of our four heroes would opt for a communitarian inclusion—unless in small primary groups.

WHAT DESCRIBES THE EMANCIPATION OF INDIVIDUALS?

If we conclusively use the standard of individuals more or less embraced by modern society, we can see four different positions, ranged from one extreme to the other. The two extremes are Luhmann and Bourdieu. To Luhmann, psychic systems are simply not part of modern society. Modern society is constituted by communication, not by individuals, and communication is only possible because our thoughts are distinguished from what we communicate. Luhmann claims that modern individuals, luckily, are emancipated from a societal communication system that claimed the impossible, namely, the transfer of thoughts into an individual psychic system. The power of society may be as hard, totalitarian, and dedifferentiated, but in spite of attempts at indoctrination, the thoughts and feelings of psychic systems are free and emancipated from modern power, and today they even have the human right to be so.

The opposite position is held by Bourdieu in *The Distinction* (1979/1984) and in his later book *Rules of Art* (1992) and his lectures *Manet* (2013). His test case can be said to be the classic Kantian good taste in art claim, which is a test case for Luhmann too. This classical Kantian theme of beauty and sublime taste is an extreme case, since it concerns the most subjective claim among the ideas we have. Feelings for beauty are apparently constituted in a very personal way, compared to our sense of justice, organization, scientific validity claims, or other activities that we all have to deal with in communion with others. Habermas claims that such acts of coordination and cooperation are far more intersubjectively constituted. Bourdieu goes much further than Habermas and argues a point not unlike Woody Allen's style of arguing: People claim that they like this or that because they have been socialized to have a taste for it, and have experienced sufficiently often that such a taste is recognized among those to whom they address their thoughts and meanings. The sense and taste of art are cultivated and ritualized by those codes of conduct used in the social setting, which each individual—even those who claim individuality and freedom from conformity—takes part in, since such ideas are current among their fellows. The individual habitus is deeply embedded into social forms, and individuals express tastes that can expose their position in the social space, close to the *avant garde* or to commonly held views.

By contrast Luhmann, in *Art as a Social System* (*Art* 1995/2000; *Schriften* 2008), analyzes art according to the self-descriptions found among artists in art catalogues and writings and speeches in which we find communication about art. Communication about art is found not only in a distanced reception of it but also among art producers; yet what one individually thinks (as a psychic system) is wisely held apart. An observer might even note that he or she does not really feel or know much in particular, but nonetheless certainly can find her way with some codes in discussions about art while still keeping a distance. Art as communication is a form that keeps its distance not only from our reception but also from artists themselves. Art therefore escapes the life story of the artist, and the art of geniuses is especially conveyed according to ideas of aura and sublimity that escape the situation of art production.

Habermas, despite studies in the history of literature, does not bother so much with art; but the Kantian test case about art is important to him in another way, since it exposes claims about what can be meant and held as viewpoints concerning political and organizational coordination and cooperation. In a sense, Habermas accepts Luhmann's viewpoint that the psychic system of the lifeworld reproduces its autonomy with the background of its own presuppositions and understandings, in contrast to communicative acts. Habermas's main concern is not the sense of art or individual situations kept apart from society, but our sense of cooperation. In principle, we cannot have opinions about how to cooperate in a neglect of those with whom we embark on cooperation. Whatever we claim should, in principle, be acceptable to those concerned with our proposals for communication. This view is close to Kant's idea that judgments of art should be subject to some form of communication (*Mitteilung*) but cannot be subsumed by rules and concepts that determine taste; yet in the politics of war and peace we certainly have to be able to express our opinions and cannot publicly hold positions that cannot be defended according to generally and universally accepted norms. Similarly for Habermas, in political and organizational cooperation, that is, in the republican social life of modern individuals, we cannot have individualized claims completely apart from others. We cannot individually and in principle claim that Jews should be exterminated (for instance, with acceptance from Jews themselves), or that Iraq should be invaded without asking the Iraqi people.

According to such criteria, Habermas has a position in between Bourdieu and Luhmann. Foucault is certainly closer to Luhmann's position, but Foucault's analysis does not reach as far as Luhmann's. At the same time, in some respects his views on subjective taste are close or even identical to Bourdieu's. Foucault embarks less on investigations of art, instead finding another area for subjectivity, namely, sexual taste. Discourses about sexual behavior and opinions have been developed since ancient Greece and have been addressed at the level of individuals. Foucault's famous analyses in *Volonté du savoir*, especially in volume 1 (1976), describe how judges, doctors, teachers, fathers, and mothers have normalized codes, vocabularies, rules, and discourses about sexuality, about what is allowed and especially what is forbidden. Paradoxically, the Victorian discourse of sexuality even forbade discussing sexuality and excluded such discussions from public concern. The growth of cities during the long Victorian decades endangered the lives of young women (and men) and exposed them to the vices of modern life: hence the emergent concern about what could not be discussed. The paradoxical result was, of course, that everyone became curious about this forbidden thing called sexuality.

This analysis offered a triple insight to Foucault. First, even some of the most subjective ideas—such as sexuality—seemed to be indeed very socially constructed. Indeed, Luhmann's books on love and seduction exposed the same social form of communication codes about intimate passion. Second, when sexuality was again freed in the so-called sexual liberation, and discourses about sexuality flourished all over, nothing guaranteed that such discursive forms did not indeed regulate, normalize, and strangulate sexual and subjective life even more. Third, Foucault told a story about the power of discourses that, far more generalized, could tell a lot of other stories about power, discourse, communication, freedom, and individuality—as if Foucault were making Grand Theory. In this sense, Foucault and Luhmann, in similar ways, expose how discourses and communication seduce and induce individual passions, yet also individual thoughts to stay at a remote distance from speech acts, and individualize sense in an existential reflection at a distance from sense offered by societally empowered discourses.

Both Foucault and Luhmann thereby exposed the extent to which subjective desires were part of social analysis in a way similar to Émile Durkheim's famous analysis of deviance in *The Rules of Sociological Method* (1895/1937, chap. 3) and in *Suicide* (1897); even such a subjective idea as the meaning and meaninglessness of an individual's own life and eventual suicide seemed to be possible to analyze in sociological terms.

Durkheim, Simmel, and Weber set standards for social research. Nevertheless, the generation of Foucault, Luhmann, Habermas, and Bourdieu certainly broadened those standards, depicting forms to be analyzed and methodologies for further investigation. Empirical research may use a form of triangulation and detect how forms conflict in certain specified cases, whereas those conflicting forms may be described according to Bourdieu and Luhmann, Habermas and Foucault, Luhmann and Foucault, Habermas and Bourdieu, and, for sure, Habermas and Luhmann. Some researchers may take only two of those authors, according to the subject analyzed or their reading capacities; others may use three or four and include still other authors. The four authors here discussed took different positions, and throughout their formative years in the 1950s and 1960s operated almost completely independently from one another, rather adhering to forms of dependencies on the classic authors as well as an independence from them, with new questions, new methods, and new philosophies. Yet only with Habermas and Luhmann do we see how many of those questions, criteria, and standards became subject to debate about possibilities and ways to go.

Too late to have a profound impact on the foundations of social thought, our four authors looked abroad to the French and German traditions in order to discover other insights and debates. They began to read one another in the 1970s, but the scarce interpretations across the Rhine do not reveal a greater understanding. Habermas in 1982 declared that he read Foucault "over and over" and published a lecture on Foucault in *The Philosophical Discourse of Modernity* from 1985. Luhmann in *Die Religion der Gesellschaft* (2000, 103) claimed that "here one could quote all the publications of Bourdieu." In 1978, Bourdieu published an article "The Force of Law" (1987c) on Luhmann's sociology of law, which he certainly misunderstood (as if Luhmann's view was close to Hans Kelsen's pure theory of law).

The result, luckily, is that we have a legacy of social thought that exposes different occupations, passions, and opposed attempts that are sufficiently similar to be compared, but sufficiently different to schematize various positions and possibilities for combination and mutual tests. When Bourdieu exposes how dedifferentiation has taken place in modern society, in education, at universities, in art, or in politics and Luhmann exposes the opposite—how differentiation has taken place—they cannot both be right. They expose forms of social analysis where their insights test each other. Accordingly, social analysis has to come to grips with how Bourdieu got it right in some sense and Luhmann got it right in another sense. Similarly, when Foucault (and Bourdieu) exposed how power is constructed in our institutions, discourses, fields, and systems, Habermas was challenged to find a way in which rationality, democracy, and freedom can develop. One important step in this effort was to go along with Luhmann to depict how the separation of powers is embedded into a much larger functional differentiation.

ENLIGHTENMENT OR UNDERENLIGHTENMENT

A conclusion is not possible. Yet some may, rightly, find it necessary, eventually, to suggest empirical studies or solutions for hard cases and impossible problems as the yardstick and milestone for theory comparison. Surely, a number of studies can enlighten their perspectives if they include discussions about the consensus or dissent, which may appear with the different and often opposed angles proposed by the power genealogy of Foucault, the field analysis of Bourdieu, the theory of differentiated communication systems by Luhmann, or the discourse ethics of communicative rationality exposed by Habermas. It is a kind of *underenlightenment* to ignore the strength of other perspectives. It is not only the object focused on that stays in the shadows through such neglect, but the research project as intervention risk that it exaggerates its unique focus and methodology, not to say the esteem, dignity, and reason of its authors.

In comparison to Foucault and Bourdieu, Luhmann and Habermas probably both underestimate stronger analytics of power. It is not obvious why this should be necessary. Luhmann, certainly, could expose a far stronger theory of power as self-reference (by definition) and as autopoietic self-observation and self-description as a historical and evolutionary emergent social phenomenon. This would add a far more general perspective to the French authors and even expose the risk of power building as well as risks for fusions of reason and rationality (Harste 2017; Andersen 2009).

Another angle is exposed by the incessant French occupation with historical, social, and bodily details in ways already exposed by Marx and Weber in studies on material rationality and by Norbert Elias in his detailed studies on the civilization process. Yet, we should not underestimate Luhmann's careful studies on historical semantics. Rather we should broaden their angles into political, organizational, legal, and pedagogic semantics of the present day, including the "essentially contested concepts," codes, and systems that appear in conflicts about such concrete semantics. Semantics is about daily words, bodily challenges, and hybrid collisions in welfare, warfare, and workfare (Andersen and Sand 2012).

EPILOGUE

Habermas's Limitations to Secularization (2019)

In November 2019, someone in China supposedly ate a bat or another animal that had not been sufficiently cooked. Such intake of an animal environment into a human bodily system could occur anywhere. We all know that this led to a severe social crisis somewhat similar to the Spanish Flu, which killed more than fifty million people in the period from 1917 to 1921. That pandemic probably had its origins in a military hospital in Arkansas, or among Chinese workers burying corpses in the trenches in Northern France, or among British troops in England or France during World War I. In the spring of 2020, the pandemic spread and the world literally shut down. Economic, political, legal, and motivational crises followed. Everybody experienced a new form of social (dis)order. In the United States, a crisis transition evolved from system to system, from health to economy, to law, to politics, and to a moral panic. This crisis transition was not unlike what Habermas analyzed in *Legitimation Crisis* (1973).

The million-dollar question became how to achieve isolation while surrounded by others. Governments tried to behave as if they themselves governed individually, whereas everybody knows that they inspired—if not directly copied—one another, from China to Italy, to Iceland, to the United States. World Society synchronized and became common—yet separated. Society experienced a classic theme from Rousseau and

Durkheim, for whom the question of how to legitimize is about how to accept a common form of separation.

This is essentially what the Habermas-Luhmann controversy is about. A most important and continuing divergence seems to appear in the question of observation (Luhmann) or participation (Habermas). The "double perspective" of observation and participation creates a hybridity between functionalism and hermeneutics (Habermas *Auch*, 1:35). Communication in society is observed and is subject to participation; if it hadn't been before, then certainly the pandemic crisis revealed it to us all. As individuals, each of us may think, perceive, and apperceive, or feel observing or participating in communication whether in school, with our families, or at work. We may unavoidably participate in linguistic performances that stabilize the significance and meaning of our perceptions as socially recognized, although such performances do not really fit our thoughts. Life and society are about common communication, in simultaneous synchronization of matters and themes isolated in risk of nonsimultaneity or simple belatedness. All kinds of metabolisms between systems and their different environments with differently coded systems came to the fore. The different metabolisms were always there, however; and they will stay with us, in society and outside of it.

At the same time, in November 2019, albeit without any connection to the pandemic, a ninety-year-old Habermas published his seminal, two-volume and 1738-page chef d'oeuvre *Auch eine Geschichte der Philosophie* (*Also a Philosophy of History*). This is an extraordinary achievement among social thinkers—and not only because of his age and his status as the last survivor of the great generation of social philosophers born in Europe before Hitler's disastrous regime. It is a well-written reconstruction of the lengthy secularization process from religion to knowledge in between history and evolution. In one word, his seminal book is about secularization from the mythical axial age to modernity. The contribution is that he attempts to clarify this often very broad and blurred concept, stage by stage, and one philosopher after another. The breath-taking scope of a historical process of philosophical thought obviously appears extremely remote from the present crisis scenario. However, deep crises always develop as transformations of deep-layered decision-making premises and their conditions: the entire web of interconnected ideas of society, man, communication, consensus and conflict, distanced observation, and part-taking subject to disruptions. Unfortunately, those trapped in "conspiracy theories" do not pore over books detailing the philosophy of science and religion. To study a classic author who wrote remotely from our present situation is always a hermeneutical exercise of meeting with another known to be essentially unknown. In the interpretation, the observation of the text must therefore turn into some form of participation in the worldview of the other. This is a learning process of decentered communication. I will first comment on the very outline of Habermas's ambition in the double volume, compared to other similar endeavors, such as Luhmann's. Second, I focus on the initial secularization embedded in the model of Trinitarian communication and the Eucharist. Third, from Luther's interpretation of the real presence of communication, there is a secularized heritage in Kant's critical philosophy of religion. Finally, I find some pitfalls in Habermas's interpretation of Kant's standard-setting deontological social theory.

HISTORY AND EVOLUTION

Habermas's late magnum opus is about evolution in the sense of irreversible advancements and learning processes in argumentation, as if philosophy and theological reflections develop in one great community of argumentation, eventually resulting in the actual society in mythologies of politics and social realities of scientific truths. And it is history in the sense that Habermas describes contingencies and social conditions together with structural, organizational, and systemic emergencies stretching back to the earliest stages of mankind, throughout the beginnings of civilization in Egypt, Mesopotamia, and early China. It gives Habermas's authorship and its position in social theory a seat alongside Weber, Durkheim, Foucault, and Luhmann. Moreover, he links his reconstruction to a narrative that in other forms is known and thoroughly studied, from Kant's teleological philosophy of history to Ernst Cassirer's three-volume *Philosophy of Symbolic Forms* (1922–1927–1929/1955). Habermas, however, does not go about that which he usually aims to do: that is, discuss using other, more contemporary theories.

Nevertheless, in his use of concepts, it is possible to follow his implicit comments on Luhmann.

Cassirer's achievement was the first advanced modern attempt at fulfilling Kant's ambition of a well-argued evolution in communication from an explanatory *Erklären* in natural history through an interpretation (*Deutung*) of civilization processes to a cultural understanding (*Verstehen*) (Kant 1790/1974: §77; Cassirer 1918/1972: 374–75). Of course, Hegel delineated the same ambition in *Vorlesungen über die Geschichte der Philosophie* and—also comparable to Habermas's endeavor—*Vorlesungen über die Philosophie der Religion*. Yet Hegel made this triple interpretation into a single perspective of the spirit, though it was divided into three: subjective, objective, and absolute.

Cassirer (1922–1925–1929/1955, 2:237), however, consequently delivered interpretations in which he conceived of how "in the development of linguistic forms we differentiated three stages which we designated as these of mimetic, analogical, and symbolic expression." As in Luhmann's social theory, the point is "the self-thematization of society from rite to myth and by means of a cognitive self-understanding of a collectivity" (Habermas *Auch*, 1:193). Moreover, "in the course of its development every religion comes to a point at which it must withstand this 'crisis' and break loose from its mythical foundations" (Cassirer, 239). Hence, already in *Critique of Judgment* (1790, §30), Kant described the freedom inherent in the interdiction of picturing God and man (e.g., Muhammad) at a certain stage of rationalized secularization. Whereas Cassirer wrote his three volumes amid the short but immense rise of German research after World War 1 and before its breakdown in 1933, Habermas published his two volumes mere weeks before the pandemic downfall of the postwar, almost-utopian paradise of modern society.

Whereas Kant wrote about immunity systems in *Critique of Judgment* (§§64–65), which co-opted parts of their environment into themselves and then learned about their self-organizing organisms, Cassirer, Luhmann, and Habermas all described how the Enlightenment learned from medieval and Reformation thought to co-opt heresies into the doxa of communication in order to maintain order. Such an endeavor is not unlike the frameworks described by Foucault and Pierre Bourdieu. This co-optation replaced the high medieval metaphysical thought of societies. Forms of *Corpus Spiritus* or corporate organisms were reformed with ideas of complex systems. Opposition and deviance had to enter government systems of rational argumentation and deliberation more than simply voting yes or no (where no one even knows what "no" means). If anything, to Habermas, the long British Brexit process was surely more important than a possible pandemic during the years he wrote this late two-volume book.

While Habermas does indeed use many pages, *Auch eine Geschichte der Philosophie* is also far better written and far more readable than his previous publications since *The Structural Transformation of the Public Sphere* (1962). The length of the book is preferable to an extremely concentrated four-hundred-page book: he uses all 1738 pages, takes the reader by the hand, and leads her through the immense material of authors and texts. Still, compared to Luhmann, many authors, texts, and clarifications in secondary literature are left aside, and excused in some modesty. However, the depths of many authors are much more elucidated. Luhmann analyzes semantics—Habermas analyzes authors.

Luhmann observes social communication, though individuals are kept at distance to it; notwithstanding, Habermas observes how authors and governors can do something about the organization of social communication. Marx, famously in the Eleventh Thesis of Feuerbach (1844), wrote that philosophers always tried to interpret the world in various ways, but what is truly important is to change it. Luhmann basically aimed to interpret observations, and Habermas to change with participation. In this late double volume, Habermas turns to interpretation and distanced observation. Nevertheless, he cannot resist commenting on the present crises. With the pandemic crises and its repercussions in social systems, we stand with one leg in each of two camps. For centuries (if not millennia), society, philosophy, and research learned about themselves in both camps. Society observed its self-descriptions and reacted to them. In the interpretation of Marx's functionalist theory of capitalism, Habermas recapitulates Marx with Luhmann's concepts of self-referential systems. Capital distorts environments and accumulates as a "differentiated" system of "self-steering," "self-alienation," "self-relating," "self-reflexive," and "self-reproduction" processes. While Marx remains in the vocabulary of an action theorist, Habermas uses "the language of systems theory," since "the self-reflexive closure [was] established by means of a transition of the systemic communication into an abstract denaturalized medium of money" (Habermas *Auch*, 2:655–56).

In the introductory chapter to *Communication Theory*, Habermas conceived a strong yet extremely demanding and methodological point developed in the philosophy of history of Kant and in Luhmann's theory of evolution. If the general conceptualization of evolution is about world as objectivity clarified in history, this cognitive achievement is conditioned by a secondary level of societal semantics about norms (Habermas) and codes (Luhmann). Society—the research community in particular—in its political, legal, and economic conditions could not develop contrary to this cognitive evolution. With Immanuel Kant's path-breaking "Copernican Revolution," the access to any metaphysics of the world and its civilizing process is achieved by postmetaphysical epistemologies. Cassirer (1922–1927–1929/1955) also describes this transformation. According to Habermas, the ontological metaphysics of world religions has transformed into epistemologies of subjective consciousness and further into communication forms. This means that long-term semantic lessons and ideas are still in use, such as ones about living in one world, about coherence, and about a series of binary codes. This is a daring point about development, and we may call it a process of differentiation, but it is also a process of rationalization, and at the same time a risky process of irrationalization. We cannot avoid the teleological a priori of performative validity claims or, as Luhmann (*Rationalität* 1981, 228) writes, the self-implication and fact of the self-reference of social self-descriptions. As long as evolution is about the emergence of systems differentiated from their environment, evolution is about risks too.

Simply put, "the world is habitable" (Habermas *Auch*, 2:205). Accordingly, Habermas's 1738 pages about social evolution must evidently end up with Habermas and his discourse theory, if not with Luhmann's notion of self-reference (2:336–40, 379). Since Kant, the point for a critical theory is that there is a risk that different and even risky processes of systemic self-reference invalidate these secularization and rationalization processes (2:660). This is why Luhmann's theory might cognitively still conceive a more critical methodology than Habermas. In an apocalyptic nuclear war or at the tipping points of ecological disaster, research and communication might still be codified along the risky vein of a negative dialectical enlightenment (1:124, 2:798–99; *Observations* 1993).

Research might accept this methodological blind spot, "observed from nowhere" (*Auch*, 1:473), and might have to accept that even enlightened research "prevents one from seeing that one does not see what one sees" (Luhmann *Theory* 1997, 2:323).

Habermas and Luhmann both conceive the bodily organic systems and the thoughts, consciousness, and feelings of psychic systems together with communicative meaning. Very importantly, they both understand this threefold differentiation in its evolutionary and historical development in bodily rituals and communicative semantics.

In the present book, I have established some reservations to Habermas's previous social theory of evolution in comparison to Luhmann's. Prior to *Auch*, Habermas's theory of the evolution of modern society had an immense gap between short descriptions of antiquity and the eighteenth-century Enlightenment. In a brief note, Habermas comments on the ambitions expressed in his lengthy article "History and Evolution" (1976) discussed in part 3. Many of Habermas's analyses, including *Communicative Action* (1981) and in particular "Second Intermediate Reflections" (section 2), fell far too short if they were intended as an attempt at offering a response to Luhmann's (at the time) much more developed analyses of societal self-descriptions in *Funktion der Religion* (1977) and the first two volumes of *Gesellschaftsstruktur und Semantik* (1980, 1981, 1989, 1995). Luhmann definitely continued to develop his approach in the last two volumes of *Gesellschaftsstruktur* (1989, 1995) and in his chapters on self-descriptions in *Law as a Social System* (1993), *Die Politik der Gesellschaft* (2000), *Die Religion der Gesellschaft* (2000), *Das Erziehungssystem der Gesellschaft* (2002), *Ideenevolution* (2008), and certainly in his final *Theory of Society* (1997).

Habermas analyses the historical secularization theme in the medium of the linguistification of sacral semantics (*Versprachlichung der Sakrale*). In this sense, he elaborates on the classical Durkheimian conception from *Communication Theory*. With Habermas's *Auch* (2019), we eventually find how Habermas, implicitly or explicitly, attempts to answer Luhmann, and probably Foucault too. Habermas coins his endeavor in terms of the concept of "genealogy," which after Nietzsche is mainly framed by Foucault, who mainly built his analytics upon discourses rooted in antiquity, the medieval, high medieval, late medieval ages, absolutism, and the eighteenth century. Nevertheless, Habermas continues to draw on a wealth of Luhmann's concepts about the functional differentiation of social communication systems' self-descriptions and self-reference (e.g., *Auch*, 1:654; and more emphatically, 1:852–85). Furthermore, in a kind of proxy debate, he enters into lengthy, fruitful discussions with the Egyptologist Jan Assmann, who worked with Luhmann in the 1980s, including a period at Dubrovnik's InterUniversity Centre, where they developed Luhmann's conception of monotheism (Assmann 1985, 1986, 1989; Luhmann *Unterscheidung* 1987). One God and one coherent interpretation of communication with God lead to the conception of one world and one world society (1:472–75). On this point, there might be an unspoken difference between Luhmann's focus on semantic distinctions and Habermas's recapitulation of Chinese philosophy, whether Confucian, Daoist, or Buddhist. With Daoism, certainly, we merely find a dynamic difference and no unity, whereas the Mediterranean heritage also distinguishes between what is a mandate from Heaven on Earth, as in Chinese philosophy (Henderson 1998). In particular, the Chinese expert and Luhmann scholar Hans-Georg Moeller (2006, 2012, 2017) has greatly elucidated the affinities of Luhmann's methodologies with Daoist thought.

EUCHARIST AS SPEECH ACT IN A COMMUNICATION PROCEDURE

More important to Habermas is the Christian idea of Trinitarian communication. Habermas recapitulates this in its formulation after the Council of Nicaea in 325 AD. The Holy Spirit appears as an interpretative formula for communication about the Lord and Jesus Christ as son (Habermas *Auch*, 1:543). Indeed, Habermas uses Luhmann's theory of social, material, and temporal forms of codified and reduced complexity and of how this constitutes meaning in communication. The communicative coherence establishes a form of simultaneity (*Gleichzeitigkeit*, cf. Habermas's sociological analogy, *Gleichursprünglichkeit*). Habermas's discussion of the Trinity (*Auch*, 1:541–45) is typical for his immanently continued discussion (or *Auseinandersetzung*) with Luhmann. On this point, Habermas continues (1:546ff.) in a suggestive interpretation of the famous philosophy of time in chapter 11 of Augustine's *Confessions*

(397/2006) and comes close to Luhmann's theory of temporality. Previously, Habermas didn't have an adequate answer to Luhmann's intensely repeated focus on time embedded in the simultaneity or even cosimultaneity of what Parsons called double contingencies (Habermas *Auch*, 1:794; Luhmann *Systems* 1984, chap. 3): for example, in intersubjectivity or in communication between God and humankind. Habermas's point is about the need to participate and not merely observe, and it is exactly for this reason that, to him, the Eucharist is supposed to be about the reality of the body of Christ and not merely the symbolic or semantic form. The Eucharist, in the liturgical form of Trinitarian communication, is about the inclusion of humankind in social speech acts and about the organizational form of society as centered or decentered. Habermas therefore sticks to this communication form and its learning processes in his treatment of the early Christian communities (1:518–19), in a recapitulation of history of ideas from Luther and the Reformation (2:43–59), and in a discussion of Kierkegaard (2:698–702). Of great importance to Habermas's—and Luhmann's—endeavors is that the liturgical struggle over the Eucharist as a form of communication was a core issue in the transformation from a substantial conception of societal metaphysics to a postmetaphysical conception.

An important entrance is Habermas's recapitulation of simultaneity in bodily gestures of human communication (1:247–52) and later (1:161–62; 2:48–51) in liturgical interpretations of the Eucharist (Wandel 2006, 94ff., 258ff.; Elwood 1999). Habermas is quite right that interpretations of substance (i.e., bread and wine as representations of Jesus Christ) created a Catholic legitimacy for the concentration of power, whereas Protestant (in particular Ulrich Zwingli's) interpretations focused more on symbolism. Habermas does not focus on the Reformist Calvinist interpretation, in which individuals, after the printing press revolution, can in principle each read, interpret, and make a difference as they may wish. However, a stronger focus on Hauke Brunkhorst's (2000, chap. 4) and Luhmann's analysis of the consequences in the aftermath of the printing press revolution (Luhmann *Theory* 2012, vol. 1, chap. 2, section 6) would enable a better and more Habermasian argumentation about the Lord's Supper. This developed as a form of procedural community and, in this sense, an institutionalization of Martin Luther's point about the real presence of Christ, conceived as a speech act of a social reality embedded in the

Eucharist, and even more so to Luther, as rituals and communicative semantics developed in prayers and in bodily performed psalms, regardless of whether individuals actually understood what was actually sung in collective rituals, for example, among children, and whether they understood the words or not. They may participate or only observe, remain at a distance or be included. During the pandemic crisis, first in Wuhan and later pretty much everywhere else, people sang from their balconies and participated in common communication, synchronically, whereas they simultaneously remained at a distance from one another, wondering about what was happening. This distance, "in a form of continued Eucharist," Habermas with Sören Kierkegaard, finally, at the end of *Auch* (2:673–80, 698–702), is observed as the lonely existential fate of the one, the author, who could merely, like Kierkegaard, write, communicate, and doubt about thoughts and experiences outside the reach of others.

In the almost conclusive "Intermediate Reflections" ("Zwischenbemerkung," in *Auch* 2:557–89), Habermas leans up against a young Hegelian perspective on the historical interdependencies of reasoning in a functional and complex society. He thinks about how autonomy can be learned, and in particular how it cannot avoid not learning. Conversely, in a more pessimist view, he recognizes a Luhmannian view of adaptability in a modern society distorted by powerful abuses of communication. This might be in the Adorno-Horkheimer sense of spin-doctors, propaganda, and ever more advanced forms of publicity. The liturgical interpretation of dependency, interdependency, and autonomy seems constitutive for modern communication: namely, as constitutionalization processes and the genealogy of communicative learning processes.

FROM LUTHER TO KANT

Psalms and the Eucharist constituted the core issue in the contested confessional conflicts. To a historical sociologist, they were about the delegation, management, and organization of society as they released and appeared after the printing press, after the discovery of the "New World," and after the military revolution with guns, fortifications, and navies, all taking place from 1500 onward. This triggered new conflicts over the constitutions of political community (or *Gemeinwesen*). In long discussions, while Habermas elucidates his argument with Kant and Hegel, he somewhat amazingly ignores a great deal of Kantian scholarship. In particular, since the 1960s, if not since Cassirer's important study *Kant's Life and Thought* from 1918, the importance of Kant's *Critique of Judgment* (1790) has been analyzed (Deleuze 1963/1997; Düsing 1968; Roviello 1984; Philonenko 1988; Riedel 1989; Makkreel 1994; Böhme 1996; Kaag 2005). Merely in a note (Habermas *Auch*, 2:362), Habermas reduces the teleological structure of the hypothesis that natural history is unavoidably observed as an evolutionary achievement, which emerged with the autonomous freedom of reasoning. Communicative evolution is thereby embedded in a transition from natural history to civilizational and cultural history (this evolution of a desacralization is extremely well studied by Habermas himself in this volume, yet had already been observed by Kant). At the end of Habermas's elucidation of Kant's philosophy of history, Habermas finally arrives at the form of nature reconciled with freedom, which is analyzed in the introduction to Kant's *Critique of Judgment*.

At this point, Kant's question of the Eucharist is decisive in Habermas's argumentation. The problem is quite subtle and should be confronted with another issue discussed by Kant: the general question of communication (*Mitteilung*) and the more differentiated quest for publicity, as in questions of war and peace. In *Auch*, Habermas does not connect these two nevertheless interconnected themes. Neither does Luhmann, though his form of analysis allows for another interpretation, somewhat more independent of Kant as a source of interpretation.

Kant is thoroughly aware that he makes two different forms of act to commitments: on the one hand, the individual acts in caution of the moral law; on the other, the individual acts in cooperation with others in order to obtain a morally conceived yet merely consequential common effort, namely, the goal of a philosophy of history (*Auch*, 2:358).

From this level, Habermas turns his attention away from the political community and its republican learning processes and toward those civilizational virtues taught by the church: "So when we see ourselves not merely as 'humans' or private people in the civil society but also as citizens of a political republic, we as moral persons 'have to contribute also as citizens in god's state on Earth and to act committed under the name of a church to the existence of such a bond'" (*Auch*, 2:359, citing Kant *Religion* 1794 Akademie Ausgabe 06, 105/B. 149, here cited from Suhrkamp 1977, 765). In *Auch*, Habermas interprets the problem with Kant's exposition of the Eucharist in the form of a church, or, rather, the Christian Church as exposed in Kant's philosophy of religion (*Die Religion innerhalb der Grenzen der blossen Vernunft*, 1794). To Habermas, the point is that the universalist duties of the subjective consciousness were realized as speech act and social reality in the form of sociality civilized by the Church. Whether in a later argument further developed by Hegel as a form of mediation (*Vermittlung*) or in an earlier argument made by Kant, the idea of transsubjectivity (Schwemmer 1970) should find an institutionalized conception in order to be realized as social bond and commitment. Here, Habermas lets Kant take the classic and (in particular) the Lutheran conception of the Eucharist as the decisive learning process. In Habermas's description, it was the Eucharist and the form it attained in the Church that taught humans to socialize and participate.

As discussed earlier, however, to Luhmann, that very process was just as much an experience of learning how to keep the distance as observer, yet remain immanent in communication. In the systems of education in schools, or argumentation in court, or observation of art, or hypothetical distance to truth in academia, it is just as important to learn and experience what reflected observation is about if observed somewhat similarly to the liturgy of churches (Luhmann *Law* 1993, chap. 8, section 10; *Erziehungssystem* 2002, 79; *Art* 1995, chap. 2; *Wissenschaft* 1990, chap. 2). As Luhmann (*Religion* 2000, 24) states in his theory of religion: "Hence the question is, who is the observer of religion? Theologians will perhaps offer the surprising answer: God. In order not themselves to be the observer? And should we believe in that?" Elsewhere, he continues to question the answer with the obvious question of who observes God, and he proposes the fallen angel: that is, the Devil (Luhmann *Religion* 2000, 167). As distanced psychic systems, humans observe that, historically, there is communication about such issues—whether in conflict or in peace. In the court, the answer would have been the judge; this would have been even more obviously the case in the legal philosophy of the tribunal of judgment, starting from the universalist linguistic pragmatics of the French chancellor Henri-François d'Aguesseau (1727) all the way to Kant himself. In this sense, Habermas, probably and paradoxically, should have stuck more to a Habermasian interpretation of functional equivalences of communicative learning processes from church to courts in the early Enlightenment. This is in contrast to *The Structural Transformation of the Public Sphere* (1962), where he so brilliantly argued along with theatrical performances in cafés and salons.

In fact, Luhmann and Habermas, both Lutherans, subscribe to Luther's idea that (absent) transcendence is present in immanence (Luhmann *Unterscheidung* 1987, 248). This corresponds to the Lutheran reading of the first three Commandments, which are inherent in the following seven Commandments (Bayer 2003, 93–96). The word becomes flesh and bread. This inherent linguistic philosophy first penetrates Habermas's thought when he sees Francisco Vitoria's *De Indis* as a preliminary "veil of ignorance," which decenters the European worldviews (Habermas *Auch*, 1:913). Later, in his reading of C. S. Peirce, the observant communication participates whenever "we" communicate. "I think" or "I believe" is immanently embedded in "we who speak" (2:782–86).

In particular, in order to eventually get to the point of participation, Habermas concludes his discussion of the importance of the Eucharist to his philosophy of communicative learning processes with Søren Kierkegaard; and yet, of course, the paradox with Kierkegaard is to keep the self at bay with the inclusive form of participation in communication by means of communication. The liturgical form, which Kant and Kierkegaard both find mysterious (if not silly), is institutionalized as "unavoidable, in the delicate question of the mystery of the internal worldly presence experienced in the *bodily words* of a spirit returned from transcendence. And Luther explains this physical presence of a transcendental power in the words of the pastor, when he comes to terms with his plastic interpretations of appropriate speech acts and symbolic gestures in the concepts of a theory that conceptualizes as speech acts do" (2:700; Habermas's italics).

Behind the Eucharist, however, in *Philosophy of Religion*, Kant had already exposed a more general form. Indeed, in *Die Religion innerhalb der Grenzen der blossen Vernunft*, from the very first phrase of the foreword (Kant 1794/1977, 649), he emphatically favors Erasmus's argument for freedom over Luther's argument for a higher dependency and commitment—without mentioning either by name. The discussion between Erasmus and

Luther is subject to Habermas's elucidation in *Auch* (2:52–59), though Erasmus's *Diatribe, or The Free Judgment* (*De libero arbitrio*, 1525) is not cited; yet Habermas cites Luther's response, *De servo arbitrio* (1526) at length. Of course, Kant's argument is not about freedom as egocentric voluntarism. On the contrary, free will is to abstain from inclinations in favor of bonds and duties. Here, a Luhmannian argument would reinforce Kant's argument as a *temporal* form of the modality of will-formation, since will is the (present) will to (future) will. Habermas's focuses more on the *social* will as socially committed will-formation: that is, both Habermas and Luhmann embed will in a form of communicative reality. Like Kant, they certainly find their analysis on Erasmus's side.

However, Habermas does offer some theological strength to Luther's position, since the problem for Luther—behind a veil of evangelic citations—is that resistance to an authoritarian claim for obedience is only possible if a higher authority can claim grace and forgiveness. Hence, to Luther, free will is not a first-order form of freedom, but rather a second-order commitment of conscientious will-formation. For example, Kant's paradox regarding the moral duty to lie or to speak the truth is clearly possible to solve for the squeezed consciousness of a person who believes that their lies are forgiven by a higher moral authority—God or a free discourse—when, for instance, the Nazi officer asks where the Jews are hidden. Habermas very well knows about this solution of the paradox. The second-order communication (with a "transcendent community of argumentation," Apel 1973) overrules the first order. To Luhmann, the long run, if not eternity, overrules the short run.

KANT'S DEONTOLOGICAL SOCIAL THEORY AS STANDARD

More dubiously, and too obsoletely neo-Kantian in its outline, over the course of the following pages (2:361–74), Habermas first ignores Kant's philosophy of communication (*Mitteilung*) and then neglects how Kant's communication theory is linked to his teleological philosophy of history. Kant did not finish this theory of the evolution in communication in *Critique of Judgment* in 1790, and he added some interpretations in *Toward Perpetual Peace* in 1795. Nevertheless, it is disappointing that Habermas did not simply mention the possibility that his own (or Luhmann's or Bourdieu's or Foucault's) undertakings had to extend that frame into a more coherent whole. Habermas continues to discuss Kant's endeavors under the neo-Kantian umbrella of a subjectivist philosophy, and he can only do so by neglecting Kant's theory of communication (*Mitteilung*) and, as mentioned, his idea of a tribunal of reasoning (Kant 1781/1787/1966, B 780–81; O'Neill 1989, chap. 1; Luhmann *Law* 1993, 340–41).

Judgment, whether in aesthetics or about war, cannot avoid communication and, even more to the point, judgment is inherently about communication, positively or negatively. Judgments of taste are not relative; they should be subject to defense as reflection, albeit not as determination.

In this community (*Gemeinsinn*) of rules and concepts, a social community (*Gemeinschaft*) is constituted as the "we." This social community involves more explicitly argued rules and concepts whenever cooperative judgments in the case of, for example, declarations of war or simply political organization are involved in a political, republican society (*Gemeinwesen*). The problem and its solution might not merely be in the intersubjectivity of mind as an embeddedness of mind in language, but in the simultaneity too, and its double contingencies of reciprocity in communication. Freedom from determination and the unavoidability of time-binding in will-formation—Luhmann's "will to will"—are still forms of subjective rights (Luhmann *Subjektive* 1981, 66).

This point leads to more common ground between Habermas and Luhmann: they both conceive the so-called papal revolution (Berman 1983) in theological dogmatics, legal dogmatics, and what could be called the organizational dogmatics. Whereas Luhmann (in *Funktion* 1977, 272–320) analyzes such a form of *corporate* dogmatics, Habermas repeatedly—I count more than fifty times—discusses organizational themes (in particular *Auch*, 1:654–75). This form of dogmatics and its counterposition in heresy emerged with the conception of corporate spirit (*Corpus Spiritus*) in the long twelfth century—from the Great Schism (1054) between the Eastern and Western Christian Church to the manifold European constitutions in the first half of the thirteenth century. Inherent in "organ-ization" we find the idea of corps and body politics (i.e., the body of Jesus) that re-presented an eternal Christ.

Here, Habermas takes Chris Thornhill (2011) and Brunkhorst's (2014a) somewhat similar analyses into account. All of them (including Luhmann), however, neglect the obvious self-reference in the constitution of power as concept, which takes power over its own definition, as if mighty might might communicate and thereby constitute itself with the concept of might or power. Along with Luhmann, Habermas even writes about "the autonomization of the Church into a thoroughly self-steering system" (*Auch*, 1:662). In the German, French, and Scandinavian languages, this self-reference to power is obvious (in German, *Macht macht Macht*; in French, *le pouvoir de pouvoir constituer pouvoir*). In addition, neither Bourdieu nor Foucault sees this system-theoretical conception (Harste 2017).

These points wrap up the differentiations between authority (*Auctoritas*) and power (*Potestas*). Similar to Chinese semantics about this distinction, which constitutes the idea of a "heavenly mandate," the extremely important historical distinction between authority and power developed between observation and doing, as a distinction between counselors and decision-makers. Reasonability and even "reason of state" developed with this distinction (Ullmann 1955, 1981).

Kant certainly, like Habermas, discusses the role of the Church in the communicative learning processes—and Habermas indeed emphasizes civilization and secularization as learning processes. However, the Church community is merely one particular form of communication institutionalized in liturgical procedures. Legal procedures in courts, theatrical procedures, parliamentary procedures, and procedures of academic discussions, as well as politeness in court and in love affairs, were all important, in particular in the aftermath of the Reformation (as well as in non-Western cultures). In the French Counterreformation, the procedures of dinner communication may have had previous learning processes in gastronomic experiences of supper, albeit a secularized Lord's Supper. Secularized processes demonstrated how communicative and bodily meaning were independent of the media of the Church; they could also certainly develop and continue as substantial meaning in another and more temporal earthly form than the Eucharist. What Kant describes in *Critique of Judgment* (§40) as "the fine distinctions" (*die feinen Unterschiede*) in dinner communication was certainly loaded with meaning (Bourdieu 1979/1984).

Habermas obviously knows very well about the commitment to publicity in the argumentation about decisions about war and peace. To Kant, this was more important than aesthetic judgments. However, Kant's famous analysis of aesthetic rationality was, to Kant, as an immensely clever philosopher, foremost a demonstration of how the obligatory communication about judgment in the case of war and peace would certainly be committed to public forms *if* he could (as he indeed did) demonstrate that judgment in cases of aesthetic judgment was committed to public communication (*Mitteilung*). Kant himself was not particularly interested in art (Böhme 1996).

Altogether, a conclusion to Habermas's critical theory of crises and their systemic tipping points is that moral panic risks imploding into fundamentalist metaphysics, as in conspiracy ideologies. This reduces the dual complexity of structurally coupled self-referential systems as well as the internal complexity of each system, scientifically, legally, economically, politically, and so on. Habermas's recent endeavor lets us remember and take account of the lengthy learning processes in which the functional differentiation of complex systems and themes ran along with the secularization of communication. If we do so, we will not escape into what sociologists call moral panics.

NOTES

INTRODUCTION

1. The second part of this essay is the only part of the book that has been translated into English: "Meaning as Sociology's Basic Concept," in Luhmann, *Self-Reference* 1990, 21–79.
2. A famous mistake, certainly, was that Habermas wrote about Luhmann's systems theory that it was "a culmination [*Hochform*] of technocratic consciousness," (H/L, 145). There is no doubt that Habermas regretted this claim, which he mixed with Carl Schmitt's legal theory of decisionism (cf. Thornhill 2007a, 502). In the situation among naïve students and scholars, in 1971, it was certainly a complete and unrooted offense—not honorable for a philosopher claiming high ethical standards in dialogue. However, I will not dwell on polemical parts of the controversy. In his final seminal *Theory of Society* (*Theory* 1997/2013, vol. 1, xi) Luhmann concluded that "The irony of the title [of H/L 1971] was that neither author wished to stand up for social technology, but we differed on what a society ought to be; and it is symptomatic that the theory first came to public attention in the form, not of a theory, but of a controversy." Cf. Marcelo Neves (2018a) about the controversy. Still those misunderstandings are repeated, for instance, in Jean-Marc Durand-Gasselin's introduction to Habermas (*Philosophical* 2018, 8, 22, 49). In Chris Thornhill's earlier *Political Theory in Modern Germany* (2000, 174–207), he tries to describe Luhmann's early political theory as if it fits into the series of German ascriptions of it as technocratic, conservative, neoconservative, close to Carl Schmitt, and so on. This attempt, I find, goes too far, since Thornhill's main argument is that Luhmann explains illusions of modern democracies, in particular in Germany's post-*Wirtschaftswunder* period and before the recession in 1975. Some of these explanations might be shared with some conservatives—by way of a classical position, one even shared a long time before with the young Marx (cf. Nisbet 1967). It must be

maintained that Luhmann already in the 1960s depicted very well the political risks of technical planning in any linear systems. In these years, such illusions about social technology certainly ruled among social-democratic parties, for instance, in Scandinavia; but this criticism does not turn Luhmann's systems theory conservative, and in particular not his theory after 1975. From that moment, it was clearly, if anything, anticommunitarian and antitotalitarian. Apart from this, I agree with Thornhill's later use of Luhmann's theory. Whereas Thornhill (in 2000) takes his departure from the overburdened "ungovernmentality" of the democratic welfare states starting in the 1970s, my point is different: namely that Luhmann and Habermas beyond actual political problems focus on the risk of a revitalized dedifferentiated "state of exception" that reduces political coordination or synchronization merely to the task of one single functional system (or its moral equivalents), whether in war, economic liberalism, social-technological planning, conservative-communitarian moralism, neonationalist populism, or a future ecofascism.

3. Moreover, Luhmann distanced himself from Parsons's conception of action systems. However, he found Parsons's analyses of "generalized symbolic media" very useful, and there is no doubt that Habermas could agree with Luhmann's words in this appreciation: "To be sure it does not make sense to claim that the Parsonian theory has failed or to say that fundamental mistakes had been built into the theory" (*Introduction* 1992/2002, 24).

1. THE HISTORICAL CONTEXT OF THE DEBATE

1. Cf. Hauke Brunkhorst and Stefan Müller-Doohm's (2018, xiiff.) interpretation of Habermas's and Luhmann's youth. Cf. "Niklas Luhmann–1997–Es gibt keine Biographie (Persönliches und Werk)," *YouTube*, www.youtube.com/watch?v=nFhQ6SrIKVo.
2. Christian Fleck (2011) documents this forced brain drain of several hundred top researchers.
3. Neo-Kantianism developed and dominated research in particular from about 1870 to 1920. These were the years of a take-off in modern science, natural science, and the cultural sciences (*Kulturwissenschaften*). The German notion of science (*Wissenschaft*) is broader and more reflective and philosophical than the American notion of "sciences." Neo-Kantianism was led, on the one hand, by an objectivist natural science oriented by Kant's *Critique of Pure Reason* (1781) and, on the other hand, by a more subjectivist core oriented toward Kant's moral philosophy in *Critique of Practical Reason* (1788). The crisis and breakdown of this dualism, under the First World War, led to new orientations, in which Kant's later historical and social philosophy in *Critique of Judgment* from 1790 opened a whole range of new conceptions, including a focus on communication, systems theory, evolution, political history, law, religion, aesthetics, education, and war and peace.
4. Moreover, they agree that Adorno failed to appreciate the critical rationalism established by Durkheim.

5. In this description, I follow Parsons's self-description in *Action Theory and the Human Condition* (1978) as well as Habermas's and Luhmann's later recapitulations of his endeavors.
6. This Cassirerian thought is important too in Bourdieu's analyses.
7. In Luhmann's "Meaning as a Basic Concept" (in *Self-Reference* 1990, 24), he accepted a translation of *Sinnzusammenhang* into "interconnected complex of meaning." In Habermas's *Communicative Action*, 1:153 Thomas McCarthy translated Weber's concept into "interconnections of meaning."
8. Whereas Luhmann, as a lawyer, never considered Carl Schmitt a serious lawyer, Habermas, as a philosopher and sociologist, in *The Structural Transformation of the Public Sphere* (1962/1975) took this former Nazi lawyer more seriously.

2. HOW A DEBATE TAKES OFF

1. Habermas later (in 1976) elucidated this part of the argument in the long and penetrating article "Universalpragmatics" (1998), originally published in a book edited by Karl-Otto Apel.
2. Specifically on trust and reputation in science, cf. Luhmann *Self-Steering* 1968, 237–38, 243.
3. Cf. Searle 1969, 20ff.; the point is also explained by Kant in *Critique of Judgment*, §§19–22, and as "the transcendental and affirmative principle of public right" in Kant 1795/1977, 109.
4. According to Martin Luther, "bread" in the Christian Eucharist might be a metaphor for the realities of social relations, for example, taking part in the Lord's Supper. In this sense, both Luhmann and Habermas are Lutherans, not Calvinists or Catholics. "Bread" is neither only symbolic nor only substantial, but part of a procedure in a dinner.
5. At the end of the line, Habermas, in particular after 2001, in several writings about the similar or functional equivalent status of religious confessions, as in his famous debate with Joseph Ratzinger (the future Pope Benedict VI), seems to accept a distinction between those theological worldviews open for interpretation and those fundamentalist worldviews closing off any discussion (Habermas *Naturalism* 2008, 114–48; *Awareness*; *Secularization*).
6. Luhmann, in 1975, wrote the introduction to the German translation of Durkheim's seminal *The Division of Labor in Society*. The introduction is translated (in Luhmann *Differentiation* 1982, 3–19).

3. INTERSUBJECTIVITY AND LIFEWORLD

1. In other words, how should our lifeworld possibly be interconnected with the lifeworld of Iraqi people?

2. At Bielefeld University, there is a huge department of sociology—perhaps the biggest in the world—and a huge department of history, separated by fifty meters, with a great library one floor below. Later, a department of historical sociology developed, in between the two departments.

4. HISTORY AND EVOLUTION

1. This common ground in Durkheim's writings could be subject to closer examination. There is a story about Durkheim—that he departed on a longer journey, like Columbus. Durkheim was a Kantian moral philosopher and discovered a new continent in *The Division of Labour in Society* (1893/1930).
2. Whereas some might find a range of similarities to Herbert Spencer's sociological systems theory in *Principles of Sociology* (1969/1876-96), the basic difference is indeed the point of self-implication and the communication paradigm.
3. This is the Kantian so-called a priori *and* synthetic achievement.
4. Later, in his seminal *Theory of Society* (1997), based on empirical accounts, Luhmann described a fourth type placed as a second stage, namely, center/periphery-differentiated societies, such as empires.
5. In 1971, however, Parsons published *The System of Modern Society*, which certainly is a much better booklet than its reputation at the time as deplorable reveals.
6. In German conceptual history, the classical reference is to the Austrian Otto Brunner's somewhat organistic *Land and Lordship: Structures of Governance in Medieval Austria* (*Land und Herrschaft*) from 1939 (translated into English in 1992). The Nazi and even pre-Nazi folkloristic vein offers narratives that Luhmann strives to keep at bay.
7. In his treatise *On the Origins of Geometry* in *Die Krisis der Europäischen Wissenschaften*, Edmund Husserl displayed how we might today think about geometric principles as universal standards, yet they appeared as unstable ideas at a certain moment, e.g., in antiquity, but then were thought as universal principles in early modernity—and then, again, relativized in the twentieth century. However more complex, this is obviously the case not only for organic achievements but for social concepts and principles as human rights, constitutions, law, bureaucratic organization, payments, war and peace, representation, and so on. Hence, sociology talks about "evolutionary universals" (Parsons 1964; Brunkhorst 2014a, 10–11; 43). In particular, Jacques Derrida (1989) made an interpretation of Husserl's *On the Origins* similar to Luhmann's evolutionary history of semantics.
8. The *Finnish Yearbook of Political Philosophy* has established something of a common ground between those different endeavors.
9. The controversies between Erasmus of Rotterdam and Martin Luther (e.g., about free will) is one example of such self-thematizations, followed by still others during the late stages of the Reformation.
10. This and the next two articles are not translated in *Communication and the Evolution of Society*.

11. In his reference to the articles, Lyotard (1979) writes "nonpreliminary..." (*Unbereitende*), as if it is a printing failure.
12. More recently, in the Luhmannian vein, Chris Thornhill published *A Sociology of Constitutions* (2011; cf. Thornhill 2008, 2010) and Hauke Brunkhorst, in a middle position between Luhmann and Habermas, published *Critical Theory of Legal Revolutions* (2014). Cf. Gorm Harste (2013b).
13. In 2000, Luhmann's brilliant student Urs Stäheli (now professor in Hamburg) published his habilitation dissertation *Sinnzusammenbrüche*, which deconstructed the Weberian notion of interconnected complexes of meaning (*Sinnzusammenhänge*), which were so important for post-1945 sociology (and even post-1914 sociology). A later, condensed summary was titled "The Hegemony of Meaning: Is There an Exit to Meaning in Niklas Luhmann's Systems Theory?" (Stäheli 2012). From the Luhmannian perspective, disconnected complexities of meaning could also be observed and are as likely as interconnected complexities of meaning. Interestingly, in an old article, Habermas speaks about the "context of guilt" (*Schuldzusammenhang*) (*Saying No* 1964/2002), namely between East and West Germany during the disrupted world of the Cold War.

5. EVOLUTION AND HISTORY

1. Those questions are adequate in the sense that they in a modernized version correspond to Kant's standard-setting *problematique* in *Critique of Judgment* (1790/1794) that grounded philosophy of history and made it relevant for social theory.
2. This topic later was to be discussed by Habermas too (in *Auch* 2019, as I describe in the epilogue).
3. This too was the unsolved "metaphysical" puzzle Gouldner (1970, 211) found in Parsons's social theory.
4. Karl-Otto Apel *Transformation der Philosophie* 1973, 2:358–435, referred to by Luhmann (in *Intersubjectivity* 1995, 175).
5. Luhmann later explained this device about "duplication" (in *Directrices*). In *Theory of Society* (1997, 1:565), he expresses the idea of a "take-off" (a concept that was lost in the translation). Cf. Brunkhorst 2014, 13, 51–53.
6. A classical analysis of the form is found in Walter Benjamin's *The Work of Art in the Age of its Technical Reproduction* (1936/1963).
7. About narratives, cf. Habermas, *Communicative Action*, 2:136–37, in addition to his article "Geschichte und Evolution" (*Rekonstruktion*, 210–13), as previously discussed in chapter 5.
8. Habermas's lecture "Myth and Ritual" at Berkeley on October 19, 2011 (www.youtube.com/watch?v=qA4iw3V001c), could indicate that *Auch* (2019) was intended to fill this gap.
9. Pierre Bourdieu's sociology of art exposes an interest-oriented position of social capital somewhere between the Hohendahl and Luhmann positions.

10. Unfortunately, these misreadings are recently repeated in the French Jean Marc Durand-Gasselin's introduction to Habermas's *Philosophical Introductions* (2018, 8, 22).

6. COMPLEXITY AND DEMOCRACY (1968–71)

1. Habermas's daughter, Rebekka Habermas, in 2016 published a study, in which chapter 9 has the title "Legitimation Through Procedures." The original title of the book in 2008 was *Diebe vor Gericht*.
2. Luhmann *Macht* 1967/2012, 87 (note 110).
3. In Luhmann (*Politische* 1967/2010, 23), a short footnote to Heinz von Foerster's publication *Self-Organizing Systems* (1961) has found a place.

7. PARADOXES OF LEGITIMACY

1. A somewhat different version followed with his book on "The Double Face of Europe" (*Das doppelte Gesicht Europas*, 2014b).
2. Let us note that, in translating Habermas's piece in 1975, Thomas McCarthy had troubles in dealing with the German concept *Bestandserhaltung*.
3. In his *Why War?* (2005) Philip Smith used Luhmann's theory of differentiated codes to differentiate crisis criteria into four narratives used in mass media and in politics to legitimate military interventions in, for example, Suez, the Gulf War, and Iraq: "business as usual," "drama," "heroization," and "apocalypse."
4. Cf. François Furet (1989), Denis Richet (1973), Isser Woloch (1994), and Pierre Rosanvallon (1990), all of which can readily be placed among the proponents for a long history behind the modern political revolution.
5. In fact, Iceland's financial crisis, almost three times deeper than the Greek one of 2008–18, hardly broke the far more sustainable social integration of Iceland and merely shook the political integration at its upper levels.
6. The nondistinction of crisis and society accompanies Luhmann's thought throughout, at least discretely. In an article published two years after German reunification, he states, "the continuous efforts of diagnosing a crisis lead to the notion that one is not dealing with this or that crisis, but with society itself" (Luhmann *Ende* 1991).
7. After Luhmann established his list of functionally differentiated systems, without changing the outlook several further candidates to the system rankings were added by systems theorists. These include, among others, systems for sport, tourism, transport, war, and garbage.
8. Two, fairly different versions or works of Luhmann are published under that same title *Organisation und Entscheidung*, in 1978 and far larger, posthumously in 2000 (translated 2018).

8. "BEFORE THE LAW" (1992–)

1. Luhmann's thought about the paradoxical risks embedded in legal procedures might very well have been influenced by his job in the 1950s: justifying procedures against Nazi officials and their confiscation of art and property.
2. A classic exposition is offered by the German Princeton historian Ernst Kantorowicz, and a number of later representations, such as Harold Berman's *Law and Revolution* (1983/2004), followed (cf. Habermas *Construction*). The French historian Françoise Autrand (1981) described the transformations in duties, habits, and mores among higher judges in France before the abstraction and homogenizing processes of law in the sixteenth century—well described by Pierre Chaunu (1993, 90–129)—and the professionalization of those judges, analyzed by François Bluche (1961). The point is not only that legal procedures underwent impressive reforms that led to positive law, but also that this led to structural couplings and interconnected procedures of obligations and moral duties in the very form of reasoning. According to a classical interpretation by François Olivier-Martin (1951/1997), still more refinements in the spirit of justice, counseling, and reasoning developed in France. These refinements in the civilizational procedures of negotiation and deliberation took place over a period of about five hundred years. Patrick Riley (1978), however, underestimates that a form of early Kantian reasoning in a "tribunal of justice" can be found in the philosophy of the Paris "Parlement" and particularly in the writings and speeches of its dominant figure, the Chancellor Jean-François d'Aguesseau (1759) (cf. Harste 2016a).
3. Cf., for example, Jacques Lenoble's comment (1996) to Habermas, although Lenoble certainly misunderstood not only Luhmann's and Teubner's systems theory but also what systems theory is about.
4. The pandemic in 2020 has demonstrated that health got priority, as previously war had. Both did so in states of exception.

9. BROADER PERSPECTIVES

1. In the article, Pierre Bourdieu criticizes the Habermas adept Peter Bürger's *Theory of the Avant-Garde* and Bürger's criticism of Bourdieu's autonomy. Bürger surely defends a classical view on art.

REFERENCE LIST

In the text, when references are indicated as, for example, 1977/1984, it is often the case that the first year to mark the original German edition, the second to mark the year of the published translation. In the remaining cases, a revised edition is marked after the original, for example, 1963/1971. If two years are given in an in-text citation with accompanying page numbers, the year indicates which publication the page numbers cite. All publication information is given in the reference list.

In this reference list, Jürgen Habermas's writings are listed according to alphabetized keywords referencing core concepts found in Brunkhorst, Kreide, and Lafont 2018; of course not all these writings are translated into English, and sometimes when they are published in compiled monographs, they are not identical to German publications. Niklas Luhmann's writings are listed chronologically and indicated with keywords referencing core concepts.

In the text, citations to Luhmann have a year after the keyword; citations to Habermas have the keyword without a year.

The translations cited come from the published translation, if available, unless otherwise noted.

JÜRGEN HABERMAS AND NIKLAS LUHMANN'S JOINT PUBLICATION

H/L Habermas, Jürgen, and Niklas Luhmann (1971). *Theorie der Gesellschaft oder Sozialtechnologie—Was leistet der Systemforschung*. Frankfurt: Suhrkamp.

JÜRGEN HABERMAS'S PUBLICATIONS

Arbeit "Arbeit und Interaktion: Bemerkungen zu Hegels Jenenser 'Philosophie des Geistes.'" In *Technik und Wissenschaft als "Ideologie."* Frankfurt: Suhrkamp, 1968.

Auch *Auch eine Geschichte der Philosophie*. Vol. 1, *Die okzidentale Konstellation von Glauben und Wissen*. Vol. 2, *Vernünftige Freiheit: Spuren des Diskurses über Glauben und Wissen*. Frankfurt: Suhrkamp, 2019.

Awareness *An Awareness of What Is Missing: Faith and Reason in a Post-Secular Age*. Cambridge: Polity, 2010. This is a coauthored publication.

Cardozo "Reply." *Cardozo Law Review*, special issue on Habermas on law and democracy, 17, nos. 4–5): 1552–57.

Communicative Action *The Theory of Communicative Action*. 2 vols. Boston: Beacon, 1987 (*Theorie des kommunikativen Handelns*. 2 vols. Frankfurt: Suhrkamp, 1981; abbreviated as TKH).

Complex "Could Complex Societies Form a Reasonable Identity?" ("Können komplexe Gesellschaften eine vernünftige Identität ausbilden?" (1974). In *Rekonstruktion* 1976.

Construction "Hauke Brunkhorst's Critical Theory of Legal Revolutions: Some Comments on Theory Construction." *Social and Legal Studies* 23, no 14 (2014): 533–46.

Dialektik "Dialektik der Rationalisierung," *Ästhetik und Kommunikation*, nos. 45/46 (1981): 126–58.

Discourse *The Philosophical Discourse of Modernity—Twelve Lectures*. Cambridge, MA: MIT Press, 1987 (*Der philosophische Diskurs der Moderne*. Frankfurt: Suhrkamp, 1985).

Diskursethik *Erläuterungen zur Diskursethik*. Frankfurt: Suhrkamp, 1991.

Divided West *The Divided West*. Cambridge: Polity, 2006 (*Der Gespaltene Westen*. Frankfurt: Suhrkamp, 2004).

Erkenntnis "Knowledge and Human Interests: A General Perspective" (1965/2005). In *Continental Philosophy of Science*, edited by Gary Gutting. London: Blackwell ("Erkenntnis und Interesse." In *Technik und Wissenschaft als "Ideologie."* Frankfurt: Suhrkamp, 1965/1968).

European *The Crisis of the European Union*. Cambridge: Polity, 2012.

Evolution *Communication and the Evolution of Society*. Boston: Beacon, 1979.

Facts (BFN) *Between Facts and Norms: Contributions to a Discourse Theory of Law and Democracy*. Cambridge, MA: MIT Press, 1996 (*Faktizität und Geltung: Beiträge zur Diskurstheorie des Rechts und des demokratischen Rechtsstaats*. Frankfurt: Suhrkamp, 1992).

Faltering *Europe: The Faltering Project*. Cambridge: Polity, 2009.

Future *The Future of Human Nature*. Cambridge: Polity, 2003.

Handeln "Handlung und System—Bemerkungen zu Parsons' Medientheorie." In *Verhalten, Handeln und System*, edited by Wolfgang Schluchter. Frankfurt: Suhrkamp, 1980.

History "History and Evolution." *Telos*, March 20, 1979, 5–44, http://journal.telospress.com/content/1979/39/5.full.pdf+html ("Geschichte und Evolution." In *Zur Rekonstruktion des historischen Materialismus*, 200–260. Frankfurt: Suhrkamp, 1976).

Inclusion *The Inclusion of the Other*. Cambridge, MA: MIT Press, 1998 (*Die Einbeziehung des Anderen*. Frankfurt: Suhrkamp, 1996).

Individuierung "Individuation Through Socialization." In *Postmetahysical Thinking*, 149–204. Cambridge, MA: MIT Press, 1992 ("Individuierung durch Vergesellschaftung." In *Nachmetaphysisches Denken*, 187–241. Frankfurt: Suhrkamp, 1988).

Justification *Justification and Application*. Cambridge, MA: MIT Press, 1991/1994.

Knowledge *Knowledge and Human Interests*. Boston: Beacon, 1971 (*Erkenntnis und Interesse*. Frankfurt: Suhrkamp, 1968/1973).

Kultur und Kritik "The Hermeneutic Claim to Universality." In *Contemporary Hermeneutics*, edited by Josef Bleicher. London: Routledge 1980. ("Die Universalitätsanspruch der Hermeneutik." In *Kultur und Kritik*. Frankfurt: Suhrkamp, 1970/1974).

Law *Law and Morality*. Tanner Lectures on Human Values, Boston University, 1986; published Salt Lake City: University of Utah Press, 1988, also https://tannerlectures.utah.edu/_documents/a-to-z/h/habermas88.pdf (in *Facts BFN* [German edition], 541–99, and not translated in the English version of *Facts BFN*).

Legitimation Crisis (LC) *Legitimation Crisis*. Boston: Beacon, 1975 (*Legitimationsprobleme im Spätkapitalismus*. Frankfurt: Suhrkamp, 1973).

Liberating *The Liberating Power of Symbols*. Cambridge, MA: MIT Press 2001 (*Vom sinnlichen Eindrück zum symbolischen Ausdrück*. Frankfurt: Suhrkamp, 1997).

Linguistic "Reflections on the Linguistic Foundation of Sociology." In Pragmatics 1988 ("Vorlesungen zu einer sprachtheoretischen Grundlegung der Soziologie." In *Vorstudien und Ergänzungen zur Theorie der kommunikativen Handelns*, 11–126. Frankfurt: Suhrkamp, 1971/1984).

Logic *On the Logic of the Social Sciences*. Cambridge: Polity, 1988 (*Zur Logik der Sozialwissenschaften*. Frankfurt: Suhrkamp, 1967/1970).

Modernity "Modernity—an Unfinished Project." In *Habermas and the Unfinished Project of Modernity*, edited by Maurizio Passerin and Seyla Benhabib, 38–58. Cambridge, MA: MIT Press, 1997.

Moral Consciousness *Moral Consciousness and Communicative Action*, Cambridge, MA: MIT Press, 1990 (*Moralbewußtsein und kommunikatives Handeln*. Frankfurt: Suhrkamp, 1983).

Moralität "Moralität und Sittlichkeit: Treffen Hegels Einwände gegen Kant auch auf die Diskursethik zu?" In *Moralität und Sittlichkeit: Das Problem Hegels und die Diskursethik*, edited by W. Kuhlmann. Frankfurt: Suhrkamp.

Myth "Myth and Ritual" at Berkeley on October 19, 2011 (www.youtube.com/watch?v=qA4iw3V001c).

Naturalism *Between Naturalism and Religion*. Cambridge: Polity, 2008 (*Zwischen Naturalismus und Religion*. Frankfurt: Suhrkamp, 2005).

Philosophical *Philosophical Introductions*. Cambridge: Polity, 2018.
Postmetaphysical *Postmetaphysical Thinking*. Cambridge, MA: MIT Press, 2001 (*Nachmetaphysisches Denken*. Frankfurt: Suhrkamp, 1988).
Postnational *The Postnational Constellation*. Cambridge, MA: MIT Press, 2001 (*Die postnationale Konstellation*. Frankfurt: Suhrkamp, 1998).
Pragmatics *On the Pragmatics of Communication*. Cambridge, MA: MIT Press, 1998.
Profiles *Philosophical Political Profiles*. Cambridge, MA: MIT Press, 1985 (*Philosophisch-politische Profile*. Frankfurt: Suhrkamp, 1981).
Rational Society *Towards a Rational Society*. Boston: Beacon, 1971.
Rekonstruktion *Zur Rekonstruktion des historischen Materialismus*. Frankfurt: Suhrkamp, 1976.
Religion *Rationality and Religion: Essays on Reason, God, and Modernity*. Cambridge, MA: MIT Press, 2002.
Reply "A Reply to My Critics." In *Habermas: Critical Debates*, edited by John Thompson and David Held. London: MacMillan, 1982.
Saying No "On the Difficulty of Saying No" (1964). In *Religion and Rationality*. Cambridge, MA: MIT Press, 2002 (in *Logic* 1967/1980).
Secularization *The Dialectics of Secularization: On Reason and Religion*. San Francisco: Ignatius Press, 2006. Coauthored with Joseph Ratzinger.
Technik *Technik und Wissenschaft als "Ideologie."* Frankfurt: Suhrkamp, 1968.
Theory and Practice *Theory and Practice*. Boston: Beacon, 1973 (*Theorie und Praxis*. 2nd ed. Frankfurt: Suhrkamp, 1963/1971).
Transformation (STPS) *The Structural Transformation of the Public Sphere*. Cambridge, MA: MIT Press, 1991 (*Strukturwandel der Öffentlichkeit*. Berlin: Luchterhand, 1962/1975).
Truth *Truth and Justification*. Cambridge, MA: MIT Press, 2003 (*Wahrheit und Rechtfertigung*. Frankfurt: Suhrkamp, 1999).
Universalpragmatics "What Is Universal Pragmatics?" In *On the Pragmatics of Communication*, 21–105. Cambridge, MA: MIT Press, 1998 ("Was heist Universalpragmatik?" In *Sprachpragmatik und Philosophie*, edited by Karl-Otto Apel. Frankfurt: Suhrkamp, 1976).
Unübersichtlichkeit *Die neue Unübersichtlichkeit*. Frankfurt: Suhrkamp, 1985.
Veröffentlichung "Zur Veröffentlichung von Vorlesungen aus dem Jahre 1935" (1953/1981). In *Profiles*, 65–71.
Vorstudien *Vorstudien und Ergänzungen zur Theorie des kommunikativen Handelns*. Frankfurt: Suhrkamp, 1984.
Wahrheitstheorien "Wahrheitstheorien" (1972). In *Vorstudien und Ergänzungen zur Theorie des kommunikativen Handelns*. Frankfurt: Suhrkamp, 1984.

NIKLAS LUHMANN'S PUBLICATIONS

Many of Luhmann's articles are found in *Soziologische Aufklärung*. 6 vols. Opladen: Westdeutscher, 1970, 1975, 1981, 1987, 1990, 1995. Here and in the text, they are abbreviated with SA and the volume number (SA 1, SA 2, etc.). Some of the articles are translated in *Differentiation* 1982; other translations are found in *Self-Reference* 1990.

Wahrheit (1962). "Wahrheit und Ideologie—Vorschläge zur Wiederaufnahme der Diskussion." In SA 1.

Ends (1964). "Ends, Domination, and System" (Engl. in *The Differentiation of Society*. New York: Columbia University Press, 1982).

Folgen (1964). *Funktionen und Folgen formaler Organisationen*. Berlin: Duncker und Humblot.

Grundrechte (1965). *Grundrechte als Institution*. Berlin: Duncker und Humblot.

Reflexive (1966). "Reflexive Mechanismen." In SA 1.

Macht (1967/2012). *Macht im System*. Frankfurt: Suhrkamp.

Politische (1967/2010). *Politische Soziologie*. Frankfurt: Suhrkamp.

Positive (1967). "Positives Recht als Ideologie." In *Ausdifferenzierung* 1981.

Sociology (1967). "Sociology as Theory of Social Systems." In SA 1 (Engl. in *Differentiation* 1982).

Self-Steering (1968). "Selbststeuerung der Wissenschaft." In SA 1 (Engl. "The Self-Steering of Research").

Trust (1968). *Vertrauen*. Stuttgart: Enke (Engl. *Trust and Power*. Chichester: Wiley, 1979).

Zweckbegriff (1968). *Zweckbegriff und Systemrationalität*. Frankfurt: Suhrkamp, 1973. (Not translated: Goal Concept and Systems Rationality).

Klassische (1969). "Klassische Theorien der Macht." *Zeitschrift für Politik* 16:149–70.

Komplexität (1969). "Komplexität und Demokratie." In *Politische Planung*. Opladen: Westdeutscher, 1970.

Legitimation (1969). *Legitimation durch Verfahren*. Frankfurt: Suhrkamp.

Love (1969/2008). *Liebe—eine Übung*. Frankfurt: Suhrkamp (Engl. *Love—a Sketch*. Cambridge: Polity, 2010).

Normen (1969). "Normen in soziologischer Perspektive." In *Die Moral der Gesellschaft*. Frankfurt: Suhrkamp, 2008.

Praxis (1969). "Die Praxis der Theorie." In SA 1.

Unterwachung (1969/2016). "Die Unterwachung oder Die Kunst, Vorgesetzte zu lenken." In *Der neue Chef*, edited by Jürgen Kaube, 90–106. Berlin: Suhrkamp.

Kausalität (1970). "Funktion und Kausalität." In SA 1, 9–30.

Political (1970). "Soziologie des politischen Systems." In SA 1 (Engl. "Sociology of the Political System." In *Differentiation* 1982).

Aufklärung (1971). "Soziologische Aufklärung." In SA 1.

Meaning (1971). "Sinn als Grundbegriff der Soziologie." In H/L 1971 (Engl. "Meaning as Sociology's Basic Concept." In *Self-Reference* 1990, 21–79).

Planung (1971). *Politische Planung*. Opladen: Westdeutscher.

Rechtsstaates (1971). "Gesellschaftliche und politische Bedingungen des Rechtsstaates." In *Planung*.

World Society (1971). "Die Weltgesellschaft." *Archiv für Rechts- und Sozialphilosophie* 57 (in SA 2) (Engl. "The World Society as a Social System." *International Journal of General Systems* 8, no. 3 [1982]: 131–38).

Politikbegriffe (1972). "Politikbegriffe und die 'Politisierung' der Verwaltung." In *Demokratie und Verwaltung*. Berlin: Speyer.

Self-Thematization (1972/1975). "Selbst-Thematisering des Gesellschaftssystem." In SA 2 (Engl. in *Differentiation* 1982).

Theory of Law (1972/1985). *Rechtssoziologie*. 2 vols. Hamburg: Rowohlt (Engl. *A Sociological Theory of Law*. London: Routledge, 1985).

Einführende (1974). "Einführende Bemerkungen zu einer Theorie symbolisch generalisierter Kommunikationsmedien." In SA 2.

Kontingenz (1974/2013). *Kontingenz und Recht*. Frankfurt: Suhrkamp.

Evolution (1975). "Evolution und Geschichte." In SA 2.

Gesellschaftstheorie (1975/2017). "Gesellschaftstheorie als Wissenschaft." *Zeitschrift für Soziologie* 46 (4): 219–48.

Innendifferenzierung (1975/2017). "Zur Innendifferenzierung des Gesellschaftssystems: Schichtung und funktionale Differenzierung." *Soziale Welt* 68 (1): 5–23.

Power (1975). *Macht*. Stuttgart: Enke (Engl. *Trust and Power*. Chichester: Wiley, 1979).

Systemtheorie (1975/2017). *Systemtheorie der Gesellschaft*. Frankfurt: Suhrkamp.

World-Time (1975). "Weltzeit und Systemgeschichte." In SA 2 (Engl. in *Differentiation* 1982).

Function (1977). *Funktion der Religion*. Frankfurt: Suhrkamp (Engl. *Religious Dogmatics and the Evolution of Societies*. New York: Edwin Mellen Press, 1984, 72–181).

Entscheidung (1978/1981). "Organisation und Entscheidung." In SA 3, 335–89.

Prozess (1978). "Geschichte als Prozess und die Theorie sozio-kultureller Evolution." In SA 2.

Temporalstrukturen (1979). "Temporalstrukturen des Handlungssystem." In *Verhalten, Halten und System*, edited by Wolfgang Schluchter. Frankfurt: Suhrkamp.

Anthropologie (1980). "Frühneuzeitliche Anthropologie: Theorietechnische Lösungen für ein Evolutionsproblem der Gesellschaft." In *Gesellschaftsstruktur*, vol. 1.

Gesellschaftsstruktur (1980, 1981, 1989, 1995). *Gesellschaftsstruktur und Semantik*. 4 vols. Frankfurt: Suhrkamp (Engl. *Structure of Society and Semantics*).

Interaktion (1980). "Interaktion in den Oberschichten: Zur Transformation ihrer Semantik im 17. und 18. Jahrhundert." In *Gesellschaftsstruktur*, vol. 1.

Temporalisierung (1980). "Temporalisierung von Komplexität: Zur Semantik neuzeitlicher Zeitbegriffe." In *Gesellschaftsstruktur und Semantik*, vol. 1.

Temporalstrukturen (1980). "Temporalstrukturen des Handlungssystems." In *Verhalten, Handeln und System*, edited by Wolfgang Schluchter. Frankfurt: Suhrkamp.

Ausdifferenzierung (1981). *Ausdifferenzierung des Rechts*. Frankfurt: Suhrkamp.

Erziehung (1981). "Theoriesubstitution in der Erziehungswissenschaft." In *Gesellschaftsstruktur*, vol. 2, 105–94.

Improbability (1981/1990). "The Improbability of Communication." In *Self-Reference* 1990, 86–98.

Ordnung (1981). "Wie ist soziale Ordnung möglich?" In *Gesellschaftsstruktur*, vol. 2, 195–286.

Rationalität (1981/2008). "Rationalität in modernen Gesellschaft." In *Ideenevolution*. Frankfurt: Suhrkamp.

Subjektive (1981) "Subjektive Rechte." In *Gesellschaftsstruktur*, vol. 2, 45–104.

Teleologie (1981). "Selbstreferenz und Teleologie in gesellschaftstheoretischer Perspektive." In *Gesellschaftsstruktur*, vol. 2, 9–44.
Welfare (1981). *Politische Theorie im Wohlfahrtsstaat*. Munich: Olzog (Engl. *Political Theory in the Welfare State*, Berlin: de Gruyter, 1990; this also includes essays from SA 4).
Differentiation (1982). *The Differentiation of Society*. New York: Columbia University Press.
Passion (1982). *Liebe als Passion*. Frankfurt: Suhrkamp (Engl. *Love as Passion: The Codification of Intimacy*. Cambridge: Polity, 1986).
Verständigung (1982). "Autopoiesis, Handlung und kommunikative Verständigung." In *Zeitschrift für Soziologie*, no. 11:366–79.
Organ (1984). "Organisation." In *Historisches Wörterbuch der Philosophie*, vol. 6, edited by J. Ritter. Stuttgart: Schwabe.
Systems (1984). *Soziale Systeme*. Frankfurt: Suhrkamp (Engl. *Social Systems*. Stanford: Stanford University Press, 1995).
Widerstandsrecht (1984). "Widerstandsrecht und politische Gewalt." *Zeitschrift für Rechtssoziologie* 6 (1): 36–45.
Epochenbildung (1985). "Das Problem der Epochenbildung und die Evolutionstheorie." In *Epochenschwellen und Epochenstrukturen im Diskurs der Literatur- und Sprachhistorie*, 11–33. Frankfurt: Suhrkamp.
Betrachtung (1986). *Die Soziologische Betrachtung des Rechts*. Würzburg: Metzner.
Ecological (1986). *Ökologische Kommunikation*. Opladen: Westdeutscher (Engl. *Ecological Communication*. Cambridge: Polity, 1989).
Lebenswelt (1986/2000). "Die Lebenswelt—nach Rücksprache mit Phänomenologen." In *Protosoziologie im Kontext—"Lebenswelt" und "System" in Philosophie und Soziologie*, Humanities Online, 2000:268–89.
Archimedes (1987). *Archimedes und Wir*. Berlin: Merve.
Circuit (1987). "Machtkreislauf und Recht in Demokratien." In SA 4.
Directrices (1987). "'Distinction directrices': Über Codierung von Semantiken und Systemen." In SA 4, 13–31.
Resistance (1987). "Widerstandsrecht und politische Gewalt." In SA 4.
Unterscheidung (1987). "Die Unterscheidung Gottes." In SA 4.
Organization (1988). "Organisation." In *Mikropolitik. Macht und Spiele in Organisationen*, edited by Willy Küppers and Günther Ortmann. Opladen: Westdeutscher (Engl. David Seidl and Kai Helge Becker, eds., *Niklas Luhmann and Organization Studies*. Copenhagen: Copenhagen Business School Press, 2005).
Wirtschaft (1988). *Die Wirtschaft der Gesellschaft*. Frankfurt: Suhrkamp (English translation of chapter 10: "Limits of Steering." *Theory Culture and Society* 14 [1]: 41–57).
Anfang (1989). "Am Anfang war kein Unrecht." In *Gesellschaftsstruktur*, vol. 3, 11–64.
Ausdifferenzierung (1989). "Die Ausdifferenzierung der Religion." In *Gesellschaftsstruktur*, vol. 3, 259–357.
Ethik (1989). "Ethik als Reflexionstheorie der Moral." In *Gesellschaftsstruktur*, vol. 3, 358–448.
Paradigm (1989). *Paradigm Lost*. Frankfurt: Suhrkamp (Engl. "Paradigm Lost: On the Ethical Reflection of Morality: Speech on the Occasion of the Award of the Hegel Prize 1988." *Thesis Eleven* 29 [1991]: 82–94; this translation is partial).

Silence (1989). *Reden und Schweigen.* Frankfurt: Suhrkamp (Engl. "Speaking and Silence." *New German Critique* 61 [1994]: 25–37; this translation is partial).
Staatsräson (1989). "Staat und Staatsräson." In *Gesellschaftsstruktur*, vol. 3, 65–148.
Erkenntnis (1990). "Erkenntnis als Realität." In SA 5.
Familie (1990). "Sozialsystem der Familie." In SA 5.
Konstruktivismus (1990). "Das Erkenntnisprogramm des Konstruktivismus und die unbekannt bleibende Realität." In SA 5.
Self-Reference (1990). *Essays in Self-Reference.* New York: Columbia University Press.
Wissenschaft (1990). *Die Wissenschaft der Gesellschaft.* Frankfurt: Suhrkamp (Engl. "The Modernity of Science." *New German Critique* 61 [1994]: 9–23; this is a translation of chapter 10).
Ende (1991). "Am Ende der kritischen Soziologie." *Zeitschrift für Soziologie* 148:147–52.
Mittelalter (1991). "Mein Mittelalter." *Rechtshistorisches Journal* 10:66–70.
Risk (1991). *Soziologie des Risiko.* Berlin: De Gruyter (Engl. *Risk: A Sociological Theory.* New York: Routledge, 2017).
Communication (1992). "What Is Communication?" In *Communication Theory*, vol. 2, no. 3:251–59 ("Was ist Kommunikation." In SA 6, 113–24).
Introduction (1992/2002). *Einführung in die Systemtheorie.* Heidelberg: Carl-Auer (Engl. *Introduction to Systems Theory.* Cambridge: Polity, 2013).
Einführung (1993/2005). *Einführung in die Theorie der Gesellschaft.* Heidelberg: Carl-Auer.
European (1993). "Europäische Rationalität." In *Beobachtungen der Moderne.* Opladen: Westdeutscher.
Law (1993). *Das Recht der Gesellschaft.* Frankfurt: Suhrkamp (Engl. *Law as a Social System.* Oxford: Oxford University Press, 2004).
Observations (1993). *Beobachtungen der Moderne.* Opladen: Westdeutscher (Engl. *Observations on Modernity.* Stanford: Stanford University Press, 1998).
Paradoxie (1993). "Paradoxie der Form." In *Kalkül der Form*, edited by Dirk Baecker. Frankfurt: Suhrkamp.
Natur (1994). "Über Natur." In *Gesellschaftsstruktur*, vol. 4.
Unity (1994). "The Idea of Social Unity in a Differentiated Society." Manuscript.
Art (1995). *Die Kunst der Gesellschaft.* Frankfurt: Suhrkamp (Engl. *Art as a Social System.* Stanford: Stanford University Press, 2000).
Bewusstsein (1995). "Die Autopoiesis der Bewusstsein." In SA 6.
Exklusion (1995). "Inklusion und Exklusion." In SA 6.
Intersubjectivity (1995). "Intersubjektivität oder Kommunikation." In SA 6.
Post-Modernism (1995). "System Theory and Post-Modernism." London School of Economics and Political Science, March 17, 1995, www.youtube.com/watch?v=EHnbWEYHkd8.
Mass Media (1996). *Die Realität der Massenmedien.* Opladen: Westdeutscher (Engl. *The Reality of the Mass Media*, Cambridge: Polity Press 2000).
Omnes (1996). "Quod Omnes Tangit: Remarks on Jürgen Habermas's Legal Theory." *Cardozo Law Review*, special issue, *Habermas on Law and Democracy* 17 (4–5): 883–900.
Shocked (1996). *Modern Society Shocked by Its Risks.* University of Hong Kong, Department of Sociology, Occasional Papers 17.

Tautologie (1996). "Tautologie und Paradoxie in den Selbstbeschreibungen der modernen Gesellschaft." In *Protest*. Frankfurt: Suhrkamp.
Theory (1997). *Die Gesellschaft der Gesellschaft*. 2 vols. Frankfurt: Suhrkamp (Engl. *Theory of Society*. 2 vols. Stanford: Stanford University Press, 2012, 2013).
Organization (2000). *Organisation und Entscheidung*. Opladen: Westdeutscher (Engl. *Organization and Decision*. Cambridge: Cambridge University Press, 2018).
Politik (2000). *Die Politik der Gesellschaft*. Frankfurt: Suhrkamp.
Religion (2000). *Die Religion der Gesellschaft*. Frankfurt: Suhrkamp (Engl. *A Systems Theory of Religion*. Stanford: Stanford University Press, 2013).
Erziehungssystem (2002). *Das Erziehungssystem der Gesellschaft*. Frankfurt: Suhrkamp.
Difference (2006). "System as Difference." *Organization* 13 (1): 37–57.
Ideen (2008). *Ideenevolution*. Frankfurt: Suhrkamp.
Moral (2008). *Die Moral der Gesellschaft*. Frankfurt: Suhrkamp.
Norms (2008). "Are There Still Indispensable Norms in Our Society?" *Soziale Systeme* 14 (1): 18–37.
Schriften (2008). *Schriften zu Kunst und Literatur*. Frankfurt: Suhrkamp.
Zettelkasten (2015). http://zettelkasten.danielluedecke.de/en/.

OTHER AUTHORS

Adorno, Theodor (1962/1969). "Fortschritt." In *Stichworte: Kritische Modelle 2*, 29–50. Frankfurt: Suhrkamp.
—— (1966). *Negative Dialektik*. Frankfurt: Suhrkamp (Engl. *Negative Dialectics*. New York: Continuum, 1973).
—— (1968). "Late Capitalism or Industrial Society?" Opening Address to the 16th German Sociological Congress. In *Modern German Sociology*, edited by Volker Meja, Dieter Misgeld, and Nico Stehr, 232–47. New York: Columbia University Press, 2019.
——, ed. (1969/1976). *The Positivist Dispute in German Sociology*. New York: Harper.
Adorno, Theodor, and Max Horkheimer (1944/1971). *Dialektik der Aufklärung*. Frankfurt: Fischer (Engl. *Dialectic of Enlightenment*. Stanford: Stanford University Press, 2002).
Agamben, Giorgio (2005). *The State of Exception*. Chicago: University of Chicago Press.
d'Aguesseau, Henri-François (1759). *Essai d'une institution au droit public*. In *Oevres T. I*. Paris: Libraires Associés.
Albert, Mathias (2000). *Zur Politik der Weltgesellschaft*. Frankfurt: Suhrkamp.
—— (2002). *Zur Politik der Weltgesellschaft: Identität und Recht im Kontext internationaler Vergesellschaftung*. Frankfurt: Suhrkamp.
—— (2016). *A Theory of World Politics*. Cambridge: Cambridge University Press.
Albert, Mathias, Lars-Erik Cederman, and Alexander Wendt, eds. (2010). *New Systems Theories of World Politics*. Basingstoke, UK: Palgrave MacMillan.
Albert, Mathias, and Lena Hilkermeier, ed. (2004). *Observing International Relations: Niklas Luhmann and World Politics*. London: Routledge.

Albert, Mathias, Oliver Kessler, and Stephan Stetter (2008). "On Order and Conflict: International Relations and the 'Communicative Turn.'" *Review of International Studies* 34 (January): 43–67.

Albert, Mathias, and Rudolf Stichweh, eds. (2007). *Weltstaat und Weltstaatlichkeit*. Wiesbaden: Verlag für Sozialwissenschaften.

Andersen, Niels Åkerstrøm (2003a). *Discursive Analytical Strategies*, London: Policy Press.

—— (2003b). "Luhmann and Koselleck: Conceptual History and the Diagnostics of the Present." In *Discoursive Analytical Strategies: Understanding Foucault, Koselleck, Laclau, and Luhmann*. Chicago: University of Chicago Press.

—— (2009). *Power at Play: The Relationships Between Play, Work and Governance*. Houndmills, UK: Palgrave.

—— (2013a). "Contract as a Form of Intersystemic Communication." In *Law and Intersystemic Communication: Understanding "Structural Coupling,"* edited by Alberto Febbrajo and Gorm Harste, 129–54. Surrey, UK: Ashgate.

—— (2013b). "Managing Intensity and Play at Work." In *Luhmann Observed: Radical Theoretical Encounters*, edited by Anders La Cour and Andreas Philippopoulos-Mihalopoulos, 203–25. Basingstoke, UK: Palgrave Macmillan.

Andersen, Niels Åkerstøm, and Inger-Johanne Sand, eds. (2012). *Hybrid Forms of Government: Self-Suspension of Power*. Basingstoke, UK: Palgrave.

Apel, Karl-Otto (1973). *Transformation der Philosophie*. 2 vols. Frankfurt: Suhrkamp. (Translated as *Transformation of Philosophy*).

Arendt, Hannah (1958). *The Human Condition*. Chicago: University of Chicago Press.

Aron, Raymond (1955). *L'opium des intellectuels*. Paris: Calmann-Lévy.

Assmann, Jan (1985). "Die Entdeckung der Vergangenheit." In *Epochenschwellen und Epochenstrukturen im Diskurs der Literatur- und Sprachhistorie*, edited by Hans Ulrich Gumbrecht and Ursula Link-Heer. Frankfurt: Suhrkamp.

—— (1986). "Viel Stil am Nil." In *Stil*, edited by Hans Ulrich Gumbrecht and Ludwig Pfeiffer. Frankfurt: Suhrkamp.

—— (1989). "Im Schatten junger medienblüte." In *Materialität der Kommunikation*, edited by Hans Ulrich Gumbrecht and Ludwig Pfeiffer. Frankfurt: Suhrkamp.

Augustine (397/2006). *Confessions*. Indianapolis: Hackett.

Austin, J. L. (1962). *How to Do Things with Words*. Oxford: Oxford University Press.

Autrand, Françoise (1981). *Naissance d'un grand corps de l'Etat: Les gens du parlement de Paris, 1345-1454*. Paris: Publications de la Sorbonne.

Backhouse-Barber, Joseph (2017). "Morality at the Close of Humanism: Subject and Social in Habermas and Luhmann." *Sociology: Thought and Action [Sociologija: Mintis ir Veiksmas]* 1:98–116.

Baecker, Dirk (1991). *Womit Banken handeln*. Frankfurt: Suhrkamp.

—— (2017). "Systems Are Theory." *Cybernetics and Human Knowing* 24 (2): 9–39.

Baker, G. P., and P. M. S. Hacker (1984). *Scepticism, Rules and Language*. Oxford: Basil Blackwell.

Barry, Peter Brian (2015). "The Kantian Case Against Torture." *Philosophy* 90:593–621.

Bayer, Oswald (2003). *Martin Luthers Theologie*. Tübingen: Mohr Siebeck.

Beck, Ulrich (1986). *Das Risikogesellschaft*. Frankfurt: Suhrkamp.
Behrens, Catherine B. A. (1985). *Society, Government and Enlightenment*. London: Thames and Hudson.
Bell, Daniel (1961). *The End of Ideology*. New York: Free Press.
—— (1973). *The Coming of Post-Industrial Society*. London: Verso.
Benjamin, Walter (1936/1963). *Das Kunstwerk im Zeitalter seiner technischen Reproduzierbarkeit*. Frankfurt: Suhrkamp.
Berman, Harold (1983/2004). *Law and Revolution*. 2 vols. Cambridge, MA: Harvard University Press.
Berman, Marshall (1983). *All That Is Solid Melts Into Air*. New York: Verso.
Bernstein, Richard (1976). *The Restructuring of Social and Political Theory*. Philadelphia: University of Pennsylvania Press.
—— (1981). *Beyond Objectivism and Relativism*. Oxford: Blackwell.
Bertalanffy, Ludwig (1968). *General System Theory*. New York: Braziller.
Bluche, François (1961). *Les magistrats du parlement de Paris au XVIIIe siècle*. Paris: Economica.
Böckenförde, Ernst-Wolfgang (1991). *Staat, Verfassung, Demokratie*. Frankfurt: Suhrkamp.
Bodin, Jean (1961). *Les six livres de la république*. Aalen: Scientia. Originally published in 1583.
Böhme, Gernot (1996). "Kants Ästhetik in neuer Sicht." In *Immanuel Kant über Natur und Gesellschaft*, edited by Gorm Harste, Thomas Mertens, and Thomas Schaeffer. Odense: Odense University Press.
Boltanski, Luc (1991). *De la justification*. Paris: Gallimard.
Boltanski, Luc, and Ève Chiapello (1999). *Le nouvel esprit du capitalisme*. Paris: Gallimard.
Borch, Christian (2011). *Niklas Luhmann*. London: Routledge.
Boucheron, Patrick, and Nicolas Offenstaedt, eds. (2011). *L'espace public au Moyen Âge—Débats autour de Jürgen Habermas*. Paris: Presses Universitaires de France.
Bourdieu, Pierre (1979/1984). *La distinction*. Paris: Les éditions du minuit. (Engl. *The Distinction*. New York: Routledge, 1984).
—— (1980). *Le sens pratique*. Paris: Les éditions du minuit (Engl. *The Logic of Practice*. Cambridge: Polity, 1990).
—— (1984). *Homo Academicus*. Paris: Les éditions du minuit (Engl. *Homo Academicus*. Stanford: Stanford University Press, 1988).
—— (1987a). "Le champ intellectuel." In *Choses dites*. Paris: Les éditions du minuit.
—— (1987b). "Legitimation and Structured Interests in Weber's Sociology of Religion." In *Max Weber, Rationality and Modernity*, edited by Sam Whimster and Scott Lash. London: Allen and Unwin.
—— (1987c). "The Force of Law." *Hastings Law Journal* 38 (5): 814–53.
—— (1989). *La noblesse d'état*. Paris: Les éditions de minuit (Engl. *The State Nobility*. Stanford: Stanford University Press, 1996).
—— (1992). *Les règles de l'art*. Paris: Seuil (Engl. *Rules of Art*. Cambridge: Polity, 1996).
—— (1994). "Dans l'esprit d'État." In *Raisons pratiques*. Paris: Seuil (Engl. "Rethinking the State." In *Practical Reason*, 35–64. Cambridge: Polity, 1998).
—— (2004). "From the King's House to the Reason of State." *Constellations* 11 (1): 16–36.

—— (2012). *Sur l'État: Cours au Collège de France, 1989–2012*. Paris: Seuil (Engl. *On the State*. Cambridge: Polity, 2014).

—— (2013). *Manet*. Paris: Seuil (Engl. *Manet*. Cambridge: Polity, 2017).

Bourdieu, Pierre, and Alain Darbel (1969/1991). *L'amour de l'art*. Paris: Les éditions du minuit. (Engl. *Love of Art*. Cambridge: Polity).

Brunkhorst, Hauke (2000). *Einführung in die Geschichte politischer Ideen*. Munich: Fink.

—— (2012). *Legitimationskrisen—Verfassungsprobleme der Weltgesellschaft*. Baden-Baden: Nomos.

—— (2014a). *Critical Theory of Legal Revolutions: Evolutionary Perspectives*. London: Bloomsbury.

—— (2014b). *Das doppelte Gesicht Europas*. Frankfurt: Suhrkamp.

—— (2014c). The Crisis of Legitimization in the World Society. Manuscript.

Brunkhorst, Hauke, Regina Kreide, and Christina Lafont (2018). *The Habermas Handbook*. New York: Columbia University Press.

Brunkhorst, Hauke, and Stefan Müller-Doohm (2018). "Intellectual Biography." In *The Habermas Handbook*, edited by Hauke Brunkhorst, Regina Kreide, and Christina Lafont, 1–26. New York: Columbia University Press.

Brunner, Otto, Werner Conze, and Reinhart Koselleck, eds. (1972–94). *Geschichtliche Grundbegriffe*. 7 vols. Stuttgart: Klett-Cotta.

Bühler, Karl (1934/1982). *Sprachtheorie*. Stuttgart: Fischer. (Engl. *Theory of Language*, Amsterdam: John Benjamins, 2011).

Butterfield, Herbert (1931/1965). *The Whig Interpretation of History*. New York: Norton.

Cassirer, Ernst (1911/1972). *Funktion und Substanz*. Darmstadt: Wissenschaftliche Buchgesellschaft (Engl. *Substance and Function*. London: Dalton, 2015).

—— (1918/1972). *Kants Leben und Lehre*. Darmstadt: Wissenschaftliche Buchgesellschaft (Engl. *Kant's Life and Thought*. New Haven: Yale University Press, 1981).

—— (1922–1925–1929/1955). *The Philosophy of Symbolic Forms*. 3 vols. New Haven: Yale University Press.

Castoriadis, Cornelius (1975). *L'institution imaginaire de la société*. Paris: Seuil (Engl. *The Imaginary Institution of Society*. Cambridge: Polity, 1997).

Chaunu, Pierre (1993). "L'administration de justice." In *L'État*, vol. 1, *Histoire économique et sociale de la France, 1450–1660*, edited by Fernand Braudel, Ernest Labrousse, Pierre Chaunu, and Richard Gascon. Paris: Presses Universitaires de France.

Cohen, Deborah (2001). *The War Comes Home: Disabled Veterans in Britain and Germany, 1914–1939*. Berkeley: University of California Press.

Cohen, Jean, and Andrew Arato (1994). *Civil Society and Political Theory*. Cambridge, MA: MIT Press.

Deleuze, Gilles (1963/1997). *La philosophie critique de Kant*. Paris: Presses Universitaires de France.

Derrida, Jacques (1989). *Husserl's On the Origins of Geometry—an Introduction*. Lincoln: University of Nebraska Press.

Deutsch, Karl (1963/1967). *Nerves of Government*. London: MacMillan.

Dummett, Michael (1976). "What Is a Theory of Meaning? II." In *Truth and Meaning*, edited by Gareth Evans and John McDowell, 67–137. Oxford: Oxford University Press.
Durand-Gasselin, Jean Marc (2018). "Introduction." In *Philosophical Introductions*, by Jürgen Habermas. Cambridge: Polity.
Durkheim, Émile (1893/1930). *De la division du travail social*. Paris: Presses Universitaires de France (Engl. *The Division of Labour in Society*. New York: Free Press, 1997).
—— (1895/1937). *Les règles de la methôde sociologique*, Paris: Presses Universitaires de France (Engl. *Rules of Sociological Method*. New York: Free Press, 1982).
—— (1897). *Le Suicide*. Paris: Presses Universitaires de France (Engl. *Suicide*. New York: Free Press, 1951).
—— (1908/1969). *Léçons de sociologie*. Paris: Presses Universitaires de France (Engl. *Professional Ethics and Civic Morals*. Mansfield: Martino, 2013).
—— (1912/1960). *Les formes élémentaires de la vie religieuse*. Paris: Presses Universitaires de France (Engl. *The Elementary Forms of Religious Life*. Oxford: Oxford University Press, 2001).
—— (1924). *Sociologie et philosophie*. Paris: Presses Universitaires de France (Engl. *Sociology and Philosophy*. New York: Routledge, 1953).
Düsing, Klaus (1968). *Die Teleologie in Kants Weltbegriff*. Bonn: Bouvier.
Easton, David (1965). *A Systems Analysis of Political Life*. New York: John Wiley.
Eder, Klaus (1976). *Die Entstehung staatlich organisierter Gesellschaften*. Frankfurt: Suhrkamp.
—— (1985). *Geschichte als Lernprozess? Zur Pathogenese politischer Modernität in Deutschland*. Frankfurt: Suhrkamp.
Eder, Klaus, Bernard Willms, Karl Tjaden, Karl Hondrich, Hartmut v. Hentig, Harald Weinrich, and Wolfgang Lipp (1973). *Theorie der Gesellschaft oder Sozialtechnologie—Beiträge zur Habermas-Luhmann Diskussion*. Frankfurt: Suhrkamp.
Eisenstadt, Shmuel (1963). *The Political System of Empires*. New York: Free Press.
Elias, Norbert (1939/1976). *Über den Prozeß der Zivilisation*. 2 vols. Frankfurt: Suhrkamp (Engl. *The Civilizing Process*. Oxford: Blackwell, 2000).
Elwood, Christopher (1999). *The Body Broken: The Calvinist Doctrine of the Eucharist and the Symbolization of Power in Sixteenth-Century France*. Oxford: Oxford University Press.
Emery, Fred, ed. (1970). *Systems Thinking*. London: Penguin.
Erasmus of Rotterdam (1525/1991). *Le libre arbitre*. In *Oevres choisies*. Paris: Paris: Libreairie générale française.
Eriksen, Erik Oddvar (2001). "Leadership in a Communicative Perspective." *Acta Sociologica* 44 (1): 21–35.
Eriksen, Erik Oddvar, and Jarle Weigaard (1997). "Conceptualizing Politics: Strategic or Communicative Action." *Scandinavian Political Studies* 20 (3): 219–41.
—— (2003). *Understanding Habermas: Communicative Action and Deliberative Democracy*. New York: Continuum.
Esposito, Elena (2011). *The Future of Futures: The Time of Money in Financing and Society*. New York: Elgar.

Febbrajo, Alberto, and Gorm Harste, eds. (2013). *Law and Intersystemic Communication: Understanding "Structural Coupling."* London: Ashgate.

Fischer-Lescano, Andreas, and Gunther Teubner (2006). *Regime-kollisionen.* Frankfurt: Suhrkamp.

Fleck, Christian (2011). *A Transatlantic History of the Social Sciences: The Third Reich and the Invention of Empirical Social Research.* London: Bloomsbury.

Foerster, Heinz von (1961). "A Predictive Model for Self-Organizing Systems." Part 1: *Cybernetica* 3:258–300; Part 2: *Cybernetica* 4:20–55.

Foucault, Michel (1969). *L'archéologie du savoir.* Paris: Gallimard (Engl. *The Archeology of Knowledge.* London: Tavistock, 1972).

—— (1970). *L'ordre du discours.* Paris: Gallimard (Engl. *The Discourse on Language.* London: Tavistock, 1972).

—— (1975). *Surveillir et punir.* Paris: Gallimard (Engl. *Discipline and Punish.* London: Penguin, 1977).

—— (1976). *La volonté de savoir.* Paris: Gallimard (Engl. *The Will to Knowledge: History of Sexuality*, vol. 1. London: Penguin, 1990).

—— (1997). *"Il faut défendre la société."* Paris: Gallimard (Engl. *"Society Must Be Defended."* London: Penguin, 2004).

—— (2004). *Naissance de la biopolitique.* Paris: Gallimard (Engl. *The Birth of Biopolitics.* New York: Palgrave, 2008).

Frank, Manfred (1983/1989). *Was ist Neo-Strukturalismus?* Frankfurt: Suhrkamp (Engl. *What Is Neostructuralism?* Minneapolis: University of Minnesota Press, 1989).

Frankenberg, Gunter (1986/2011). "Down by Law: Irony, Seriousness, and Reason." *German Law Review* 12 (1): 300–37.

Frege, Gottlob (1892/1962). "Über Sinn und Bedeutung." In *Funktion, Begriff, Bedeutung.* Göttingen: Vandenhoeck und Ruprecht.

Friedrich, Carl (1941/1949/1968). *Constitutional Government and Democracy.* Boston: Ginn.

Fröbel, Folker, Jürgen Heinrichs, and Otto Kreye (1997). *Die neue internationale Arbeitsteilung.* Hamburg: Rowohlt.

Fukuyama, Francis (1992). *The End of History and the Last Man.* London: Hamilton.

Furet, François (1989). *La révolution française.* Paris: Seuil (Engl. *Revolutionary France, 1770–1880.* Oxford: Blackwell, 1992).

Gadamer, Hans-Georg (1960/2004). *Wahrheit und Methode.* Tübingen: Mohr (Engl. *Truth and Method.* New York: Continuum).

Giddens Anthony (1976). *New Rules of Sociological Method.* London: Hutchinson.

—— (1979). *Central Problems in Social Theory.* London: MacMillan.

—— (1984). *The Constitution of Society.* Cambridge: Polity.

—— (1990). *The Consequences of Modernity.* Cambridge: Polity.

Giegel, Hans-Joachim (1992). "Diskursive Verständigung und systemische Selbststeuerung." In *Kommunikation und Konsens in modernen Gesellschaft.* Frankfurt: Suhrkamp.

Goffman, Erving (1971). *Relations in Public.* New York: Harper and Row.

Gouldner, Alvin (1970). *The Coming Crisis of Western Sociology.* London: Heinemann.

Gumbrecht, Hans-Ulrich (2004). *Production of Presence.* Stanford: Stanford University Press.

Gumbrecht, Hans Ulrich, and Ursula Link-Heer (1985). *Epochenschwellen im Diskurs der Litteratur- und Sprachhistorie*. Frankfurt: Suhrkamp.
Gumbrecht, Hans Ulrich, and Ludwig Pfeiffer, eds. (1986). *Stil: Geschichten und Funktionen eines kulturwissenschaftlichen Diskurselements*. Frankfurt: Suhrkamp.
———, eds. (1988). *Materialität der Kommunikation*. Frankfurt: Suhrkamp.
———, eds. (1991). *Paradoxien, Dissonanzen, Zusammenbrüche*. Frankfurt: Suhrkamp.
Günther, Klaus (1986/2011). "The Pragmatic and Functional Indeterminacy of Law." *German Law Journal* 12 (1): 407–29.
Hamilton, Peter (1992). *Talcott Parsons: Critical Assessments*. 4 vols. London: Routledge.
Harste, Gorm (1996). "Kant und Luhmann über Teleologie in Natur und politische Kommunikation." In *Immanuel Kant über Natur und Gesellschaft*, edited by Gorm Harste, Thomas Mertens, and Thomas Scheffer. Odense: Odense University Press.
——— (1997). "The Paradoxes of Risk Society." *Conditions for Social Progress—UN Report*, Ministry of Foreign Affairs, Copenhagen, 95–110.
——— (2001). "Early Reflexive Modernity." In *The Transformation of Modernity*, edited by Michael Carleheden and Michael Jacobsen. Aldershot, UK: Ashgate.
——— (2003). "The Emergence of Autopoietic Organisation." In *Autopoietic Organization Theory*, edited by Tore Bakken and Tor Hernes. Oslo: Abstrakt Forlag.
——— (2004). "Society's War." In *Observing International Relations: Niklas Luhmann and World Politics*, edited by Mathias Albert and Lena Hilkermeier. London: Routledge.
——— (2009). "Kant's Theory of European Integration." *Jahrbuch für Recht und Ethik* 17:53–84.
——— (2013a). "The Improbable European State: Its Ideals Observed with Social Systems Theory." In *New Agendas in Statebuilding*, edited by Robert Egnell and Peter Halden. London: Routledge.
——— (2013b). "The Big, Large and Huge Case of State-Building—Studying Structural Couplings at the Macro Level." In *Law and Intersystemic Communication: Understanding "Structural Coupling,"* edited by Alberto Febbrajo and Gorm Harste. London: Ashgate.
——— (2015). "The Democratic Surplus that Constitutionalised the European Union." In *The Evolution of Intermediary Institutions in Europe*, edited by Poul Kjaer and Eva Hartmann. London: Palgrave.
——— (2016a). "The Missing Link in the Philosophy of Enlightenment: Reasonability, Will and Separation of Powers in the Philosophy of Henri-François d'Aguesseau." In *Ethics, Democracy, and Markets*, edited by Giorgio Baruchello, Jacob Rendtorff, and Asger Sørensen. Aarhus: NSU Press.
——— (2016b). "Summary: Critique of the War Reason: A Perspective on Self-Referential Systems, 11th–21st Centuries." In *Kritik af Krigens Fornuft*, 721–40. Aarhus: Aarhus University Press.
——— (2017). "Autopoietic Power." *Cybernetics and Human Knowing* 24 (2): 41–67.
——— (2020). "Crisis Transitions in the World Risk Society." In *Corona: Weltgesellschaft in Ausnahmezustand?*, edited by Markus Heidungsfelder and Maren Lehmann. Weilerswist: Velbrück.
Hegel, Georg Wilhelm Friedrich (1807/1972). *Phänomenologie des Geistes*. Frankfurt: Suhrkamp. (Engl. *Phenomenology of Spirit*. Oxford: Oxford University Press, 1977).

——— (1821/1972). *Grundlinien zur Philosophie des Rechts*. Frankfurt: Ullstein (Engl. *Philosophy of Right*. London: Dover, 1896/2005).
Heidegger, Martin (1927/1972). *Sein und Zeit*. Tübingen: Niemeyer (Engl. *Being and Time*. Oxford: Blackwell, 1962).
Heisler, Martin, ed. (1974). *Politics in Europe*. New York: McKay.
Henderson, John (1998). *The Construction of Orthodoxy and Heresy: Neo-Confucian, Islamic, Jewish, and Early Christian Patterns*. Albany: State University of New York Press.
Hinrichs, Ernst (1989). *Ancien Régime und Revolution*. Frankfurt: Suhrkamp.
Hohendahl, Peter (1985). "Habermas' Critique of the Frankfurt School." *New German Critique*, no. 35:3–27.
Horkheimer, Max (1922/1987). *Zur Antinomie der teleologischen Urteilskraft*. In *Gesammelte Schriften*, vol. 2. Frankfurt: Fischer.
——— (1925/1987). *Über Kants "Kritik der Urteilskraft" als Bindeglied zwischen theoretischer und praktischer Philosophie*. In *Gesammelte Schriften*, vol. 2. Frankfurt: Fischer.
——— (1937/1968). "Traditionelle und kritische Theorie." In *Traditionelle und kritische Theorie*. Frankfurt: Suhrkamp (Engl. in *Critical Theory*. New York: Continuum, 2002).
Hoy, David, and Thomas McCarthy (1994). *Critical Theory*. Cambridge, MA: Blackwell.
Huntington, Samuel (1996). *The Clash of Civilizations and the Remaking of World Order*. New York: Simon and Schuster.
Husserl, Edmund (1928/1962). *Cartesianische Meditationen*. Husserliana, vol. 5. Haag: Martinus Nijhof (Engl. *Cartesian Meditations*. Boston: Kluwer Academics, 1988).
——— (1937/1962). *Die Krisis der europäischen Wissenschaften und die transzendentale Phänomenologie*. Haag: Martinus Nijhof (Engl. *Husserl's Crisis of the European Sciences*. Cambridge: Cambridge University Press, 2011).
Hutter, Michael (1993). "The Emergence of Bank Notes in the 17th Century England." *Sociologica Internationalis* 31:23–39.
Jay, Martin (1973). *The Dialectical Imagination: A History of the Frankfurt School and the Institute of Social Research, 1923–1950*. Berkeley: University of California Press.
Jencks, Charles (1977). *The Language of Post-Modern Architecture*. London: Academy.
Joerges, Christian (1996). "Taking Law Seriously." *European Law Journal* 2 (2): 105–35.
Joerges, Christian, and Michelle Everson (2020). "The Legal Proprium of the Economic Constitution." In *The Law of Political Economy: Transformation in the Function of Law*, edited by Poul Kjaer. Cambridge: Cambridge University Press.
Joerges, Christian, Poul Kjaer, and Tommi Ralli (2011). "A New Type of Conflicts Law as Constitutional Form in the Postnational Constellation." *Transnational Legal Theory* 2 (2): 153–65.
Kaag, John (2005). "Continuity and Inheritance: Kant's 'Critique of Judgment' and the Work of C. S. Peirce." *Transactions of the Charles S. Peirce Society* 41 (3): 515–40.
Kant, Immanuel (1781/1787/1966). *Kritik der reinen Vernunft*. Stuttgart: Reclam (Engl. *Critique of Pure Reason*. New York: MacMillan, 1929).
——— (1783/1977). *Beantwortung der Frage: "Was ist Aufklärung?"* In *Werkausgabe*, vol. 11. Frankfurt: Suhrkamp (Engl. "An Answer to the Question: What Is Enlightenment?" In

Practical Philosophy, edited by Mary J. Gregor. Cambridge: Cambridge University Press, 1999).
—— (1788/1974). *Kritik der praktischen Vernunft*. In *Werkausgabe*, vol. 7. Frankfurt: Suhrkamp (Engl. *Critique of Practical Reason*. New York: Classic, 2010).
—— (1790/1974). *Kritik der Urteilskraft*. In *Werkausgabe*, vol. 10. Frankfurt: Suhrkamp (Engl. *Critique of Judgment*. Oxford: Oxford, 2007).
—— (1794/1977). *Die Religion innerhalb der Grenzen der blossen Vernunft*. In *Werkausgabe*, vol. 8. Frankfurt: Suhrkamp (Engl. *Within the Boundaries of Mere Reason*. Cambridge: Cambridge University Press, 2018).
—— (1795/1977). *Zum ewigen Frieden*. In *Werkausgabe*, vol. 11. Frankfurt: Suhrkamp (Engl. *Towards Perpetual Peace*. New Haven: Yale University Press, 2006).
King, Michael, and Chris Thornhill (2003). *Niklas Luhmann's Theory of Politics and Law*. Basingstoke, UK: Palgrave.
Kjaer, Poul (2006). "Systems in Context: On the Outcome of the Habermas/Luhmann-Debate." *Ancilla Iuris*: 66–77.
—— (2010). *Between Governing and Governance: On the Emergence, Function and Form of Europe's Post-National Constellation*. London: Hart.
—— (2014). *Constitutionalism in the Global Realm—a Sociological Approach*. London: Routledge.
Kjaer, Poul, Gunther Teubner, and Alberto Febbrajo, eds. (2011). *The Financial Crisis in Constitutional Perspective: The Dark Side of Functional Differentiation*. Oxford: Hart.
Koselleck, Reinhart (1959/1988). *Kritik und Krise*. Frankfurt: Suhrkamp (Engl. *Critique and Crisis: Enlightenment and the Pathogenesis of Modern Society*. Cambridge, MA: MIT Press).
—— (1979). *Vergangene Zukunft*. Frankfurt: Suhrkamp (Engl. *Futures Past: On the Semantics of Historical Time*. New York: Columbia University Press, 2004).
—— (2000). *Zeitschichten*. Frankfurt: Suhrkamp.
Koskenniemi, Martii (2006). "Constitutionalism as a Mindset—Reflections on Kantian Themes About International Law and Globalization." *Theoretical Inquiries in Law* 8 (1): 9–36.
Krause, Detlef (1996). *Luhmann-Lexikon*. Stuttgart: Enke.
Kripke, Saul (1982). *Wittgenstein on Rules and Private Language*. Cambridge, MA: Harvard University Press.
Kuhn, Thomas (1962). *The Structure of Scientific Revolutions*. Chicago: University of Chicago Press.
Lawrence, T. E. (1935/1997). *Seven Pillars of Wisdom*. London: Wordsworth.
Lenoble, Jacques (1996). "Law and Undecidability." *Cardozo Law Review*, special issue on Habermas on Law and Democracy, 17 (4–5).
Lorenzen, Paul (1974). *Konstruktive Wissenschaftstheorie*. Frankfurt: Suhrkamp.
Lukacs, Georgy (1923/1971). *History and Class Consciousness*. Cambridge, MA: MIT Press.
Luther, Martin (1526/2017). *Om den trælbundne vilje (De servo arbitrio)*. Copenhagen: Eksistensen.

Lyotard, Jean-François (1979). *La condition postmoderne*. Paris: Les éditions du minuit (Engl. *The Postmodern Condition*. Minneapolis: University of Michigan, 1984).
MacCormick, John (2009). *Weber, Habermas, and the Transformations of the European State*. Cambridge: Cambridge University Press.
MacIntyre, Alisdair (1981). *After Virtue?* Notre Dame: University of Notre Dame.
Makkreel, Rudolf (1994). *Imagination and Interpretation in Kant: The Hermeneutical Import of the Critique of Judgment*. Chicago: University of Chicago Press.
Marx, Karl (1845/1974). *Die deutsche Ideologie*. In MEW 3. Berlin: Dietz (Engl. *The German Ideology*. New York: Prometheus, 1998).
—— (1848/1964). *Manifest der kommunistischen Partei*. In MEW 4. Berlin: Dietz (Engl. *The Communist Manifesto*. London: Penguin, 2002).
—— (1867–94/1977). *Das Kapital*. 3 vols. MEW 23, 24, 25. Berlin: Dietz.
Mathiessen, Ulf (1983). *Die Dickicht der Lebenswelt*. Stuttgart: Enke.
Maturana, Humberto, and Francisco Varela (1979). *Autopoiesis and Cognition: The Realization of the Living*. Boston Studies in the Philosophy of Science. Dordrecht: Reidel.
Maus, Ingeborg (1986a). "Verrechtlichung, Entrechtlichung und der Funktionswandel von Institutionen." In *Rechtstheorie und Politische Theorie im Industriekapitalismus*. Munich: Fink.
—— (1986b). "Entwicklung und Funktionswandel der Theorie des bürgerlichen Rechtsstaat." In *Rechtstheorie und Politische Theorie im Industriekapitalismus*. Munich: Fink.
—— (1992). *Zur Aufklärung der Demokratietheorie*. Frankfurt: Suhrkamp.
McCarthy, Thomas (1978). *The Critical Theory of Jürgen Habermas*. Cambridge, MA: MIT Press.
—— (1985). "Complexity and Democracy, or The Seducements of Systems Theory." *New German Critique*, no. 35:27–54.
Menéndez, Agustin, and John Erik Fossum, eds. (2011). *Law and Democracy in Neil MacCormick's Legal and Political Theory: The Post-Sovereign Constitution*. Berlin: Springer.
Merleau-Ponty, Maurice (1945/2012). *Phénomenologie de la perception*. Paris: Gallimard (Engl. *Phenomenology of Perception*. New York: Routledge, 2012).
Miller, Max (1994). "Intersystemic Discourse and Co-Ordinated Dissent: A Critique of Luhmann's Ecological Communication." *Theory, Culture and Society* 11:101–21.
Moeller, Hans-Georg (2006). *Luhmann Explained: From Souls to Systems*. Chicago: Open Court.
—— (2012). *The Radical Luhmann*. New York: Columbia University Press.
—— (2017). "On Second-Order Observation and Genuine Pretending: Coming to Terms with Society." *Thesis Eleven*, December.
Montesquieu, Charles (1749). *De l'esprit de loix*. 4 vols. Amsterdam: Chatelain (Engl. *The Spirit of Laws*. Cambridge: Cambridge University Press, 1989).
Narr, Wolf-Dieter, Dieter Runze, Elmar Koenen, Karl Steinbacher, Lothar Eley, Bernhard Heidtmann, and Peter Hejl (1973). *Theorie der Gesellschaft oder Sozialtechnologie—Beiträge zur Habermas-Luhmann Diskussion*. Frankfurt: Suhrkamp.
Neves, Marcelo (2018a). "The Epitome of Technocratic Consciousness." In *The Habermas Handbook*, edited by Hauke Brunkhorst, Regina Kreide, and Christina Lafont, 98–104. New York: Columbia University Press.

——— (2018b). "System and Lifeworld." In *The Habermas Handbook*, edited by Hauke Brunkhorst, Regina Kreide, and Christina Lafont, 632–36. New York: Columbia University Press.
Nisbet, Robert (1967). *The Sociological Tradition*. London: Heineman.
Nobles, Richard, and David Schiff (2013). *Observing Law Through Systems Theory*. Oxford: Hart.
O'Connor, James (1973/2017). *The Fiscal Crisis of the State*. London: Routledge.
Offe, Claus (1972). *Strukturprobleme des kapitalistischen Staates*. Frankfurt: Suhrkamp (Engl. *Contradictions of the Welfare State*. New York: Routledge, 2019).
Olivier-Martin, François (1951/1997). *L'absolutisme français* and *Les parlements contre l'absolutisme traditional au XVIIIe siècle*. Paris: LGDJ.
O'Neill, Onora (1989). *Constructions of Reason*. Cambridge: Cambridge University Press.
Parsons, Talcott (1951). *The Social System*. New York: Free Press.
——— (1963/1969). "On the Concept of Power." In *Sociological Theory and Modern Society*. New York: Free Press.
——— (1964). "Evolutionary Universals in Society." *American Sociological Review* 29:1–6.
——— (1966). *Societies—Evolutionary and Comparative Perspectives*. Englewood Cliffs, NJ: Prentice-Hall.
——— (1971). *The System of Modern Societies*. Englewood, NJ: Prentice-Hall.
——— (1971/1977). "Comparative Studies and Evolutionary Change." In *Social Systems and the Evolution of Action Theory*. New York: Free Press.
——— (1977). *Social Systems and the Evolution of Action Theory*. New York: Free Press.
——— (1978). *Action Theory and the Human Condition*. New York: Free Press.
Parsons, Talcott, and Neil Smelser (1958). *Economy and Society*. New York: Free Press.
Paterson, John (2013). "Contracts and Hedgings in Self-Referential Systems." In *Law and Intersystemic Communication*, edited by Alberto Febbrajo and Gorm Harste. London: Ashgate.
Philonenko, Alexis (1988). *L'oeuvre de Kant 1–2*. Paris: Vrin.
Piketty, Thomas (2013). *Capital in the Twenty-First Century*. Cambridge, MA: Harvard University Press.
——— (2020). *Capital and Ideology*. Cambridge, MA: Harvard University Press.
Poggi, Gianfranco (1978). *The Development of the Modern State*. Stanford: Stanford University Press.
Porter, Bruce (1994). *War and the Rise of the State*. New York: Free Press.
Quillet, Jeaninne (1972). *Les Clefs du pouvoir au moyen âge*. Paris: Flammarion.
Rasch, William (2000). *Niklas Luhmann's Modernity: The Paradoxes of Differentiation*. Stanford: Stanford University Press.
Rawls, John (1993). *Political Liberalism*. New York: Columbia University Press.
Richet, Denis (1973). *La France modern—l'esprit des institutions*, Paris: Flammarion.
Rickert, Heinrich (1910/1986). *Kulturwissenschaft und Naturwissenschaft*. Stuttgart: Reclam.
Riedel, Manfred (1989). *Urteilskraft und Vernunft: Kants ursprüngliche Fragestellung*. Frankfurt: Suhrkamp.
Riley, Patrick (1978). "The General Will Before Rousseau." *Political Theory* 6 (4): 485–516.

Ritzer, George (2014). *Sociological Theory*. New York: McGraw-Hill.
Rorty, Richard (1979). *Philosophy and the Mirror of Nature*. Princeton: Princeton University Press.
Rosa, Helmut (2005). *Beschleunigung*. Frankfurt: Suhrkamp (Engl. *Social Acceleration*. New York: Columbia University Press, 2015).
Rosanvallon, Pierre (1990). *L'État en France de 1789 à nos jours*. Paris: Seuil.
Rousseau, Jean-Jacques (1762/1971). *Du contrat social*. In *Oevres completes*, vol. 2. Paris: Seuil (Engl. *The Social Contract*. Indianapolis: Hackett, 1987).
Roviello, Anne-Marie (1984). *L'institution kantienne de la liberté*. Bruxelles: Ousia.
Schluchter, Wolfgang, ed. (1980). *Verhalten, Handeln und System*. Frankfurt: Suhrkamp.
Schmitt, Carl (1922/1996). *Politische Theologie*. Berlin: Duncker und Humblot (Engl. *Political Theology*. Chicago: University of Chicago Press, 1985).
Schwemmer, Oswald (1970). *Philosophie der Praxis*. Frankfurt: Suhrkamp.
Searle, John (1967) "How to Derive 'Ought' from 'Is.'" In *Theories of Ethics*, edited by Philippa Foot. Oxford: Oxford University Press.
—— (1969). *Speech Acts*. Cambridge: Cambridge University Press.
Simmel, Georg (1892/1989). *Über soziale Differenzierung*. In *Gesamtausgabe*, vol. 2. Frankfurt: Suhrkamp.
—— (1900/2009). *Die Philosophie des Geldes*. Cologne: Anaconda (Engl. *The Philosophy of Money*. London: Routledge, 1990).
—— (1908). *Soziologie*. Leipzig: Duncker und Humblot (Engl. *The Sociology of Georg Simmel*. New York: Free Press, 1964).
—— (1923). "Die Mode." In *Philosophische Kultur*. Berlin: Wagenbach (Engl. "The Philosophy of Fashion." In *Simmel on Culture—Selected Writings*, 187–205. London: Sage).
Simon, Herbert (1945). *Administrative Behavior*. New York: Free Press.
Simon, Herbert, and James March (1958). *Organizations*. Oxford: Blackwell.
Smith, Philip (2005). *Why War? The Cultural Logic of Iraq, the Gulf War, and Suez*. Chicago: University of Chicago Press.
Spencer, Herbert (1969/1876–96). *Principles of Sociology*, London: MacMillan.
Spencer Brown, George (1969). *Laws of Form*, London: Allen and Unwin.
Stäheli, Urs (2000). *Sinnzusammenbruche*. Frankfurt: Suhrkamp.
—— (2012). "The Hegemony of Meaning: Is There and Exit to Meaning in Niklas Luhmann's Systems Theory?" *Revue internationale de philosophie* 66 (259): 105–22.
Stetter, Stephen, ed. (2007). *Territorial Conflicts in World Society: Modern Systems Theory, International Relations and Conflict Studies*. London: Routledge.
Stichweh, Rudolf (1991). *Der frühmoderne Staat und die europäische Universität*. Frankfurt: Suhrkamp.
—— (2000). *Die Weltgesellschaft*. Frankfurt: Suhrkamp.
Stolleis, Michael (1994). *Recht im Unrecht*. Frankfurt: Suhrkamp.
Strecker, David (2018). "The Theory of Society: The Theory of Communicative Action (1981): A Classical Social Theory." In *The Habermas Handbook*, edited by Hauke Brunkhorst, Regina Kreide, and Christina Lafont, 360–82. New York: Columbia University Press.
Taylor, Charles (2007). *A Secular Age*. Cambridge, MA: Harvard University Press.

Teubner, Gunther (1986/2011). "'And God Laughed...': Indeterminacy, Self-Reference and Paradox in Law." *German Law Review* 12 (1): 376–406.
—— (1987). "Hyperzyklus in Recht und Organisation." In *Sinn, Kommunikation und soziale Differenzierung*, edited by Hans Haferkamp and Michael Schmid. Frankfurt: Suhrkamp.
—— (1989/1993). *Recht als autopoietisches System*. Frankfurt: Suhrkamp (Engl. *Law as an Autopoietic System*. Oxford: Blackwell, 1993).
—— (1997). "The King's Many Bodies: The Self-Destruction of Law's Hierarchy." *Arena Papers*, 22. Oslo.
—— (2006). "From Coincidentia Oppositorum, Hybrid Networks Beyond Contract and Organization." In *Festschrift in Honor of Lawrence Friedman*, edited by Robert Gordon and Mort Horwitz. Stanford: Stanford University Press.
—— (2007). "In the Blind Spot: The Hybridization of Contracting." *Theoretical Inquiries in Law* 8:51–71.
Teubner, Gunther, and Andreas Fischer-Lascano (2007). "Fragmentierung des Weltrechts." In *Weltstaat und Weltstaatlichkeit*, edited by Mathias Albert and Rudolf Stichweh. Wiesbaden: VS.
Thornhill, Chris (2000). *Political Theory in Modern Germany* (2000). Cambridge: Polity.
—— (2007a). "Niklas Luhmann, Carl Schmitt and the Modern Form of the Political." *European Journal of Social Theory* 10 (4): 499–522.
—— (2007b). *German Political Philosophy: The Metaphysics of Law*. London: Routledge.
—— (2008). "Towards a Historical Sociology of Constitutional Legitimacy." *Theory and Society* 37:161–97.
—— (2010). "Niklas Luhmann and the Sociology of Constitution." *Journal of Classical Sociology* 10:315–37.
—— (2011). *A Sociology of Constitutions: Constitutions and State Legitimacy in Historical-Sociological Perspective*. Cambridge: Cambridge University Press.
Tocqueville, Alexis (1835/2002). *Democracy in America*. Chicago: University of Chicago Press.
—— (1856/1988). *L'ancien régime et la révolution*. Paris: Flammarion (Engl. *The Old Regime and the Ancient Regime*. London: Random House).
Tönnies, Ferdinand (1887/2010). *Gemeinschaft und Gesellschaft*. Darmstadt: Wissenschaftliche Buchgesellschaft (Engl. *Community and Society*. New York: Dover; reprint from Michigan State University Press, 1957).
Ullmann, Walter (1955). *The Growth of the Papal Government in the Middle Ages*. London: Methuen.
—— (1981). *Gelasius I, 492–496*. Stuttgart: Hiersemann.
Vanderstraeten, Ralph (2000). "Autopoiesis and Socialization: on Luhmann's Reconceptualization of Communication and Socialization." *British Journal of Sociology* 51 (3): 581–98.
Wagner, Gerhard (1997). "The End of Luhmann's Social Systems Theory." *Philosophy and the Social Sciences* 27:387–409.
Waldenfels, Bernhard (1985). *In Netzen der Lebenswelt*. Frankfurt: Suhrkamp.
Walzer, Michael (1977). *Just and Unjust Wars*. New York: Basic.
—— (1983). *Spheres of Justice*. New York: Basic.

Wandel, Lee Palmer (2006). *The Eucharist in the Reformation*. Cambridge: Cambridge University Press.
Watts Miller, W. (1996). *Durkheim, Morals and Modernity*. London: UCL.
Weber, Max (1904/1985). "Die 'Objektivität' sozialwissenschaftlicher und sozialpolitischer Erkenntnis." In *Wissenschaftslehre*. Tübingen: Mohr (Engl. "'Objectivity' in Social Sciences and Social Policy." In *Methodology of the Social Sciences*. New York: Routledge, 2017).
—— (1919/1988). "Politik als Beruf." In *Gesammelte Politische Schriften*. Tübingen: Mohr (Engl. *Politics as Vocation*. Minneapolis: Fortress, 1965).
—— (1920). *Die protestantische Ethik und der Geist des Kapitalismus*. In *Gesammelte Aufsätze zur Religionssoziologie*, vol. 1. Hamburg: Severus, 2014. (Engl. *The Protestant Ethic and the Spirit of Capitalism*. Eugene: Cascade, 2010).
—— (1922/1980). *Wirtschaft und Gesellschaft*. Tübingen: Mohr (Engl. *Economy and Society*. Berkeley: University of California Press, 1978).
—— (1922/1985). *Wissenschaftslehre*. Tübingen: Mohr (Engl., partial, *Methodology of the Social Sciences*. New York: Routledge, 2017).
Wehler, Hans-Ulrich (1973). *Das Deutsche Kaiserreich, 1871–1918*. Göttingen: Vandenhoeck und Ruprecht (Engl. *The German Empire, 1871–1918*. Leamington Spa: Berg, 1985).
Weiler, Joseph H. H. (1999). *The Constitution of Europe*. Cambridge: Cambridge University Press.
Wellmer, Albrecht (1969). *Kritische Gesellschaftstheorie und Positivismus*. Frankfurt: Suhrkamp (Engl. *Critical Theory of Society*. New York: Seabury, 1971).
—— (1986). *Ethik und Dialog*. Frankfurt: Suhrkamp.
—— (1992). "Konsens als Telos der sprachlichen Kommunikation?" In *Kommunikation und Konsens in modernen Gesellschaften*, edited by Hans-Joachim Giegel, 18–30. Frankfurt: Suhrkamp 1992.
Wiethölter, Rudolf (1986/2011). "Prozeduralization of the Category of Law." *German Law Journal* 12 (1): 465–73.
—— (1989). "Ist unserem Recht der Prozess zu machen?" In *Zwischenbetrachtungen—Im Prozess der Aufklärung: Jürgen Habermas zum 60. Geburtstag*, edited by Axel Honneth, Thomas McCarthy, Claus Offe, and Albrecht Wellmer. Frankfurt: Suhrkamp.
Willke, Helmut (1992). *Ironie des Staates*. Frankfurt: Suhrkamp.
—— (1997). *Supervision des Staates*. Frankfurt: Suhrkamp.
—— (2001). *Systemtheorie III: Steuerungstheorie*. Stuttgart: Lucius und Lucius.
Wittgenstein, Ludwig (1952/1984). *Philosophische Untersuchungen*. Frankfurt: Suhrkamp (Engl. *Philosophical Investigation*. Oxford: Blackwell, 1953).
Woloch, Isser (1994). *The New Regime*. New York: Norton.
Wright, Georg Henrik von (1971). *Explanation and Understanding*. London: Routledge.
Zolo, Danilo (1992). *Democracy and Complexity: A Realist Approach*. University Park: Pennsylvania State University Press.

In Habermas's books, lists of references are normally included with indexes to authors. Luhmann's books, on the contrary, usually contain references to concepts. Yet Luhmann refers to Habermas in many of his publications. Accordingly his publications have useful conceptual indexes but no indexes for authors. In the following, I have indicated some of Luhmann's references to Habermas. Sometimes, the references do not mark the name of Habermas but obviously refer to his positions. The list that follows is not complete.

Macht 1975:133
Gesellschaftsstruktur und Semantik Bd. 1 1980:11, 237
Gesellschaftsstruktur und Semantik Bd. 2 1981:269
Gesellschaftsstruktur und Semantik Bd. 4 1995:138
Soziale Systeme 1984:106, 110, 112, 352, 643, 652
Ökologische Kommunikation 1986:59–60, 75, 170, 215, 249–54 (a response to Habermas 1985:424–444)
Soziologische Aufklärung 4 1987:16, 138–39, 154
Die Wissenschaft der Gesellschaft 1990:109–10, 610, 710, 715
Die Kunst der Gesellschaft 1995:152, 163
Die Gesellschaft der Gesellschaft 1997:11, 35, 36, (90), 173–75, 177, 200, 229–30, (245), 618, 766, 775, 797, (826), 986, 1027, 1029, 1030–32, (1078), 1098.
Die Politik der Gesellschaft 2000:42, 52, 124, 125, 220, 265, 282, 291, 301, 352, 362–63, 368, (417)
Ideenevolution 2008:134, 210
"Globalization as World Society" 1997:69

INDEX

1960s, 5, 7, 31, 34, 37, 40, 44, 46, 49, 69, 71, 197, 211ff, 223, 229, 231, 249, 336, 357
1968, 40, 48f, 82, 133, 165, 211ff, 241
1970s, 3, 7, 33, 52, 56, 71f, 103, 117, 141, 150–57, 164, 170, 172, 176, 256, 262, 275, 327, 336, 344
1980s, vii, 3, 14, 134, 158, 170, 171, 179, 201f, 221, 265, 284, 296, 327f,
1990s, 118, 134, 284f, 300f, 329f
Abuse, 48f, 112, 162, 183, 335, 356
Acquis communautaire, 280, 295, 313
Action, action theory, 36–37, 45, 57, 60–61, 79ff, 87, 105, 113, 122, 157, 161, 159, 189–93, 214, 224, 256, 264, 351
Adenauer, Konrad, 27
Administrative law, 305
Administrative, strategic rationality, 257–65
Adorno, Theodor, 4, 5, 24, 27, 29f, 31ff, 44, 124, 133, 137, 153, 164, 204, 206, 221f, 269, 327, 337, 356, 366
Aguesseau, Jean-François, 312, 358, 371
Albert, Mathias, ix, 275,
America, 3, 134, 166, 190, 252, 326, 328, 330
American Revolution, 219
American way of warfare, 330, 336

Anderson, Perry, 162
Apel, Karl-Otto, 33, 68, 77, 89, 181f, 360
Apocalypse, 251, 279, 352
Arato, Andrew, ix, 216
Arendt, Hannah, 47, 335
Argumentation, 16, 41, 65, 77, 79, 81ff, 109, 115, 181, 287, 289, 321–22, 349, 351, 358, 360, 363
Aristotle, 92, 153, 166, 195, 220, 221, 274, 305
Aron, Raymond, 94,
Asceticism, 305
Augustine, Aurelius, 146, 149, 177, 354
Austin, John, 64, 73, 206, 207
Autonomy, 46, 82, 84, 182, 220, 269, 303, 310, 342, 356
Autopoiesis, 123, 179f, 204ff, 287, 295, 345
Axial Age, 348

Bachrach, Peter, 293
Baecker, Dirk, 25, 141, 196, 256
Balkan wars, 319
Baratz, Morton, 293
Bauman, Zygmunt, 28, 99
Beauty 83, 116, 171, 341
Beauvoir, Simone de, 328

Benjamin, Walter, 195, 197
Berkeley, 29
Berlusconi, Silvio, 227
Berman, Harold, 162, 194f, 361, 371
Bertalanffy, Ludwig von, 29, 61, 62, 204, 205
Biden, Joe, 6, 276
Bielefeld, 4, 41, 84, 118, 149, 158f, 184
Böckenförde, Ernst-Wolfgang, 315
Bodin, Jean, 145, 146, 183, 195
Boltanski, Luc, 156, 327,
Bonn, 27
Bourgeois, 46, 98, 127, 175, 263, 277
Braudel, Ferdinand, 196
Brunkhorst, Hauke, ix, 33, , 144f, 146, 183, 189, 194, 233, 276, 295, 297, 322, 355, 362, 366, 369, 373
Buddhism, 174, 354
Burden of proof, 66, 312
Bush, George Walker, 15, 67, 79, 226, 227, 291, 330
Butterfield, Herbert, 207f, 333

Canon law, 115, 296
Capitalism, 76, 95, 138ff, 141, 151, 154, 178, 196, 250, 254, 257f, 264
Cassirer, Ernst, 39ff, 67, 68, 336, 349ff, 352, 357, 367
Catastrophe, 41, 234, 279
Categorization, 26, 67, 111, 168ff, 192, 334
Chancellery, 46, 186, 358, 371
Change, 28, 63, 76, 93, 143, 148ff, 160ff, 185–87, 226ff, 240, 249, 251, 262, 279, 298, 313
Charity, 305
Children, 17f, 27, 67, 188, 254, 261, 279, 314, 328, 356
China, 347, 114, 140, 152, 168, 277, 300, 322
Chinese philosophy, 23, 69, 354, 362
Christ, 354–55, 361, 367
Christian community, 355
Christianity, 174–75, 328, 354, 358, 361
Church, 144, 151, 159, 174f, 177, 259, 358f, 362f
Class relations, 44, 48, 154, 184, 232, 247

Classification, 35, 254, 334
Clausewitz, Karl von, 67, 159, 334
Clima, 8, 16, 239, 276
Clinton, Bill, 319
Coffee breaks, 279, 325
Cognition, cognitive, 12, 43, 50, 90, 136, 141, 165, 206, 312, 338
Cohen, Jean, 216
Colbert, Jean-Baptiste, 219
Collision, 276, 346
Colonize, 159, 277, 301
Commandments, Ten, 295, 359
Commission (European), 27
Common law, 314, 316
Communication, 13, 56, 81, 110, 126, 151, 189, 194–95; code, 17ff, 23, 36, 158, 174–75, 182ff, 275, 343; history, 193ff; system, 10, 18ff, 21, 83, 86, 183, 187, 204, 243, 270
Communicative action, 56, 105, 113, 189, 192, 195, 298
Communism, 164
Community (*Gemeinschaft*), 15, 135, 181, 193, 284 , 328–29, 355, 357, 361
Complainers, 282
Complexity, 50, 55, 58ff, 62, 74–77, 136, 184, 197, 211ff, 218–28, 255, 363
Conceptual history, semantic history, 40, 47, 68, 118, 142f, 158, 162, 172, 188, 190, 303, 322, 368
Condition, 21, 83, 92, 109f, 148, 187, 190, 229, 247, 251, 257, 259
Confession, 25, 241, 356
Confidentiality, 79, 121, 188, 227, 243
Conflict, 15, 31, 43, 83, 85ff, 100, 105, 137f, 148, 173, 184, 185, 200, 213, 229, 259, 266, 270ff, 280ff, 292, 310f, 343, 356
Conformity, 43, 86, 264, 341
Confucianism, 174, 354
Consensus, 7–10, 43, 64, 71f, 85–86, 105, 111, 116, 125, 138, 190, 213ff, 229f, 251ff, 276–78, 292
Constative, 122
Convergence, 108

Cooperation, 14, 24, 35, 63ff, 75, 112, 116, 199, 267, 278, 342, 361
Co-optation, 215, 350
Coordination, 12, 36, 57, 63–65, 90, 100ff, 178, 189, 198, 199ff, 251, 272, 342
Co-originality, 102, 300
COP21 Paris Agreement, 276, 280
Copernican revolution, 352
Corporate spirit (*Corpus Spiritus*), 212, 250, 261, 296, 350, 361
Corporatism (neocorporate), 215, 217, 275, 276
Corpus Juris, 296
Cosmopolitan, viii, 147, 329
Councils, 86f, 222, 354
Crime, 295, 317
Crisis, 22, 41, 160, 219, 231ff, 236–42, 245–47, 347
Critic, criticism, 15, 34, 39, 43, 91, 98, 104, 123, 176, 196ff, 272, 277, 289, 332, 335
Critical theory, 29ff, 41, 74, 91, 94, 170, 172, 181, 277ff, 352, 363
Croatia, 7
Cultural fascism, 307
Cultural sense (*Kulturbedeutung*), 286
Culture, 25, 114f, 149, 205, 250, 261, 264, 289
Customary law (oral law), 308f
Customary law (traditional law), 308f
Cybernetics, 61, 198, 204, 235

Danger, 282, 293
Daoism, 354
Debate, controversy, 3–6, 8ff, 15, 29, 32–33, 46f, 51ff, 55–57, 67, 75, 77ff, 89f–91, 107, 117ff, 124, 133ff, 140, 156, 163ff, 165, 175, 197, 201–2, 213, 222, 224, 235, 238, 247, 266, 284, 293, 295, 297, 305, 318ff, 325–29, 331, 344, 354
Decency, 36, 44, 128
Decisionism, 99, 259, 365
Dedifferentiation, 115, 289, 344
Deliberatiion, deliberative democracy, 15, 46, 64f, 72, 217–18, 222, 229, 249, 252, 276, 297, 306, 351, 371

Dependency (path dependencies, form dependencies), 194, 249, 281, 297, 344, 356
Descombes, Vincent, 327
Deutsch, Karl, 37, 179, 216ff, 282
Dialogue, 4, 6, 63, 80, 82, 85–86, 112ff, 119ff, 125, 194, 250, 276, 279, 317
Differentiation, 10–11, 13, 16, 18, 19, 25, 36, 63
Dindic, Zoran, 329
Diplomacy, 8, 276ff, 292
Directives, 280
Discourse: Foucault and, 44, 142, 270, 331f, 342ff, 353; Habermas and, 24, 66, 81, 88, 91, 106–17, 129f, 141, 181, 206, 247, 252, 261, 279, 288, 306f, 352
Discourse ethics, 24, 88, 91, 129f, 181, 322
Discursive argumentation, 111–15, 127, 128ff
Discussion, 3, 7, 11f, 15, 27, 44, 45–48, 65ff, 74ff, 83–86, 92, 116–17, 127, 129, 151, 168, 176, 201ff, 207, 224, 325, 341, 354ff, 359
Disputes, 25, 30ff, 158, 296f
Distance, viii, 17, 25–27, 42f, 134, 163, 251, 260, 322, 341f, 343, 356, 358
DNA, 189
Domat, Jean, 309
Domination, 13, 75ff, 88, 98, 142, 214, 250, 333, 338
Downing, Brian, 162
Doxa, 337, 338, 339, 350
Dubrovnik, viii, 7, 196, 329, 354
Durkheim, Émile, 4, 10, 13, 15, 35ff, 43, 64, 68, 78, 101f, 104, 111, 135ff, 142, 144ff, 151, 153, 159, 167, 171ff, 175, 182, 185, 189ff, 198ff, 206, 211, 217ff, 220, 222, 238, 249, 286, 301, 315, 326, 328, 343, 348f, 353, 383, 367, 368
Duties, 167, 297, 318, 360, 371
Dworkin, Ronald, 305

Eastern Europe, 298f, 300f, 329f, 361
Easton, David, 37, 216ff, 257, 282
Economy, 18, 37, 68, 138, 141, 169f, 248, 253, 256–57, 258, 277, 281, 310, 332
Eder, Klaus, 150, 191, 233

Education, 18, 90, 122, 144, 185, 218f, 222, 257, 259, 268, 338, 344, 358
Egypt, 191, 349, 354
Electronic media, 301
Embeddedness, 14, 43, 56, 87, 111, 117, 253, 275, 293, 322, 334f, 341, 345, 349, 359, 361
Enlightenment, 6, 11, 14, 23, 40, 42–47, 66, 95f, 103, 115, 127ff, 134, 167, 170, 181, 199, 222, 249, 286, 296, 303–4, 312, 331–35, 345ff, 350, 359
Environment (*Umwelt*), 20, 24, 37, 79–80, 125, 136f, 139, 154, 155, 159, 198, 203, 206, 241, 252, 254f, 264, 268ff, 275–81, 302, 309–11, 314, 339ff, 347ff, 350ff
Equality, 231, 256, 265, 280, 294
Erasmus, Desiderius, 119, 195, 359ff
Eriksen, Erik Oddvar, ix, 291
Escalation, viii, 234, 310f, 319
Esposito, Elena, ix, 141, 196, 256f,
Essentially contested concepts, 278, 346
Eternity, 177f, 225, 360
Ethical reflections, 288
Ethics, 9, 14, 128f, 135, 168, 189, 250, 255, 263, 288f, 293, 307, 315
Etzioni, Amitai, 319
EU, European Union, 234, 280, 295, 300, 319
Eucharist, 124, 174, 195, 354–59, 362
Eurocentric, the, 179
Europe, vii, 6, 9, 15, 25–32, 38f, 56, 114, 139, 151, 159–61, 166, 196, 205, 219, 224ff, 231ff, 280, 295, 300ff, 320, 328, 332, 336, 348, 359
Everyday, 16, 42, 78, 84, 109, 112, 116, 117f, 212, 242f, 258, 261, 289, 306, 321
Evidence, 115, 289f, 325
Evolution, 10, 115, 130–73, 183, 187ff, 193–94, 200, 205, 246, 249, 308, 349ff, 352ff, 357
Exams, 337, 338
Exchange, 18, 164, 177f
Excluded third, 294
Exclusion, 23–24, 175, 234, 314, 330ff, 339–40
Existentialism, 126, 336ff, 356
Explanation (*Erklären*), 20, 33f, 60ff, 67–68, 95, 139, 159, 162, 184, 310

Facebook, 279
Fact of self-reference, 179–82
Fairness, 294
False, falsify, 43, 86–87 111, 114, 140, 170, 337
Family, 27, 279, 311
Fascism, 332, 333, 337, 366
Febbrajo, Alberto, ix, 141, 233
Feedback, 37, 204, 216, 224, 275
Ferguson, Niall, 196
Field, 90, 147, 182f, 270, 337–40, 344
Figuration, 186
First order/second order, 199, 203, 205, 246, 286–87, 309, 338f, 360
Fischer, Joschka, 86, 291
Fischer-Lascano, Andreas, 276, 295
Foerster, Heinz von, 179, 205,
Forecourt, 47, 222, 293
Forgiveness, 305, 360
Founding Fathers, 194, 304, 332
France, 27, 172, 211, 239, 249f, 297, 328, 332f, 371
Frank, Manfred, 327
Frankfurt, vii, 5, 29–32, 41, 74, 91, 219, 232
French Revolution, 92, 219f, 236, 248
Friedrich, Carl, 218
Friend/foe, 330
Fröbel, Folker, 233
Functional differentiation, 46, 101, 137, 145, 199, 218ff, 228, 247, 288, 290, 335, 345, 353, 363

Genealogy, 142, 167, 270, 331, 349, 353, 356
Germain, Randall, 196
German, vii, 3, 4–7, 15, 25–33, 51–52, 65, 86, 94, 106, 112, 133ff, 146, 156, 159f, 161, 163, 164f, 175, 176, 203, 215, 231ff, 263, 278, 299, 310, 316, 320, 326, 328f, 330, 333f, 350, 362, 365, 369
Girard, Réne, 327
Gorbachev, Mikhail, 279, 285, 299, 329
Göttingen, 27
Grace, 305, 360
Grand Theory, 38, 175, 331, 334
Gratian, 296

Great Generation, 337, 346
Guilt, 17, 168, 263, 282, 305, 310, 369
Gumbrecht, Hans-Ulrich, ix, 142, 159, 196ff
Gummersbach, 26
Günther, Klaus, 294f, 301, 326

Habitus, 270, 334, 341
Hallstein, Walter, 27
Hard case, 317, 345
Hart, Herbert L., 287
Hegel, Georg Wilhelm Friedrich, viii, 3, 12, 15, 26, 44f, 68, 76, 116, 152ff, 163, 166ff, 170, 179f, 184, 193, 200, 202f, 204ff, 253, 301, 315, 317, 326, 328f, 350, 356, 357, 358
Heidegger, Martin, 30, 44, 62, 112, 123, 328f, 336f
Heinrich, Dieter, 153,
Heinrich, Jürgen, 213
Hercules judge, 293, 312
Heritage, 12, 26f, 31, 38, 41, 43, 47, 73, 167, 328, 349, 354
Hermeneutics, 33, 62, 90, 111ff, 119f, 143, 157, 161, 348, 349
Hierarchy, 76, 143, 165, 219
Hintze, Otto, 162
History, 133–210, 349ff; and emergence, 160, 175f, 178, 194, 236, 303, 352; historical research, 140, 148; historical sociology, 47, 128, 139, 148, 162, 179f, 181, 296, 356; historical stages, 127, 139, 150, 153ff, 207, 244, 349, 350, 368
Hitler Youth 26
Hjelmslev, Louis, 336
Hobbes, Thomas, 146, 166, 183, 188, 214, 286, 298, 305
Hohendahl, Peter, 196ff
Hollywood, 329
Holocaust, 26, 99
Holy Spirit, 200, 354
Homogeneity, 187
Honesty, 312
Honor, 128, 168, 186, 305, 316

Horkheimer, Max, 29f, 30ff, 41, 91, 137, 202, 206, 278,
Human duties, 318f
Human rights, 102, 303ff, 317–18, 330, 368
Humanity, humanities, 37, 40, 71, 90, 206, 226, 227, 274, 277
Husserl, Edmund, 7, 41f, 44, 76, 78ff, 82, 112, 121, 123, 124f, 203, 242f, 368
Hutter, Michael, 256

Idealized speech situation, 81, 86
Illusion, illusio, 10, 86, 274, 337ff, 339, 366
Impartiality, 291
Improbability of communication, 140, 302
Inclusion, 23ff, 150, 175ff, 194, 234, 314, 331, 339ff
Industrial revolution, 144
Innovation, 126, 140, 150, 158, 161, 177, 186f, 305
Institution, 10, 14, 47, 103, 106, 116ff, 142, 144, 159, 218, 236, 261, 266, 287ff, 297, 307, 359
Intellectual history, 4, 7, 15, 26, 28, 29, 32, 40, 43ff, 165, 205, 232, 325
Interaction, 16, 23, 45, 47, 56, 81f, 84, 94ff, 112, 154, 157, 165, 186,188f, 192, 195, 243, 276, 279, 306f
Interlocking, 288f, 335
International law, 276, 300, 322
Internet, 161, 299, 301, 319, 329
Interpenetration, 78, 120
Interpretation, understanding (*Verstehen*), 11, 14, 39, 49, 59, 62, 108, 112ff, 120, 121, 143, 145, 157, 161, 171, 183, 192, 207f, 241, 249, 263, 270, 295, 297, 308–9, 338, 349–50, 351, 354–59
Intersubjectivity, 7, 58, 69ff, 81ff, 85f, 112ff, 118–25, 355, 361
Intertextuality, 174, 184, 310–11
Irreversible advancement, 260, 349
Is . . . ought, 114
IUC (InterUniversity Centre), viiff, 196

Jakobson, Roman, 336
Jencks, Charles, 327
Jesus Christ (Jesus of Nazareth), 354, 355, 361
Joerges, Christian, 295, 300, 310
Journal, newspaper, 13, 47
Juridification (*Verrechtlichung*), 282, 315
Just war (*jus ad bellum*), 66, 292, 330, 333, 342, 357, 361f, 361f
Justice in war (*jus in bello*), 145, 295, 330

Kafka, Franz, 340
Kant, Immanuel, 3f, 6, 10, 12f, 14f, 16f, 26, 30, 35, 37, 39, 44f, 50f, 64f, 67ff, 73, 77, 83, 85, 100, 102, 110, 116, 123, 127f, 136, 139, 154, 156, 163, 166ff, 170, 179–82, 184, 195, 197, 201, 203, 205ff, 220, 242, 253, 276, 286, 288, 297f, 299, 301, 315, 317f, 326, 328, 333, 341ff, 349ff, 352, 356–63, 366, 367, 368, 369 , 370
Kantorowicz, Ernst, 163, 371
Keynesianism, 3, 234, 257
Kierkegaard, Søren, 126f, 153, 170, 180, 221, 355ff, 359
Kindleberger, Charles, 196
King, Martin Luther, 24
King, Michael, viii, 282
Kjaer, Poul, ix, 141, 233, 295, 300
Knowledge, 11, 12, 30, 41ff, 68ff, 73, 87, 92f, 114, 126, 152, 169, 181, 191, 202, 275, 314, 338, 348
Kohlberg, Lawrence, 138, 154, 188
Kojève, Alexandre, 328
Koselleck, Reinhardt, 47, 118ff, 127ff, 142, 149, 157ff, 161ff, 163f, 201, 236

Late capitalism, 266
Latent, latency, 37, 43, 144
Latour, Bruno, 327
Law, 17, 27, 45ff, 48, 99, 102, 115, 135, 140, 284–324
Law of nations, 132, 147, 270, 300, 322
Law-making, 313
Legal, legality, 14, 115, 148–51, 288, 290, 292, 294, 316, 319–20; argumentation, 115, 237, 284, 286, 294–96, 306–15; philosophy, 282, 285, 299, 317, 358; positivism, 31, 92, 194, 294, 304; reasoning, 294, 296, 309–10, 314; revolution, 163
Legitimacy, critique of legitimacy, viii, 15, 66, 86, 103, 252, 211–82
Legitimation crisis, 251–66, 280
Leibniz, Gottfried, 80, 166, 203
Liability, 295, 310
Liberal, 319, 328
Liberalism, 3, 165, 290, 328–29, 366
Liberation, 26, 60, 139, 343
Lifeworld, 21, 41ff, 69
Lindblom, Charles, 169
Linguistic, 5, 40, 47, 56f, 63, 73–82, 108–22, 140–43, 178, 190, 266, 291, 310, 313, 336–37, 350, 358f; philosophy (of language), 50, 57, 313, 359; turn, viii, 7, 87, 194
Literature, 5, 27, 55, 159, 342, 352
Locke, John, 166
Logic, 6, 23, 32, 33f, 42, 44, 47, 110f, 128–29, 182, 260, 266, 287, 307, 325, 336
Loose communication, 21
Louis XVI, 249
Lüneburg, 26–27
Luther, Martin, 349, 355–60, 367, 368
Lyotard, Jean-François, 4, 28, 52, 78, 89, 124, 164, 202, 211, 327, 329, 369

Maastricht Treaty, 319
Machiavelli, Niccolò, 146, 183, 188
MacIntyre, Alisdair, 328
Macron, Emmanuel, 234f, 251
MacWorld, 329
Mafia, 310, 321
Mann, Michael, 162
March, James, 169, 259
Marx, Karl (Marxism), 3, 7, 10, 31f, 33, 43ff, 48f, 50f, 65, 76, 95, 100, 102, 138ff, 143f, 150–54, 157, 170f, 175, 178f, 184, 196, 198, 201, 204f, 207, 212, 232f, 238ff, 250, 256, 258, 261, 266, 325ff, 329, 345, 351f, 365
Material rationality, 14, 169, 286f, 290, 333, 345

Maus, Ingeborg, 33, 290f, 315,
McCarthy, Thomas, viii, 5, 29, 51, 77, 158, 196–99, 367, 370
Me Too, 289
Medicine, 242, 332
Meeting, 47, 84, 129, 180, 222, 278f
Member, 23, 106, 127, 151, 175f, 189, 195, 293
Merkel, Angela, 251
Merleau-Ponty, Maurice, 121, 243, 328
Mertens, Thomas, ix
Metacommunication, 57, 107, 183, 279
Metaphysics, 6, 25, 204, 232, 350, 352f, 363
Military (military power, state, exercises), 25, 49f, 67, 145, 151, 186, 195, 218, 222, 249, 254, 259, 299, 303, 314, 333–34, 347, 370
Military revolution, 356
Misgeld, Dieter, 196
Modernity, 11, 13, 48, 146, 167, 168, 175, 188, 191, 201–3, 219, 237, 249f, 297, 333, 348
Moeller, Hans-Georg, ix, 354
Monetarism, 3
Montesquieu, Charles, 116, 166, 183, 194f, 199, 213, 247, 296f, 332
Moore, Barrington, 162
Morality, 23, 28, 151, 155, 189, 192, 194, 281, 285, 288–93, 300, 310; moral argumentation, 288, 297; moral philosophy, 35f, 141, 303, 366; moral theory, 288
Morin, Edgar, 327
Mothers, 67
Münch, Richard, 38
Music, musicality, 19, 55, 170, 333
Mythology, 191ff, 349
Myths, 126, 191ff, 278, 348, 350f

Nationalism, 146, 164, 322, 329
Natural law, 102, 285, 294, 296, 303f, 317, 335
Nature, 37, 114, 204ff, 248, 254, 263, 264, 276ff
Natural science, 29, 37, 40, 48ff, 366
Nazism, 218, 332f
Necessity (*necessitas*), 229, 336

Negative dialectic, 352
New York, viii, 29f
News, 14, 47, 112, 225
Nixon, Richard, 49, 79
Noble/aristocracy, 128, 175, 185, 194, 218, 222, 224, 231, 248, 317, 333
Nobles, Richard, ix, 51, 185, 296, 312ff
Nominalism, 322
Nonidentity, 153f, 204, 221f
Norm, 13, 35ff, 64–66, 101ff, 111, 114ff, 151, 159, 235, 243, 245, 250, 262, 265, 287f, 292f, 297, 315–16, 352

O'Connor, James, 233
Obama, Barack, 79
Offe, Claus, 233
Ontogenetic, 188
Ordoliberal, 310
Organic, organism, 77, 80, 137, 142, 160, 204, 246, 350, 353
Organization, 8, 12, 14, 22–23 45, 48ff, 64, 100, 135, 156f, 165, 175, 178, 188, 192f, 194ff, 199, 212f, 217ff, 224–25, 228–29, 241, 244–45, 249–50, 259–60, 274, 293, 342, 355f, 361
Oxford, 44, 73, 336

Pandemic crisis, 277, 348, 350, 356
Paradise, 350
Paris Agreement (COP 21), 276, 280
Parliament, 47, 222, 224, 321, 333, 362
Parsons, Talcott, 18, 36–39, 50, 83, 104, 136, 141, 143–45, 163, 172, 175–79, 182, 192, 195, 200, 205f, 213, 216, 335, 355, 366, 367, 368
Paterson, John, 256
Peace of Constance (1183), 297
Peirce, Charles Sanders, 110, 201, 359
Pence, Mike, 244
Performative act (linguistic), 20, 47, 56, 63f, 66, 71, 81, 291, 309f, 348, 359
Pessimism, 100ff, 334f, 356
Philosophy of history, 10, 139, 180, 352, 357, 360

Physiocrats, 332
Piety, 305
Plan, 42f, 48, 50, 155, 229, 258, 261, 268, 366
Plato, 92, 194, 195
Politeness, 6, 65, 321, 338, 362
Politics, 57, 72, 75, 99, 127, 147, 216–33, 265, 271–74, 281–83, 293, 300, 321; political argumentation, 72, 115, 286; political integration, 251, 300; political philosophy, 6, 30, 330; political rationality, 75, 333; political society, community (*Gemeinwesen*), 12, 15, 193, 287, 329, 357, 361; political system, 22ff, 216f, 223–29, 240, 249, 254, 260, 272–80, 302
Porter, Bruce, 218
Positive law, 45f, 49, 99–103, 285, 303f, 335, 371
Positivism, 31–34, 49, 51, 68, 92
Postmodern, 99, 143, 164, 201f, 319, 327ff
Power, 10f, 21, 28ff, 46, 87f, 97ff, 140, 142, 178ff, 193, 217–18, 241, 244, 258, 260, 270–72, 328, 301–3, 331–35, 338, 343–45, 362ff
Power circuit, 212–17, 224
Practice, 33, 41, 44, 80, 113, 117, 270, 334, 336, 339
Pragmatics, 73, 90ff, 109, 111, 121, 321, 358
Praxis, viii, 33, 222, 329,
Precedence, 16, 148, 280, 309
President, 65, 108, 122, 226, 276
Preventive war, 330
Preventive, precaution, protection, 16, 258, 277f, 282, 301, 314, 317ff
Privacy, 185f
Privilege, 46, 65, 92, 103, 113, 126, 232, 247, 250, 320
Procedures, 11, 45, 49, 64, 115, 117, 138, 212, 237ff, 250, 284–97, 304, 307ff, 311ff, 314, 354, 362, 367, 371
Prussia, 333
Psalms, 356
Psychiatry, 60, 61
Psychic systems, 17, 19f, 71, 79, 83f, 120ff, 123, 128, 140, 174, 187, 204, 269f, 337, 341ff, 353, 358

Psychoanalysis, 43, 65, 120
Public, 3, 8, 11, 15, 48, 80, 68, 156, 194, 217, 236, 248, 250, 281, 291, 304f, 363
Punishment, 17, 305

Rape, 120, 124, 289f
Rasmussen, David, 196
Rationality, 40, 95, 169–71, 254f, 290, 332, 345; aesthetic, 75, 108, 363; communicative, 14ff, 71, 75, 85, 95, 106, 165, 225, 286, 345; formal, 169, 286, 333; goal, 169; procedural, 288, 290f; systems, 33, 35, 68, 88; value, 169
Rationalizations, 10, 13, 42, 104, 116, 151, 168–71, 189, 286, 333, 352f
Rawls, John, 4, 65, 128, 199, 305, 319, 328
Reading, 38, 55, 112, 119, 121, 152, 163, 167ff, 246, 297, 307, 344, 359
Reagan, Ronald, 79, 227
Real presence, 349, 355
Reason, 12, 47, 64, 127, 128, 130, 156, 170ff, 205, 328, 332, 345, 366
Reason of state, 170f, 186, 318, 330, 362
Reasoning, 8, 12, 15, 41, 47, 65, 101ff, 117, 127–28, 138, 182, 205, 232, 236–37, 246, 265, 294–96, 307, 309–15, 334, 336, 361, 371
Reconstruction, 6, 30, 41, 61, 68, 72, 86, 89, 118, 138ff, 141ff, 150ff, 155, 164, 172, 175ff, 237, 264, 296f
Redescription, 128, 173, 298f, 311
Reduction of complexity, 16ff, 34, 59, 76ff, 80, 98, 121, 138, 244, 307
Reformation, 25, 138, 177, 195ff, 305, 350, 355, 362f, 368
Reformist, reformed, 153, 195, 351, 355
Relief, 25, 178, 290f
Religion, 22, 90, 124, 147, 151, 154, 158ff, 168, 172–75, 190, 192, 200, 258, 281, 321, 340, 348–61
Republic (*Gemeinwesen*), 15, 155, 193, 220, 285, 342, 357, 361
Republicanism, 220
Resistance, 48, 335, 360

Resonance, 276, 279
Restaurants, 12, 99, 105f, 279
Revolution, 149, 231, 339, 361; printing press, 146, 161, 177, 187, 195, 197, 301, 355ff; organizational, 219; political, 248
Rights, 15, 24, 45f, 102, 238, 274f, 303–6, 314, 317ff, 340
Risk, 86, 130, 141, 155, 162, 177, 196, 206f, 231–35, 241–43, 255, 258f, 260, 269ff, 274, 276, 279–83, 345, 352, 366
Roman law, 194, 296, 319
Roosevelt, Eleanor, 24
Rosa, Hartmut, 262
Rosanvallon, Pierre, 370
Rousseau, Jean-Jacques, 166, 213, 215ff, 218, 221, 286, 296, 303f, 320, 332, 347
Rumsfeld, Donald, 49, 86, 291

Sand, Inger-Johanne, ix, 300, 346
Sandel, Michael, 328
Sartre, Jean-Paul, 12, 325, 328, 336f
Saussure, Ferdinand, 336
Scandinavia, ix, 268, 291, 362, 366
Schelling, Friedrich, 27
Schiff, David, ix, 51, 185, 296, 312ff
Schism, 361
Schmitt, Carl, 99ff, 200, 251, 259, 279, 330, 365, 367
Schmoller, Gustav, 219
Scotus, Duns, 322
Searle, John, 33, 73, 114, 206f
Secularization, 166, 161, 177, 200, 347–60
Self, selves, 20, 359
Self-description, self-thematization, self-descriptive systems, 92, 145ff, 163, 174ff, 182–83, 199ff, 271, 341, 345; self-determination, 220ff, 273ff, 303; self-implication, 136–38, 171, 181, 362; self-legalizing, vii; self-observation, self-observing systems, 145, 345; self-organization, self-organizing systems, 179, 205, 217; self-reference, self-referential systems, vii, 18–22, 57ff, 122f, 141, 158, 171, 179–82, 205, 215, 217, 272ff, 272, 338f, 352f, 362f; self-referential power, 195, 215, 270–73, 341, 362; self-reflection, 145; self-regulative systems, 82–84, 127, 190f, 198, 244, 245
Semantics, 17ff, 39, 40, 44, 134, 158, 162ff, 181–87, 192ff, 199–201, 213, 221, 271, 302, 305, 318, 345ff, 351, 356, 362, 368
Serbia, 329
Sexuality, 343ff
Shame, 168, 305f
Simmel, Georg, 10, 43, 64, 73f, 136, 161, 186f, 256, 326, 344
Simon, Herbert, 61f, 169, 259
Social philosophy, 3, 55, 203, 325, 331, 366
Social reality, 63, 108, 355, 358
Social state (*Sozialstaat*), 299
Society of procedures (*Verfahrensgemeinschaft*), 287
Socrate, 41, 48
Sonderweg (German special path), 159, 208, 333
Sophocle, 285
Spencer Brown, George, 23, 126, 135, 198, 223
Spinoza, Baruch de, 166, 188
Spruyt, Hendrik, 162
Standard, 5, 7, 27, 83, 89, 114, 119, 129, 149, 170, 176, 201, 277ff, 294, 298ff, 326ff, 338f, 340, 343f, 349, 360, 368, 369
State of exception, 15, 279, 316, 318f, 330f, 366
Steering, 13, 42, 155, 198, 235, 238–40, 243–48, 253, 256, 259f, 268ff
Stichweh, Rudolf, 89, 159, 275
Stigma, 331
Stolleis, Michael, 115
Strauss, Leo, 330
Structural coupling, 18, 76, 241, 249, 256, 259, 265, 300f, 304f, 309, 371
Structuralism, 39, 336ff
Subject-free communication, 301
Sublime, 341ff
Supercode, 338
Switzerland, 27

Symbolically generalized, 36, 38, 45, 156, 178, 271
Symbols/diablos, 83, 124, 126, 143f, 161, 164, 175f, 178, 189, 241
Systems theory, vii ff, 11, 16, 29–30, 36ff, 57–58, 88, 90–92, 104, 117, 142, 179, 196ff, 202–6, 216ff, 246, 268, 302, 338–39
Systems, vii, ff, 17–23, 38, 49–50, 60–62, 74–77, 80, 84, 86, 91f, 136f, 140, 148ff, 155ff, 165, 182f, 188ff, 234, 238, 240–45, 255, 276–80

Take-off, 183, 189, 246, 369
Television, 337
Temporal binding, 148f, 177, 279, 292
Temporal horizons, 66, 141, 148–49, 229, 281f
Temporality, 47, 82ff, 129, 149f, 156, 176f, 229, 337, 355
Teubner, Gunther, 141, 233, 266, 275f, 287, 295f, 300, 319, 322f, 371
Text, 174, 177, 183, 184, 190, 308, 310, 311
Theater, 47ff, 51, 222
Themes, 7f, 10, 17, 43–47, 55, 57, 75, 84, 129, 153, 163f, 183, 221, 229, 237, 260, 279, 307, 326ff, 348, 361, 363
Theology, ix, 11, 77f, 85, 90, 104, 124, 148, 153, 166, 168, 170, 172, 174ff, 177, 182, 192ff, 200f, 241, 295, 333, 349, 354–61
Third Reich, 15, 26
Thornhill, Chris, ix, 6, 25, 34, 241, 259, 282, 295, 297, 362, 365, 366, 369
Tilly, Charles, 162
Transform, 57, 63, 139, 187, 191f, 194
Tribunal (of justice, reasoning), 127, 236, 268, 297, 317, 335f, 358, 361, 371
Trinity, Trinitarian communication, 354
Trivial machine, 314
Trump, Donald, 6, 112, 226f, 234, 244, 251, 263, 275f, 279, 280, 316, 322
Trust, 45f, 70, 101, 121ff, 126, 178, 188, 196, 226ff, 234, 242–48, 261ff, 290, 321

Truth, 6, 12, 57ff, 69–73, 85–94, 100, 108–15, 128, 141, 156, 188, 202, 322, 325, 336, 360
Turn-taking, TK 47
Twitter, 279

Undeterminacy, 79f, 173, 200
United Nations, 278, 322
U.S. army, 329

Veil of ignorance, 339
Vendetta, 310
Veterans, 125, 168, 299
Vision, 23, 261, 276, 281, 337, 338ff
Vitoria, Francisco, 359

Wagner, Richard, 163
Walzer, Michael, 9, 328
War, viii, 9, 15, 16, 18, 19, 26–30, 31, 33, 51, 76f, 112, 118, 125, 165, 168, 187, 218, 224, 229ff, 241, 248, 254, 263f, 265, 279, 285, 291f, 299f, 319, 326, 328, 330ff, 332, 335, 347, 350, 352, 369
War systems, 76, 84, 86, 139, 146, 149, 170, 178, 182f, 186, 193, 197, 200, 256, 259, 274, 281, 300, 311, 346, 366, 370f
Weber, Max, 4, 10, 14, 34–37, 39ff, 45, 48–50, 68f, 73ff, 100ff, 104, 105f, 137, 142, 144f, 151, 163, 167–75, 176, 178, 182, 185, 189, 191, 195, 201, 215, 219f, 247f, 256, 286ff, 290, 299, 301, 305, 308f, 310, 313, 326, 331, 333f, 336, 340, 343, 345, 349, 367, 369
Weimar, 219, 229
Welfare state, 24, 126, 175, 215, 231–33, 260, 266, 274, 331, 346, 366
Western Europe, 300ff, 319, 361
Will, 24f, 97, 120f, 129, 149f, 161, 226, 237, 258, 288, 298, 304, 311, 321f, 360ff, 368
Will-formation, 12, 37, 105, 216, 223, 259, 263, 265, 288, 290, 304, 316, 318, 361
Wittgenstein, Ludwig, 31, 33, 67f, 73, 78ff, 124, 202, 206f, 336
Wolfowitz, Paul, 330

Woloch, Isser, 196
Women, 343
Work/labor, 13, 35f, 44, 95, 101, 204, 217, 256, 261, 266
World complexity, 79
World in itself (*an sich*, external world), 59, 62, 76ff, 79–82, 125ff, 135, 203, 276, 279, 339ff
World society, viii, 147ff, 154ff, 161f, 167, 171, 191, 194, 212, 227, 234, 241ff, 274ff, 285, 329f, 295, 353

World, world history, 28f, 39, 59, 85, 90, 110, 166, 146, 148f, 170f, 255, 315, 318, 347, 352f, 356, 369
Worldviews, 98, 147, 162, 192, 232, 241, 275, 349, 359, 367
Written law, 47, 308f

Yin-Yang, 23

Zolo, Danilo, 233

GPSR Authorized Representative: Easy Access System Europe, Mustamäe tee
50, 10621 Tallinn, Estonia, gpsr.requests@easproject.com

www.ingramcontent.com/pod-product-compliance
Lightning Source LLC
Chambersburg PA
CBHW021928290426
44108CB00012B/766